Research Ethics in Behavior Analysis

Research Ethics in Behavior Analysis

From Laboratory to Clinic and Classroom

Edited by

David J. Cox
Institute for Behavioral Studies, Endicott College, Beverly, MA, United States

Noor Y. Syed
SUNY Empire State College and the Center for Autism Advocacy: Research, Education, and Supports, Saratoga Springs, NY, United States; Anderson Center International, Staatsburg, NY, United States; Endicott College, Beverly, MA, United States

Matthew T. Brodhead
Department of Counseling, Educational Psychology, and Special Education, Michigan State University, East Lansing, MI, United States

Shawn P. Quigley
Melmark, Andover, MA, United States; Berwyn, PA, United States; Charlotte, NC, United States

ELSEVIER

ACADEMIC PRESS

An imprint of Elsevier

Academic Press is an imprint of Elsevier
125 London Wall, London EC2Y 5AS, United Kingdom
525 B Street, Suite 1650, San Diego, CA 92101, United States
50 Hampshire Street, 5th Floor, Cambridge, MA 02139, United States
The Boulevard, Langford Lane, Kidlington, Oxford OX5 1GB, United Kingdom

Notices

Knowledge and best practice in this field are constantly changing. As new research and experience broaden our understanding, changes in research methods, professional practices, or medical treatment may become necessary.

Practitioners and researchers must always rely on their own experience and knowledge in evaluating and using any information, methods, compounds, or experiments described herein. In using such information or methods they should be mindful of their own safety and the safety of others, including parties for whom they have a professional responsibility.

To the fullest extent of the law, neither the Publisher nor the authors, contributors, or editors, assume any liability for any injury and/or damage to persons or property as a matter of products liability, negligence or otherwise, or from any use or operation of any methods, products, instructions, or ideas contained in the material herein.

ISBN: 978-0-323-90969-3

For information on all Academic Press publications visit our website at
https://www.elsevier.com/books-and-journals

Publisher: Nikki P. Levy
Acquisitions Editor: Joslyn T. Chaiprasert-Paguio
Editorial Project Manager: Timothy J. Bennett
Production Project Manager: Omer Mukthar
Cover Designer: Greg Harris

Typeset by TNQ Technologies

Dedication

This is dedicated to those who model perseverance through adversity. For my colleagues in the Autistic Community and Anderson Center International—thank you for enriching the lives of so many and for making the world a better place. — Noor

I would like to thank Reviewer 2 for all the encouragement they have provided throughout the years. — Matt

This book is dedicated to the millions of past, present, and future research participants. Your gift of your time and your body to scientific endeavors is humbling. Without you, none of us would likely have the careers we do. Thank you. — David

I want to recognize the individuals that did not consent to research. Their stories are the pillars of research ethics. — Shawn

Contents

3. Equity, diversity, inclusion, and accessibility in research
Noor Y. Syed, Leanna Mellon and Sarah Kristiansen

4. On staying open: thoughts on the ethics of seeking funding for basic behavioral research
David P. Jarmolowicz and Rogelio Escobar

5. Obtaining resources to support research in applied clinical settings
Amber L. Valentino and Olivia M. Onofrio

6. Subject recruitment, consent, and assent

*Allison N. White, Jessica L. Herrod, Holly M. Long
and Matthew T. Brodhead*

7. Ethical considerations with balancing clinical effectiveness with research design

*Wayne W. Fisher, Ashley M. Fuhrman, Brian D. Greer,
Vivian F. Ibañez, Kathryn M. Peterson and Cathleen C. Piazza*

11. Supporting the replication of your research

Heather J. Forbes, Jason C. Travers and Jenee Vickers Johnson

Contributors

Shahla Ala'i-Rosales, University of North Texas, Denton, TX, United States

Matthew T. Brodhead, Department of Counseling, Educational Psychology, and Special Education, Michigan State University, East Lansing, MI, United States

Jeremiah M. Brown, Department of Family and Community Medicine, University of Kentucky College of Medicine, Lexington, KY, United States; Department of Psychology, Louisiana State University, Baton Rouge, LA, United States; Optum Labs, Eden Prairie, MN, United States; Department of Human Nutrition, Foods, and Exercise, Fralin Biomedical Research Institute at VTC, Virginia Tech, Blacksburg, VA, United States

Traci M. Cihon, University of North Texas, Denton, TX, United States

David J. Cox, Institute for Behavioral Studies, Endicott College, Beverly, MA, United States

Alicia Re Cruz, University of North Texas, Denton, TX, United States

W. Brady DeHart, Department of Family and Community Medicine, University of Kentucky College of Medicine, Lexington, KY, United States; Department of Psychology, Louisiana State University, Baton Rouge, LA, United States; Optum Labs, Eden Prairie, MN, United States; Department of Human Nutrition, Foods, and Exercise, Fralin Biomedical Research Institute at VTC, Virginia Tech, Blacksburg, VA, United States

Rogelio Escobar, School of Psychology, National Autonomous University of Mexico, Mexico City, Mexico

Wayne W. Fisher, Children's Specialized Hospital—Rutgers University Center for Autism Research, Education, and Services, Somerset, NJ, United States; Department of Pediatrics, Rutgers Robert Wood Johnson Medical School, New Brunswick, NJ, United States

Heather J. Forbes, West Virginia University, Morgantown, WV, United States

Ashley M. Fuhrman, Children's Specialized Hospital—Rutgers University Center for Autism Research, Education, and Services, Somerset, NJ, United States; Department of Pediatrics, Rutgers Robert Wood Johnson Medical School, New Brunswick, NJ, United States

Shawn P. Gilroy, Department of Family and Community Medicine, University of Kentucky College of Medicine, Lexington, KY, United States; Department of Psychology, Louisiana State University, Baton Rouge, LA, United States; Optum Labs, Eden Prairie, MN, United States; Department of Human Nutrition, Foods, and Exercise, Fralin Biomedical Research Institute at VTC, Virginia Tech, Blacksburg, VA, United States

Brian D. Greer, Children's Specialized Hospital−Rutgers University Center for Autism Research, Education, and Services, Somerset, NJ, United States; Department of Pediatrics, Rutgers Robert Wood Johnson Medical School, New Brunswick, NJ, United States

Jill M. Harper, Melmark New England, Andover, MA, United States

Jessica L. Herrod, Department of Communication Sciences and Special Education at the University of Georgia, Athens, GA, United States

Vivian F. Ibañez, Children's Specialized Hospital−Rutgers University Center for Autism Research, Education, and Services, Somerset, NJ, United States; Department of Pediatrics, Rutgers Robert Wood Johnson Medical School, New Brunswick, NJ, United States; University of Florida, Gainesville, FL, United States

David P. Jarmolowicz, Department of Applied Behavioral Science, University of Kansas, Lawrence, KS, United States; Cofrin Logan Center for Addiction Research and Treatment, University of Kansas, Lawrence, KS, United States; Healthcare Institute for Improvements in Quality, University of Missouri-Kansas City, Kansas City, MO, United States

Jenee Vickers Johnson, University of Kansas, Lawrence, KS, United States

Brent A. Kaplan, Department of Family and Community Medicine, University of Kentucky College of Medicine, Lexington, KY, United States; Department of Psychology, Louisiana State University, Baton Rouge, LA, United States; Optum Labs, Eden Prairie, MN, United States; Department of Human Nutrition, Foods, and Exercise, Fralin Biomedical Research Institute at VTC, Virginia Tech, Blacksburg, VA, United States

Mikahil N. Koffarnus, Department of Family and Community Medicine, University of Kentucky College of Medicine, Lexington, KY, United States; Department of Psychology, Louisiana State University, Baton Rouge, LA, United States; Optum Labs, Eden Prairie, MN, United States; Department of Human Nutrition, Foods, and Exercise, Fralin Biomedical Research Institute at VTC, Virginia Tech, Blacksburg, VA, United States

Sarah Kristiansen, Endicott College, Beverly, MA, United States

Holly M. Long, Department of Counseling, Educational Psychology, and Special Education, Michigan State University, East Lansing, MI, United States

James K. Luiselli, Melmark New England, Andover, MA, United States

Videsha Marya, Institute for Behavioral Studies, Endicott College, Beverly, MA, United States; Village Autism Center, Marietta, GA, United States

Leanna Mellon, SUNY New Paltz, New Paltz, NY, United States

Fernanda S. Oda, Department of Applied Behavioral Science, University of Kansas, Lawrence, KS, United States

Olivia M. Onofrio, Trumpet Behavioral Health, Lakewood, CO, United States

Kathryn M. Peterson, Children's Specialized Hospital—Rutgers University Center for Autism Research, Education, and Services, Somerset, NJ, United States; Department of Pediatrics, Rutgers Robert Wood Johnson Medical School, New Brunswick, NJ, United States

Cathleen C. Piazza, Children's Specialized Hospital—Rutgers University Center for Autism Research, Education, and Services, Somerset, NJ, United States; Graduate School of Applied and Professional Psychology, Rutgers University, New Brunswick, NJ, United States

Malika Pritchett, University of Kansas, Lawrence, KS, United States

Derek D. Reed, Department of Applied Behavioral Science, University of Kansas, Lawrence, KS, United States

Victoria D. Suarez, Institute for Behavioral Studies, Endicott College, Beverly, MA, United States; Centria Autism, Farmington Hills, MI, United States

Noor Y. Syed, SUNY Empire State College and the Center for Autism Advocacy: Research, Education, and Supports, Saratoga Springs, NY, United States; Anderson Center International, Staatsburg, NY, United States; Endicott College, Beverly, MA, United States

Jason C. Travers, Temple University, Philadelphia, PA, United States

Amber L. Valentino, Trumpet Behavioral Health, Lakewood, CO, United States

Allison N. White, Department of Counseling, Educational Psychology, and Special Education, Michigan State University, East Lansing, MI, United States

Preface

The fact that you are reading this book suggests you might be like us—research and ethics junkies interested in how research and ethics intersect for the behavior analytic scientist and practitioner. But, you may ask, "Why do we need a book about research ethics in behavior analysis? Research ethics and behavior analysis have both been around for a while. What possibly can be gained by adding another book to this mix?" We invite you to explore these questions with us now as we dive into the unique attributes of behavior analytic research.

First, behavior analysis is somewhat unique among scientific fields that span research and practice. Many areas of human subjects research emphasize randomized controlled trials and other group designs to study intervention effectiveness. Here, the methods employed by researchers differ significantly from the methods used by practitioners to evaluate interventions for individual patients (e.g., medical doctors, licensed psychologists). As a result of this difference in methodological approaches between researchers and practitioners, authors writing about research ethics will often address the ethical conduct of group design research and ethical claims around generalizing group design research to individuals within the studied populations. In contrast, the methods used by behavior analytic researchers can be directly replicated by practitioners who seek to employ empirically supported methodologies for behavior change. The generalizability of research methods (e.g., single-case research design) to practice creates unique ethical challenges and questions specific to the behavior analytic community that traditional research ethics texts often fail to address (see Normand & Donohue, *in press*). This book attempts to fill that gap.

Second, research ethics can sometimes feel like a set of rules we need to follow, a set of Institutional Review Board (IRB) boxes we need to check, and a series of responses that allow us to avoid contacting aversive contingencies. Often, these regulatory actions can seem annoying or counterproductive to the research process. In fact, anyone who has conducted research can probably share with you at least one story of IRB oversight gone awry (see Briggs, 2022, for a particularly notable rant)! Once the regulatory boxes are checked, researchers often feel they can get on with the real work in knowing what they are doing is "good." But ethics involves claims about what's right and what's wrong; ethical decisions are made daily and throughout the research process; and ethics is also about inspiring and helping us do better. Thus, this book attempts to highlight how claims about right and wrong are woven into the fabric of decisions that researchers make throughout the research process. This book also highlights how ethical research conduct can lead you to conducting higher quality research with greater impact.

As editors of a textbook centering around ethical research practices, we believe that higher quality research first comes by acknowledging biases within the research process, both covert and overt. The ability and opportunity to engage in research is a social privilege and carries many associated costs for actually conducting research and having the free time to write and publish papers. The behavior analytic field is composed primarily of practitioners, many of whom dedicate their careers towards improving the lives of others. The emotional, physical, and mental strain, coupled with other responsibilities, may leave practitioners with little time or energy to engage in the research and publication processes. Such processes are generally a significant time commitment, which may not be feasible for all. Too, research tools, such as statistical analyses platforms and literature databases, are typically a high cost and can only be accessed by those who have funding sources or an institutional affiliation. IRB requirements can also be expensive, as these often require certifications that are not free or widely available. In one editor's rant, while doing research with colleagues in Kenya, they found that the cost of certification and Kenyan IRB came to an amount that was the average equivalent of almost two month's national salary! Such an amount that would not be feasible for most without external funding.

It is critically important that we acknowledge the current criticisms, and subsequent challenges, the field is facing. As this text is going to press, over 70% of certified behavior analysts identify as working in the field of autism (BACB, n.d.), yet we are hearing strong outcries against applied behavior analysis from members of the autism and autistic communities. Further, most behavior analytic research has been conducted in North America, primarily in the United States, which limits the inclusivity and applicability of our research. These disparities and challenges can lead to a gap between what we *know* and what we *do,* a phenomenon often referred to as the **know-do gap** in implementation science framework (e.g., Booth, 2011; Pakenham-Walsh, 2004). Without bridging these gaps, we may begin to question whether our research is truly socially significant.

Though such logistical challenges may feel disheartening, shining a light on areas for growth in our research ethics helps us identify how to move forward. These criticisms have been an impetus for important discussions centering how to engage in community-based and compassionate research in behavior analysis. We can begin conditioning the reporting of participant and research identities as a reinforcer, create research teams that represent the broader community, and engage in participatory research to increase social significance of our goals, acceptability of our treatments, and perhaps, the generalizability of our findings. Most importantly, however, we may find that these strategies will begin bridging the inclusivity research gap in our field, therefore, creating an equitable culture that continues to be the heart of behavior analysis.

Finally, many existing texts on research ethics focus on broad ethical theories and principles. As a result, the reader is often left to independently generalize those topics to the unique and varied situations they encounter while conducting research. This can be a challenging exercise, especially for newer researchers. Thus, rather than organize this text around a theory (or three), we sought to organize this text around researcher behavior. Specifically, this text follows the prototypical research pipeline to demonstrate how every stage in the research process involves ethical considerations, ethical traps, and opportunities to be better researchers. As a result, we hope the book helps you to become fluent in identifying the relevance of ethical conversations in your daily empirical work and become enthusiastic about seeking them out. To slightly tweak for emphasis an oft-quoted phrase stemming from Herrnstein (1970): All research behavior involves ethical choice. We hope, by the end of this text, you agree.

To close, we would be remiss if we failed to use this space to thank the many contributors to this book. If you have not yet seen, the table of contents is packed with a stellar group of individuals who each have pushed the boundaries of current conversations at the intersection of research in behavior analysis and research ethics. Their thoughtful, reflective, and insightful prose left us inspired and energized to be better researchers and stewards of this beautiful science we call "behavior analysis." We hope you enjoy reading this text as much as we enjoyed bringing it into your home.

—David, Noor, Matt, and Shawn

REFERENCES

BACB (n.d.). About behavior analysis. Retrieved from: https://www.bacb.com/about-behavior-analysis/.

Briggs, R. (March 23, 2022). *The abject failure of IRBs*. *The Chronical of Higher Education*. https://www.chronicle.com/article/the-abject-failure-of-irbs.

Booth, A. (2011). Bridging the 'Know-do gap': a role for health information professionals?. *Health information and libraries journal, 28*(4), 331−334. https://doi.org/10.1111/j.1471-1842.2011.00960.x.

Herrnstein, R. J. (1970). On the law of effect. *Journal of the Experimental Analysis of Behavior, 13*(2), 243−266. https://doi.org/10.1901/jeab.1970.13-243.

Normand, M. P., & Donohue, H. E. (2022). Research ethics for behavior analysts in practice. *Behavior Analysis in Practice*. https://link.springer.com/article/10.1007/s40617-022-00698-5.

Pakenham-Walsh, N. (2004). Learning from one another to bridge the "know-do gap". *British Medical Journal, 329*(7475), 1189. https://doi.org/10.1136/bmj.329.7475.1189

Chapter 1

From Fuller to Fawcett: a human rights history of research ethics in behavior analysis*

Malika Pritchett[1], Shahla Ala'i-Rosales[2], Traci M. Cihon[2] and Alicia Re Cruz[2]
[1]*University of Kansas, Lawrence, KS, United States;* [2]*University of North Texas, Denton, TX, United States*

At some basic level, there is agreement that science is a fundamental means of understanding ourselves and the world in which we live. Beyond that simple agreement, there is a world of complications, particularly in the arena of behavior change, and the ethics of how and why we come to understand the processes and outcomes of change. The purpose of this chapter is to provide a historical analysis of how the ethics of behavior change research has evolved and is continually evolving, from ensuring basic protections from harm to nurturing clear and meaningful benefit for participants. Our central focus is on key historical events that have contributed to the emergence and urgency of rules and guidelines that direct ethical research practices with human participants, especially those who are vulnerable, and how those rules have translated to policies and safeguards. This history is placed within a larger framework of evolving conceptions of the role of research in human rights and human progress and the unique position of behavior analytic research and practice. We begin with a conceptual analysis and exploration of systems contingencies that can lean toward devaluing, disrespecting, and potentially harming people who are research participants, or that can lean toward respecting, cherishing, and potentially increasing well-being for people who are research participants.

---

* Portions of this manuscript were completed as part of the first author's dissertation for the PhD in Health Services Research with a concentration in Behavior Analysis at the University of North Texas.

Research Ethics in Behavior Analysis. https://doi.org/10.1016/B978-0-323-90969-3.00011-6

Introduction: our growing understanding of research ethics

Science "is a search for order, for uniformity, for lawful relations among the events in nature" (Skinner, 1953, p. 13), and the purpose of science is to generate knowledge, often through research or experimentation. The science of behavior analysis is dedicated to understanding and describing the role of the environment and its impact on the fundamental datum of analysis—the response of organisms (Skinner, 1938, 1953). Organism responses are an unique and extremely complex datum for analysis due to continuous, elaborate movement cycles (Kubina & Yurich, 2012; Skinner, 1938); behavior "is changing, fluid, and evanescent, and for this reason it makes great technical demands upon the ingenuity and energy of the scientist" (Skinner, 1953, p. 15). Moreover, the activity of research itself is a constellation of human behaviors that includes the development of experimental questions, operational definitions, measurement systems, selection of dependent variables and independent variables, and more. Research activity that involves humans also includes decisions about who is part of the research, and how and why they are included. Agreement among scientists regarding which research areas are pursued and how they are pursued (and recognized) is made by members of the scientific community (e.g., funding agencies, university research labs, journal reviewing bodies).

Research can be characterized as social behavior or "the behavior of two or more people with respect to one another or in concert with respect to a common environment" (Skinner, 1953, p. 297). Skinner (1953) discussed the 'common environment' as a 'social environment' or 'culture' that includes social stimuli and social reinforcers. The combination of social stimuli and reinforcers that comprise our social environments forms networks of contingencies that establish, evoke, shape, reinforce, and punish social behaviors. The social behaviors of the members of the scientific community also serve to establish and maintain the networks of contingencies in our social environments and cultures. The contingencies in the social environment affect the members of the research group and are established and upheld by the members of the group (e.g., participants, researchers, editors, professors, students).

When research is conceptualized as social behavior, it allows for contextual descriptions and analyses of the variety of contingencies that establish and maintain researcher behaviors within the research context and subsequently the translation of the research to broader scientific communities and society (Goldiamond, 1978, 1984). Ethical considerations arise when behavior scientists/analysts, and especially applied behavior scientists/analysts, engage other humans in their research endeavors (e.g., co-investigators, participants, and the larger scientific community). These human-to-human research interactions have dramatic implications for humanity in the present as well as in the future, at cellular, individual, community, and global levels (Benjamin, 2013).

Behavior analysts not only engage in behaviors and practices related to the research process but are also "members of the social systems within which they conduct research" (Pritchett et al., 2021, p. 17; see also Goldiamond, 1978, 1984). This dual role, created through a recursive relationship between social behavior and practices and the social environment, creates the conditions under which "the individual [researcher] acquires from the group an extensive repertoire of manners and customs ... all of which depend in part on the practices of the group [scientific community] of which he is a member" (Skinner, 1953, p. 415). For instance, the behaviors and practices that exemplify the *purpose of research* evolve, as do the behaviors and practices related *to how and why research questions emerge* in a given scientific community. There is a recursive relationship between the social behaviors involved in conducting research with humans and the social environment that selects these behaviors and practices, both of which are constantly changing over time and in relation to one another.

Simultaneously, this dual role creates a dual obligation for behavior analytic researchers. The research-related behaviors and practices "generate ethical behavior and the extension of these practices to manners and customs ... A culture [the social environment] ... is thus enormously complex and extraordinarily powerful" (Skinner, 1953, p. 419) in determining our behaviors and practices, including those of the researcher in behavior analysis. Notably, this recursive relationship affects the behaviors of the researchers and the environmental selecting events (e.g., motivating contexts, resources and conditions, consequences; see also Mattaini, 2013). They contribute to why experiments are conducted, how and why we ask and pursue different research questions, how research and its findings are communicated to scientists and society, and the practices and directions of our research ethics.

Conceptualizing research as social behavior suggests that, while behavior analysts strive to engage in research that advances our understanding as to how to improve conditions for people, they also operate within systems that have other goals and contingencies (Pritchett et al., 2021; see also Goldiamond, 1978, 1984). The behavior analyst's obligations to the research participant, society, and the institutions in which they work have the potential to create competing contingencies (Bandura, 1978; Stolz, 1978), especially in cases for which there are acknowledged or hidden vulnerabilities or power imbalances.

Ethical dilemmas ... arise when the professional and the individual whose behavior is to be changed are from different social classes or have different statuses (and hence have different values for differential access to reinforcers), when the voluntary nature of the involvement of the persons whose behavior is to be changed is compromised in any way, when their competence to enter into an agreement regarding the intervention is questionable, or when people are subjected to interventions they do not realize are in effect.

(Stolz, 1978, p. 18)

Benjamin (2013) describes a parallel tension in the life sciences and the biotech sector:

The life sciences and the burgeoning biotech industry are especially vulnerable to conflicts between commercial, medical, and broader social interests, as the application of commercial logic to (and commodification of) the human body leads us full circle to the dangerous medical practices of World War II — and even prior to that, to American chattel slavery.

(p. 4)

Such responsibilities are further highlighted when we consider the implications and development of ethics in relation to consent. There are many cases of persons, discussed in detail later in this chapter, in marginalized positions in society, who were involuntarily forced to participate in biomedical and behavioral research—individuals such as Mrs. Henrietta Lacks (Skloot, 2011), the subject in Fuller (1949), and the men in Tuskegee (Tuskegee University, n.d.). In each of the cases, subjects were treated as if their lives were less; they were considered subhuman. The information and understandings gained from these research programs and the research subjects became commodities that produced profits. Those whose bodies and behavior produced the knowledge did not profit from the knowledge, and in most cases neither did the marginalized communities to which they belonged. The commodification of the knowledge gained was a direct product of the diminished value of their lives relative to the lives and rights of other members of society; they were used to benefit others. It was not until much later that advocacy and outrage for these individuals produced several, sometimes simultaneous global responses, and society responded with counter controls and protections that are now built into the research process (cf., Stolz, 1978; Wood, 1975).

Timelines of protections and the development of a science of behavior change

To understand the context and development of ethics standards and policies in behavior analytic research practice, it is helpful to view a timeline of events (see Table 1.1), consider the relations between and among these events, and explore how the progression of behavior analysis fits with other global movements. Historical analyses are by their nature complicated and biased from the perspectives of those who write the history. The authors of this chapter focused the lens purposefully toward events that indicate an evolution in care for the well-being of participants. Our lens is influenced by culturo-behavior systems science (see Cihon & Mattaini, 2019, 2020), human rights, and womanist philosophies (e.g., Walker, 2004; Maparyan, 2012). The timeline is intentionally presented thematically and as a non-linear summary of the central issues related to evolution of human rights protections and social justice.

TABLE 1.1 Key events related to ethical codes and protections outside of and within behavior analysis.

Year	Key events outside of behavior analysis	Key events within behavior analysis
1945		First program in behavior analysis created at Columbia University Teacher's College
1947	Nuremberg Code released	
1948	Universal Declaration of Human Rights (UDHR) released	*Walden Two* published by B. F. Skinner
	Declaration of Geneva	
1949		*Operant Conditioning of a Vegetative Human Organism* published by Fuller
1953	Wichita jury study	First formal code of ethics developed by the American Psychological Association (APA)
1956	Willowbrook hepatitis studies commence in New York	
1957		Society for the Experimental Analysis of Behavior (SEAB) formed
1958		*Journal of the Experimental Analysis of Behavior (JEAB)* established
1961	Milgram's 'obedience to authority' experiments commence	
	Draft of Declaration of Helsinki released	
1962	Pappworth's paper on "human guinea pigs" published in popular magazine *Twentieth Century*	
1963	Jewish Chronic Disease Hospital Study	*Application of Operant Conditioning Procedures to the Behavior Problems of an Autistic Child* published by Wolf et al.
1964	Declaration of Helsinki adopted by World Medical Association	
	US Civil Rights Act of 1964	
	Britain's Medical Research Council publishes statement on regulations of medical research	
1965	Voting Rights Act of 1965	

Continued

TABLE 1.1 Key events related to ethical codes and protections outside of and within behavior analysis.—cont'd

Year	Key events outside of behavior analysis	Key events within behavior analysis
1966	Beecher's paper on unethical research published in *New England Journal of Medicine*	
	First institutional research ethics committee in South Africa formed at University of Witwatersrand	
	Australia's NHMRC publishes Statement on Human Experimentation and Supplementary Notes	
	Cervical cancer experiments commence at New Zealand's National Women's Hospital	
1967	Pappworth's book *Human Guinea Pigs: Experimentation on Man* published	
1968		*Journal of Applied Behavior Analysis* (*JABA*) founded; *Some Current Dimensions of Applied Behavior Analysis* published by Baer et al.
1970	*Tearoom Trade* by Laud Humphreys published	
	Pedagogy of the Oppressed by Paulo Freire published	
1971	San Antonio contraception study	*Beyond Freedom and Dignity* published by B. F. Skinner
	Zimbardo's mock prison experiments at Stanford University commence	*The Modification of Human Behavior: The Ethics of Human Control* panel presentation held at an international symposium on human rights, retardation, and research sponsored by the Joseph P. Kennedy Foundation
		Individual Rights and the Federal Role in Behavior Modification, a 3-year study started by Senate appointed

TABLE 1.1 Key events related to ethical codes and protections outside of and within behavior analysis.—cont'd

Year	Key events outside of behavior analysis	Key events within behavior analysis
		members of the Subcommittee on Constitutional Rights of the Committee on the Judiciary
		APA appoints Task Force on Behavior Therapy
1972	Tuskegee syphilis trials conclude after running for 40 years	Sunland Training Center abuse investigation launched
	Willowbrook hepatitis studies conclude after running for 16 years	
	Geraldo Rivera's documentary *Willowbrook: The Last Great Disgrace* broadcast on network television	
1973	*Zap! You're Normal* published by Yafa in Playboy Magazine	*Behaviorism* journal founded (changed to *Behavior & Philosophy* in 1990)
	Big Brother and Psychotechnology published by Chorover	
1974	Congress passes the National Research Act (PL 93-348)	Association for Behavior Analysis (ABA; later renamed the Association for Behavior Analysis International [ABAI]) founded
	Law Enforcement Assistance Administration (LEAA) bans funding for the use of behavior modification programs in prisons	First Drake Conference on Professional Issues in Behavior Analysis
	US Senate Subcommittee on Constitution Rights of the Committee of the Judiciary publishes 600+ page report on federal support for research on behavior modification and implications for individual rights	APA publishes response to LEAA funding restrictions
	US National Commission for the Protection of Human Subjects of Biomedical and Behavioral Research (The National Commission) created as part of the National Research Act	Board of Social and Ethical Responsibility of the APA meets for the first time, meetings continue through 1976

Continued

TABLE 1.1 Key events related to ethical codes and protections outside of and within behavior analysis.—cont'd

Year	Key events outside of behavior analysis	Key events within behavior analysis
	Behavior Mod published by Hilts	*Toward a Constructional Approach to Social Problems: Ethical and Constitutional Issues Raised by Applied Behavior Analysis* published by Goldiamond
		Protection of Human Subjects and Patients: A Social Contingency Analysis of Distinctions Between Research and Practice, and its Implications published by Goldiamond
		Individual Rights and the Federal Role in Behavior Modification report published
1975		Midwest Association for Behavior Analysis founded
		The Ethics of Helping People published by B. F. Skinner
		Proceedings from the first Drake Conference on Professional Issues in Behavior Analysis published
1977	Canada's Council's Consultative Group on Ethics publishes report on ethical principles for researchers and review committees	*Behaviorism and Ethics* published by Krapfl and Vargas
	Medical Research Council of South Africa (MRCSA) publishes Guidelines on Ethics for Medical Research	
	The People Shapers published by Packard	
1978	Medical Research Council of Canada publishes *Ethics in Human Experimentation*	*Social Validity: The Case for Subjective Measurement or How Applied Behavior Analysis is Finding its Heart* published by Wolf
		Behaviorists for Social Action Journal (*BFSAJ*) and Behaviorists for Social Action (BSA) Special Interest Group of ABAI are founded; BSA later (ca.

TABLE 1.1 Key events related to ethical codes and protections outside of and within behavior analysis.—cont'd

Year	Key events outside of behavior analysis	Key events within behavior analysis
		1980s) changes its name to Behaviorists for Social Responsibility (BFSR); BFSAJ changes name to *Behavior Analysis and Social Action (BASA)* in 1982 and to *Behavior & Social Issues (BSI)* in 1991
		Findings from the APA Commission on Behavior Modification, *Ethical Issues in Behavior Modification* published by Stolz
1979	*Belmont Report* published by the National Commission	*On the Usefulness of Intent for Distinguishing Between Research and Practice, and its Replacement by Social Contingency* by Goldiamond published in Belmont Report Appendix Volume II
1980	Indian Council of Medical Research (ICMR) publishes *Policy Statement on Ethical Considerations Involved in Research on Human Subjects*	ABAI presidential debates on application and analysis started
1981	Report of the US President's Commission for the Study of Ethical Problems in Medicine and Biomedical and Behavioral Research released, recommending that a Common Rule for all federally funded research be developed	ABAI presidential debates on application and analysis concluded
1982	Council for International Organizations of Medical Sciences with World Health Organization first proposes International Ethical Guidelines for Biomedical Research Involving Human Subjects	
1986	Project Follow Through, largest federally sponsored educational experiment to determine best strategies for teaching at-risk students (grades K-3rd) commences and runs through 1977	
1987	South Africa's Human Sciences Research Council published its Code of Research Ethics	*Some Still-Current Dimensions of Applied Behavior Analysis* published by Baer et al.

Continued

TABLE 1.1 Key events related to ethical codes and protections outside of and within behavior analysis.—cont'd

Year	Key events outside of behavior analysis	Key events within behavior analysis
	Willowbrook State School closes	US Department of Education provides funding for non-aversive behavior management research and training center
1988	New Zealand's "Cartwright Inquiry" reports on the treatment of cervical cancer at New Zealand's National Women's Hospital	*The Right to Effective Behavioral Treatment* published by Van Houten et al.
1989	United Nations Convention on the Rights of the Child	ABAI releases position statement on clients' right to effective behavioral treatment
		Coercion and its Fallout published by Sidman
1990	Norwegian Parliament approves establishment of three national committees for research ethics	*Balancing the Right to Habilitation with the Right to Personal Liberties: The Rights of People with Developmental Disabilities to Eat Too Many Doughnuts and Take a Nap* published by Bannerman et al.
		Toward a Technology of "Nonaversive" Behavioral Support published by Horner et al. introducing the term "positive behavioral support"
1991	"Common Rule" (CRF 46) adopted by 16 US Federal departments and agencies	*Some Values Guiding Community Research and Action* published by Fawcett
	Interim Guidelines on Ethical Matters in Aboriginal and Torres Strait Islander Research released in Australia	*Social Validity Assessments: Is Current Practice State of the Art?* published by Schwartz and Baer
1992	Australian Health Ethics Committee (AHEC) established	
	Research ethics committees established in Denmark	
1993	Vancouver Protocol published by International Committee of Medical Journal Editors	

TABLE 1.1 Key events related to ethical codes and protections outside of and within behavior analysis.—cont'd

Year	Key events outside of behavior analysis	Key events within behavior analysis
1994	US Advisory Committee on Human Radiation Experiments formed	
	Canada's three key research Councils (MRC, NSERC and SSHRC) release Statement on Integrity in Research and Scholarship	
	US Advisory Committee on Human Radiation Experiments reports published; President Clinton apologizes to the citizens who were subjected to these experiments, their families, and communities	
1995	Australian Commonwealth Government releases Report of the Review of the Role and Functioning of Institutional Review Committees	
1996	President Clinton apologizes to Tuskegee experimental subjects	
	National Health Council in Brazil adopts Guidelines and Norms Regulating Research Involving Human Subjects (Resolution 196/96)	
1997	Joint NHRMC/AV-CC Statement and Guidelines on Research Practice released in Australia	
	Canada's Tri-Council Policy Statement: Ethical Conduct for Research Involving Humans	
1998		Behavior Analyst Certification Board (BACB) established; First discipline specific and national ethics code released including a section on research ethics
1999		*Journal of Positive Behavior Interventions (JPBI)* founded

Continued

TABLE 1.1 Key events related to ethical codes and protections outside of and within behavior analysis.—cont'd

Year	Key events outside of behavior analysis	Key events within behavior analysis
2000	United States Federal Policy on Research Misconduct	*European Journal of Behavior Analysis* (*EJOBA*) founded
	Canadian interagency Advisory Panel on Research Ethics (PRE)	
	National Committee for Ethics in Social Science Research in Health (NCESSRH) in India publishes Ethical Guidelines for Social Science Research in Health	
2001	*Values and Ethics: Guidelines for Ethical Conduct in Aboriginal and Torres Strait Islander Health Research* published in Australia	
2002	American Anthropology Association's El Dorado Task Force final report	*Is it Morally Defensible to Use the Developmentally Disabled as Guinea Pigs* published by Malott
	Council for International Organizations of Medical Sciences most recent revision of International Ethical Guidelines for Biomedical Research Involving Human Subjects	
	Association of Internet Researchers' recommendations on ethical decision-making and internet research	
2003	Canadian PRE's Working Party report *Giving Voice to the Spectrum*	
2004	RESPECT Principles for Ethical Socio-Economic Research	
	2004 Health Act in South Africa	
2005	EUREC Declaration to establish a European Network of Research Ethics Committees	*Ethics for Behavior Analysts* published by Bailey and Burch
	OHRP sets out preliminary criteria for determining whether institutions outside the United States offer protections equivalent to their "Common Rule"	

TABLE 1.1 Key events related to ethical codes and protections outside of and within behavior analysis.—cont'd

Year	Key events outside of behavior analysis	Key events within behavior analysis
	British ESRC's Research Ethics Framework	
2006	Australian Code for the Responsible Conduct of Research and National Statement on Ethical Conduct in Human Research	
	NESH publishes guidelines for cultural and social studies in Norway	
2007	Swedish Research Council's *Good Research Practice* guide	
	Forum for Ethical Review Committees in Thailand produces guidelines for research on human subjects	
	South Korean Ministry of Science and Technology's *Guides for Securing Research Ethics*	
2008	Canadian PRE's Working Party report on ethical issues in internet-based research	Pennsylvania becomes the first state to license behavior analysts
		Association for Professional Behavior Analysts (APBA) founded
		BACB adds Board Certified Behavior Analyst-Doctoral (BCBA-D) designation
2009	British ESRC revises Framework for Research Ethics	
	Finnish National Advisory Board on Research Integrity publishes principles for the social sciences and humanities	
	Qatar's Guidelines, Regulations and Policies for Research Involving Human Subjects	

Continued

TABLE 1.1 Key events related to ethical codes and protections outside of and within behavior analysis.—cont'd

Year	Key events outside of behavior analysis	Key events within behavior analysis
2010	Second edition of Canada's Tri-Council Policy Statement: Ethical Conduct for Research Involving Humans (TCPS 2)	ABAI releases position statement on restraint and seclusion
	Te Ara Tika drafted for Māori research ethics	
	Singapore Statement on Research Integrity adopted by the second World Conference on Research Integrity	
	Saudi Arabia's System of Ethics of Research on Living Subjects	
2011	*The Immortal Life of Henrietta Lacks* published by Rebecca Skloot	
	NIH and NSF revise their conflict-of-interest rules for funded research	
	The Office of Human Research Protections announces proposed changes to the Common Rule to enhance human subject protections and reduce investigator burden.	
	Canada's Tri-Agency Framework: Responsible Conduct of Research	
2012	Australian Institute of Aboriginal and Torres Strait Islander Studies (AIATSIS) Guidelines for Ethical Research in Australian Indigenous Studies	
2013	NIH reaches agreement with the Lacks family giving the family control of data access and acknowledgment in scientific publications	
	The New Brunswick Declaration: A Declaration on Research Ethics, Integrity and Governance	
	International Committee of Medical Journal Editors (ICMJE) releases its Recommendations for the Conduct,	

TABLE 1.1 Key events related to ethical codes and protections outside of and within behavior analysis.—cont'd

Year	Key events outside of behavior analysis	Key events within behavior analysis
	Reporting, Editing, and Publication of Scholarly Work in Medical Journals	
2020	World Health Organization (WHO) declares COVID-19 a pandemic	
2021	Lacks family sues Thermo Fisher Scientific for commercializing HeLa cell line	Massachusetts Association for Applied Behavior Analysis (MassABA) *Position Statement on the Use of Electric Shock as an Intervention in the Treatment of Individuals with Disabilities* released
	George Floyd Uprisings	*Behavior Analysis in Practice* Journal releases special issue on racism and police brutality
		Behavior Analysis in Practice Journal releases special issue on culture
		Social Justice is the Spirit and Aim of an Applied Science of Behavior: Moving from Colonial to Participatory Research Practices published by Pritchett et al.
		Quality of Life for People with Disabilities: Why Applied Behavior Analysts Should Consider This a Primary Dependent Variable published by Schwartz and Kelly

Information included in Table 1.1 was selected from several sources (Beirne & Sadavoy, 2022; Curry, 2013; Israel, 2014; Luke et al., 2017; Michael, 1980; Resnik, 2021; Rutherford, 2006; Sailor et al., 2009; Stolz, 1978; US House of Representatives: History, Art & Archives, 2008; Wood, 1975). Table 1.1 generally reveals a pattern, within and outside of behavior analysis, of disruptions that occurred across the globe and of systems that have and are responding through discourse and policy revisions, shaping our research practices, and shifting the boundaries of research ethics. For example, in 1968, the *Journal of Applied Behavior Analysis* was founded. One of the primary stated purposes was to produce socially important research (Baer et al., 1968). The journal and the commentary emerged at a time of heightened civil rights activity in the United States (US) and in response to a need for an applied publication venue. What constitutes applied, and the lineage, is a topic of study itself (Morris et al., 2013). Determining what is important (and to whom it is important) turned out to be a complicated endeavor, and discourse continues as to how this can be ethically accomplished (e.g., Schwartz & Baer, 1991; Schwartz & Kelly, 2021; Wolf, 1978).

Formal expressions of concern can take many forms. For example, the general public has long expressed concerns regarding "the deliberate alteration of human behavior" (Stolz, 1978, p. 1; see also Hilts, 1974; Rutherford, 2006). As the Department of Health, Education, and Welfare started to expand guidelines and regulations that had previously focused on medical research to also consider practices in social and behavioral research (ca., early 1960s), behavior analytic research and practice were becoming more widespread in education (e.g., Project Follow Through; Bushell et al., 1975), community settings (e.g., Achievement Place; Braukman et al., 1975), psychiatric hospitals, and prisons. The public's discomfort and fear of behavioral control combined with the discovery of severe misapplications of behavioral technologies (Risley, 1975) gained the attention of groups such as the American Civil Liberties Union concerned with the use of behavioral interventions in prisons and members of Congress concerned with the potential for behavior change programs to infringe on constitutional law and individual rights. Responses to the public outcry included targeted inquiries into specific programs such as the Special Treatment and Rehabilitative Training program and formal investigation of grant funded behavioral intervention programs conducted in prisons. Specific programs were terminated; the Law Enforcement Assistance Administration funds for behavioral intervention programs were suspended, and the National Research Act (PL 93−348) was passed. Professional organizations (e.g., the American Psychological Association and the Association for the Advancement of Behavior Therapy) formed commissions, task forces, and committees that issued public statements and reports (Stolz et al., 1975), and concerned behavior scientists held conferences focused solely on discussions of ethical and professional issues in behavior analysis (e.g., the Drake conference; Wood, 1975). These social outcries and the responses from social, political, and disciplinary institutions served as catalysts for discussions regarding the regulation of professional activities from both within (e.g., Florida Association for Behavior Analysis) and outside the scientific community (e.g., Americans with Disabilities Act). They also serve as examples of some of the first analyses and discussions of the ethical issues in behavior analytic research and practice, and many of the topics and themes remain salient today as evidenced in our current ethics codes (BACB, 2020).

Public expressions of dissatisfaction with behavioral interventions are key indicators of social invalidity and serve as opportunities for change (Schwartz & Baer, 1991). Responses to social outcries can affect meaningful change, especially for research participants, so long as research behaviors and practices evolve in response. Often, however, researchers and practitioners may ignore or dismiss some voices in favor of others, and responses to public outcries can be unnecessarily delayed, slowing scientific advancements, and prolonging individual suffering. This may be especially true when the voices are louder and are accompanied by powerful aversive contingencies (e.g., loss of funding, positions). Populations that are generally more subject to societal disparities are more likely to be exploited.

Exploitation for knowledge

Necropolitics

Who can use who? Who controls the course and the value of individual lives? "Necropolitics" is the term used to describe the societal systems that exert power over who is afforded life and who is expendable by death (Mbembé & Meintjes, 2003). Manifestations of power over the lives of others are best understood through the relations of dominant persons who are in positions to determine the value of human lives relative to their societal positions that give them power over persons of lesser autonomy. This power might start with use of groups of persons and go as far as to determine the extermination of groups of persons. Through this process, lives perceived as lesser become entities to be possessed, used, and transformed by the dominant group (Foucault, 1997; Mbembé & Meintjes, 2003).

When seen from the lens of the present day, there are many historical actions in the name of biomedical and behavioral research that would produce outrage and policy changes, especially when those research practices occurred disproportionately on people who are vulnerable. Humans have suffered inhumane treatments because they are poor, disabled, or imprisoned; and because racism, sexism, nationalism, religious hatred, and other forms of domination allowed one group to use another group to advance their own knowledge base and well-being (Office for Human Research Protections, 2016).

Probably the most notorious examples of research atrocities were against Jewish people by Nazi physicians conducting research in World War II concentration camps. Humans who were prisoners, already subjugated to inhumane conditions, were further tortured in scientific experiments, such as the injection of toxic substances and objects into their bodies, to observe their physical and behavioral responses (Rice, 2008). Society reacted. The Nazi physicians were prosecuted for crimes against peace and humanity in The Nuremberg Trials in Nuremberg, Germany. The outcomes of these trials occasioned the first waves of initiatives dedicated to defining human rights and developing protections for human research subjects (Rice, 2008; Slavicek & Forsdahl, 2009).[1] On December 10, 1948, the United Nations General Assembly articulated the first international declaration about basic human rights, The Universal Declaration of Human Rights (UDHR) (United Nations, 1948). The United Nations states:

> *Human rights are rights inherent to all human beings, regardless of race, sex, nationality, ethnicity, language, religion, or any other status. Human rights include the right to life and liberty, freedom from slavery and torture, freedom of opinion and expression, the right to work and education, and many more. Everyone is entitled to these rights, without discrimination.*

(United Nations, n.d.)

The UDHR was created in the midst of several other initiatives throughout the world. How human rights were to be protected and by whom in the context of biomedical and behavioral research were outlined in ethical standards created specifically in response to violations of the protection of human research subjects. For example, the Nuremberg Code (1947), the Declaration of Geneva (1948), and the Declaration of Helsinki (1964) are all policies directed toward preventing human rights violations (Rice, 2008; Slavicek & Forsdahl, 2009). At the same time that Nazi physicians were being tried for egregious crimes against humanity in Germany, events were taking place in the United States that would further evolve the intentional protection of research subjects, especially those who are vulnerable to the oppressions of their societal contexts.

Ironically, the "mother of modern medicine" (Nelson, 2017; Smith, 2018) was the quintessential example of exploitation and oppression. The scientific understandings that became possible using Mrs. Lacks' cells have resulted in countless lives saved, scientific discoveries, Nobel prizes, and numerous medical advances, including contributions to the development of COVID-19 vaccines (Wolinetz & Collins, 2020). An explicit example of necropolitics, Mrs. Lacks cells were obtained without consent, compensation, or acknowledgment; and the treatment she received during the Jim Crow era in Baltimore, Maryland, was not comparable to the treatment of White, affluent peers (Skloot, 2011). In a book popular in both scientific and lay communities, *The Immortal Life of Henrietta Lacks*, Skloot details the dramatic and traumatic events of Mrs. Lacks life. She arrived at Johns Hopkins Hospital on January 29, 1951. She was Black, young, a mother, and poor. Mrs. Lacks was in excruciating pain. Her cervix was scraped for pathological tests. The samples

---

1. Over the last 20+ years, there has been shift from the use of "subjects" to "participants" to describe the individuals who volunteer to participant in human research. Readers will note that both terms occur throughout the chapter. We have maintained the use of "subjects" when this is the term used in the original source or when we are describing an event in its historical context.

were sent for examination. They were also sent for research purposes, unrelated to her well-being and without her consent. These cells became extraordinarily noteworthy in that instead of quickly dying, as other cell specimens had, they multiplied rapidly, an important feature for scientific preparations. These unique "HeLa" cells are still harvested by the trillions and integral for medical use and research today. Mrs. Lacks, a victim of generations of generational societal trauma, died of cervical cancer, unknown and in poverty and pain 9 months after her visit to Johns Hopkins Hospital.

The events that transpired after Mrs. Lacks entered the hospital are examples of human rights violations in the context of biomedical research. Pivotal questions related to these kinds of circumstances emerged in the years following: Who gives consent and what are the conditions and context in which consent is obtained? How is consent obtained? To what extent can a person with marginalized social status, with severely restricted treatment options, suffering from severe pain, provide truly informed and meaningful consent? Would Mrs. Lacks agree as to how her cells have been and continue to be used today? When specimens leave human bodies to whom do they belong? Who has the right to decide? Who profits from another person's body? Parallel ethical questions can be found in the context of research about human behavior.

A parallel example in behavioral research is illustrated by Fuller (1949), a seminal publication in human operant conditioning. He describes the patient:

> … an opportunity was offered to us to conduct an operant conditioning experiment on an 18-yr-old inmate of a feeble-minded [sic] institution, whose behavior was that of a 'vegetative idiot.' [sic] The term 'vegetative' [sic] clearly describes his condition. He lay on his back and could not roll over; he could, however, open his mouth, blink, and move his arms, head and shoulders, to a slight extent. He never moved his trunk or legs. The attendant reported that he never made any sounds; but in the course of the experiment vocalizations were heard. He had some teeth but did not chew. He had been fed liquids and semi-solids all his life. While being fed, he sometimes choked and would cough vigorously.

(Fuller, 1949, p. 588)

Through experimental operant conditioning sessions, Fuller (1949) demonstrated success in shaping arm raising responses using a sugar milk solution following 15 hours of food deprivation. The subject was an unnamed, nonconsenting resident of a state institution. Moreover, Fuller considered his subject at the bottom of a scale of human worth; he writes, "Perhaps by beginning at the bottom of the human scale the transfer from rat to man can be effected [sic]" (p. 590). Nevertheless, Fuller is widely cited in introductory textbooks as one of the first demonstrations of human operant conditioning (Cooper et al., 2019) and touted as important to the development of an applied science of human behavior. Despite its historical significance that highlights the generality of behavior principles across species, the experiment now begs ethical questions similar to the case of Mrs. Lacks. What did lack of consent imply about the worth of this person in the eyes of the researcher and the scientific community? Was the subject of Fuller's experiment able to meaningfully consent to participate? What knowledge or understanding of the experimental procedures did they have? Was there any person there to meaningfully advocate for or protect the subject? In what way did the conditioning of an arm-raising response benefit the subject? What were the conditions under which this person was selected for this experiment? Fuller notes that "an opportunity was offered to us" (p. 588), but would the subject of Fuller's experiment consider the experiment an "opportunity" as well?

The experiments conducted on Mrs. Lacks and the unnamed subject of Fuller's experiment are extremely unsettling. It is clear, however, throughout the end of the 19th and beginning of the 20th century, these and other similar events were largely ignored. Biomedical and behavioral research procedures did not change until the outcry that followed the Tuskegee Syphilis Study conducted by the US Public Health Service from 1932 to 1972 at the Tuskegee Institute in Tuskegee, Alabama. Over the course of 40 years, 600 subjects were enrolled in a study of the short- and long-term effects of syphilis. All of the subjects were Black male sharecroppers in Alabama. They were poor, forced to work in questionable sharecropping arrangements, and had not been afforded or allowed opportunities to learn to read and write. In exchange for participation in a study about "bad blood," they were offered medical exams, transportation, meals, and burial costs. None of the men knew the purpose of the research was, in fact, to study the course of untreated syphilis, and that 5 years after the study began penicillin had become a recognized treatment for the disease. For 35 years, the subjects and their families were denied treatment. They were unaware that the true purpose of the research was to study the outcomes and effects of untreated syphilis *post-mortem*. Their deaths were conducive to the knowledge being gained and their deaths considered acceptable (Tuskegee University, n.d.). This was necropolitics.

Protections

Once the Tuskegee study was publicly understood, in a context of changing views on the worth of Black Americans, public outrage increased. The outrage was mounted during a period in history when US society was shifting policies about civil and human rights. That is, during a period of great unrest, citizens who could vote were deciding that Black people should be afforded civil rights, that people with disabilities should be afforded education, and that poverty was an injustice to be fought and dismantled. Such events led to the establishment of the first national institution dedicated to bioethics policy, the National Commission for the Protection of Human Subjects of Biomedical and Behavioral Research. The task of the commission was fourfold: (1) to analyze the boundaries between biomedical and behavioral research, including defining acceptable medical practices, (2) to assess risks and benefits in human subject research, (3) to develop guidelines for how human subjects can be selected for research, and (4) to define informed consent in research settings (CDC, 2020).

Knowledge seeking with protections

Belmont report

The National Research Act of 1974 (PL 93−348) established the National Commission for the Protection of Human Subjects of Biomedical Behavioral Research in the United States. Members of the Commission gathered for monthly discussions for 4 years and "one of the charges to the Commission was to identify the basic ethical principles that should underlie the conduct of biomedical and behavioral research involving human subjects and to develop guidelines which should be followed to assure that such research is conducted in accordance with those principles" (Office for Human Research Protections, 2016, para. 1). The result was the Belmont Report, which outlines three ethical principles: respect, beneficence, and justice. The associated guidelines were designed to serve as a minimum standard for protection of humans participating in biomedical and behavioral research (Office for Human Research Protections, 2016).

Respect. Autonomy is a central organizing principle related to respect. Individuals should be considered autonomous or free to act of their own accord; and in the event they have compromised autonomy, they should be protected (Office for Human Research Protections, 2016). This requires the researcher to both acknowledge the value of autonomy and to protect persons with compromised autonomy. Persons without autonomy are especially vulnerable due to an inability to express their personal goals, opinions, and choices, and to be free from coercion when choices are made available (Bannerman et al., 1990). Respect is diminished when acts of agency are extinguished or punished by the researcher by repudiation or denial of freedom to make decisions, or by withholding information necessary to make informed decisions (Office for Human Research Protections, 2016). Respect is also diminished when societal structures and policies place individuals in a position of little or no agency.

In most cases of research involving human participants, ensuring respect for persons involves arranging protections for participants such that they may enter research voluntarily and with adequate information. In some cases, there are groups of people with vulnerabilities that need more extensive protection due to circumstances that severely restrict liberty (Office for Human Research Protections, 2016). Moreover, persons with multiple intersections of identity (e.g., race, class, religion, gender, disability status, sexual orientation) may experience a compounding effect of vulnerability that deserves particular care and protection (Crenshaw, 1989). For example, Mrs. Lacks' race, level of education, and socioeconomic status are all factors that increased her vulnerability and marginalization in society. Her options for medical care were extremely limited, which set the occasion for her to unknowingly become a human research subject. Mrs. Lacks "was a black woman born of slavery and sharecropping who fled north for prosperity, only to have her cells used as tools by white scientists without her consent" (Skloot, 2011, p. 197).

Persons with vulnerabilities have compromised capacity to independently make meaningful and informed decisions about their lives. Factors that can reduce autonomy include, but are not limited to, age, cognitive ability (e.g., mental illness, intellectual disability), and health status (Office for Human Research Protections, 2016). In some cases, legal guardians, parents, and/or custodians are given the authority to provide consent for others. Research participants without the ability (by their own and/or society's capacity) to clearly consent to the risks and benefits of research (e.g., adults with intellectual disabilities, children with or without developmental disabilities) depend on assistance in the decision-making process. As a result of these conditions that can compromise meaningful and informed consent, additional protections such as obtaining child assent and parental/guardian consent are now considered necessary (Committee on Bioethics, American Academy of Pediatrics, 1995; Office for Human Research Protections, 2016; Rossi et al., 2003).

It is currently expected that the principle of respect for persons is maintained throughout the research process rather than as a discrete event that occurs only at the outset of the research when consent forms are signed. Moreover, the extent to which protections are applied are individualized, periodically reevaluated, and adjusted when necessary. This is dictated by the needs of the participant, as evaluated by independent reviewers. These research practices ensure the optimal reduction of risk and maximization of benefit (Office for Human Research Protections, 2016).

Beneficence. Beneficence is the guiding principle to protect the well-being of the research participant. Beneficence is defined as the researcher's obligation to do no harm while ensuring maximum benefit and minimal risk. Such cost–benefit analyses are ethically complex and variable due to the difficulty of the decision-making process. The researcher must determine if the potential risks for participants are justifiable in relation to the potential benefits of the research (Office for Human Research Protections, 2016; see also Stolz, 1978 for a more detailed discussion of risk–benefit analyses in behavioral research). Fuller (1949), for example, demonstrated the success of an operant conditioning procedure used to shape an arm-raising response, an experiment that proved beneficial for behavioral scientists and society. However, the behavior that was increased did not expand the subject's repertoire in a way that improved their quality of life; the target response was likely selected for ease of measurement, not to benefit the subject. Additionally, deprivation of sustenance for 15 hours did not contribute to the subject's emotional, physical, or medical well-being. The principle of beneficence reminds researchers that the benefits of the research should be incurred first by the research participant and *then* extended to members of society (Office for Human Research Protections, 2016).

Justice. The principle of justice in biomedical and behavioral research addresses the over and underselection of populations with vulnerabilities for research participation, calling into question who should bear the burden of the research experience and what members of society receive the benefits of the research. Historically, persons with vulnerabilities have been overselected for some lines of research participation (see also Malott, 2002), bearing the burden of research due to their inability to understand, self-advocate, or escape the research context because of their marginalized and disempowered positions in society. Acts of injustice occur when benefits are unfairly denied or when burdens are unduly applied. Equitable distribution of benefits among various persons and their positions in society requires researchers to comprehend equality, inequality, and how to distribute research burdens across persons based on these qualifiers (Office for Human Research Protections, 2016). Perhaps most importantly,

> the selection of research subjects needs to be scrutinized in order to determine whether some classes (e.g., welfare patients, particular racial and ethnic minorities, or persons confined to institutions) are being systematically selected simply because of their easy availability, their compromised position, or their manipulability, rather than for reasons directly related to the problem being studied.

(Office for Human Research Protections, 2016, para. 24)

For example, The Tuskegee Syphilis Study included a homogeneous group of poor, Black, male, sharecroppers who had been generationally denied access to education due to enslavement and civil rights restrictions. They bore the burden of research participation such that the impact of syphilis could be studied before and after they died. Moreover, despite their contributions to the knowledge base that produced the treatment (Tuskegee University, n.d.), they were purposefully denied the benefits of a treatment to cure the disease that was discovered shortly after the study was initiated.

Institutional review boards

The ethical principles in the Belmont Report established a minimum standard for protection of human participants in biomedical and behavioral research. These minimum standards are regulated through agencies specifically established to ensure protections preemptively and during the research process. The agencies are typically referred to as Institutional Review Boards (IRBs). IRBs are mandated to regulate processes and outcomes along several dimensions. For example, there are requirements that the composition of the IRB membership includes scientific, nonscientific, and community members and that those members have experience and training regarding the needs of vulnerable populations. There are specific application criteria regarding respect, beneficence, and justice to be addressed when applying for permission to conduct research with human participants, and there are specific approval criteria that involve appropriateness of the informed consent process, participant selection, monitoring, confidentiality, and minimization of harm. In a commentary on the IRB process, Grady (2015) notes, "although ethical principles underlying research with human subjects have not changed, their implementation and actualization requires refinement and adaptation to respond to changing scientific and social contexts" (p. 1153). The IRB process, like the research process, is responsive to the system contingencies and to the members of the system. The procedural safeguards put into place are in a state of evolution, balancing the pursuit of knowledge and the well-being of research participants and communities. Procedures and policies like those of the IRB are continually modified through ethics discourse as widening groups of people are involved in the process of knowledge production and human rights protections.

Collaborative knowledge seeking for well-being

Participatory action research

Finally, and perhaps one of the most significant historical events in the context of this chapter is the emergence of Participatory Action Research (PAR). PAR is an approach with an impressive array of progenitors from diverse research sectors, beginning as early as the 1940s, highlighted by Freire in the 1970s, and established in the 1990s as a new scientific paradigm for dismantling oppressive structures in the production of knowledge and betterment (see Jacobs, 2018). PAR was first introduced to behavior analysis by Fawcett in 1991 and revisited 30 years later by Pritchett et al. (2021) and Fawcett (2021). PAR is a research methodology characterized by active participation of research participants to address real-world problems. Research questions are developed in collaboration between researchers and participants and emerge from the participants' current concerns and those of the communities to which they belong. Thus, the research engagement is directly applicable to improvement of the participants' lives, by including their concerns, needs, and voices, and directly challenges the traditional researcher-driven relationships, neutralizing power imbalances between persons in the research context, and avoiding colonial relationships (Fawcett, 1991; Pritchett et al., 2021). PAR also emphasizes the emancipation of persons suffering from oppressive societal conditions denoting an explicit social justice agenda. Participants are active members in problem solving and knowledge seeking opportunities dedicated to improvement of lived conditions (see for example, Baum et al., 2006; Jacobs, 2018). In the context of behavior analytic research, participatory approaches increase the likelihood of generating socially valid research goals, procedures, and outcomes (Wolf, 1978), avoiding rejection (Schwartz & Baer, 1991), while encouraging active engagement of people who have been systematically and historically marginalized, resulting in valued benefits for diverse groups of people *and* valuable knowledge about behavior change (Fawcett, 1991).

Shifting perspectives: context, epistemology, ontology, and axiology

This chapter is intentionally placed within an evolutionary, ecological, and culturo-behavioral systems science framework. We deliberately shifted between context and details. Research ethics are necessarily nonlinear and recursive. Ethical decision-making requires shifting between molar and molecular perspectives. Research ethics, and specifically the ethics of our research care, are evolving; and they are evolving with a global context that operates within changing discourses about the nature of our existence in relationship to one another. In the late 1970s, Bandura (1978) noted that

> *a psychological [behavioral] technology operates within the values, ideologies, and power structures of a social system … Ethical dilemmas arise repeatedly when practitioners bear the double responsibility of furthering institutional goals while at the same time attempting to serve diverse individual interests. When these aims do not coincide, questions arise about whether the individuals or the institutional practices require change. The direction in which such value dilemmas are resolved rests partly on how much power the various constituencies exercise in determining the functions and practices of social institutions.*

> (p. x)

The ethics of epistemologies focus on the procedures and methods of how we obtain knowledge and what is considered viable knowledge and under what conditions. As can be seen by the timeline and through publications in behavior analysis (Table 1.1), there is also a growing body of scholarship that is centered on the social justice aspects of our research and practices (e.g., Pritchett et al., 2021; Sadavoy & Zube., 2021). Social justice issues raised in these arenas are closely tied to our discourses, within and outside of behavior analysis, related to our worldviews. That is, how we, as a species, view the ideas about the reality of our existence (ontological) and the value of those realities across members of our species (axiological). The discourses around values and ideologies, and who is participating in the discourse, are rapidly changing and are evidenced by recent events in the United States and across the world.

Uprisings, agency, and pandemics

The Unites States may have reached an inflection point in the wake of the painful and public murder of Mr. George Floyd and other similar events, in challenging systemic racism and a long history of injustices against Black individuals. The research enterprise must admit to its own ugly scars of institutional racism, from the unethical Tuskegee syphilis experiments on Black men, to the recently troubling revelations that Black researchers are significantly less likely to receive funding from the National Institutes of Health (NIH) than their White counterparts, and that research involving healthcare disparities is less likely to be funded (Ginther et al., 2011).

The importance of scientists understanding the history of research ethics in the context of human rights abuses cannot be understated, especially given the persistent outcries of persons who have historically been defined by the dominant caste as lesser or subhuman. In an increasingly globalized world, human interconnectedness is more and more apparent, and the urgency to protect all of humanity is more vital (Karlberg & Farhoumand-Sims, 2006). In fact, there is a growing worldview that the well-being or suffering of one individual can only be viewed in the context of the well-being or suffering of the human collective. To accept and promote this ideology in our research is a value, a value that compels us to seek social justice for all members of the species (Maparyan, 2012) and to not value the benefits of one group over another.

The spread of the COVID-19 virus and its many variants across the planet unveiled many disparities in life and life expectancy. In the United States, for example, the COVID-19 pandemic reduced the life expectancy for Black and Latino persons at a rate of 3—4 times more than White persons (Andrasfay & Goldman, 2021; Woolf et al., 2021). Subsequently, the American Public Health Association (APHA) reported many cities in the United States have declared racism a public health crisis (APHA, 2021). Although emerging conversations regarding the impact of these "converging pandemics" have increased, science continues to operate under a "veneer of neutrality" (Benjamin, 2019) in which perceived objectivity assumes data are simply numbers rather than numerical representations of human life. The science of behavior can learn from the past, especially from colleagues in more entrenched disciplines such as medicine, and learn to engage in practices that prevent the science of behavior from becoming (perhaps further) complicit in widening these disparities in the name of research and experimentation as has medicine.

Accordingly, even though we care, we are still learning what that means and under what conditions care is expressed. We are still learning how much we have not cared. We are still learning how much damage has been done. We are still learning what not to do. We are still learning what to do (e.g., What and who do we protect? What does well-being mean? What is global justice?). The social environments, cultures, and networks of contingencies internal and external to our own scientific communities can provide us with clues. Social outcries to scientific research, for example, are indicators of social invalidity and opportunities for behavioral researchers and practitioners to learn and evolve (Schwartz & Baer, 1991). Social invalidity and the commodification of the knowledge gained through behavioral research are less likely to occur if measures of social validity are held to the same esteem as internal validity. Social invalidity is not the opposite of social validity; rather, social validity is, on the one hand, a method for understanding what and how a particular individual or group can benefit (Fawcett, 1991; Schwartz & Kelly, 2021; Wolf, 1978) and, on the other hand, can serve as a framework to understand counter control and what happens when people who disagree with behavior analytic research or practice elect to refuse portions of or outright reject the entire science (Schwartz & Baer, 1991). They are indicators of colonial research practices and coercive research contexts (Pritchett et al., 2021). One of many ways to prevent the emergence of socially invalid research and increase socially valid research is through participatory and collaborative research practices (e.g., PAR). Moreover, while converging pandemics/crises amplify, exemplify, and horrify, they also make necessary an evolutionary response (even if one is not ready). Social disruption often requires us to see things in a very different way. Crises and disruptions are opportunities for change and thus for paradigm shifts (Risley, 2001).

Within our own scientific community, we can be cognizant of the networks of contingencies in our social environments and cultures. For example, when

> [u]tilizing behavioral methods for remedial purposes, one must distinguish between social regulation and treatment. Social regulation subordinates the interest of the individual to the group, prescribed conduct by institutional means, and authorizes coercive measures to force compliance; and agents of social regulation work mainly to further institutional goals. In the case of treatment, the interests of the individual are given priority, personal consent and choice about direction of change are possible, the right to terminate the relationship is recognized, and the agent of change works mainly for the benefit of the individual seeking help.
>
> (Bandura, 1978, p. x)

Ignoring Bandura's concerns in the context of research puts behavior analysts/scientists at risk for engaging in research practices that are dehumanizing and threaten the inherent dignity of all humans behind the objective veneer of science (Benjamin, 2019). Shifting our orientation in behavior analytic research toward participatory practices creates space for collaboration with research participants rather than researcher-dominated research engagements in which persons are treated as objects (i.e., subjects) of inquiry from which data are extracted.

The science of behavior change is powerful and changing behavior makes a difference in the trajectory of lives. By necessity, ethics are at the center of every behavior change research endeavor. The science of behavior analysis has made significant knowledge advancements, perhaps at times at the expense of human rights (Pritchett et al., 2021). However, advancements at the expense of human rights can and should be avoided as we move into new frontiers of exploration and inquiry. Consider the decades of research in functional analysis of challenging behaviors (e.g., Iwata et al., 1982/1994). This work has proved instrumental in the treatment and prevention of severe challenging behaviors and it exemplifies Bandura's (1978) description of social regulation. The future of behavior change, however, is in the ultimate eradication of "the structures, the system, the forms of societal control" (Holland, 1978, p. 163) that produce the "problems" and the prevention of the emergence of challenging behaviors altogether (Ala'i-Rosales et al., 2019). This distinction and intentional shift in conceptualizations of care emphasize quality of life as the primary dependent variable and as the goal for all persons engaged in behavior analytic research (Schwartz & Kelly, 2021). Similar to Tuskegee, when a cure for syphilis was discovered a little over a decade after the study started, one of the most egregious human rights violations was that these men were allowed to suffer illness and die, rather than receive lifesaving treatment. In behavior analysis, there are areas in which we have learned enough about the contingencies that produce difficulty and distress that we can now focus on well-being and the prevention of suffering. Suffering can be avoided. Cihon et al. (2020) suggest that,

> behavior scientists must examine their own contingencies, the interlocking contingencies, and the metacontingencies of their own cultures and communities, always taking multiple perspectives and prioritizing collaboration as a preeminent practice. We must establish and sustain a culture that supports cultural practices that help others and improve the world.

(p. 213)

Conclusion: advancing our understanding of research ethics

The brief history of research ethics presented in this chapter highlights how global, social, political, and economic movements have influenced the development of procedural safeguards and institutional guidelines for research in behavior analysis. A clear understanding of the evolutionary history of research ethics within and outside of behavior analysis helps to see the trajectory toward human rights and social justice ethics. It has become conceivable for behavior analysts to envision research practices that encourage the full and active participation of the individuals who are involved, to contribute to create nonoppressive structures, and to avoid egregious human rights violations of the past. Although minimum standards for behavioral research exist (e.g., IRB, Belmont Report, Human Rights Committees), there is an increasing ethical obligation to go beyond the minimum standards, ensuring humane and ethical practices and participant well-being are at the core of all research activities, not simply as an afterthought or a social validity box that is checked on a list of minimum requirements at the conclusion of the experiment.

A brief history of research ethics presented here also emphasizes how the learned experiences of the scientific communities outside of behavior science have influenced behavioral research ethics. Disciplines such as biology, medicine, and public health have longer histories and experiences in research ethics than behavior science. They have also developed explicit subdisciplines, such as bioethics and medical ethics, which intentionally advance scientific practices and technologies. Behavior science and behavioral technologies have evolved considerably in the last several decades, notably in the domains of theory, experimental analysis of behavior, applied behavior analysis, and clinical practice. However, behavior science has not emphasized the need for an explicit focus on behavioral ethics as a separate but interrelated domain, despite early calls to do so in response to the rapid spread of the use of behavioral technologies seen in the 1960s and 1970s (see Stolz, 1978; Wood, 1975). As behavioral technologies have advanced and the application thereof has become more widespread, particularly with individuals with autism/autistics and as applied to individuals who engage in severe challenging behavior(s), there is a growing collective of individuals who are expressing public concern with behavior analytic research practices. Their voices, identities, and narratives are important and should be included in the framing and reframing of behavior analytic research practices. The system is disrupted and we would all benefit from systematic responses, such as a discipline specific domain such as bioethics in medicine, which is explicitly dedicated to human rights and the study of behavioral ethics. Topics of research might include developing an understanding of the environmental contingencies that reinforce or punish ethical behaviors, developing instructional programs and strategies that explore how to train ethical decision-making skills (Brodhead, 2015), and exploring different research strategies and tactics that increase participation and occasion genuine choice-making through measurement of inverse relationship of degrees of freedom and coercion (Goldiamond, 1974).

Behavior analysts are members of specific scientific communities and are also part of a rapidly changing world. It may be easier in either community to react after harm has occurred than to be proactive and preventative. At the same time, the trend is clear—disruptions will become more challenging and harmful as the injustices are more obvious and preventable. Behavior analytic researchers can respond to the trend and engage in the critical self-reflection necessary to prevent harm before it arises and to promote benefit for humanity. Current and aspiring behavior analysts no longer need to wait for social outcry to change the behaviors, practices, and contingencies of our scientific community; we can be proactive.

We beseech the readers of this volume to create a research culture in which the time and behavior of each participant are worthy of justice, respect, and beneficence; where the ethics of how to collaborate and design scientific and human research practices are central; the practices in which we engage are continually and critically revisited; and one in which ethical concerns expressed from all persons involved in the research, regardless of perceived rank or position of authority (e.g., professors, funding agencies, researchers, participants, graduate students, research assistants, community members, students, etc.) are welcomed and heard. In many cases the behavioral researcher might find oneself in a position in which the institutional contingencies appear in conflict; these contingencies need not be upheld at the expense of human rights. Our science is progressive (Leaf et al., 2016) and the boundaries of institutional contingencies can be expanded while simultaneously upholding the inherent dignity of persons. New ways can be developed, and history has suggested we are capable of envisioning new and innovative ways to move forward alongside, rather than at the expense of, humanity. Behavioral technologies are powerful, and behavioral researchers are subject to the systemic contingencies that perpetuate injustices and oppression as well as those that perpetuate justice, human rights, and freedom from coercion. In our dual roles as researchers and members of society, we can lean toward the latter and join the trend that cherishes and nurtures the sanctity of all human life.

References

Ala'i-Rosales, S., Cihon, J. H., Currier, T. D. R., Ferguson, J. L., Leaf, J. B., Leaf, R., McEachin, J., & Weinkauf, S. M. (2019). The big four: Functional assessment research informs preventative behavior analysis. *Behavior Analysis in Practice, 12*(1), 222−234. https://doi.org/10.1007/s40617-018-00291-9

American Public Health Association. (October 2021). *Analysis: Declarations of racism as a public health crisis.* https://www.apha.org/-/media/Files/PDF/topics/racism/Racism_Declarations_Analysis.ashx.

Andrasfay, T., & Goldman, N. (2021). Reductions in 2020 US life expectancy due to COVID-19 and the disproportionate impact on the Black and Latino populations. *Proceedings of the National Academy of Sciences, 118*(5), 1−6. https://doi.org/10.1073/pnas.2014746118

Baer, D. M., Wolf, M. M., & Risley, T. R. (1968). Some current dimensions of applied behavior analysis. *Journal of Applied Behavior Analysis, 1*(1), 91−97. https://doi.org/10.1901/jaba.1968.1-91

Bandura, A. (1978). Foreword. In S. B. Stolz, & Associates (Eds.), *Ethical issues in behavior modification* (pp. ix−x). Jossey-Bass Publishers.

Bannerman, D. J., Sheldon, J. B., Sherman, J. A., & Harchik, A. E. (1990). Balancing the right to habilitation with the right to personal liberties: The rights of people with developmental disabilities to eat too many doughnuts and take a nap. *Journal of Applied Behavior Analysis, 23*(1), 79−89. https://doi.org/10.1901/jaba.1990.23-79

Baum, F., MacDougall, C., & Smith, D. (2006). Participatory action research. *Journal of Epidemiology and Community Health, 60*(10), 854–857. https://doi.org/10.1136/jech.2004.028662

Behavior Analyst Certification Board. (2020). *Ethics code for behavior analysts*. Author. https://www.bacb.com/wp-content/uploads/2020/11/Ethics-Code-for-Behavior-Analysts-210902.pdf.

Beirne, A., & Sadavoy, J. A. (Eds.). (2022). *Understanding ethics in applied behavior analysis: Practical applications*. Routledge.

Benjamin, R. (2013). *People's science: Bodies and rights on the stem cell frontier*. Stanford University Press.

Benjamin, R. (2019). *Race after technology: Abolitionist tools for the new Jim code*. Polity.

Braukman, C. J., Fixsen, D. L., Kirigin, K. A., Phillips, E. A., Phillips, E. L., & Wolf, M. M. (1975). Achievement place: The training and certification of teaching parents. In S. W. Wood (Ed.), *Issues in evaluating behavior modification* (pp. 131–152). Research Press.

Brodhead, M. T. (2015). Maintaining professional relationships in an interdisciplinary setting: Strategies for navigating nonbehavioral treatment recommendations for individuals with autism. *Behavior Analysis in Practice, 8*, 70–78. https://doi.org/10.1007/s40617-015-0042-7

Bushell, D., Jackson, D. A., & Weis, L. C. (1975). Quality control in the behavior analysis approach to project follow through. In S. W. Wood (Ed.), *Issues in evaluating behavior modification* (pp. 107–125). Research Press.

Centers for Disease Control and Prevention. (2020). *The U.S. Public health Service syphilis study at Tuskegee: Research implications*. https://www.cdc.gov/tuskegee/after.htm.

Cihon, T. M., & Mattaini, M. A. (2019). Editorial: Emerging cultural and behavioral systems science. *Perspectives on Behavior Science, 42*(4), 699–711. https://doi.org/10.1007/s40614-019-00237-8

Cihon, T. M., & Mattaini, M. A. (Eds.). (2020). *Behavior science perspectives on culture and community*. Springer.

Cihon, T. M., Walker, D., Kazaoka, K., & Pritchett, M. (2020). Ethics for cultural and community applications of behavioral science. In T. M. Cihon, & M. A. Mattaini (Eds.), *Behavior science perspectives on culture and community* (pp. 195–219). Springer. https://doi.org/10.1007/978-3-030-45421-0_9

Committee on Bioethics, American Academy of Pediatrics. (1995). Informed consent, parental permission, and assent in pediatric practice. *Pediatrics, 95*(2), 314–317. https://doi.org/10.1542/peds.95.2.314

Cooper, J. O., Heron, T. E., & Heward, W. L. (2019). *Applied behavior analysis* (3rd ed.). Pearson Education.

Crenshaw, K. (1989). *Demarginalizing the intersection of race and sex: A black feminist critique of antidiscrimination doctrine, feminist theory and antiracist politics* (Vol. 140, pp. 139–267). University of Chicago Legal Forum.

Curry, K. (2013). The sunland training centers: Florida's Institutes for children with intellectual disabilities. *Health Review, 10*(6), 14–24. https://digitalcommons.unf.edu/fphr/vol10/iss1/6.

Fawcett, S. B. (1991). Some values guiding community research and action. *Journal of Applied Behavior Analysis, 24*(4), 621–636. https://doi.org/10.1901/jaba.1991.24-621

Fawcett, S. B. (2021). A reflection on community research and action as an evolving practice. *Behavior and Social Issues, 30*, 535–544. https://doi.org/10.1007/s42822-021-00083-x

Foucault, M. (1997). *Il faut défendre la société [We must defend society]*. Gallimard/Seuil.

Fuller, P. R. (1949). Operant conditioning of a vegetative human organism. *The American Journal of Psychology, 62*(4), 587–590. https://doi.org/10.2307/1418565

Ginther, D. K., Schaffer, W. T., Schnell, J., Masimore, B., Liu, F., Haak, L. L., & Kington, R. (2011). Race, ethnicity, and NIH research awards. *Science, 333*(6045), 1015–1019. https://doi.org/10.1126/science.1196783

Goldiamond, I. (1974). Toward a constructional approach to social problems: Ethical and constitutional issues raised by applied behavior analysis. *Behaviorism, 2*(1), 1–84. https://doi.org/10.5210/bsi.v11i2.92

Goldiamond, I. (1978). The professional as a double-agent. *Journal of Applied Behavior Analysis, 11*(1), 178–184. https://doi.org/10.1901/jaba.1978.11-178

Goldiamond, I. (1984). Training parent trainers and ethicists in nonlinear analysis of behavior. In R. F. Dangel, & R. A. Polster (Eds.), *Parent training: Foundations of research and practice* (pp. 504–546). The Guilford Press.

Grady, C. (2015). Institutional review boards: Purpose and challenges. *Chest, 148*(5), 1148–1155. https://doi.org/10.1378/chest.15-0706

Hilts, P. J. (1974). *Behavior mod*. Harper's Magazine Press.

Holland, J. G. (1978). Behaviorism: Part of the problem or part of the solution. *Journal of Applied Behavior Analysis, 11*(1), 163–174. https://doi.org/10.1901/jaba.1978.11-163

Israel, M. (2014). *Research ethics and integrity for social scientists: Beyond regulatory compliance*. SAGE.

Iwata, B. A., Dorsey, M. F., Slifer, K. J., Bauman, K. E., & Richman, G. S. (1982/1994). Toward a functional analysis of self-injury. *Journal of Applied Behavior Analysis, 27*(2), 197–209. https://doi.org/10.1901/jaba.1994.27-197

Jacobs, S. D. (2018). A history and analysis of the evolution of action and participatory action research. *Canadian Journal of Action Research, 19*(3), 34–52. https://doi.org/10.33524/cjar.v19i3.412

Karlberg, M., & Farhoumand-Sims, C. (2006). Global citizenship and humanities scholarship. *International Journal of the Humanities, 2*(3), 2189–2198.

Kubina, R. M., & Yurich, K. K. L. (2012). *The precision teaching book*. Greatness Achieved.

Leaf, J. B., Leaf, R., McEachin, J., Taubman, M., Ala'i-Rosales, S., Ross, R. K., Smith, T., & Weiss, M. J. (2016). Applied behavior analysis is a science and, therefore, progressive. *Journal of Autism and Developmental Disorders, 46*(2), 720–731. https://doi.org/10.1007/s10803-015-2591-6

Luke, M. M., Roose, K. M., Rakos, R. F., & Mattaini, M. A. (2017). The history and current status of *behavior and social issues*: 1978–2016. *Behavior and Social Issues, 26*, 111–127. https://doi.org/10.5210/bsi.v26i0.7728

Malott, R. W. (2002). Notes from a radical behaviorist: Is it morally defensible to use the developmentally disabled as Guinea pigs? *Behavior and Social Issues, 11*, 105–106. https://doi.org/10.5210/bsi.v11i2.90

Maparyan, L. (2012). *The womanist idea*. Routledge. https://doi.org/10.4324/9780203135938

Mattaini, M. A. (2013). *Strategic nonviolent power: The science of satyagraha*. Athabasca University Press.

Mbembé, J., & Meintjes, L. (2003). Necropolitics. *Public Culture, 15*(1), 11–40. https://www.muse.jhu.edu/article/39984.

Michael, J. (1980). Flight from behavior analysis pesidential address ABA 1980. *The Behavior Analyst, 3*, 1–21. https://doi.org/10.1007/bf03391838

Morris, E. K., Altus, D. E., & Smith, N. G. (2013). A study in the founding of applied behavior analysis through its publications. *The Behavior Analyst, 36*, 73–107. https://doi.org/10.1007/BF03392293

Nelson, K. (2017). *Henrietta Lacks (HeLa): The mother of modern medicine*. National Museum of African American History and Culture [Oil on linen] https://npg.si.edu/object/npg_NPG.2018.9.

Office for Human Research Protections. (2016). *The Belmont report*. https://www.hhs.gov/ohrp/regulations-and-policy/belmont-report/index.html.

Pritchett, M., Ala'i-Rosales, S., Cruz, A. R., & Cihon, T. M. (2021). Social justice is the spirit and aim of an applied science of human behavior: Moving from colonial to participatory research practices. *Behavior Analysis in Practice*, 1—19. https://doi.org/10.1007/s40617-021-00591-7

Resnik, D. B. (November 16, 2021). *Research ethics timeline*. National Institute of Environmental Health Sciences. https://www.niehs.nih.gov/research/resources/bioethics/timeline/index.cfm.

Rice, T. W. (2008). The historical, ethical, and legal background of human-subjects research. *Respiratory Care, 53*(10), 1325—1329.

Risley, T. R. (1975). Certify procedures not people. In S. W. Wood (Ed.), *Issues in evaluating behavior modification* (pp. 159—181). Research Press.

Risley, T. R. (2001). Do good, take data. In W. T. O'Donohue, D. A. Henderson, S. C. Hayes, J. E. Fisher, & L. J. Hayes (Eds.), *A history of the behavioral therapies: Founders' personal histories* (pp. 267—287). Context Press.

Rossi, W. C., Reynolds, W., & Nelson, R. M. (2003). Child assent and parental permission in pediatric research. *Theoretical Medicine and Bioethics, 24*(2), 131—148.

Rutherford, A. (2006). The social control of behavior control: Behavior modification, individual rights, and research ethics in America, 1971—1979. *Journal of the History of the Behavioral Sciences, 42*(3), 203—220. https://doi.org/10.1002/jhbs.20169

Sadavoy, J. A., & Zube, M. L. (Eds.). (2021). *A scientific framework for compassion and social justice: Lessons in applied behavior analysis*. Routledge. https://doi.org/10.4324/9781003132011

Sailor, W., Dunlap, G., Sugai, G., & Horner, R. (Eds.). (2009). *Handbook of positive behavior support*. Springer. https://doi.org/10.1007/978-0-387-09632-2

Schwartz, I. S., & Baer, D. M. (1991). Social validity assessments: Is current practice state of the art? *Journal of Applied Behavior Analysis, 24*(2), 189—204. https://doi.org/10.1901/jaba.1991.24-189

Schwartz, I. S., & Kelly, E. M. (2021). Quality of life for people with disabilities: Why applied behavior analysts should consider this a primary dependent variable. *Research and Practice for Persons with Severe Disabilities, 46*(3), 159—172. https://doi.org/10.1177/154079692 11033629

Skinner, B. F. (1938). *The behavior of organisms: An experimental analysis*. D. Appleton-Century Company. Cambridge.

Skinner, B. F. (1953). *Science and human behavior*. Macmillan.

Skloot, R. (2011). *The immortal life of Henrietta Lacks*. Crown Publishers.

Slavicek, G., & Forsdahl, G. (2009). Ethics and regulatory aspects in medical research. *International Journal of Stomatology & Occlusion Medicine, 2*, 45—49. https://doi.org/10.1007/s12548-009-0007-y

Smith, R. P. (May 15, 2018). *Famed for 'immortal' cells, Henrietta Lacks is immortalized in portraiture*. Smithsonian Magazine. https://www.smithsonianmag.com/smithsonian-institution/famed-immortal-cells-henrietta-lacks-immortalized-portraiture-180969085/.

Stolz, S. B. (1978). *Ethical issues in behavior modification*. Jossey-Bass.

Stolz, S. B., Wienckowski, L. A., & Brown, B. S. (1975). Behavior modification: A perspective on critical issues. *American Psychologist, 30*(11), 1027—1048. https://doi.org/10.1037/0003-066X.30.11.1027

Tuskegee University. (n.d.). *About the USPHS syphilis study*. https://www.tuskegee.edu/about-us/centers-of-excellence/bioethics-center/about-the-usphs-syphilis-study.

United Nations. (1948). *Universal declaration of human rights*. https://www.un.org/sites/un2.un.org/files/udhr.pdf.

United Nations. (n.d.). Human rights. https://www.un.org/en/global-issues/human-rights#: ~ :text= Human%20rights%20are%20rights%20inherent,and%20education%2C%20and%20many% 20more.

US House of Representatives: History, Art & Archives. (2008). *Constitutional amendments and major civil rights acts of congress referenced in black Americans in congress.* https://history. house.gov/Exhibitions-and-Publications/BAIC/Historical-Data/Constitutional-Amendments-and-Legislation/.

Walker, A. (2004). In *In Search of our mothers' gardens: Womanist prose.* Mariner Books.

Wolf, M. M. (1978). Social validity: The case for subjective measurement or how applied behavior analysis is finding its heart. *Journal of Applied Behavior Analysis, 11*(2), 203—214. https:// doi.org/10.1901/jaba.1978.11-203

Wolinetz, C. D., & Collins, F. S. (2020). Recognition of research participants' need for autonomy: Remembering the legacy of Henrietta Lacks. *JAMA, 324*(11), 1027—1028. https://doi.org/ 10.1001/jama.2020.15936

Wood, W. S. (Ed.). (1975). *Issues in evaluating behavior modification.* Research Press.

Woolf, S. H., Masters, R. K., & Aron, L. Y. (2021). Effect of the Covid-19 pandemic in 2020 on life expectancy across populations in the USA and other high income countries: Simulations of provisional mortality data. *British Medical Journal, 373*(1343), 1—9. https://doi.org/10.1136/ bmj.n1343

Chapter 2

Ethical principles and values guiding modern scientific research

David J. Cox[1], Victoria D. Suarez[1,2] and Videsha Marya[1,3]
[1]*Institute for Behavioral Studies, Endicott College, Beverly, MA, United States;* [2]*Centria Autism, Farmington Hills, MI, United States;* [3]*Village Autism Center, Marietta, GA, United States*

An undeniable fact is that scientific research has continuously improved the lives of humans (Pinker, 2018). The computers on which we draft this chapter; the rapid development of a COVID-19 vaccine; the broad dissemination of research findings; electronic data collection by Registered Behavior Technicians (RBTs) during Applied Behavior Analysis (ABA) sessions—all were made possible by the research activities of scientists. However, research does not always work out as planned and sometimes research directly harms people, animals, or the environment.

When harms wrought through research become public, the overarching profession often develops ethical guidelines demonstrating the profession as a whole does not accept such conduct (Emanuel et al., 2008). For example, the Nuremberg Code is a set of rules designed to protect research participants developed in response to the atrocities enacted by Nazi doctors during World War II (Annas & Grodin, 2008). And, the Developmental Disabilities Assistance and Bill of Rights Act (1975), the Education for All Handicapped Children Act (1975), and the Civil Rights of Institutionalized Persons Act (1980) were developed in response to the mistreatment of disabled individuals at the Willowbrook State School (Lynch, 2021).

Research within behavior modification received increased public attention in the 1970s due to concern about aversive conditioning procedures and other questionable methods of behavior control (e.g., use of electric shock; Rutherford, 2006). In response, the Subcommittee on Constitutional Rights of the Committee on the Judiciary investigated the ethics involved in the increasingly popular "science of human behavior" being researched to change human

Research Ethics in Behavior Analysis. https://doi.org/10.1016/B978-0-323-90969-3.00008-6

behavior. The investigation showed that the individual rights of research participants were not always fully upheld and culminated in the 1972 court case of *Wyatt v. Stickney* (Rutherford, 2006). As a result of the scandals leading to *Wyatt v. Stickney* (Rutherford, 2006), the guidelines of least restriction were developed, which argued that individuals have the right to the least restrictive interventions necessary to achieve socially valid behavioral goals—including within research contexts.

Ethical guidance born from research scandal or misconduct serves a clear function. Specifically, the developed ethical guidelines often act to protect future vulnerable research participants from experiencing similar harms. Relatedly, it's impossible to track, observe, measure, and test every decision and step that comprises each research protocol the world over. Ethical guidance born from scandal focuses the limited resources we have on minimally acceptable behavior and behavior that has the potential to cause the most harm to others and to the profession. Finally, ethical guidance born from scandal also signals to the broader public that the behavior of those few "bad apples" is not how research is typically conducted in that field and that such behavior is not tolerated by the larger researcher community.

However, developing ethical guidelines only in response to misconduct can have drawbacks. First, this approach narrowly focuses on what researchers should not do. For example, this approach can limit the function and scope of ethical guidelines to preventing researcher misconduct, preventing harm to research participants, and creates contingencies to punish misconduct or behaviors that lead to participant harm. But ethics is more than catching people doing bad things. Ethics is focused on asking the questions "How can we conduct the best research?" and "What does it mean to conduct good research?" Stated differently, ethics also involves what behaviors we should engage in, not just what people should not do.

Second, developing ethical guidelines only in response to misconduct would also mean advances in research ethics would first require a misstep that the profession then finds a way to avoid in the future. This kind of reactive approach is limited because it only seeks to resolve a specific issue or set of related issues. In contrast, developing a broader research ethics approach antecedent to the occurrence of misconduct can allow researchers to develop tools and technologies that help other researchers maximize the good that is accomplished through research in addition to mitigating harms and avoiding misconduct.

In this chapter, we focus on principles and values of research ethics that provide a framework for decision making in research contexts beyond simply avoiding harms that occurred during past scandals. Whereas the remaining chapters in this book focus on ethical topics related to specific research activities, in this chapter we provide a broader framework through which to view, analyze, and engage in ethical decision-making relative to the research-related behaviors of behavior analysts. Specifically, we focus on principles that can be used to guide ethical behavior within a research-related context. And, once a principled decision has been made, how you might evaluate whether the principled approach chosen was the "right" choice. We accomplish this across three major sections. First, we describe the function of conducting research, the function of ethical rules and decision models, and the function of ethical theories. Next, we describe principles and values of modern research ethics that become the content of rules, decision models, and ethical theories. Lastly, we highlight common paradigms of research oversight and decision-making that readers can use on conjunction with the first two sections in their daily research activities.

On terms and functions

The function of conducting research. To understand *what* someone should do in a specific situation, it helps to understand the function of the behavior. *What* is considered ethical research behavior is not different. To understand *what* research-related behaviors are considered "right," it helps to understand the function of conducting research in behavior analysis broadly, as well as for the individual researcher. Because the function of behavior is likely to vary from individual to individual, it is impossible to cover all possible functions in a single chapter. Nevertheless, we can talk about commonly reported—and professionally supported—functions of conducting research that are likely to influence the ethical decisions that researchers make.

One function of conducting research in behavior analysis might be to improve our basic understanding of environment—behavior relationships. In behavior analysis, much of this research falls under the umbrella label of the experimental analysis of behavior (i.e., EAB—see Part III of Madden et al., 2013 for more robust coverage of this topic). But what is "good" basic research? How do researchers choose a "good" basic research question to ask? And, what is the "right" way to disseminate and communicate about basic research findings so that all behavior analysts can benefit from their work? Ethical values shape how different people answer these questions (and many others! see Chapter 4) within the experimental analysis of human and nonhuman behavior.

A second function of research in behavior analysis might be to obtain generalizable knowledge that improves lives beyond those of the research participants. For example, research published in the *Journal of Applied Behavior Analysis* and *Behavior Analysis in Practice* is largely "good" to the extent that readers can generalize the processes and procedures to produce similar or better outcomes for the individuals they serve. However, applied research is hard work and may involve many tries that lead to researcher error or dissatisfactory outcomes. Thus, an adverse effect of applied research is that the participants from research studies might be at risk of gaining less from the study than it costs them in time and effort compared to the benefits the researcher attains from publishing (i.e., the participants are exploited). But what does "good" applied research look like, and how do we avoid exploiting research participants? Ethical values shape how different people answer these questions (and many others! see Chapter 6) within applied research in behavior analysis.

A third possible function of research might be professional or personal goals. For instance, researchers might be motivated to publish their research to further their career in academia lest they perish (Kumar, 2008; Van Fleet et al., 2006); or students completing graduate studies might be motivated to fulfill educational requirements by conducting research. In these contexts, research is unlikely to be published and students are unlikely to obtain their degree if their research violates commonly accepted rules and methods for the ethical conduct of research. At the extreme, where research integrity becomes questioned or dishonesty is substantiated, the career of a researcher can be ruined leading to the opposite of what an academic researcher is likely after (e.g., Wakefield's article linking MMR vaccine and autism; Godlee et al., 2011; see Marcus, 2021a for a curated website containing such events). Similarly, students who engage in unethical research conduct during their graduate studies may have their degrees revoked—again resulting in the opposite of the function students may be engaged in research (e.g., Flaherty, 2017; Marcus, 2021b; McCook, 2018).

In total, the specific function of engaging in research behaviors is likely to vary widely across the many individuals that consider themselves behavior analysts. It seems likely that such variability in controlling contingencies will lead to varied patterns of responding, and that the resulting research products (e.g., publications) from one individual will play a functional role in the research behavior of other behavior analysts. Understanding why you are conducting research helps narrow the field of ethical rules and principles to those most relevant to the function of your research-related behavior. This can be quite helpful because—as we describe more later in the chapter—the list of rules and principles can be quite extensive.

Function of ethical rules and decision models. Principles of research ethics are instances of verbal behavior. As verbal stimuli, they can influence the behavior of researchers based on their role in respondent and operant contingencies. The specific function of any one principle of research ethics will likely vary from person-to-person (e.g., mand, metaphorical tact) and the conditions under which those verbal stimuli covary with consequence events. But verbal behavior also allows humans to learn about some contingencies without experiencing contingencies directly (e.g., Baron & Galizio, 1983; Catania & Matthews, 1982; Hayes et al., 1986). In turn, humans can learn to behave in ways that optimize their performance toward whatever outcome they pursue. For example, certified behavior analysts might have never implemented a novel preference assessment procedure published in the *Journal of Applied Behavior Analysis*. But, after reading rules about how to implement the preference assessment methodology, they can implement the procedure at work the very next day. Similarly, having read ethical rules and guidelines on what to do in varying contexts, behavior analytic researchers might be more likely to engage in behaviors the profession deems as "good" or "right" relative to the broader function of conducting research in the profession.

Ethical rules and decision models help researchers to know *what* to do in a given context (e.g., Marya et al., 2022). Historically, this area of ethical literature is referred to as normative ethics—*what* someone ought to do in a situation (e.g., Boone, 2017). For simpler situations, one or more guidelines might directly inform the researcher *what* behavior the larger profession of behavior analysts claims is correct. For example, the professional and ethical compliance code for behavior analysts indicates that researchers should give appropriate credit to collaborators involved in completed research activities (BACB, 2021 Code 6.08) and data should be published accurately and completely without omitting or fabricating data (BACB, 2021 Code 6.11). Thus, if a behavior analyst is tasked with publicly displaying their research, *what* behaviors should be carried out are relatively clear (e.g., give appropriate coauthor credit, provide accurate data).

Decision models often are created to help researchers identify *what* to do in more complex situations. Decision models (as different from causal models; Marya et al., 2022) are often designed to help the model user make the best decision in the situation toward meeting a predefined goal. Decision-making models accomplish this by serving as a textual prompt to help the model user consider the relevant variables and options, which may have gone unconsidered without the model prompt. Decision models are helpful as they walk the user through a chain of behaviors that increase the likelihood that the model user makes a "better" decision than had they not used the model. Throughout the rest of the book, you will see many examples of individual rules and guidelines as well as examples of decision models to help you with ethical decision making as it relates to research conduct of behavior analysts.

Function of stating principles and values. Whereas guidelines and decision models can help someone identify *what* to do in a context, guidelines and decision models do not necessarily tell you *why* you should engage in that behavior. For many individuals, it is not very convincing to simply state that someone should do something. A fair question to ask is why they should believe that what's being told to them as the "right" thing to do is, in fact, the "right" thing to do. Ethical principles, ethical values, and ethical theories are aimed at justifying *why* researchers should follow the rules and advice for how to behave. These ethical principles, values, and theories are often referred to as *normative* ethical behaviors (e.g., Boone, 2017).

Different people have different preferences for how they rank the importance of ethical values, principles, and theories (e.g., Bailey, 2021; Cox, 2021; Witts et al., 2020). For example, across two experiments, Cox (2021) evaluated *what* behavior analysis students considered the "right" thing to do in certain

ABA scenarios and *why* that behavior was the "right" thing to do. In both experiments, participants consistently differed on *what* behavior they considered was 'right' and *why* their selection was right. For example, some participants preferred to determine what was right based on reference to the then current BACB Code of Ethics (2014), whereas other participants preferred to determine what was right based on which behavior was most likely to lead to the most benefit (or least harm) to the client. In total, different participants' justification for *why* their choice was right could be described by different ethical theories.

Function of ethical theories. Ethical theories might be considered functionally similar to the role that clinical decision models serve for practitioners. Clinical decision models help a practitioner aggregate information about the client, their culture and values, the known research literature, and the practical constraints of the intervention context to determine what intervention should be implemented. Similarly, ethical theories help a researcher aggregate information about various claims of "right" and "wrong," metrics for measuring and assessing those claims, and the practical constraints of the decision context to determine what might be the "most right" (or "least wrong") behavior to emit in a situation.

For example, consider the ethical theory called contract theory. Contract theory argues that "correct" or "right" behavior is fulfilling one's obligations as outlined in a fair social contract willingly entered by two or more people (e.g., Rawls, 1971). Contracts might be formally documented in legal writings or contracts might be more informal rules contacted through our learned history (e.g., if you get in line at the grocery store you will be checked out in turn). A researcher who receives grant funding to support their research originally submitted an application that detailed what research they would conduct and how much it would cost. Under contract theory, "right" or "good" researcher conduct would be using those grant funds only for the research activities that they contracted with the grant agency to perform. Using those funds for different research activities (e.g., obtaining pilot data for an unrelated project) or for non-research-related activities might be considered "wrong" researcher conduct from a contract theory standpoint.

As a second example, consider the ethical theory called consequentialism (aka utilitarianism). Consequentialism argues—generally—that "right" or "good" behavior is that which maximizes benefit or minimizes harm for the greatest number of people (e.g., Marino, 2010). When determining whether a line of research[1] is ethically justified or not under consequentialism, "good" research questions might be those that have the greatest likelihood of

---

1. We define a line of research as a preplanned sequence of experiments designed to ask and answer a particular question comprehensively and empirically. This contrasts with experiments developed as one-off studies without explicit consideration to the next steps needed to fully answer the research question and fit within a larger research literature.

benefitting the greatest number of people or helping to minimize harm that many people experience. Pursuing lines of research that have minimal impact to benefitting or minimizing harms that humans or nonhumans experience might be challenging to ethically justify if the researcher prefers a consequentialist ethical framework to guide their decision-making.

Summary. Fig. 2.1 shows one way to visualize the relationship between ethical principles and values, ethical theories, and researcher behavior as they relate to the function of behavior analysts conducting research. As you contact various claims about what you should or ought to do when conducting research in behavior analysis, we hope you ask the question, "Why should I follow that rule or guideline about how to conduct research, analyze data, or to disseminate research findings?" To answer this question, the rest of this chapter highlights some tools, terminology, and frameworks for analyzing *why* you should engage in the rules, guidelines, and decision processes outlined in the remaining chapters of this book.

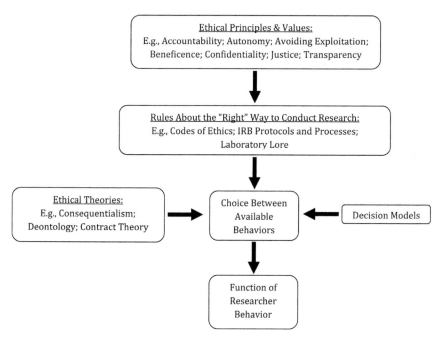

FIGURE 2.1 The relationship between ethical principles/values, ethical theories, researcher conduct, and the function of researcher behavior. Ethical principles/values are verbal stimuli that lead researchers to derive rules for what behaviors can be tacted as "good" or "ethical" research conduct. Many rules can describe many different "correct" ways to conduct research. Ethical theories and decision models help the researcher choose between incompatible behaviors when needed. This chain of behaviors is followed by consequences that functionally control researcher conduct in future similar situations.

Principles and values of modern research ethics

The Belmont report

The National Commission for the Protection of Human Subjects of Biomedical and Behavioral Research (hereafter referred to as "The Commission") was created following the National Research Act of 1974. The Commission developed a document titled the Belmont Report that provided three ethical principles. The purpose of these ethical principles was to provide a set of guidelines for conducting research with human participants. In addition to outlining those principles, the Belmont Report provided three demonstrations for how to apply those principles.

The first principle discussed in the Belmont Report was respect for persons (The Commission, 1978). In its raw form, the principle of respect for persons makes the ethical claims that individuals should be treated as "autonomous agents" and that individuals with "diminished autonomy" have the right to be protected (The Commission, 1978). Translated for the present context, the principle of respect for person's claims that individuals have the right to be presented with all available response options and the opportunity to choose among those responses so long as the chosen option does not lead to significant harm to the research participant or to other people. However, some individuals (e.g., infants or some individuals with developmental disabilities) might make choices that could lead to significant harm to themselves or others; they may not fully understand the options being presented to them; or they may not fully understand the consequences that follow from each response. Individuals in these situations might require another individual (e.g., parent, caregiver, legal guardian) to choose for them so as to avoid harm and maximize their well-being.

The second principle discussed in the Belmont Report was beneficence (The Commission, 1978). The principle of beneficence claims that people should be treated in a manner that secures their well-being. What exactly constitutes "well-being" can be defined differently by different people (e.g., Diener & Suh, 2000) and research in behavior analysis suggests different people often have different preferences (e.g., intersubject differences in preference assessment results; Kodak et al., 2009; Verriden & Roscoe, 2016). However, broadly speaking, two general rules are often used to guide behaviors consistent with improving the well-being of others. One rule is to "do no harm" (i.e., nonmaleficence; The Commission, 1978) and the second rule is to "maximize possible benefits while minimizing possible harms."

The final principle discussed in the Belmont Report was justice (The Commission, 1978). Justice in this specific context generally refers to the equitable distribution of benefits and costs that result from research. When carrying out research, injustice can occur in at least two ways. First, research injustice occurs if the amount of benefit that a participant contacts from research is less than the amount that the individual has a right to receive. Second, research injustice occurs if the burden or costs of research are not fairly distributed among those who participate in research. Rules about—and data collection on—what counts as the equitable distribution of benefits and burdens can differ depending on the preferred methodology espoused by the decision-maker (The Commission, 1978). Regardless, the basic principle of equitable distribution of benefits and burdens is the principle upon which these rules typically are argued to rest.

The ethical principles delineated in the Belmont report have served as an ethical framework for the protection of human participants and have since been applied toward the development of the principles that are central to several codes of ethics (e.g., American Counseling Association, 2014; American Dental Association, 2020; AOTA, 2015). As examples, the application of the respect of person's principle has influenced the informed consent process where participants (or their legal representative) are provided with all the information about the study in a way that is comprehensible and allows for them to choose whether to participate. The beneficence principle when applied requires the researcher to assess the potential risks and anticipated benefits with the intention toward minimizing harm and maximizing benefits. Finally, the justice principle advocates for fair treatment for all participants, requires that the selection of participants is done in a fair and impartial manner, and forbids exploitation of vulnerable individuals.

Additional principles of research ethics

The Belmont Report arguably set a foundational example for how people can cooperate to derive principles of research ethics involving human subjects and how to apply them to research-related decisions. However, the field of research ethics is broad and deep with several journals devoted to theoretical and empirical advances in this area (e.g., *Research Ethics, Journal of Empirical Research on Human Research Ethics, Ethics & Human Research*). Though the three principles of research ethics espoused in the Belmont Report continue to be endorsed by scientists and the regulatory bodies that oversee their work (e.g., Adashi et al., 2018; White, 2020), many additional principles of research ethics have been discussed in the literature. Next, we briefly review some of these additional principles of research ethics you might find helpful when making decisions along your research journey. Table 2.1 provides a one-page overview of these ethical principles and values of modern research ethics.

Nonmaleficence — Minimizing Harm. Though included in the Belmont Report as a rule logically following from beneficence, nonmaleficence can be considered a principle used for ethical decision-making independent of beneficence. Nonmaleficence is often described by the maxim to "Do no harm." Whereas beneficence is focused on maximizing the good that results from a decision, nonmaleficence is focused on minimizing or avoiding harm

TABLE 2.1 List of principles and values in research ethics.

Principle	Description of principle	Relation to research in behavior analysis
Respect for persons	Present individuals with available response options and the opportunity to choose among responses so long as the option does not lead to significant harm to themselves or others	• Obtain informed consent and/or assent • Involve others when the individual cannot make a safe choice
Beneficence	"Do no harm," maximize possible benefits, and minimize possible harms	• Review by Institutional Review Boards (IRBs), Research Review Committees (RRCs) • Conduct risk–benefit analyses
Justice	Equitable distribution of benefits and costs that result from research	• Ensure equal and/or fair treatment between participants
Nonmaleficence	Focus on minimizing or avoiding harm	• Ongoing review and oversight • Conduct risk–benefit analyses
Avoiding exploitation	Fair distribution of benefits and burdens of research among the people involved	• Amount of compensation is fair and delivered without undue influence • Data used only for approved and predetermined research questions • Additional protections when conducting research with vulnerable populations
Protecting anonymity and confidentiality	Protection of identifiable and confidential information	• Ensure that any personal health and identifiable information about the participants will not be disclosed or accessible • Information will not be discussed or shared without permission • Procedures for safe keeping (storing, transporting, etc.) are created
Transparency and accountability	Research data and methods are visible in a way that allows others to view, analyze, and replicate them	• Transparent communication of research methods to allow other researchers to replicate an experiment within a publication • A priori documentation of methods and procedures • Documentation of all data/outcomes including incomplete data
Collegiality in the social Enterprise of science	Having respect for and working together with other researchers toward the common goal of advancing the science	• Communicate with other researchers in critiquing and supporting ideas • Detailed description of experimental methods to allow for replication • Free or cheap access to experimental data and tools
Objectivity and avoiding bias	Awareness of personal biases and past learning histories	• Consider biases at all stages of research • Involving colleagues and other neutral parties to review the research • Seek ways to combat bias

that results from a decision. For example, when conducting research on varying approaches to identify the function of self-injurious behavior (SIB), the principle of nonmaleficence might be used to justify the inclusion of early session termination criteria, the use of physical or chemical restraints, or focusing a functional analysis only on behavior that reliably precedes SIB (i.e., precursor behavior). Nonmaleficence is often tied to beneficence as they are typically involved in conversations about risk—benefit calculations and whether the benefit gained by the research participant or the larger field is worth the costs associated with carrying out the research—all things being equal (i.e., there is a favorable risk—benefit ratio for each participant; Lund, 2012; see Chapter 4 for a more thorough discussion).

Avoiding exploitation. There may be occurrences during one's research career wherein the function of the researchers' scientific behavior (as described above) might conflict with the function the participant has chosen to participate in the study. For example, the function of your behavior as a researcher might be to see whether a robust observation from the laboratory setting (e.g., the generalized matching equation) translates into a clinical setting within which you work (e.g., allocation of behavior to eating vegetables compared to desserts). However, the function of your participant's presence in that same study might be to help increase the healthiness of their overall diet. It's unknown the extent to which the function of researcher and participant behavior typically align. But when the motivation for partaking in research differs between the researcher and the participant, the possibility for exploitation increases.

Exploitation occurs when there is an unfair distribution of benefits and burdens of research among the people involved (Emmanuel et al., 2008; Wertheimer, 1999). Similar to benefits and harms, avoiding exploitation is another fundamental principle of research ethics upon which ethical decisions can be justified (e.g., exploitation can occur even if the transaction is mutually advantageous and consensual; Wertheimer, 1999). Avoiding exploitation is often invoked to support ethical research decisions such as identifying the right amount of compensation research participants should receive without being undue influence, the limits of research participant data use beyond the scope of the original research question (i.e., data ownership), and additional protections when conducting research with vulnerable populations (e.g., rigorous informed consent process and additional institutional oversight).

Protecting anonymity and confidentiality. Confidentiality in the literal sense means that whatever information has been shared between two parties will not be discussed or shared without permission. Within the context of behavior analytic research, confidentiality and anonymity imply that researchers will ensure that any personal health information and personally identifiable information about the participants will not be disclosed or accessible (Wiles et al., 2008). Research participant's right to remain anonymous and for their health and personal information to remain confidential are principles used to support practices such as how researchers describe and name participants in published research as well as the rules many Institutional Review Boards (IRBs) have surrounding data storage, data security, and data maintenance protections.

Transparency and accountability. Transparency and accountability are newer ethical principles meant to guide researcher decision-making. In the context of research, transparency can be defined as ensuring visibility of research methods, data, analyses, and researchers' interpretation of outcomes such that others can readily evaluate the research (Moravcsik, 2019). In the context of research, accountability can be defined as the analysis, creation, maintenance, and alteration of contingencies surrounding research conduct that maximizes the integrity of research (see the journal *Accountability in Research*). Together, transparency in research refers to behaviors that researchers engage in that allow systems of accountability to operate as designed to maximize the quality and integrity of the research being conducted and the accurate interpretation of data obtained through research.

Transparency and accountability are often discussed most prominently as it relates to the dissemination of research findings through publications or presentations (Moravscsik, 2019). However, to adequately engage in those behaviors at the end of the research process, researchers would need to engage in a documented sequence of behaviors throughout the research process (e.g., see remaining chapters in this book). For example, to transparently write or present on research methods in a manner that allows other researchers to replicate your experiment, you would need to adequately document what is what you did when conducting the experiment, which may have been months or years prior to the time of writing.

Collegiality in the social enterprise of science. Collegiality in the social enterprise of science and respect for colleagues is another ethical principle that is related to—but distinct from—transparency and accountability. Science is largely a social enterprise. Though an individual can engage in research and learn about the world in isolation (e.g., Skinner, 1945, p. 293; Tourinho & Neno, 2003), understanding how the findings of an experiment fit with past knowledge requires the participatory behavior of many different individuals. For example, past researchers must have documented and submitted their findings for publication. Other people must have engaged in the behaviors necessary for the experiment to be published and accessible online or via print. And, once an individual researcher completes a study, still other researchers are required to provide feedback and critique of the study during peer review. Finally, an unpublished or unread study likely influences the future behavior of only the researchers who conducted the study. To have an impact and move the collective body of knowledge labeled as a "science of behavior" forward, additional researchers would have to make use of the experimental findings obtained by the individual researcher.

Research suggests there are certain behavioral patterns that influence the cooperation between individuals toward a common goal (e.g., Driskell et al., 2018; Olivola et al., 2020). Some patterns of behavior help facilitate cooperation between scientists that comprise a field of study (e.g., behavior analysis). Some of these behaviors include: publishing experimental methods with enough detail to allow for replication; storing and documenting experimental data in a manner that allows easy or free access; creating and documenting experimental tools in a manner that allows easy or free access; how we communicate with other researchers in critiquing and supporting ideas; and how we establish experimental roles and authorship order. The remaining chapters in this book offer many more examples of claims for how we should interact with colleagues and participants throughout the research process under the ethical claim that it is "good" to foster collegiality in the social enterprise of science.

Objectivity/avoiding bias. "Every way of seeing is a way of not seeing" (Burke, 1935, p. 70). Data obtained via empirical research is typically a visual stimulus (e.g., table, graph) to which researchers are then taught how to respond during graduate training and through their interactions with colleagues. Because our responses to obtained data are determined by our learned history and each person has a unique learned history, it is possible that different individuals will respond differently to the exact same set of data (e.g., Cox & Brodhead, 2021). As a result, researchers are likely biased to some degree when interpreting obtained data, choosing methodological approaches for conducting research, choosing research questions, how to recruit research participants, and how to review published research or manuscripts submitted for publication. Thus, researchers are generally considered to have an ethical obligation to be aware that they might be biased throughout the research process and to take steps to mitigate any biases that may exist.

Summary. The Belmont Report laid the foundation for how people can work together to create rules and contingencies that afford researchers the opportunity to advance scientific fields forward while maintaining or enhancing the rights, dignity, and well-being of research participants. Over the past 40+ years, additional ethical principles and values have been developed and incorporated into research practices of scientists the world over. These include nonmaleficence; avoiding exploitation; protecting anonymity and confidentiality; transparency and accountability; collegiality in the social enterprise of science; and objectivity and avoiding bias. Table 2.1 provides a summary description of each of these principles and their relation to research in behavior analysis.

Paradigms of research oversight and decision-making

Principles and values of research ethics are verbal stimuli that can lead researchers to derive rules about "right" or "good" researcher conduct (Fig. 2.1).

For example, consider a situation where a researcher wants to conduct research on SIB in children with Autism Spectrum Disorders. The ethical principles of *nonmaleficence* and *beneficence* might lead to the following rule of researcher conduct: "Expose participants to the minimal amount of SIB that answers the research question and improves their well-being." Similarly, the ethical value of *collegiality in science* might suggest that research should always be conducted with quality and rigor to maximize the likelihood that research results are useful to the scientific field. Thus, *beneficence, nonmaleficence*, and *collegiality in science* might lead to the following rule of researcher conduct: "Use the research design and number of sessions that best allows you to adequately answer the research question while exposing participants to only minimal amounts of SIB with primary concern for improving their well-being."

In some situations, the rules derived from the ethical principles and values relevant to a research context might be incompatible with each other. Continuing the above example, there might be a situation wherein the ethical value of *collegiality in science* conflicts with the ethical principles of *nonmaleficence* and *beneficence*. Perhaps the appropriate methodology to adequately answer the research question is a reversal design (Sidman, 1960) where each phase lasts at least five sessions. However, reversing back to a baseline condition reexposes the research participant to the conditions known to evoke SIB and removes the environmental conditions known to reduce SIB (assuming the intervention phase was successful). In these situations where different ethical principles or values suggest incompatible behaviors for the researcher (i.e., an ethical dilemma), researchers must choose among the incompatible behaviors to continue carrying out the research project. Paradigms of research oversight and decision-making can help researchers faced with ethical dilemmas as they provide a benchmark against which to evaluate different response options.

Theories of Bioethics. One set of paradigms for research oversight and decision-making are the common theories of bioethics. Though many different ethical theories exist (e.g., Marino, 2010), arguably the most commonly discussed ethical theories in research ethics are consequentialism, deontology, contract theory, and principlism. We reviewed consequentialism and contract theory earlier in the chapter and so we won't rehash those here.[2] However, deontology argues that researchers can determine what behavior is most "right" or "good" by adhering to as many rules as possible that outline their duties and obligations that are relevant to the decision context. And, principlism (Beauchamp & Childress, 2001) argues that ethical reasoning occurs by weighing ethical principles commonly understood and accepted by society to determine the most "right" or "good" behavior.

---

2. For a more detailed review of several common ethical theories from the discipline of bioethics and from the lens of behavior analysis, see — Brodhead et al. (2018, 2022) and Cox (2021).

Theories of bioethics help with research oversight and decision-making by providing a benchmark for which to evaluate research decisions being made. Taking a consequentialist approach would require you to calculate the overall net benefit and harm to all relevant stakeholders (e.g., participants, researcher, scientific community) and choose the research design and protocol components that maximize benefit or minimizes harm. Taking a deontological approach would require you to identify all duties of "right" conduct that are fulfilled or broken for different research design and protocol components; and, then to choose path that fulfills the most (or breaks the least) rules of "good" researcher conduct. Taking a contract theory approach would turn on the details of any contracts you have entered with funding agencies, the research participants via informed consent, other members of the research team, and (arguably) the larger scientific field in conducting and contributing high-quality practical and useable research. Ideally, these contracts would have been setup as to avoid conflict among social contracts. However, if conflict exists, then the "right" thing to do would be the behavior that meets the most contractual arrangements and working to rectify the contracts that you are unable to meet. Lastly, a principled approach requires the researcher to identify all relevant principles that apply to a decision, identify what each principle requires, and choose the course that best blends the behavioral requirements resulting from those principles.

In sum, different ethical theories have different benchmarks around what the "most ethical" or "least ethical" behaviors are when conducting research. Engaging in ethical research behavior can be helped by identifying which ethical theory you most align, or of which is espoused by the people governing your research (e.g., IRBs, Funding Agency). Once known, you should identify the requirements the identified ethical theory places on your behavior while conducting research so that you can fulfill those requirements.

Historical Paradigms of Research Oversight and Participant Inclusion. Emanuel and Grady (2008) offered an alternative way to categorize paradigms of ethical research oversight centered on the role of the relationship between the researcher and the research participant during the research process. These four paradigms are: researcher paternalism; regulatory protectionism; participant access; and community partnership. Arguably, research oversight in the United States has shifted from primarily a "researcher paternalism" framework to a "community partnership" framework (Emanuel & Grady, 2008). However, all four frameworks are used by many researchers and IRBs, each incorporates different values and provides a different approach to ethically evaluating researcher behavior, and disagreement persists over which paradigm—and which components of each paradigm—is best (Emanuel & Grady, 2008). Table 2.2 summarizes each paradigm and its corresponding characteristics.

Researcher paternalism rests on the assumption that individual researchers are generally benevolent, they make decisions that protect research participants, and they know the best way to conduct research to produce the most

TABLE 2.2 Paradigms of research oversight and participant inclusion.

Paradigm	Assumption about research	Role of the research participant	Relation between health care and health research	Underlying ethical theory for decision-making	Driving set of ethical principles
Researcher Paternalism	Research is tool to protect society against disease and societal problems.	Passive Subject	Distinct from Each Other	Consequentialism	Overall risk-benefit ratio to society
Regulatory Protectionism	Researchers will engage in harmful and unethical practices if unregulated.	Vulnerable Patient	Research Threatens Patient Care	Principlism	Independent review of protocols to ensure it meets minimal principles
Participant Access	Cutting-edge, life-saving research is a benefit patients should not be denied.	Informed Consumer	Research separated and Communicated as Distinct from Care-as-usual	Deontology	Rights-based approach with patient autonomy and protection through robust informed consent
Collaborative Partnership	Patients from the targeted population and their communities should be involved throughout the research process.	Active Participants and Collaborators	Research and Practice are Complementary	Contract Theory	Collegiality in science (Including Participants)

social value (Emanuel & Grady, 2008; Halpern, 2004). This approach was influenced by World War II where society placed emphasis on the sacrifice of the individual for the betterment of society. For biomedical research, this emphasis was translated into an assumption that research is a tool to be used to benefit society in protection against disease and societal problems (Emanuel & Grady, 2008). Researchers, in turn, likely are the best positioned experts to make decisions about what research—if successful—is likely to be most useful to society. As a result, research participants are considered passive subjects and an overall risk—benefit ratio creates the driving principles under the ethical theory of consequentialism. Lastly, under this approach, health-related research and healthcare are distinct from each other.

Regulatory protectionism was developed in response to the many research scandals during the 20th century that suggested some biomedical researchers will place their research agenda above the well-being of the research participants (e.g., the Tuskegee Syphilis Experiment —Jones, 1981; The Jewish Chronic Disease Hospital case—Beecher, 1966). As a result of these harms to participants in the name of science, regulatory protectionism was developed out of the assumption that researchers need to be watched and regulated by a third-party to protect research participants from contacting unethical and harmful practices (Emanuel & Grady, 2008). This approach views research participants as vulnerable patients such that independent third-party reviewers (e.g., IRBs) should use a principled approach to ensure that patients' well-being is not threatened by participating in research and that minimal ethical principles and standards are met.

Regulatory protectionism created systems where research review committees effectively controlled access to cutting-edge, health-related research. This became problematic with new health crises in the 1970s and 1980s (e.g., AIDS) where treatments that could save lives were still experimental, being researched, and difficult to access. Out of this context rose the paradigm of *participant access*, which argues that individuals have a right to access experimental treatments; and those individual rights outweigh society's attempt to control our behavior (i.e., research is a benefit we should not be denied; Delaney, 1989; Emanuel & Grady, 2008). Under this approach, research participants are considered to be informed consumers of research and are protected via a robust informed consent process that clearly differentiates research from care-as-usual. The *participant access* paradigm leverages deontology as the primary ethical theory arguing that researchers and participants each have duties they must uphold before, during, and after research has been conducted. Throughout the research process, individual participant autonomy drives what is considered ethical research. That is, if the informed consent process is robust, ethical research is research where the participant can choose whether to continue participating.

Relying on robust informed consent processes has obvious flaws. People rarely read the fine print when they sign up for a new media account, they rarely read nutrition facts when they buy food at the grocery store, and—yes, sadly—they rarely read the fine print when signing informed consent documents to participate in research. Further, all three paradigms to this point have started with researchers who have an idea for improving healthcare via basic or applied research and then determining the most ethical way to enroll participants. The reviewed paradigms to this point assume the informed consent process perfectly conveys information to rational consumers of healthcare, and that the researchers are best positioned to know what's likely the next most important topic to study for the population they hope to help. But many of these assumptions are likely to be less than perfectly accurate.

The *collaborative partnership* paradigm was developed in response to these shortcomings. This paradigm rests on the assumption that ethical research can only be conducted by involving participants and their communities throughout the research process (i.e., planning, conduct, and dissemination; Emanuel & Grady, 2008). This approach was influenced by advances in the fields of genomics (e.g., Weijer et al., 1999), increased frequency of research being conducted in developing countries and with cultures different from those of the researchers (e.g., Angell, 1997; Weijer & Emanuel, 2000), and by increased calls by some participants to be involved during the planning stages of research (Weijer & Emanuel, 2000; Weijer et al., 1999). Under this paradigm, research participants become active collaborators throughout the entire research process with research and practice being complementary. Contract theory is the primary ethical theory via the importance of social relationships, and the ethical principle of collegiality in the social enterprise of science (including participants) is the primary ethical principle driving oversight.

Similar to theories of bioethics, historical paradigms of research oversight can help researchers ethically evaluate their interactions with, and the roles of, research participants throughout the research process. Taking a researcher paternalism approach would require conducting a risk—benefit ratio and engaging participants in a manner that ensures the maximum benefit to society results from the research. Taking a regulatory protectionist approach would have the researcher focus on existing IRB rules and regulations to guide interactions with research participants with the assumption that the approach approved by the IRB is sufficiently ethical. Taking a participant access approach would require engaging with participants to determine what they value relative to consenting to research to identify the ideal informed consent contract for conducting a research project. Lastly, taking a collaborative partnership approach would involve enrolling one or more participants as a part of the research team so they could have input throughout the research process (i.e., from determining the experimental question, to designing the protocol, through conducting the research, and finally publishing the results). Importantly, because each approach carries a different benchmark for what is ultimately the "right" way to incorporate research participants when making research-related decisions, each approach might ethically justify a behavior similar to or different from the other theories.

The functional application of ethical principles and values to guide research

Depending on which paradigm one uses, the functional application of the above principles and values may lead to different research topographies. Fig. 2.2 shows

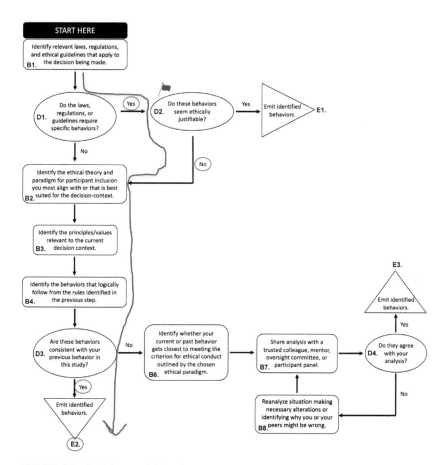

FIGURE 2.2 Decision model for incorporating principles/values of research ethics when engaged in a decision-making process within research contexts. Rectangles represent behaviors (B) the model user should emit while making a decision; ovals represent questions and decision points (D); and triangles represent endpoints (E) where the user has identified an ethically justified solution. Red flags and lines follow the decision path of the in-text example of someone who is legally capable of providing informed consent, but the researcher is concerned they do not fully understand the requirements and conditions of the study.

a decision model that may help researchers apply the principles and values of research ethics throughout the research process. This model was developed by adapting common models for clinical ethical decision-making (e.g., Brodhead et al., 2018; Rhodes & Alfandre, 2007) to the research context and by incorporating the relationship between ethical principles/values, ethical theories, researcher conduct, and the function of researcher behavior (Fig. 2.1).

Few researchers are likely to conduct research outside of some kind of institutional affiliation. Thus, when faced with a decision point, researchers should ensure that they have identified all laws, institutional policies, regulations, and ethical guidelines to which they are required to adhere when conducting research (B1, Fig. 2.2). For many researchers, these likely involve regulations and policies set forth by their university IRBs and IACUC (institutional animal care and use committee), any regulations or policies set forth by agencies the researcher hopes will, or currently does, fund their project (e.g., NIH, NSF), and any laws or regulations governing the type of research they are interested in conducting (e.g., HIPAA, HITECH, FERPA, FDA). To the extent that the relevant laws, policies, and guidelines clearly suggest specific behaviors (respond "Yes" at D1, Fig. 2.2) and seem ethically justifiable (respond "Yes" at D2, Fig. 2.2), the researcher can likely just follow the policies, laws, and guidelines (E1, Fig. 2.2).

However, in some situations, simply following the identified behaviors outlined in regulation and law might be challenging. This might occur because the policies, laws, or guidelines seem ethically suspect (e.g., Thoreau, 1849). Or this may occur because the behaviors are incompatible, suggest a behavior that seems unethical, or existing rules may not explicitly relate to a decision that needs to be made. For example, suppose an adult who is their own conservator and has a complex disability is recruited to participate in research. Given that they are an adult and their own conservator, the law indicates they can be asked to give consent to participate in the research. When going through the informed consent process, the researcher feels that the individual may not understand the research conditions to the extent that their consent is being provided with full awareness of the research requirements and conditions (red flag, Fig. 2.2). What should the researcher do?

In this example, the behaviors suggested by law, regulations, and ethical guidelines as outlined in the approved informed consent document do not seem ethically justifiable (respond "No" at D2, Fig. 2.2), the next step would be to identify the ethical paradigm with which you most align (e.g., regulatory protectionism; collaborative partnership; B2, Fig. 2.2). Once chosen, you can use the ethical paradigm to identify the relevant benchmarks, principles, and values for ethical behavior (B3, Fig. 2.2). Continuing our example, someone using the regulatory protectionism paradigm would use principlism and the viewpoint that the potential participant might be vulnerable. In contrast, someone using the collaborative partnership paradigm would take a contract theory approach and want to ensure that the potential participant—as a collaborator—fully understands everything entailed in the social contract both are agreeing.

Once the model user has identified the values and principles that will need to be upheld, the next step is to translate those principles/values into behavior (B4, Fig. 2.2; e.g., Skinner, 1945). For the regulatory protectionist researcher, the behaviors that follow would be sticking to the protocols for informed consent reviewed and approved by the IRB. If the researcher followed those protocols to the letter, they would be ethically justified to accept the participant's consent and move forward in the decision model. For the collaborative partnership researcher, the behaviors that follow might be to consult with your research team member with a similar complex disability. That individual might shed light on how the complex disability could influence the validity of the participant's consent. This consultation would then likely lead the researcher to either be comfortable with the participant's consent or to recognize that follow-up questions and conversations are warranted.

At this point, the model user would have identified an ethical paradigm (B2), identified the relevant principles and values (B3), and translated these to behaviors (B3). Because the identified behaviors meet socially determined benchmarks of "right" or "good" researcher behavior within one socially derived paradigm (Baum, 2004; Skinner, 1953), to the extent that the identified behaviors in B4 are compatible with past and current behaviors the researcher emits, the researcher would be ethically justified to emit the identified behaviors (E2, Fig. 2.2). At this point, the researcher would be ethically justified via the principles and values hierarchically ranked from the ethical paradigm guiding ethical decision-making. In short, they could carry on with their research feeling confident their decision was ethically justified.

However, sometimes conflict might occur between the recommended behaviors and either past or current behaviors (respond "No" at D3, Fig. 2.2). For example, the behaviors translated from the chosen ethical paradigm might require deviation from an approved IRB protocol, or how you treat this participant might differ in significant ways from how you have treated past participants. In this situation, the researcher would need to analyze which behavior (the previously emitted responses or the current responses) is more consistent with the ethical paradigm and corresponding rules used to guide their ethical decision making (B6, Fig. 2.2).[3]

Once analyzed, the researcher should share their analysis with the social group from which the conflict emerged (e.g., the IRB for regulatory

---

3. Behavioral consistency over time and across contexts is often considered a primary characteristic of ethics (e.g., Markkula Center for Applied Ethics, 1988). However, it is important to note this does not negate ethical situationism (e.g., Kamteker, 2004; Mower, 2013; c.f. Sabini & Silver, 2005) wherein ethically justified behavior is similar/dissimilar along generalization gradients (e.g., Guttman & Kalish, 1956; Zaman et al., 2019) derived from the contextual stimuli that control ethical behavior.

protectionist researcher; the participant panel for the collaborative partnership researcher; B7, Fig. 2.2). If this social check-and-balance agrees with the analysis (respond "Yes" at D4, Fig. 2.2), then the researcher can emit the identified behaviors (E3, Fig. 2.2), and they could carry on with their research feeling confident their decision was ethically justified. If the social check-and-balance disagrees with the analysis (respond "No" at D4, Fig. 2.2), then the researcher would need to reanalyze the situation and either: alter their analysis based on the errors and feedback received from the social check-and-balance; or, identify how their peers' assessment was wrong (B8, Fig. 2.2). The researcher would then continue this process of peer-review until everyone agrees as to the ethically appropriate route forward. At this point, the researcher could carry on with their research feeling confident their decision was ethically justified.[4]

Future directions

The literature and behaviors associated with research ethics are continuously shaped by historical events, current events, and the interlocking behavior of the many people required to successfully conduct a research experiment and disseminate the resulting findings. In this chapter, we have highlighted the principles and values of research ethics that are commonly used to make claims about what "good" or "bad" research looks like and the underlying ethical paradigms for creating benchmarks and criteria with which to judge those claims. There are at least two areas of future research and scholarship that may improve our understanding of ethical claims for researcher conduct in the field of behavior analysis.

One future direction for research and scholarship surrounds the current preferences for principles, values, and paradigms for research oversight in behavior analysis. Currently, it is unknown the extent to which different researchers in behavior analysis prefer different principles and values, or the extent to which different researchers are using different paradigms to set criteria for "good" researcher conduct. Recent research suggests that behavior analysts faced with the same decision context are likely to make different decisions (Cox & Brodhead, 2021), disagree on which behaviors are considered the most ethical (Cox, 2021), and disagree on the best way to justify and set criteria for what counts as "good" behavior (Cox, 2021). These disagreements should be considered, debated, and resolved if we believe there is such a thing as "good" researcher conduct (e.g., moral objectivism) or we want to

---

4. Consider a second example wherein a potential research participant appears to have the skills to provide sufficient informed consent and does/does not want to participate in a study. However, they have a legal guardian that disagrees with their choice. How might the model from Fig. 2.2 lead to an ethically justified decision? If interested, the first author would love to hear your analysis via email: dcox@endicott.edu

avoid being impacted by the unethical behavior of people conducting research under the label of "behavior analysis."

A second future direction for research and scholarship involves more rigorous testing of the decision model offered in this chapter. Though the decision model was developed using ethical decision models familiar to researchers and practitioners of behavior analysis, it is unknown whether the model: would consistently lead researchers to make the best decisions in all research contexts; is complete in the steps required to make the best decision; or includes unnecessary steps. Research on ethical research conduct exists for many other scientific disciplines (e.g., *Research Ethics, Journal of Empirical Research on Human Research Ethics, Ethics & Human Research*). Conducting similar research specific to the scientific behaviors of behavior analysts would seemingly lead to similar field-wide benefits.

Conclusion

Conducting research in behavior analysis requires a lot of time, effort, skill, and resources. The goal of much of that research is to improve the lives and well-being of the research participants or of individuals who might be impacted by the research findings. To conduct "good" research, many rules and regulations exist that suggest *what* decisions the researcher should make. But, *why* that is the best decision to make is a fair question to ask. In this chapter, we outlined principles, values, and paradigms of research oversight commonly used to create criteria for evaluating claims of *what* researchers should do. We also outlined a decision model that researchers can use to make tractable those principles, values, and paradigms of research oversight into their research practices. Throughout the rest of the book, we hope you continuously ask, "Why should I engage in these research-related behaviors?", "How can I operationally define good behavior in this context?", and "What criteria am I using to know I am engaging in ethical research conduct?". We hope this chapter provides you with the some of the tools and language to begin asking those questions and answering them relative to the function of your own research-related behaviors.

References

Adashi, E. Y., Walters, L. B., & Menikoff, J. A. (2018). The Belmont report at 40: Reckoning with time. *American Journal of Public Health, 108*(10), 1345−1348. https://doi.org/10.2105/AJPH.2018.304580

American Counseling Association. (2014). *ACA code of ethics.* https://www.counseling.org/resources/aca-code-of-ethics.pdf.

American Dental Association. (2020). *Principles of ethics and code of professional conduct.* https://www.ada.org/ ~ /media/ADA/Member%20Center/Ethics/ADA_Code_Of_Ethics_November_2020.pdf?la=en.

Angell, M. (1997). The ethics of clinical research in the third world. *New England Journal of Medicine, 337*, 847–849.

Annas, G. J., & Grodin, M. A. (2008). The nuremberg code. In E. J. Emanuel, C. C. Grady, R. A. Crouch, R. K. Lie, F. G. Miller, & D. D. Wendler (Eds.), *The Oxford textbook of clinical research ethics*. Oxford University Press.

AOTA. (2015). Occupational therapy code of ethics. *American Journal of Occupational Therapy, 69*. https://doi.org/10.5014/ajot.2015.696S03, 6913410030.

Bailey, J. S. (2021). Practical vs theoretical ethics: A response to Cox. *Journal of Applied Behavior Analysis, 54*(1), 192–196. https://doi.org/10.1002/jaba.788

Baron, A., & Galizio, M. (1983). Instructional control of human operant behavior. *The Psychological Record, 33*, 495–520.

Baum, W. M. (2004). *Understanding behaviorism*. Wiley-Blackwell.

Beauchamp, T. L., & Childress, J. F. (2001). *Principles of biomedical ethics* (5th ed.). Oxford University Press. ISBN: 0-19-51433209.

Beecher, H. K. (1966). Ethics and clinical research. *New England Journal of Medicine, 274*, 1354–1360.

Behavior Analyst Certification Board. (2014). *Professional and ethical compliance code for behavior analysts*. Author.

Boone, B. (2017). *Ethics 101: From altruism and utilitarianism to bioethics and political ethics, an exploration of the concepts of right and wrong*. Adams Media.

Brodhead, M. T., Cox, D. J., & Quigley, S. P. (2018). *Practical ethics for effective treatment of Autism Spectrum disorder*. Elsevier Inc. ISBN: 9780128140987.

Brodhead, M. T., Cox, D. J., & Quigley, S. P. (2022). *Practical ethics for effective treatment of Autism Spectrum disorder* (2nd ed.). Elsevier Inc.

Burke, K. (1935). *Permanence and change: An anatomy of purpose*. New York: New Republic, Incorporated.

Catania, A. C., & Matthews, B. A. (1982). Instructed versus shaped human verbal behavior: Interactions with nonverbal responding. *Journal of the Experimental Analysis of Behavior, 38*, 233–248. https://doi.org/10.1901/jeab.1982.38-233

Cox, D. J. (2021). Descriptive and normative ethical behavior appear to be functionally distinct. *Journal of Applied Behavior Analysis, 54*, 168–191. https://doi.org/10.1002/jaba.761

Cox, D. J., & Brodhead, M. T. (2021). A proof of concept analysis of decision-making with time-series data. *The Psychological Record, 71*. https://doi.org/10.1007/s40732-020-00451-w

Delaney, M. (1989). The case for patient access to experimental therapy. *Journal of Infectious Diseases, 159*(3), 416–419. https://www.jstor.org/stable/30137467.

Diener, E., & Suh, E. M. (2000). *Culture and subjective well-being*. The MIT Press. ISBN: 0-262-04182-0.

Driskell, J. E., Salas, E., & Driskell, T. (2018). Foundations of teamwork and collaboration. *American Psychologist, 73*(4), 334–348. https://doi.org/10.1037/amp0000241

Emanuel, E. J., & Grady, C. C. (2008). Four paradigms of clinical research and research oversight. In E. J. Emanuel, C. C. Grady, R. A. Crouch, R. K. Lie, F. G. Miller, & D. D. Wendler (Eds.), *The Oxford textbook of clinical research ethics*. Oxford University Press.

Emanuel, E. J., Wendler, D. D., & Grady, C. C. (2008). An ethical framework for biomedical research. In E. J. Emanuel, C. C. Grady, R. A. Crouch, R. K. Lie, F. G. Miller, & D. D. Wendler (Eds.), *The Oxford textbook of clinical research ethics*. Oxford University Press.

Flaherty, C. (September 1, 2017). *Killing a doctorate*. Inside Higher Ed.. https://www. insidehighered.com/news/2017/09/01/ohio-state-revokes-arizona-professors-phd-questioning-her-findings-video-games

Godlee, F., Smith, J., & Marcovitch, H. (2011). Wakefield's article linking MMR vaccine and autism was fraudulent. *British Medical Journal, 342*, c7452. https://doi.org/10.1136/bmj.c7452

Guttman, N., & Kalish, H. I. (1956). Discriminability and stimulus generalization. *Journal of Experimental Psychology, 51*(1), 79−88. https://psycnet.apa.org/doi/10.1037/h0046219.

Halpern, S. A. (2004). *Lesser harms: The morality of risk in medical research*. University of Chicago Press. ISBN: 9780226314518.

Hayes, S. C., Brownstein, A. J., Zettle, R. D., Rosenfarb, I., & Korn, Z. (1986). Rule-governed behavior and sensitivity to changing consequences of responding. *Journal of the Experimental Analysis of Behavior, 45*, 237−256. https://doi.org/10.1901/jeab.1986.45-237

Jones, J. H. (1981). *Bad blood: The Tuskegee Syphilis experiment* (2nd ed.). The Free Press.

Kamtekar, R. (2004). Situationism and virtue ethics on the content of our character. *Ethics, 114*(3), 458−491. https://doi.org/10.1086/381696

Kodak, T., Fisher, W. W., Kelley, M. E., & Kisamore, A. P. (2009). Comparing preference assessments: Selection- versus duration-based preference assessment procedures. *Research in Developmental Disabilities, 30*, 1068−1077. https://doi.org/10.1016/j.ridd.2009.02.010

Kumar, M. N. (2008). A review of the types of scientific misconduct in biomedical research. *Journal of Academic Ethics, 6*(3), 211−228. https://doi.org/10.1007/s10805-008-9068-6

Lund Research. (2012). *Principles of research ethics*. https://dissertation.laerd.com/principles-of-research-ethics.php.

Lynch, J. A. (2021). Evolving exhibits: Struggles over public memory in developing "the Willowbrook mile". *American Behavioral Scientist*, 00027642211003151.

Madden, G. J., Dube, W. V., Hackenberg, T. D., Hanley, G. P., & Lattal, K. A. (2013). *APA handbook of behavior analysis: Volume I: Methods and principles*. American Psychological Association.

Marcus, A. (2021a). *Retraction watch: Tracking retractions as a window into the scientific process*. https://retractionwatch.com/.

Marcus, A. (May 26, 2021b). *Two Japanese universities revoke PhDs, one for plagiarism and one because of cell line contamination*. Retraction Watch https://retractionwatch.com/2021/05/26/two-japanese-universities-revoke-phds-one-for-plagiarism-and-one-because-of-cell-line-contamination/.

Marino, G. (2010). *Ethics: The essential writings*. Modern Library. ISBN: 978-0-8129-7778-3.

Markkula Center for Applied Ethics. (1988). *Consistency and ethics*. https://www.scu.edu/ethics/ethics-resources/ethical-decision-making/consistency-and-ethics/.

Marya, V. G., Suarez, V. D., & Cox, D. J. (2022). Ethical decision-making and evidenced-based practices. In J. Leaf, J. Cihon, J. L. Ferguson, & M. J. Weiss (Eds.), *Handbook of applied behavior analysis interventions for Autism*. Springer Nature.

McCook, A. (July 18, 2018). *A University is revoking a student's PhD — but not because of misconduct*. Retraction Watch https://retractionwatch.com/2018/07/18/a-university-is-revoking-a-students-phd-but-not-because-of-misconduct/.

Moravcsik, A. (2019). *Transparency in qualitative research*. SAGE Research Methods Foundations. https://doi.org/10.4135/9781526421036

Mower, D. S. (2013). Situationism and confucian virtue ethics. *Ethical Theory and Moral Practice, 16*, 113−137. https://doi.org/10.1007/s10677-011-9312-9

National Commission for the Protection of Human Subjects of Biomedical and Behavioral Research. (1978). *The Belmont report: Ethical principles and guidelines for the protection of human subjects of research* [Bethesda, Md.]: The Commission.

Olivola, C. Y., Kim, Y., Merzel, A., Kareev, Y., Avrahami, J., & Ritov, I. (2020). Cooperation and coordination across cultures and contexts: Individual, sociocultural, and contextual factors jointly influence decision making in the volunteer's dilemma game. *Journal of Behavioral Decision Making, 33*(1), 93–118. https://doi.org/10.1002/bdm.2135

Pinker, S. (2018). *Enlightenment now*. Penguin Books.

Rawls, J. (1971). *A theory of justice*. Belknap Press. ISBN: 978-0-674-00078-0.

Rhodes, R., & Alfandre, D. (2007). A systematic approach to clinical moral reasoning. *Clinical Ethics, 2*, 66–70. https://doi.org/10.1258/147775007781029582

Rutherford, A. (2006). The social control of behavior control: Behavior modification, individual rights, and research ethics in America, 1971–1979. *Journal of the History of the Behavioral Sciences, 42*(3), 203–220. https://doi.org/10.1002/jhbs.20169

Sabini, J., & Silver, M. (2005). Lack of character? Situationism critiqued. *Ethics, 115*(3), 535–562. https://doi.org/10.1086/428459

Sidman, M. (1960). *Tactics of scientific research: Evaluating experimental data in psychology*. Authors Cooperative, Inc.

Skinner, B. F. (1945). The operational analysis of psychological terms. *Psychological Review, 52*(5), 270–277. https://psycnet.apa.org/doi/10.1037/h0062535.

Skinner, B. F. (1953). *Science and human behavior*. The Free Press.

Thoreau, H. D. (1849). *On the duty of civil disobedience*. The Project Gutenberg. https://www.gutenberg.org/files/71/71-h/71-h.htm.

Tourinho, E. Z., & Neno, S. (2003). Effectiveness as truth criterion in behavior analysis. *Behavior and Philosophy, 31*, 63–80. https://www.jstor.org/stable/27759447.

Van Fleet, D. D., Ray, D. F., Bedeian, A. G., Downey, H. K., Hunt, J. G., Griffin, R. W., Dan Dalton, D., Vecchio, R. P., Kacmar, K. M., & Feldman, D. C. (2006). The journal of management's first 30 years. *Journal of Management, 32*(4), 477–506. https://doi.org/10.1177/0149206306286715

Verriden, A. L., & Roscoe, E. M. (2016). A comparison of preference-assessment methods. *Journal of Applied Behavior Analysis, 49*, 265–285. https://doi.org/10.1002/jaba.302

Weijer, C., & Emanuel, E. J. (2000). Protecting communities in biomedical research. *Science, 289*, 1142–1144.

Weijer, C., Goldsand, G., & Emanuel, E. J. (1999). Protecting communities in research: Current guidelines and limits of extrapolation. *Nature Genetics, 23*, 275–280.

Wertheimer, A. (1999). *Exploitation*. Princeton Press.

White, M. G. (2020). Why human subjects research protection is important. *The Ochsner Journal, 20*(1), 16–33. https://doi.org/10.31486/toj.20.5012

Wiles, R., Crow, G., Heath, S., & Charles, V. (2008). The management of confidentiality and anonymity in social research. *International Journal of Social Research Methodology, 11*(5), 417–428. https://doi.org/10.1080/13645570701622231

Witts, B. N., Brodhead, M. T., Adlington, L. C., & Barron, D. K. (2020). Behavior analysts accept gifts during practice: So now what? *Behavior Analysis: Research and Practice, 20*(3), 196–202. https://doi.org/10.1037/bar0000117

Zaman, J., Ceulemans, E., Hermans, D., & Beckers, T. (2019). Direct and indirect effects of perception on generalization gradients. *Behaviour Research and Therapy, 114*, 44–50. https://doi.org/10.1016/j.brat.2019.01.006

Further reading

Behavior Analyst Certification Board. (2020). *Ethics code for behavior analysts.* Author.

Dittrich, A. (2020). Who has the last word? Radical behaviorism, science, and verbal behavior about verbal behavior. *Perspectives on Behavior Science, 43,* 343–359. https://doi.org/10.1007/s40614-020-00249-9

NIH. (2016). *Guiding principles for ethical research.* https://www.nih.gov/health-information/nih-clinical-research-trials-you/guiding-principles-ethical-research.

Normand, M. P. (2019). The language of science. *Perspectives on Behavior Science, 42,* 675–688. https://doi.org/10.1007/s40614-017-0123-8

Chapter 3

Equity, diversity, inclusion, and accessibility in research*

Noor Y. Syed[1,2,4], Leanna Mellon[3] and Sarah Kristiansen[4]
[1]*SUNY Empire State College and the Center for Autism Advocacy: Research, Education, and Supports, Saratoga Springs, NY, United States;* [2]*Anderson Center International, Staatsburg, NY, United States;* [3]*SUNY New Paltz, New Paltz, NY, United States;* [4]*Endicott College, Beverly, MA, United States*

Equity, diversity, inclusion, and access in research

At the core of applied behavior analysis (ABA) lie seven dimensions: applied, behavioral, analytic, generality, conceptually systematic, effective, and technological. Originally proposed by Baer and colleagues in 1968, the seven dimensions continue to be taught in behavior analytic course sequences today (Behavior Analyst Certification Board, 2017; Cooper et al., 2020; Pastrana et al., 2018). While each dimension carries equal weight and has shaped the direction of our work as behavior analysts, the dimension of *applied* is paramount in understanding the importance of diversity in behavior-analytic research.

> *The label applied is not determined by the research procedures used but by the interest*
>
> *which society shows in the problems being studied. In behavioral application,* ***the behavior, stimuli, and/or organism under study are chosen because of their importance to man and society*** *[emphasis added], rather than their importance to theory.*
>
> (Baer et al., 1968, p. 92).

---

* Noor Syed identifies as Brown, Pakistani, Filipino, Muslim, and as Cisgender Female. Leanna Mellon identifies as White, Jewish, and Cisgender Female. Sarah Kristiansen identifies as White, Roman Catholic, and Cisgender Female. The authors have no conflicts of interest to declare. Correspondence concerning this chapter should be addressed to Noor Syed, SUNY Empire State College and the Center for Autism Advocacy: Research, Education, and Supports, 2 Union Avenue, Saratoga Springs, NY 12866.

Research Ethics in Behavior Analysis. https://doi.org/10.1016/B978-0-323-90969-3.00012-8
63

Considering this, behavior analysts must be highly cognizant of engaging in research based on the needs, preferences, and strongest contextual fit for the communities and cultures in which they are conducting research.

The *applied* dimension makes clear that behavior analytic research and practice are applied when it is relevant to society and the people within society. Therefore, the practices and research must be reflective of the needs of people living in different communities and with different cultures throughout society. Behavior analyst researchers, or scientist-practitioners, must be aware of, and responsive to, the culture of those with whom they are working, as well as how their own culture intersects. In addition, we should approach the dimension of *generality* through the lens of philosophic doubt as culture and cultural evolution involve complex and interlocking contingencies that form verbal communities unique to each identity, subculture, and intersectionality. Does behavior change generalize across cultures? If we target self-help skills through behavior analysis based on our own cultural experiences, for example, would our targets be appropriate in another culture? It is important to consider the identities and cultures of behavior analytic researchers as compared to the participants. For example, it is not uncommon for research in autism to be conducted without ongoing autistic community input and involvement (Keating, 2021).

Our goal for this chapter is to engage in open, respectful discussion surrounding culture, identity, and diversity as related to behavior analytic research and to thoughtfully analyze how we can promote equity in our practices. We will begin by assessing what might be considered evidenced-based practices within behavior analysis through an analysis of diversity. The chapter will then focus on walking applied researchers through the steps of the research process, with equity, diversity, inclusivity, and accessibility (EDIA) in mind. These sections will analyze ethical challenges and provide recommendations surrounding the following applied research processes: creating research teams, culturally responsible participant recruitment, and proactive measures against colonialist research practices. We will then provide background on barriers and recommendations related to becoming a researcher and will end the chapter by providing guiding questions to support equity within research.

It is important to note that it is impossible to cover the extensive considerations that should be devoted to EDIA in behavior analytic research in one chapter. Further, we posit that EDIA continues to be an area of growth in behavior analysis. Many of the recommendations given in this chapter represent long-term goals and major cultural shifts in how ABA research is conducted that will be shaped through meeting shorter-term objectives. It is our hope these topics function as an antecedent for ongoing dialogue surrounding EDIA in applied behavior analysis.

EDIA and evidenced-based practice

The most recent edition of the Behavior Analyst Certification Board's (BACB) Ethics Code for Behavior Analysts ("Ethics Code") identifies the following variables related to diversity: "age, disability, ethnicity, gender expression/ identity, immigration status, marital/relationship status, national origin, race, religion, sexual orientation, and socioeconomic status" (BACB, 2020, p. 4). One definition of diversity is "the state of having people who are different races or who have different cultures in a group or organization" (Merriam-Webster, n.d.); one product of including diverse individuals is that it fosters an environment where different ideas are present. Further, Sugai et al. (2012) defined culture as similar learning histories that are shaped by environment and context.

We extend the Sugai et al. (2012) definition to consider that culture also consists of shared behaviors arranged by verbal communities through punishment and reinforcement contingencies (Syed et al., 2022). Behaviors are maintained through interlocking contingencies, in which the behavior of each individual functions to affect the behaviors of others with similar identities (i.e., beliefs and values) until a common culture is formed (Glenn et al., 2016). Skinner (1981) acknowledged the importance of the social environment as one of three levels that jointly produce human behavior and emphasized the role that culture has on impacting behavior. It is important to recognize the impact of the social environment on the behaviors of the participants, researchers, and the scientific community and how it has influenced the current state of the field of ABA.

One's identity can be a product of their learning history and the history of a particular verbal community, culture, or environment of which they are a member. However, it is important to avoid defining groups by a single dimension as a single individual can have multiple identities (Gorski, 2016; Hugh-Pennie et al., 2021; Hughes Fong et al., 2016; Ladson-Billings, 2018). In fact, intersectionality is a conceptual framework of how multiple identities may interact in a way that influences a person's environment, experiences, and opportunities (Crenshaw, 1989). Similarly, there may be several subcultures within larger cultural groups (Castro-Hostetler et al., 2021; Hughes Fong et al., 2016; López & Gonzalez-Barrera, 2016). The inclusion of people from diverse backgrounds can foster an environment for different ideas to be present, and the lack of diversity can result in the opposite (AlShebli et al., 2018; Hong & Page, 2004).

The majority of published behavior analytic research to date has been conducted in the English language and is a product of Western culture, primarily the United States (Alai-Rosales et al., 2022). Such a publication history may lack broader cultural diversity (across geographic regions and primary languages, as examples), therefore limiting contextual generalizability of research findings and what might be considered evidenced-based practice

(EBP). EBP implies interventions with empirical support; in other words, strategies derived from research that has historically demonstrated their effectiveness. Such strategies are the cornerstone of behavior analysis.

Slocum et al. (2014) proposed evidenced-based practice to be understood as a "professional decision-making framework that draws on the best available evidence, client values and context, and clinical expertise" (p. 53). It is important, therefore, to consider evidenced-based practices within our field as dynamic and contextual rather than as prescriptive interventions; empirical support may be insufficient to classify a practice as an EBP (Slocum et al., 2014). For example, research conducted in organizational behavior management (OBM) suggests that feedback may be key in improving employee performance (Wilder et al., 2009). The topography of feedback and history of reinforcement for feedback delivery, however, may differ across cultures, necessitating studies in performance feedback across diverse identities.

Ethical decision-making to incorporate EDIA considerations during the research process

In examining the role of EDIA in research, it is important to understand that there are many ethical decision-making opportunities within the research process where diversity, or a lack of diversity, can impact the research that gets conducted, disseminated, and acted upon in ABA. These opportunities may include forming a research team, participant recruitment, and proactive measures to prevent colonialist research. The next sections of this chapter will walk the reader through these components of the research process, describe the current state as indicated by the published literature, and give recommendations for addressing current barriers.

Forming a diverse research team

Recent demographic data show that the field of behavior analysts is lacking in racial and ethnic diversity, particularly with professionals with a BCBA credential and BCBA with a doctoral designation (BCBA-D; BACB, n.d.). ABA research is often designed by BCBAs and implemented by either BCBAs or by paraprofessionals, including Registered Behavior Technicians (RBTs), under the supervision of a BCBA. The data in Table 3.1 compare the proportion of BCBAs relative to the number of paraprofessional RBTs, the US adult population (18 years and over) and the US child population (18 years and younger). Several over and underrepresentations at the BCBA and RBT level are apparent in these data, but the disparities among BCBAs are of particular note when looking at issues of EDIA in applied research. Based on these data, it is likely that research goals are selected by White BCBAs (70.42% of all self-reported BCBAs) even though only 53% of children, who are often participants of applied behavior analytic education research, are White.

TABLE 3.1 Percentage distribution of race and ethnicity from the 2020 US Census and BACB.

Race/ethnicity	Percent of population under 18 years	Percent of population 18 years and over	Percent of BCBA and BCBA-D certificants	Percent of RBT certificants
White	53	64.1	70.42	46.18
Black or African American	13.9	12	3.85	12.95
American Indian and Alaska Native	1.4	1.1	0.28	0.42
Asian	5.5	6.1	6.7	5.81
Native Hawaiian and other Pacific Islander	0.3	0.2	0.38	0.74
Hispanic or LatinX	15.7	16.8	10.3	27.09

Note. Data on BACB certificants are reported as of November 19, 2021. BCBA/BCBA-D certificants had a 98% response rate and 8.07% respondents selected "No Answer." RBTs certificants had a 98.5% response rate and 6.81% respondents selected "No Answer." Census data on race/Ethnicity were reported as "alone" in that category and therefore do not include individuals with multiple racial/ethnic identities. Census data were reported as Hispanic or Latino.

Mismatches in culture and language between applied researchers and participants can hinder communication and the implementation of research (Kouyoumdjian et al., 2003). A mismatch in the culture of the researcher and the participant is a concern because the researcher decides what gets studied and research topics may reflect what the researcher interprets as socially important issues to a community when they do not have a shared learning history with that community. Mismatches also pose a challenge in recommending socially significant goals if the researcher does not share the values and experiences of the participants. For example, a researcher may recommend an intervention in an immigrant family that teaches a young child not to hug strangers, operationally defining a stranger as someone they have not yet met. When the child meets their grandparents for the first time, they do not hug their family, which may be a major sign of disrespect in a culture. If the researcher had learned about the significance of hugging in that culture a different dependent variable may have been chosen. This example, specifically, highlights the importance of designing research with the inclusion, or at least input, from members of the community in which research is being conducted.

Addressing disparities in forming a research team

If the cultural identities of a research team are not aligned with the participants, the researcher should make efforts to familiarize themselves with the culture and expectations of the community *before* finalizing protocols and dependent variables. Members of the community or identity being included in studies should be given the opportunity to be a part of the research process. One way this could be done is by partnering with local universities or community colleges with similar fields of study to see if students would like to gain research experience. Creating a team that reflects the values of the identities being studied is a beginning step in conducting responsible, culturally inclusive, research.

Responsible participant recruitment

Psychological research has historically been representative of White, Western, and English-speaking participants (Apfelbaum et al., 2012; Henrich et al., 2010). While factors related to diversity are not the only important variable when analyzing human learning and behavior, these factors should not be considered as arbitrary variables (Skinner, 1981). Learning histories, which may differ based on a multitude of variables related to diversity, play an important role in conditioning reinforcers. The social environment, which varies across different cultures, communities, and neurotypes, impact the contingencies that affect behavior and learning (Skinner, 1981). Primary reinforcers may even differ based on diverse factors. For example, the presence of food may be a much stronger establishing operation for an individual experiencing hunger regularly compared to someone for whom food is plentiful, making socioeconomic status a relevant variable to consider.

The Belmont report (National Commission for the Protection of Human Subjects of Biomedical and Behavior Research, 1979) specified that it is imperative to include diverse participants in research to avoid repeating historically disproportionate research risks within some communities. It is difficult, however, to determine the current impact of assumptions about variables related to diversity on research in behavior analysis because demographic information is not being widely reported—and this is not unique to the field of behavior analysis. One study reported that as much as 96% of subjects in research on human psychology and behavior are from Western, industrialized, rich, and democratic (WEIRD) backgrounds, despite that only being representative of 12% of the world population (Henrich et al., 2010). Here, a concern is that a lack of diversity in research participants may perpetuate one-size-fits-all approaches to consumers of research, which does not meet the needs of the individuals we serve or their communities (Ladson-Billings, 2008; Zarcone et al., 2019).

Inclusion criteria of specific diagnoses may also act as a barrier in conducting research with diverse participants, as a particular diagnosis or educational classification may be reflective of existing biases and inequities in diagnostics. Many diagnostic assessments, as well as special education classifications, utilize clinical judgment in the diagnostic and classification processes and are therefore susceptible to the biases of those conducting the assessment (Atkins-Loria et al., 2015; Cruz & Rodl, 2018; Donovan & Cross, 2002; Kramarczuk Voulgarides et al., 2017; Salend et al., 2002). Research in the field of special education has focused on several prominent court cases surrounding biases of norm referenced standardized tests (Salend et al., 2002; Salend & Garrick Duhaney, 2005) and cases have legally challenged the use of Intelligence Quotient (IQ) tests in special education classification due to racial and cultural bias (Larry P. v. Riles, 1979; Diana v. Board of Education; Parents in Action of Special Education v. Hannon, 1980). Similarly, research has provided evidence to support cultural biases when implementing the widely used Autism Diagnostic Observation Schedule (ADOS) (Adamou et al., 2018; Harrison et al., 2017) related to the use and recognition of eye contact and facial expressions. Additionally, differences in language and play may be factors in the significant item level bias on the ADOS and other diagnostic tools (Harrison et al., 2017). Further, BIPOC (Black Indigenous Persons of Color) children have historically received medical diagnoses significantly later in life, are often misdiagnosed, and receive less support services when compared to their White peers (Castro-Hostetler et al., 2021; Chapa, 2004; Magaña et al., 2013; Mandell et al., 2002; Rosales et al., 2021).

Strict research study inclusion criteria related to diagnosis or diagnostic instruments, therefore, may function as a barrier to including diverse participants. In many geographic regions, for example, diagnoses may be challenging to obtain due to limited knowledge or resources (Durkin et al., 2015). The researchers must consider whether requiring a diagnosis to participate in research is equitable in the environment in which research is being conducted as this could unintentionally exclude participants from groups that do not have equitable access to diagnosis. If focusing research with a specific population, such as White male autistic individuals, consider the benefit and consequences to limiting research participants to that specific group. For example, working only with White male autistic participants may provide evidence toward answering a specific research question, but it would limit access to the intervention for those outside of the group and the generality of findings. Ideally, in this example, autistic research team members and/or consultants can provide guidance as to potential consequences of such research and the rationale for these decisions should be easily accessible for IRB members, participants, and subsequent consumers of the research.

Another inclusion criterion that may serve as an unintentional barrier to diversity in research is attendance requirements for participation in research. Specific attendance requirements could exclude participants who must commute to research sites and lack access to reliable transportation or practice religions that do not follow the Christian calendar and require participation during religious holidays; this includes participants and their families who engage in daily prayer multiple times a day that could impact scheduling intervention sessions. In addition, the researcher must consider the feasibility requirements that participating in their research necessitates. For example, research may be conducted in settings that are not easily accessible for participants, such as in a clinic that is not located near public transportation. Such a study may inadvertently require participants to have ready access to private transportation. Even if the research setting is located near a public transportation hub, traveling to a research site would require funding for the transportation, which may also discriminate against populations that do not have this funding for transportation readily available. Telehealth has been emerging as a useful research tool in addressing some of these barriers (Barkaia et al., 2017; Tomlinson et al., 2018; Tsami et al., 2019); however, such research requires access to remote technology such as computers, mobile devices, electricity, and Internet access.

Addressing EDIA issues with participant recruitment

Researchers might consider compensation or incentives to participate in research to counterbalance costs associated with barriers such as travel, time away from employment, and childcare. They may also schedule research to occur at times that are convenient for the participants and offer a variety of scheduling options. Researchers must judiciously consider each inclusive criterion for their research participants as well as the overall goal of the impact of their research in order to determine if exclusionary criteria act as a barrier to including participants who they would like to benefit from the research. If participants do not have ready access to technology, researchers might provide access and equipment. Providing access and equipment to technology may be financially challenging, so it would be important to assess whether grant or other funding opportunities are available. It may be, however, that after all options to include participants are explored, there are still barriers to ensuring a diverse field of participants can be secured. In this case, we are not suggesting that a study not take place. Rather, the research should analyze whether the study would contribute to the behavior analytic literature as written. If this is the case, this should be written as a limitation within the discussion section of the article with a call for researchers with more resources to replicate findings with a more diverse group. If not, researchers may want to find other ways to engage in research that would allow more representative participants to be included.

Responsible Reporting of Demographic Data. The seventh edition of the American Psychological Association Publication Manual (APA, 2020) contains a section on bias-free language that suggests researchers report the identities of participants as they are reported by the participant. This suggestion is feasible to include in single-case design research studies since such information is often presented for each participant rather than being clustered together as in group design studies. APA (2020) also advises that language implying binaries be avoided. For example, implying that female is the opposite of male is a binary approach that ignores other identities such as nonbinary, gender-nonconforming, and transgender. Similarly, using binary language such as white and minority, or white and nonwhite, can both ignore multiple identities while incorrectly implying that the experience of being inside or outside of dominant culture has a uniform impact on the environment and behavior.

Emphasis can be placed on reporting diversity metrics in behavior analytic research. The first reporting guidelines for researchers were published in 1996 when the Consolidated Standards on Reporting Trials (CONSORT) statement was delivered (Schulz et al., 2010). The CONSORT guidelines initially gave recommendations for large group researchers utilizing randomized group designs but were subsequently revised in 2015 and 2016 to be more applicable to behavior analytic research. These revisions included the CONSORT Extension of N-1 Trials (CENT; Vohra et al., 2105) and Single Case Reporting Guidelines in Behavioral Interventions (SCRIBE) guidelines (Taylor, LeBlanc, & Nosik, 2018). CONSORT, for example, requires information only on eligibility for participants. See Table 3.2 for demographic reporting recommendations per guideline.

Researchers should also carefully consider language used to categorize or describe participants. For example, disability advocates have begun championing identity-first, rather than person-first language (Dunn & Andrews, 2015), so it may be more appropriate to use the term "Deaf person" rather than "person who is hard of hearing" when working within the Deaf community. The research team should ideally ask preference from the disabled community and participants themselves regarding terminology. If the team or researcher is unable to ascertain preference, they may choose to note this in their manuscript and use both person- and identity-first language interchangeably. Race and ethnicity should be described using capital letters (e.g., Black, White, and Brown); "underrepresented" is more appropriate than "minority" when used to describe participants (APA, 2020). While it is beyond the scope of this chapter to review all examples of bias-free language, it is recommended that researchers seek knowledge in understanding and using appropriate terminology as related to age, gender identity, socioeconomic status, disability, sexuality, and racial identity (see Chapter 5 in APA, 2020 for a full summary). Best practice in language related to reporting participant characteristics is continuously evolving; therefore, it is important to keep abreast of changes.

TABLE 3.2 Tools providing guidance on the reporting of demographic variables in research.

Guiding publication	Intended use	Recommendations for inclusion of demographic information
CONSORT (2010) *(Consolidated Standards of Reporting Trials)*	CONSORT was published to guide those conducting research using randomized controlled trials.	· Eligibility criteria for participants · Settings and locations where the data were collected
CENT (2015) *(CONSORT Extension for Reporting N-of-1 Trials)*	CENT was published to provide guidance to those conducting medical or behavioral research with a single participant (N-of-1).	· Diagnosis or disorder, diagnostic criteria, comorbid conditions, and concurrent therapies. · Make sure that the demographic information included does not make the participant easily identified to the general public.
SCRIBE (2016) *(Single Case Reporting Guidelines in Behavioral Interventions)*	SCRIBE was published to guide researchers conducting single-case experimental designs.	· State the inclusion and exclusion criteria, if applicable, and the method of recruitment. · For each participant, describe the demographic characteristics and clinical (or other) features relevant to the research question, such that anonymity is ensured.
APA Publication Manual (2020)	This manual was published as a set of guidelines for authors and edits to ensure clear, concise, and consistent publications.	· Describe participants with an appropriate level of specificity and include the most relevant characteristics · When describing demographics such as race, ethnicity, or disability, consult with the participants to determine how they would like to be identified (e.g., person-first vs. identity-first language). · When including age as a relevant characteristic for groups, use specific age ranges (e.g., 51–60-year, vs. over 65).

How to Use This Table:
- Authors should not see this table as a checklist. Rather, the table offers reminders for important demographic information that should be included in manuscripts to best inform the reader.
- All published guidelines (CONSORT, CENT, and SCRIBE) are freely available via open access at the following links:
  - CONSORT: CONSORT 2010 Statement: updated guidelines for reporting parallel group randomized trials | Trials | Full Text (biomedcentral.com).
  - CENT: CONSORT extension for reporting N-of-1 trials (CENT) 2015 Statement | The BMJ.
  - SCRIBE: Single-Case Reporting Guideline In Behavioral Interventions (SCRIBE) 2016 Statement | Physical Therapy | Oxford Academic (oup.com).
- If an individual does not own a copy of the APA publication manual, free support can be found on the manual's website: https://apastyle.apa.org.

Researchers are also encouraged to offer participation in studies outside of the readily available research group to increase diversification in a participant pool, and we must be cautious not to overgeneralize our findings to different cultural groups. As discussed earlier, Henrich et al. (2010) note that the publications in top psychological and behavioral journals are based on samples that may lack global representation. Such a lack of representation does not allow psychological and behavioral research to make broad claims about the effectiveness of behavior analytic interventions and methodologies, and we run the risk of describing our findings and protocols to be evidenced-based without considering context (Slocum et al., 2014). It may be more accurate to describe current behavior analytic strategies as effective for the specific population in which the interventions were studied, but they may not be considered evidenced-based as described by Slocum et al. (2014). Without increased data on demographics (e.g., Jones et al., 2020), we may have less support for evidenced-based interventions than we initially realized, significantly limiting the ability to assess generalization of findings. In promotion of equity, behavior analytic researchers should adjust our requirements for investigators such that additional emphasis in research is placed on explicitly discussing and defending generalizability (Heinrich et al., 2010).

Proactive measures to prevent colonialist research practices

A study conducted by Pritchett et al. (2021) investigated applied behavior analytic experiments published in the *Journal of Applied Behavior Analysis* (*JABA*) through the lens of respect, beneficence, and justice (National Commission for the Protection of Human Subjects of Biomedical and Behavioral Research, 1979) and analyzed these studies for the presence of community-based practices, which incorporate the participation of individuals and communities into research. Results of the study indicated a lack of reporting for all measures associated with respect for persons and beneficence, further supporting a historically colonial model of research in behavior analysis. The discrepancies in reporting from Pritchett and colleagues' findings suggest that, historically, the field of behavior analysis has lacked participatory research practices that incorporate community values into the selection of intervention procedures (2021). Pritchett et al. (2021) further describe three features of behavior analytic research: (a) commodities, or the exchange of behavior data for conditioned reinforcers such as publications, (b) the "taking" of data from a person to the benefit of the experimenters, and (c) colonialist research relationships in which human participant behavior functions at the discretion of the researcher, who holds the tokens—in other words, research contingencies may occur that function as coercive conditions, subsequently leading to colonialist research practices.

Researchers can engage in a number of actions to proactively prevent colonialist research practices. Creating a research team that includes members of the community, and actively incorporating these individuals into decisions regarding dependent variables and intervention procedures, can help ensure that these components of the research process reflect the values of the population being studied. The reader should note that responsible research practices begin with careful selection of the research team so that guidance can be given throughout the research process by those aligned with the culture being studied. When engaging in applied research, researchers should openly acknowledge the narrow scope of their research question, discuss these limitations, and ensure that research is relevant to the population being studied.

Participants should be continuously advised that their participation is voluntary, and they can rescind it at any time for any reason, including if they feel the research is no longer appropriate or acceptable. Assent protocols for participants should be individualized and designed with input from the participant to the greatest extent possible and from relevant parties such as caregivers.

Researchers have an ethical responsibility to keep the well-being of their participants as their top priority when conducting research. As the field of behavior analysis strives to become increasingly diverse, this will include purposeful development of a researcher's skills surrounding cultural awareness (Hughes Fong et al., 2016, 2017), which has been defined as "encompass(ing) the ability for one to examine their own cultural beliefs and values and understand how the culture of others can shape behavior and interactions with others" (Conners & Cappell, 2021, p. 2).

Hughes Fong (2021) recommends that researchers evaluate the cultural practices of participants before beginning a behavior analytic intervention that may be in contradiction with these practices. Leland and Stockwell (2019) built further upon these ideas by giving guidance on projects that do not lie within the researcher's culture as related to individuals who are transgender-nonconforming. They advise that it is the researcher's responsibility to receive ongoing supervision and training on cultural awareness as it pertains to the group that they are studying. Failure to do so may affect social significance of the goal and findings, as well as social validity. Researchers should remember that though the field of applied behavior analysis may provide us with technology to change behavior, participants ultimately have the right to choose whether they will participate in research through informed consent and assent processes. Our recommendation to researchers echoes that of Hughes Fong (2021)—studies should be guided by the community that participants are a member of to promote the highest level of social validity and likelihood of generalization following a study's conclusion. The research question studied should be one that is important to members of the participant's cultural affiliation.

Barriers to becoming researchers and published authors: analysis through an EDIA lens

Finally, the authors of this chapter felt it was important to draw attention to EDIA challenges in becoming a researcher, accessing resources for research, presenting their findings in peer-reviewed conference proceedings, and becoming published. It is difficult for someone to engage in research, much less research that is mindful of EDIA practices, without access to resources such as literature repositories, data analysis tools, and sufficient time to dedicate to research. Access to some literature may be found within academic and professional organization settings, but membership to these organizations may not be financially feasible. Behavior analytic journals, such as *Behavior Analysis in Practice, the Journal of Applied Behavior Analysis,* and *The Analysis of Verbal Behavior*, are generally not open access, and a recent review found that there are few Open Education Resources (OERs) for behavior analysts (Howard, 2019). Therefore, unless individuals have an institutional or organizational affiliation that provides access to journals, the cost is often unaffordable. Furthermore, although some professional organization memberships include academic journal access, memberships to these organizations may be expensive and do not cover all the behavior analytic journals that are behind paywalls.

Much research is conducted in academic settings. In the United States, tenure and promotion in academia are more likely to lead to a release of responsibility, which allows more time for research and writing. It is interesting to note then that data from the American Council of Education in 2016 show fewer female faculty have a rank of associate professor or higher, and promotion is often linked with records of research and scholarship in academia (Johnson, 2017). Female faculty report engaging in more hours of university and professional service (Guarino & Borden, 2017), which often comes at the expense of spending time on research and scholarship. The disparity in academic ranks between men and women is also present in behavior analysis (Li et al., 2017). Li et al. (2017) investigated publicly available rank and salaries of 103 faculty members from 16 universities accredited through the Association for Behavior Analysis International (ABAI) and found that, although 52.4% of the faculty sample was women, twice as many men were full professors, the highest tenured academic rank. Further, mean salaries of male faculty at each academic rank (assistant, associate, full) were higher than those of women at the same rank. Inequity is also present across race. BIPOC faculty often engage in disproportionately more mentorship and service activities (Barber et al., 2020; Jordan et al., 2021; Rodríguez et al., 2015), with many of these additional service demands being initiatives geared toward diversity, equity, and inclusion (Rodríguez et al., 2015). As discussed earlier, intersectionality can further amplify existing barriers (Makino & Oliver, 2019) making it even more difficult for female BIPOC faculty to engage in research and scholarship and remain employed in positions that encourage research (Chancellor, 2019; Cirincione-Ulezi, 2020).

In addition, research is often conducted by graduate students and others in academia. Despite the fact that the number of BIPOC students earning degrees in behavior analysis increased steadily from 2021 to 2017, this is still a small proportion of the students earning these degrees (Levy et al., 2021), and this growth rate may not match the growth rate of diverse populations who will participate in applied research. This is a particular concern regarding research because graduate student research is one major source of published research in the field of behavior analysis. Racial and ethnic diversity of higher education faculty, staff, and administration, who often guide student research, does not reflect today's student population (Espinosa et al., 2019). Given the lack of diversity in higher education, where much of research is conducted, post-secondary institutions should consider ways to promote equity in recruitment and support BIPOC candidates and professors with mentorship and resources throughout the academic process of applying, interviewing, onboarding, and engaging in ongoing responsibilities associated with higher education professions.

Graduate programs in applied behavior analysis should consider ways to increase accessibility of their coursework, including giving credit for prior learning experiences and professional development, minimizing cost and increasing access to required course material (for example, analyzing which textbooks are truly necessary and whether they are available across the world), providing multiple ways to engage with material, such as through podcasts, webinars, allowing choices with assignments, and presenting a worldview of curricula. Graduate programs may seek to provide scholarships and supports to their program and for other academic opportunities whenever possible and may partner with organizations who are interested in funding employees to become students, therefore creating a career path. Doing so will begin to create a culture of academia that is increasingly accessible to individuals of increased diverse identities and backgrounds, which may in turn lead over time to an increasingly diverse body of researchers.

Several behavior analytic professional organizations at state, regional, and international levels have made commitments to support research related to diversity, equity, and inclusion such as the Association for Behavior Analysis International (ABAI), the Association for Professional Behavior Analysts (APBA), Black Applied Behavior Analysts (BABA), and New York State Association for Behavior Analysts (NYSABA), with varying degrees of progress (Syed et al., 2022). In such professional organizations, current research is often disseminated through membership websites, conferences, special interest groups, committee work, and continuing education events. The cost of conferences, online events, and membership, however, may serve as a barrier to accessing current research. Many conferences are expensive, even when factoring in membership discounts, and may require additional funds for travel and lodging. The scheduling of conferences may be during a workweek, which could preclude behavior analysts who do not have the ability to miss work. Conversely, conferences scheduled over the weekends can make attendance difficult for those who have familial obligations. Further, child and family care may make conference attendance prohibitive or add to the burden of one caregiver. Conferences scheduled on major holiday weekends may make travel and lodging more cost-prohibitive for some professionals. Additionally, the scheduling of conferences on holidays that are not widely observed or on the Sabbath serves as a barrier for the participation of behavior analysts from some communities. Conferences are an important part of the research dissemination and learning processes; however, there are several existing barriers for many groups of people that may prevent attendance.

Additionally, some existing data suggest possible barriers related to EDIA in the publication process. There is evidence that covert and overt biases impact the peer-review process (Fox et al., 2016; Fox & Paine, 2019; Helmer et al., 2017; Lee et al., 2013; Lerback & Hanson, 2017; Resnik & Elmore, 2016; Resnik et al., 2008; Silibiger & Stubler, 2019), and these biases may influence what is studied and known (Knobloch-Westerwick et al., 2013; Kranak et al., 2021). For example, Fox and Paine (2019) analyzed binary gender (male and female) for over 23,000 manuscripts submitted to six journals specializing in ecology and evolution. Results suggested that though male and female authors were equally likely to be sent for peer review, female authors overall received worst scores and were more likely to be rejected. A recent study on the submitted and published manuscripts in *JABA* from 2015 to 2019 found that veteran authors are $2.5\times$ more likely to have submissions accepted for publication than new authors (Kranak et al., 2021), which could be a challenge as the field of behavior analysis engages in efforts to diversify and expand research interests. Kranak et al. (2021) found no evidence of gender bias in the rate of submission (66%) and publication (67%) for manuscripts submitted to *JABA* from 2015 to 2019, but that is a disproportionately low number of female authors submitting for publication in a field that is 86.37% female (BACB, n.d.). Disis and Slattery (2010) warned that knowledge is limited when research from only a small group of people is published. The experiences, interests, and communities of the researchers influence what topics will be researched and the types of research questions they address in their research. Similarly, the type of research that is published and then disseminated influences practice, especially in the behavior analytic field since empirical research is paramount to its practice (Kranak et al., 2021).

The abovementioned barriers have a cascading effect on inequity within a core part of the research process, namely becoming a researcher and supporting researchers from underrepresented communities. We offer several recommendations to consider, however, in promoting equity in research dissemination. Mentorship and sponsorship can be a significant tool in supporting those who have historically encountered barriers, such as individuals who identify as women and BIPOC in academia (Cirincione-Ulezi, 2020). Organizations in behavior analysis may offer scholarships or other financial support to increase membership, therefore providing more access to resources, avenues to support the ability to engage in and share research, and resources toward conference attendance, specifically to support wider attendance. Additionally, researchers should consider how they can ensure that published works are widely disseminated and barriers to access scholarly works are minimalized, such as supporting open science repositories (e.g., https://psyarxiv.com/). Reporting of inclusive and community-informed demographic data should be prioritized, and all relevant parties within the research and publication processes (e.g., primary investigators, peer reviewers, and editors, to name a few) should receive education on barriers experienced by historically disenfranchised groups, potential biases, and participatory-based research practices. Finally, we must consider broadening types of research that are supported within behavior analysis, particularly as related to our understanding of equity, diversity, inclusion, and accessibility. For example, Cirincione-Ulezi (2020) used qualitative research methodology in an influential and insightful paper discussing barriers that Black women face in accessing leadership positions in behavior analysis. Although qualitative studies are infrequently published in behavior analytic journals compared to quantitative and are often not taught in research design coursework, the research conducted by Cirincione-Ulezi (2020) had a strong impact in identifying barriers faced by this community.

Conclusion and self-assessment guiding questions

It is clear that EDIA in research is a systemic challenge, and historical barriers to increased EDIA are found in areas such as formation of research teams, participant recruitment, and in colonialist practices. Additionally, there are inequities in supporting underrepresented communities to conduct research. To begin addressing these barriers, behavior analytic researchers can begin engaging in self-awareness practices to promote EDIA in research. Below we present a practical list of recommendations for behavior analysts to consider throughout the research process.

1. Research team: Is the research team made up of a diverse body of individuals? Does the population with whom I am conducting research have an active role in the research?
   a. Example: When designing a study investigating the effect of performance feedback on employee outcomes in Saudi Arabia, the research team is composed of individuals from applicable cultures and religions from within the Saudi Arabian community.
2. Research questions: Are my research questions informed by the community? Have I investigated literature outside of one cultural group or

geographic area? Does my investigation meet the definition of *applied*? Are the questions culturally responsive?

    a. Example: Based on feedback with community members in a major metropolitan city, a researcher working within a school decides to implement a training procedure with teachers to increase recognition for mental health support needs with their students.

3. Participant recruitment: Have I engaged in behaviors to promote equity in my participant recruitment, such as mitigating financial and logistical constraints that may be experienced by potential participants, evaluating inclusionary and exclusionary criteria, and actively engaging in recruitment methods that will reach a diverse demographic?

    a. Example: When conducting research to investigate the effects of an acceptance and commitment therapy protocol on perceived stress with caregivers of family members who have had traumatic brain injuries, the researcher offers an extremely flexible schedule and the ability to have respite care during training sessions.

4. Interventions and procedures: Are my proposed methods acceptable to the community with whom I am conducting research? In addition to consent, are assent procedures in place?

    a. Example: When designing an intervention to increase vocal verbal behavior in young children, the researcher creates a separate assent protocol for each participant based on caregiver input.

5. Ethical data analysis and decision making: Are all decisions contextually made in regard to cultural contingencies? If I make this decision, how will it affect the individual acting as a participant in the study? How does my instructional history and intersectionality interact with the participant's history? What are my biases and how do these affect my decisions?

    a. Example: When designing a research study to teach vocal verbal identification of common objects for adults who have been significantly impacted by a stroke, the researcher discloses to all relevant parties that they are impacted by stroke within their own family. The researcher creates a decision-making protocol with the research team to support objective, data-based decisions.

6. Dissemination: How can I share this research on widely accessible platforms? Have I clearly stated cultural considerations regarding my investigation? Is the research shared in accessible language?

    a. Example: The researcher actively seeks grants to support open access for their manuscripts that have been accepted for publication. They provide an overview of their findings via a platform that is both free and widely available globally, such as https://psyarxiv.com/.

7. Supporting underrepresented scholars in becoming a researcher and conducting research: How can I support colleagues from underrepresented groups in the research and publication processes?

    a. Example: I petition a professional organization I am affiliated with to provide more opportunities and access to continuing education opportunities, such as scholarships for conferences. I also support a BIPOC mentorship program that focuses on preparing scholars for academic positions.

It is important to note that the above list is by no means exhaustive. Too, we understand that many of the ideas proposed here may seem great "in theory," but are much more challenging to put into practice. For example, the high cost of open access may be prohibitive to those who do not have grant funding. In addition, translation services are costly and disseminating via webinar is not a peer-reviewed process, which eliminates an important safeguard in literature. However, as the behavior analytic community moves toward increased equitable practice, we may collectively find solutions for the more challenging problems. We will also begin to shape the culture of research collectively toward EDIA. Ideally, researchers will work to ensure that all levels of their research teams are representative of a diverse group of cultures, biases are constantly being examined, research questions and decisions are created through a worldview, and data analysis and corresponding decision-making are contextual. Contingencies surrounding our research agenda should be examined closely, and we must have honest conversations about what reinforces our behavior as we engage in research. We must also consider how we can continuously increase diversity within the population of researchers. Methods to decrease burdens to inclusion within research should be examined, especially for our colleagues who are women or members of BIPOC communities. Increasing universal access to resources should continue to be a goal for the field so that those who would like to contribute to our literature-base find themselves equally positioned to do so. Finally, a behavior-analytic worldview should be consistently represented in all phases of our research.

There is no denying the findings of our research thus far have contributed greatly to our understanding of behavioral principles, which has allowed the field to engage in work that has contributed in a positive, meaningful way to many consumers of behavior analysis. We especially applaud researchers who have emphasized the importance of social validity and social significance (e.g., Wolf, 1978) and who have reminded us of the importance of translational research (Mace & Critchfield, 2010). EDIA in research is a lifelong learning process that requires continuous reflection. What reinforces our engaging in this work? Does this research represent community-based practices and is it inclusive of EDIA in all forms possible, from planning to execution? In our humble opinion, behavior analytic research has a unique ability to give power to voices that have been historically disenfranchised, moving not only our field, but the world forward toward equity.

References

Adamou, M., Johnson, M., & Alty, B. (2018). Autism diagnostic observation schedules (ADOS) scores in males and females diagnosed with autism: A naturalistic study. *Advances in Autism, 4*(2), 49–55. https://doi.org/10.1108/AIA-01-2018-0003

Alai-Rosales, S., Pritchett, M., Linden, A., Cunningham, I., & Syed, N. (2022). Be humble, learn, and care: Culturally responsive evidence-based practice. In J. B. Leaf, J. H. Cihon, J. L. Ferguson, & M. J. Weiss (Eds.), *Handbook of applied behavior analysis intervention for autism*. Springer.

AlShebli, B. K., Rahwan, T., & Lee Woon, W. (2018). The preeminence of ethnic diversity in scientific collaboration. *Nature Communications, 9*, 1–10. https://doi.org/10.1038/s41467-018-07634-8

American Psychological Association. (2020). *Publication manual of the American psychological association* (7th ed.). https://doi.org/10.1037/0000165-000

Apfelbaum, E. P., Norton, M. I., & Sommers, S. R. (2012). Racial color blindness: Emergence, practice, and implications. *Current Directions in Psychological Science, 21*(3), 205–209. https://doi.org/10.1177/0963721411434980

Atkins-Loria, S., Macdonald, H., & Mitterling, C. (2015). Young African American men and the diagnosis of conduct disorder: The neo-colonization of suffering. *Clinical Social Work Journal, 43*(4), 431–441. https://doi.org/10.1007/s10615-015-0531-8

Baer, D. M., Wolf, M. M., & Risley, T. R. (1968). Some current dimensions of applied behavior analysis. *Journal of Applied Behavior Analysis, 1*, 91–97. https://doi.org/10.1901/jaba.1968.1-91

Barber, P. H., Hayes, T. B., Johnson, T. L., & Márquez-Magaña. (2020). Systemic racism in higher education. *Science, 369*(6510), 1441. https://doi.org/10.1126/science.abd7140

Barkaia, A., Stokes, T. F., & Mikiashvili, T. (2017). Intercontinental telehealth coaching of therapists to improve verbalizations by children with autism. *Journal of Applied Behavior Analysis, 50*(3), 582–589. https://doi.org/10.1002/jaba.391

Behavior Analyst Certification Board. (2017). *BCBA task list* (5th ed.) https://www.bacb.com/wp-content/uploads/2020/08/BCBA-task-list-5th-ed-211019.pdf.

Behavior Analyst Certification Board. (2020). *Ethics code for behavior analysts*. https://www.bacb.com/wp-content/uploads/2020/11/Ethics-Code-for-Behavior-Analysts-2102010.pdf.

Behavior Analyst Certification Board. (n.d). BACB certificant data. Retrieved from https://www.bacb.com/BACB-certificant-data.

Castro-Hostetler, M., Greenwald, A. E., & Lewon, M. (2021). Increasing access and quality of behavior-analytic services for the LatinX population. *Behavior and Social Issues, 30*, 1–26. https://doi.org/10.1007/s42822-021-00064-0

Chancellor, R. L. (2019). Racial battle fatigue: The unspoken burden of Black women faculty in LIS. *Journal of Education for Library and Information Science, 60*(3), 182–189. https://doi.org/10.3138/jelis.2019-0007

Chapa, T. (2004). *Mental health services in primary care settings for racial and ethnic minority populations*. U.S. Department of Health and Human Services Office of Minority Health. https://minorityhealth.hhs.gov/Assets/pdf/Checked/1/Mental_Health_Services_in_Primary_Care_Settings_for_Racial2004.pdf.

Cirincione-Ulezi, N. (2020). Black women and barriers to leadership in ABA. *Behavior Analysis in Practice, 13*, 719–724. https://doi.org/10.1007/s40617-020-00444-9

Conners, B. M., & Cappell, S. T. (2021). *Multiculturalism and diversity in applied behavior analysis: Bridging theory and application.* Routledge.

Cooper, J. O., Heron, T. E., & Heward, W. L. (2020). *Applied behavior analysis.* Pearson UK.

Crenshaw, K. (1989). Demarginalizing the intersection of race and sex: A black feminist critique of antidiscrimination doctrine. *feminist Theory and Antiracist Politics, 1*(8), 139−167. University of Chicago Legal Forum.

Cruz, R. A., & Rodl, J. E. (2018). An integrative synthesis of literature on disproportionality in special education. *The Journal of Special Education, 52*(1), 50−63. https://doi.org/10.1177/0022466918758707

Diana v. Board of Education, No. C-70-37 RFP (N.D. Cal).

Disis, M. L., & Slattery, J. T. (2010). The road we must take: Multidisciplinary team science. *Science Translational Medicine, 2*(22), 1−5. https://doi.org/10.1126/scitranslmed.3000421

Donovan, M. S., & Cross, C. T. (Eds.). (2002). *Minority students in special and gifted education/ Committee on minority representation in special education.* Academic Press.

Dunn, D. S., & Andrews, E. E. (2015). Person-first and identity-first language: Developing psychologists' cultural competence using disability language. *American Psychologist, 70*(3), 255.

Durkin, M. S., Elsabbagh, M., Barbaro, J., Gladstone, M., Happe, F., Hoekstra, R. A., Lee, L., Rattazia, A., Stapel-Wax, J., Stone, W. L., Tager-Flusberg, H., Thurm, A., Tomlinson, M., & Shih, A. (2015). Autism screening and diagnosis in low resource settings: Challenges and opportunities to enhance research and services worldwide. *Autism Research, 8*(5), 473−476.

Espinosa, L. L., Turk, J. M., Taylor, M., & Chessman, H. M. (2019). *Race and ethnicity in higher education: A status report.* Washington, DC: American Council on Education.

Fox, C. W., Burns, C. S., & Meyer, J. A. (2016). Editor and reviewer gender influence the peer review process but not peer review outcomes at an ecology journal. *Functional Ecology, 30*(1), 140−153. https://doi.org/10.1111/1365-2435.12529

Fox, C. W., & Paine, C. E. T. (2019). Gender differences in peer review outcomes and manuscript impact at six journals of ecology and evolution. *Ecology and Evolution, 9*(6), 3599−3619. https://doi.org/10.1002/ece3.4993

Glenn, S. S., Malott, M. E., Andery, M. A. P. A., Benvenuti, M., Houmanfar, R. A., Sandaker, I., Todorov, J. C., Tourinho, E. Z., & Vasconcelos, L. A. (2016). Toward consistent terminology in a behaviorist approach to cultural analysis. *Behavior and Social Issues, 25*(1), 11−27.

Gorski, P. (2016). Rethinking the role of "culture" in educational equity: From cultural competence to equity literacy. *Multicultural Perspectives, 18*(4), 221−226. https://doi.org/10.1080/15210960.2016.1228344

Guarino, C. M., & Borden, V. M. H. (2017). Faculty service loads and gender: Are women taking care of the academic family? *Research in Higher Education, 58,* 672−694. https://doi.org/10.1007/s11162-017-9454-2

Harrison, A. J., Long, K. A., Tommet, D. C., & Jones, R. N. (2017). Examining the role of race, ethnicity, and gender on social and behavioral ratings within the autism diagnostic observation schedule. *Journal of Autism and Developmental Disorders, 47,* 2770−2782. https://doi.org/10.1007/s10803-017-3176-3

Helmer, M., Schottdorf, M., Neef, A., & Battaglia, D. (2017). Gender bias in scholarly peer review. *ELife, 6,* 1−18. https://doi.org/10.7554/eLife.21718

Henrich, J., Heine, S. J., & Norenzayan, A. (2010). Most people are not WEIRD. *Nature, 466*(1), 29. https://doi.org/10.1038/466029a

Hong, L., & Page, S. E. (2004). Groups of diverse problem solvers can outperform groups of high-ability problem solvers. *Proceedings of the National Academy of Sciences of the United States of America, 101*(46), 16385−16389. https://doi.org/10.1073/pnas.0403723101

Howard, V. J. (2019). Open educational resources in behavior analysis. *Behavior Analysis in Practice, 12*, 839−853. https://doi.org/10.1007/s40617-019-00371-4

Hugh-Pennie, A., Hernandez, M., Uwayo, M., Johnson, G., & Ross, D. (2021). Culturally relevant pedagogy and applied behavior analysis: Addressing educational disparities in PK-12 schools. *Behavior Analysis in Practice, 14*, 1−9. https://doi.org/10.1007/s40617-021-00655-8

Hughes Fong, E. (2021). Standards for culturally sensitive practice of applied behavior analysis. In B. M. Conners, & S. T. Cappell (Eds.), *Multiculturalism and diversity in applied behavior analysis: Bridging theory and application* (pp. 19−27). Routledge.

Hughes Fong, E., Catagnus, R. M., Brodhead, M. T., Quigley, S., & Field, S. (2016). Developing the cultural awareness skills of behavior analysts. *Behavior Analysis Practice, 9*, 84−94. https://doi.org/10.1007/s40617-016-0111-6

Hughes Fong, E., Ficklin, S., & Lee, H. Y. (2017). Increasing cultural understanding and diversity in applied behavior analysis. *Behavior Analysis: Research and Practice, 17*(2), 103−113. https://doi.org/10.1037/bar0000076

Johnson, H. L. (2017). *Pipelines, pathways, and institutional leadership: An update on the status of women in higher education.* American Council on Education. https://www.acenet.edu/Documents/HES-Pipelines-Pathways-and-Institutional-Leadership-2017.pdf.

Jones, S. H., St Peter, C. C., & Ruckle, M. M. (2020). Reporting of demographic variables in the journal of applied behavior analysis. *Journal of Applied Behavior Analysis, 53*(3), 1304−1315. https://doi.org/10.1002/jaba.722

Jordan, A., Shim, R. S., Rodrigues, C. I., Bath, E., Alves-Bradford, J. M., Eyler, L., Trinh, N. H., Hansen, H., & Mangurian, C. (2021). Psychiatry diversity leadership in academic medicine: Guidelines for success. *American Journal of Psychiatry, 178*(3), 224−228. https://doi.org/10.1176/appi.ajp.2020.20091371

Keating, C. T. (2021). Participatory autism research: How consultation benefits everyone. *Frontiers in Psychology, 12*, 1−6.

Knobloch-Westerwick, S., Glynn, C. J., & Huge, M. (2013). The Matilda effect in science communication: An experiment on gender bias in publication quality perceptions and collaboration interest. *Science Communication, 35*(5), 603−625. https://doi.org/10.1177/1075547012472684

Kouyoumdjian, H., Zamboanga, B. L., & Hansen, D. L. (2003). Barriers to community mental health services for Latinos: Treatment considerations. *Clinical Psychology: Science and Practice, 10*(4), 394−422. https://doi.org/10.1093/clipsy.bpg041

Kramarczuk Voulgarides, C., Fergus, E., & King Thorius, K. A. (2017). Pursuing equity: Disproportionality in special education and the reframing of technical solutions to address systemic inequities. *Review of Research in Education, 41*(1), 61−87. https://doi.org/10.3102/0091732X16686947

Kranak, M. P., Rooker, G. W., Carr, C. J., Bradtke, P., Falligant, J. M., & Hausman, N. (2021). Evaluation of accepted and rejected submissions in the journal of applied behavior analysis: Gender and experience. *Journal of Applied Behavior Analysis, 54*(3), 117−1187. https://doi.org/10.1002/jaba.828

Ladson-Billings, G. (2008). Yes, but how do we do it? In W. Ayers, G. Ladson-Billings, G. Michie, & P. A. Noguera (Eds.), *City kids, city schools: More reports from the front row* (pp. 162−177). New Press.

Ladson-Billings, G. (2018). The social funding of race: The role of schooling. *Peabody Journal of Education, 93*(1), 90−105. https://doi.org/10.1080/0161956X.2017.1403182

Larry P. v. Riles, 495 F. Supp. 926 (N.D. Cal. 1979). https://law.justia.com/cases/federal/district-courts/FSupp/495/926/2007878/.

Lee, C. J., Sugimoto, C. R., Zhang, G., & Cronin, B. (2013). Bias in peer review. *Journal of the American Society for Information Science and Technology, 64*(1), 2−17. https://doi.org/10.1002/asi.22784

Leland, W., & Stockwell, A. (2019). A self-assessment tool for cultivating affirming practices with transgender and gender-nonconforming (TGNC) clients, supervisees, students, and colleagues. *Behavior Analysis in Practice, 12*(4), 816−825.

Lerback, J., & Hanson, B. (2017). Journals invite too few women to referee. *Nature, 541*(7638), 455−457. https://doi.org/10.1038/541455a

Levy, S., Siebold, A., Vaidya, J., Truchon, M. M., Dettmering, J., & Mittelman, C. (2021). A look in the mirror: How the field of behavior analysis can become anti-racist. *Behavior Analysis in Practice.* https://doi.org/10.1007/s40617-021-00630-3

Li, A., Wallace, L., Ehrhardt, K. E., & Poling, A. (2017). Reporting participant characteristics in intervention articles published in five behavior-analytic journals, 2013−2015. *Behavior Analysis: Research and Practice, 17*(1), 84−91. https://doi.org/10.1037/bar0000071

López, G., & Gonzalez-Barrera, A. (2016). *Afro-latino: A deeply rooted identity among U.S. Hispanics.* Pew Research Center. https://www.pewresearch.org/fact-tank/2016/03/01/afro-latino-a-deeply-rooted-identity-%20among-u-s-hispanics/.

Mace, F. C., & Critchfield, T. S. (2010). Translational research in behavior analysis: Historical traditions and imperative for the future. *Journal of the Experimental Analysis of Behavior, 93*(3), 293−312. https://doi.org/10.1901/jeab.2010.93-293

Magaña, S., Lopez, K., Aguinaga, A., & Morton, H. (2013). Access to diagnosis and treatment services among Latino children with autism spectrum disorders. *Intellectual and Developmental Disabilities, 51*(3), 141−153. https://doi.org/10.1352/1934-9556-51.3.141

Makino, K., & Oliver, C. (2019). Developing diverse leadership pipelines: A requirement for 21st century success. *Organization Development Review, 51*(1), 4−10.

Mandell, D. S., Listerud, J., Levy, S. E., & Pinto-Martin, J. A. (2002). Race differences in the age at diagnosis among medicaid-eligible children with autism. *Journal of the American Academy of Child & Adolescent Psychiatry, 41*(12), 1447−1453. https://doi.org/10.1097/00004583-200212000-00016

Merriam-Webster. (n.d.). Merriam-Webster.com dictionary. Retrieved December 17, 2021, from https://www.merriam-webster.com/dictionary/diversity?utm_campaign=sd&utm_medium=serp&utm_source=jsonld.

National Commission for the Protection of Human Subjects of Biomedical and Behavioral Research. (1979). *The Belmont report: Ethical principles and guidelines for the protection of human subjects of research.* Office for Human Research Protections. https://www.hhs.gov/ohrp/regulations-and-policy/belmont-report/read-the-belmont-report/index.html.

Parents in Action on Special Ed.(PASE) v. Hannon, 506 F. Supp. 831 (N.D. Ill. 1980). https://law.justia.com/cases/federal/district-courts/FSupp/506/831/1654128/.

Pastrana, S. J., Frewing, T. M., Grow, L. L., Nosik, M. R., Turner, M., & Carr, J. E. (2018). Frequently assigned readings in behavior analysis graduate training programs. *Behavior Analysis in Practice, 11*(3), 267−273. https://doi.org/10.1007/s40617-016-0137-9

Pritchett, M., Ala'i-Rosales, S., Re Cruz, A., & Cihon, T. M. (2021). Social justice is the spirit and aim of an applied science of human behavior: Moving from colonial to participatory research practices. *Behavior Analysis in Practice.* https://doi.org/10.1007/s40617-021-00591-7

Resnik, D. B., & Elmore, S. A. (2016). Ensuring the quality, fairness, and integrity of journal peer review: A possible role of editors. *Science and Engineering Ethics, 22*(1), 169−188. https://doi.org/10.1007/s11948-015-9625-5

Resnik, D. B., Gutierrez-Ford, C., & Peddada, S. (2008). Perceptions of ethical problems with scientific journal peer review: An exploratory study. *Science and Engineering Ethics, 14*(3), 305–310. https://doi.org/10.1007/s11948-008-9059-4

Rodríguez, José, Campbell, K. M., & Pololi, L. (2015). Addressing disparities in academic medicine: What of the minority tax? *BMC Medical Education, 15*, 6. https://doi.org/10.1186/s12909-015-0290-9

Rosales, R., Leon, A., Serna, R. W., Maslin, M., Arevalo, A., & Curtin, C. (2021). A first look at applied behavior analysis service delivery to Latino American families raising a child with autism spectrum disorder. *Behavior Analysis in Practice*, 1–10. https://doi.org/10.1007/s40617-021-00572-w

Salend, S. J., & Garrick Duhaney, L. (2005). Understanding and addressing the disproportionate representation of students of color in special education. *Intervention in School and Clinic, 40*(4), 213–221. https://doi.org/10.1177/10534512050400040201

Salend, S. J., Garrick Duhaney, L. M., & Montgomery, W. (2002). A comprehensive approach to identifying and addressing issues of disproportionate representation. *Remedial and Special Education, 23*(5), 289–299. https://doi.org/10.1177/07419325020230050401

Schulz, K. F., Altman, D. G., & Moher, D. (2010). CONSORT 2010 statement: Updated guidelines for reporting parallel group randomised trials. *Trials, 11*(1), 1–8. https://doi.org/10.1186/1745-6215-11-32

Silibiger, N. J., & Stubler, A. D. (2019). Unprofessional peer reviews disproportionately harm underrepresented groups in STEM. *PeerJ, 7*, e82457. https://peerj.com/articles/8247.pdf.

Skinner, B. F. (1981). Selection by consequences. *Behavioral and Brain Sciences, 7*(4), 477–481. https://doi.org/10.1017/S0140525X0002673X

Slocum, T. A., Detrich, R., Wilczynski, S. M., Spencer, T. D., Lewis, T., & Wolfe, K. (2014). The evidence-based practice of applied behavior analysis. *The Behavior Analyst, 37*(1), 41–56. https://doi.org/10.1007/s40614-014-0005

Sugai, G., O'Keeffe, B. V., & Fallon, L. M. (2012). A contextual consideration of culture and school-wide positive behavior support. *Journal of Positive Behavior Interventions, 14*, 197–208. https://doi.org/10.1177/1098300711426334

Syed, N., Russell, C., Marshall, K., Tereshko, L., & Driscoll, N. (2022). Embedding intercultural responsiveness in graduate coursework and supervision training. In A. DeSouza, & D. Crone-Todd (Eds.), *Behavior analysis in higher education: Teaching and supervision*. Vernon Press.

Taylor, B. A., LeBlanc, L. A., & Nosik, M. R. (2018). Compassionate care in behavior analytic treatment: Can outcomes be enhanced by attending to relationships with caregivers? *Behavior Analysis in Practice, 12*(3), 654–666. https://doi.org/10.1007/s40617-018-00289-3

Tomlinson, S. R., Gore, N., & McGill, P. (2018). Training individuals to implement applied behavior analytic procedures via telehealth: A systematic review of the literature. *Journal of Behavioral Education, 27*(2), 172–222. https://doi.org/10.1007/s10864-018-9292-0

Tsami, L., Lerman, D., & Toper-Korkmaz, O. (2019). Effectiveness and acceptability of parent training via telehealth among families around the world. *Journal of Applied Behavior Analysis, 52*(4), 1113–1129. https://doi.org/10.1002/jaba.645

Vohra, S., Shamseer, L., Sampson, M., Bukutu, C., Schmid, C. H., Tate, R., ... Moher, D. (2015). CONSORT extension for reporting N-of-1 trials (CENT) 2015 Statement. *BMJ, 350*. https://doi.org/10.1136/bmj.h1738

Wilder, D. A., Austin, J., & Casella, S. (2009). Applying behavior analysis in organizations: Organizational behavior management. *Psychological Services, 6*(3), 202.

Wolf, M. (1978). Social validity: The case for subjective measurement or how applied behavior analysis is finding its heart. *Journal of Applied Behavior Analysis, 11*(2), 203—214. https://doi.org/10.1901/jaba.1978.11-203

Zarcone, J., Brodhead, M., & Tarbox, J. (2019). Beyond a call to action: An intrdouction to the special issue on diversity and equity in th epractice of behavior analysis. *Behavior Analysis in Practice, 12*(4), 741—742. https://doi.org/10.1007/s40617-019-00390-1

Chapter 4

On staying open: thoughts on the ethics of seeking funding for basic behavioral research

David P. Jarmolowicz[1,2,3,a] and Rogelio Escobar[4]

[1]Department of Applied Behavioral Science, University of Kansas, Lawrence, KS, United States; [2]Cofrin Logan Center for Addiction Research and Treatment, University of Kansas, Lawrence, KS, United States; [3]Healthcare Institute for Improvements in Quality, University of Missouri-Kansas City, Kansas City, MO, United States; [4]School of Psychology, National Autonomous University of Mexico, Mexico City, Mexico

This chapter will be different. The ethical implications of seeking funding for basic behavior analytic research are not something covered in the Behavior Analysis Certification Board's (BACB) Professional and Ethical Compliance Code for Behavior Analysts (PECCBA)—nor is it covered in other prominent codes. Moreover, we are not Board-Certified Behavior Analysts (BCBA), nor do we intend to become one. As such, our conceptualization of ethics is independent of "the code." Instead, our conceptualization sticks closer to Sidman (1960)'s assertion that to be a good researcher you need to be a good person.

On the danger of ethical codes

Many readers may remark that being a good person is not particularly well defined. We will concede that is both true and uncomfortable. This difficulty comes from many behavior analysts being most acquainted with defining behaviors topographically (Cooper et al., 2020). "When I used to help people" (Jarmolowicz, 2018, p. 172), this lack of a clear topographical definition would

---

[a] Sadly, Dr. David Jarmolowicz passed away before he could see this chapter printed. He will be remembered by family, friends, and colleagues as a flawless example of what being a good person means. This chapter is a permanent product of his commitment to understanding ethical behavior and his efforts to exhort others to behave always thinking on the greater good. He will be greatly missed.

Research Ethics in Behavior Analysis. https://doi.org/10.1016/B978-0-323-90969-3.00004-9

have bothered us. Put simply, few could readily identify what "being a good person" looks like.

A traditional behavior analytic solution to this definitional dilemma would be to determine what sorts of behavior good people engage in and provide clear operational definitions of those topographies. When using that approach, those topographies would constitute ethical behavior. Professionally, these topographical definitions are often formalized through ethical codes. In doing so, one's proficiency with professional ethics can be equated with their understanding of and adherence to the ethical code (Bailey & Burch, 2016). Put another way, one's ethical repertoire can be judged by how well they can state the relevant rules and the extent to which they follow them. This rules-based approach has the advantage of rapidly generating topographically similar ethical behavior across a large number of professionals. For the BACB, this has the potential to yield uniform ethical responding across 100,000+ certified professionals—an admirable goal.

Ethical dilemmas, however, are highly variable. Behavior analysts work across a wide range of settings, with a wide range of consumers, targeting a wide range of behavioral concerns. Ethical codes do their best to identify topographies that cut across a wide swath of situations (i.e., combinations of consumers, settings, and behavioral concerns). For example, regardless of the situation, the PECCBA is right to note that client's information should be kept confidential (2.06). Similarly, regardless of the situation, informed consent should be obtained from all human subjects prior to their participation in research activities (9.03). Even the most thoughtfully constructed ethical codes, however, may be found wanting as novel situations are encountered.

Ethical codes failing to keep pace with emerging professional situations is not new. In the face of these challenges, there are at least two avenues to address this situation—both of which have their own costs. (1) You could word items in the professional code vaguely, so that the original items have some ability to stretch as you encounter new situations. In doing so, the code sacrifices operational precision—one of the main advantages of codifying practices—to gain additional situational breadth. (2) You can modify ethical codes as new circumstances emerge. This process retains the code's original precision but is slow and can yield unapproachably long ethical codes that are—at best—challenging for new professionals to master.

A different path

Given the challenges with ethical codes, and the PECCB's relatively limited guidance for supporting/conducting basic research, a different approach is necessary. This approach entails the weighing of the proximal and distal costs/benefits of every choice. While this approach is cumbersome, and not nearly as scalable as ethical codes, it retains the flexibility needed for an area that is defined by breaking new ground while remaining tractable. The current chapter will outline this general approach, then use that approach to consider the ethical costs and benefits of seeking funding for basic research.

Utilitarian ethics

The definition of ethics, or moral philosophy, has been discussed by a myriad of philosophers from the ancient Greece until recent times. Most agree that ethics is concerned with what is good and evil, right and wrong, and with what we ought to do. As such, ethics can be applied to particular fields in which it is necessary to state rules that direct people to act not only for their own good but also but the good of others (e.g., Lattal & Clark, 2007). Applied ethics, therefore, is concerned with developing codes of behavior that ought to be followed in specific situations. Normative ethics, by contrast, is concerned with the criteria of what is ethic or moral and the origin of such criteria.

A central question for normative ethics is how ethical criteria were created in the first place. Two main theories offer answers to this question: deontological and consequential or teleological ethics. There are numerous variations of the two theories to be explained in this paper. Suffice to say that consequential theories define what is ethical in terms of the effects of the actions, and deontological ethics define what is ethical in terms of the rightness of the action independently of the effects. Most theories of normative ethics can be related to a deontological or a consequentialist view. For example, utilitarian theories of ethics based on the notion of the greatest good (or benefit) for the largest number of people state that we ought to do what produces the greatest good. Thus, individual sacrifices could justify an action if it produces the greatest good. In contrast, from a deontological perspective one has to do what is right, even if the effects are catastrophic. From this perspective, however, it is problematic to establish where the concept of rightness came from if it is independent of the goodness of the action.

The issues with the different theories that describe what we ought to do are in the domain of ethical philosophy. There is debate, however, on the feasibility of objectively defining, and empirically investigating, the concepts of ethics. In other words, if ethical statements could be equated to empirical descriptions, then ethics could be studied from a scientific perspective. Equating prescriptive statements or *ought* statements to descriptive or *is* statements, however, has been recurrently questioned. Hume (1739-1740/ 2001) stated that what we *ought to do* cannot be logically derived from *what is*. Specifically, a prescriptive statement (e.g., we ought to help others) cannot be derived from descriptive premises (e.g., helping others is good). This principle, known as the *is-ought problem* or Hume's Law, impedes the creation of rules of ethical conduct from empirical descriptions.

A similar argument was formulated by Moore (1903/1993). Using *good* as his fundamental moral concept, Moore noted that we *ought to do* what produces the most *good* (i.e., a utilitarian perspective; see also Mill, 1863/1906).

He contended, however, that it is incorrect to define *good* in naturalistic terms. This principle is known as the naturalistic fallacy. According to Moore, trying to define *good* is like trying to define *yellow*. Specifically, when asked for the meaning of *yellow*, we can provide examples of yellow objects or a description in terms of wave length but we cannot define yellow. To Moore, *good* is similarly indefinable. It is an irreducible term. These principles, which state that prescriptive statements or injunctions cannot be derived from descriptions and values cannot be equated to facts, have been used to argue that the study of ethics eludes a scientific analysis (e.g., Hinnman, 1979; Popper, 1945/1966; Rand, 1982; Staddon, 2004, 2009). This argument, however, would be pre-empted by an empirical description of values and prescriptive statements (cf. Searle, 1964). As Hinde (2002) suggested, in any attempt to study ethical behavior in naturalistic terms, it is necessary to define the concepts empirically.

In what Hocutt (1977) lauded as possibly the most important work of moral philosophy in our times, Skinner (1971) challenged Moore (1903/1993) and Hume (1739-1740/2001)'s arguments by suggesting that unlike other sciences, such as physics, that have little to say about ethics, behavioral sciences are in a particularly advantageous position for describing what is good and bad and for stating what we *ought to do* (see also, Hocutt, 2009; Rottschaefer, 1980). Elaborating on a pragmatic standpoint (e.g., Dewey & Tufts, 1908; James, 1896), the cornerstone of Skinner's analysis is that good things are positive reinforcers and bad things are negative reinforcers. Skinner's analysis of ethics emphasizes the functional relation between behavior and its consequences. Saying that good things are positive reinforcers means that they are produced by the preceding behavior and bad things defined as negative reinforcers means that they are escaped/avoided by the preceding behavior (see also, Hinnman, 1979). According to Skinner's analysis of verbal behavior (Skinner, 1957), the words "good" and "bad" can be tacts emitted given the discriminative properties of certain stimuli associated with positive or negative reinforcers. People's description of what is good and bad results from the exposure to stimuli that, as a result of our reinforcement and evolutionary history, function as reinforcers (see also, Rottschaefer, 1980). In contrast to Moore's naturalistic fallacy, Skinner posits that value judgments are trained in a similar way as tacts that describe events (cf., Day, 1977, who proposed an analysis in terms of mands). For example, saying that an object is yellow does not involve a different process from saying that spaghetti is good or that being punched is bad.

If the analysis ends at this level, ethics would be an entirely personal issue defined by the balance of positive and negative reinforcers maintaining the individual's behavior. One could say that ice cream is good if it positively reinforces behaviors that obtain it. If we, however, dislike ice cream and avoid eating it we would be more inclined to say that ice cream is bad. To guard against such unanchored relativity, Skinner (1971) suggested that good things should also be analyzed in terms of what is good for others. Others judge the individual's behavior as good when it provides reinforcement not only for the individual, but also for them.

Skinner's (1971) analysis not only included what is good for the individual and others but also what is good for the culture. Skinner differed from Hume (1739-1740/2001) in that he suggested that rules and norms are created based on what is "good for the culture" (p. 144). Defining what is *good* "for the culture", however, is complicated. Stating that *good* things are positive reinforcers and *bad* things are negative reinforcers may be useful as a description of individual behavior, but it is difficult to determine if something is *good* for the culture (e.g., Hinman, 1979). Furthermore, Skinner (1971) did not provide a way to determine what is good for a culture, instead saying:

> *"Why should I be concerned about the survival of a particular kind of economic system?" The only honest answer to that kind of question seems to be this: "There is no good reason why you should be concerned, but if your culture has not convinced you that there is, so much the worse for your culture." (p. 137)*

Skinner (1969) defined culture in terms of the contingencies acting on a group of individuals, rather than the collective behavior of this group of individuals. Specifically, Skinner noted that "A culture is not the behavior of the people 'living in it'; it is the 'it' in which they live-the contingencies of social reinforcement which generate and sustain their behavior." (p. 13). As such, these contingencies are maintained by the individuals in the group who, through a particular history of reinforcement, have been taught to maintain them. It can be said that cultural practices survived because they promote cultural survival. As Hayes and Tarbox (2007) stated "Skinner adopted survival as the absolute standard of goodness in his system" (p. 706). In this sense, it is necessary to state rules for promoting practices that contribute to the survival of those who practice them and avoid the occurrence of behavior that decreases the probability of survival of those immersed in the culture.

Whether or not Skinner's model of ethics (Skinner, 1971) derives rules that help individuals solve value conflicts has been debated (Chiesa, 2003; Day, 1977; Garrett, 1979, 1987; Graham, 1977; Rottschaefer, 1980; Vogeltanz & Plaud, 1992). For some (Ruiz & Roche, 2007; Staddon, 2004; Zuriff, 1987), Skinner's analysis does not elude Moore (1903/1993)'s naturalistic fallacy and Hume (1739-1740/2001)'s *is-ought problem* because it only describes facts that cannot be evaluated. Furthermore, Waller (1982) suggested that the survival of a culture is not necessarily related to the quantity or quality of reinforcers distributed among individuals participating in it. A culture can survive by delivering minimal reinforcement for the behavior of the individuals involved. Therefore, promoting cultural survival cannot be used exclusively as the criterion for solving value conflicts.

Given the naturalistic basis of Skinner's system of ethics, its adequacy can be empirically determined. For example, suspected controlling variables can be manipulated to examine their effect on choice. If this experimental approach proves fruitful, the sufficiency of the entire framework can then be judged by determining the extent to which this ethical fine-tuning resolves value-based conflicts. This experimental approach may be challenging, but it may be a particularly viable path toward a behavioral science of ethics.

The initial challenge is figuring out where to start. The concept of unit price (P) may help clarify the contingencies to consider when assessing behavior as ethical/unethical. Unit price, a quantification of the cost−benefit ratio translated from the consumer demand theory for use in laboratory settings (Hursh, 1980; Hursh et al., 1988; Lea & Roper, 1977), can be calculated from four elements (Hursh et al., 1988):

$$P = \frac{R \times E}{A \times V} \tag{4.1}$$

Where (R) represents the response requirement, (E) represents the effort involved in the response, (A) represents the amount of reinforcement, and (V) represents the value of the reinforcers. Although it has been suggested that benefits cannot be equated with reinforcers (Vargas, 1977), unit price emphasizes not only the stimulus that can be used as a reinforcer but also on the behavior that produces it. Importantly, when categorizing one's behavior as ethical or unethical, it is the balance of costs/benefits for all impacted individuals, not just the actor.

Ethical and unethical behavior can be conceptualized as concurrent choices. Ethical behavior can be defined as choosing to respond in ways that either decrease or have no effect on the unit price of other impacted individuals' reinforcers. By contrast, unethical behavior increases the unit price of others' reinforcers.[1] Although there is at least one previous attempt to define ethical behavior as concurrent choices (Schnaitter, 1977), by taking advantage of unit price, our model facilitates analysis of both the consequences of ethical/unethical choices and of the response requirements/effort necessary to produce the reinforcers.

This model can be extended to a wide range of ethical and unethical behaviors. Fig. 4.1 shows a diagram of the different outcomes resulting from variations in unit price for the individual and the effects on others' unit price. The diagonal line shows an equalitarian distribution of costs and benefits. For example, in the upper-left corner of the diagram, an individual can choose an alternative that increases the unit price for his behavior and reduces the price

---

1. These Cost/Benefit judgments can differ markedly from the "good vs. bad" we learned from society. For example, if an individual regularly uses drugs, but it does not harm them or anyone else, there is nothing problematic about that behavior (Hart, 2021). In fact, increasing the potency of the user's drugs would be ethical (increases V) provided that it does not result any additional costs to the user or others. Similarly, given that this use did not harm the patient or others, preventing drug use in this situation could be unethical (i.e., decreases A).

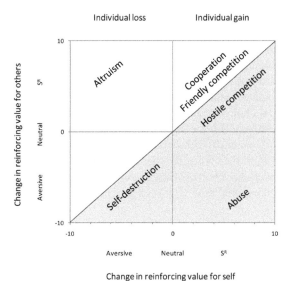

FIGURE 4.1   Diagram of the different behavioral classifications resulting from variations in unit price for the individual and the resulting unit price for others. The *diagonal line* shows an equalitarian distribution of costs and benefits. *Shaded areas* indicate unethical choice.

for others' behavior. This is commonly referred as altruism and can be considered as a special case of ethical behavior. Skinner described this type of behavior on individuals that are considered "heroes" in a community and sacrifice themselves for the good of others (Skinner, 1971, p. 135). Altruism has been defined as behavior of one organism that relieves another organism from "distress" (Rice & Gainer, 1962) and alternatively as the case in which an organism foregoes an opportunity for reinforcement to give it to another organism (Hake et al., 1975). Although, one can behave ethically without "self-sacrifice," the presence or absence of "self-sacrifice" could be considered as part of a continuum in the distribution of benefits among community members typically described as doing what is "good." Considering altruism as a special case of ethical behavior links ethical behavior to a large body of literature examining altruistic behavior (e.g., Weiner, 1977).

Some cases of unethical behavior entail choosing alternatives that result in aversive stimulation for both the individual and other members of the group (Fig. 4.1, lower left corner). For example, if we put our health in danger, we jeopardize our future contribution to society. Furthermore, if this risky behavior results in debilitation, the group's costs now entail our care and may even waste resources unnecessarily by needing other's assistance. Other cases of unethical behavior can also be described by our model. For example, "obedience to authority" often referred to as "psychology of evil" (e.g., Milgram, 1963; Zimbardo, 2007) in which the individual chooses his own relief (i.e., a negative reinforcer) over avoiding punishing others' behavior. In Milgram's experiments (see also, Burger, 2009), the individual was presented with two choices. One alternative was to comply with the request of authority figure, thus avoiding his discontent, and punish other's behavior. The other alternative was to refuse punishing other's behavior and contact the aversive stimulation associated with the discontent of the authority figure. Needless to say, the unethical choice is the alternative that involves avoiding the authority's discontent by punishing other's behavior (Fig. 4.1, bottom right corner). This example of unethical behavior makes it clear that understanding the variables that control the choice of ethical alternatives is needed to prevent the occurrence of unethical choices. How to relate the concept of unit price with the use of aversive stimulation is, however, a matter that still needs empirical support.

Applying utilitarian ethics to supporting basic research

Running a program of basic research is both fun and challenging. Many that have undertaken such an endeavor will focus on the thrill associated with generating new data that shape the very way that you think about data, or of the thrill their mentees feel as they slowly master the form, or the lightbulb moment as the behavioral science that we teach in the classroom suddenly make sense to students as they assist in answering new and exciting questions. For those that continue with this path, these positive moments overshadow many of the challenges.

But there are notable challenges—acquiring the funds to keep going often being the largest of them. The reality is that conducting basic research is expensive. For the nonhuman researcher, acquiring and caring for animals are often an ongoing expense—requiring a steady stream of research funds. For the human researcher, compelling subjects to participate in your study can be costly—particularly if you intend to collect repeated measures. These expenses cumulate in the frequent submission of grant funding applications. This in itself does not present any ethical concerns. These costs, however, should be considered on a case-by-case basis.

Costs. Conceptualizing the seeking of funding for basic research from the standpoint of utilitarian ethics requires a comprehensive accounting of the ethical costs and benefits associated with seeking research support. Based on the ever-moving target we are discussing, the list will not be comprehensive, nor will the costs outlined here apply to every case. They do, however, provide a justifiable starting point for the current discussion. First, we will discuss a number of elements that may often be viewed as costs of seeking funding for basic research.

Mission creep. In training, behavior analysts are often taught that we have the way of the right and the good. The sufficiency of our system is often so deeply emphasized that any divergence from that orthodoxy is met with suspicion. And being a heretic can be uncomfortable—a considerable cost for many young researchers.

The problem is that funding for basic science follows the innovation in basic science. Thus, making the case for research doing the Kuhnian mopping up (Kuhn, 1962) for a wholly sufficient system may be a fool's errand. As a result, many basic researchers work collaboratively with scientists from other disciplines—with innovation coming from the coordinated analysis of multiple dimensions of the phenomenon. For instance, in a systematic line of research on medication decision-making in patients with multiple sclerosis, the first author collaborated with neurologists and clinical psychologists to coordinate our behavioral economic analyses with relevance to the respective clinical communities (Bruce, Bruce, et al., 2018; Bruce et al., 2016; Bruce, Jarmolowicz, et al., 2018; Jarmolowicz et al., 2016, 2017, 2018, 2020). Similarly, in our efforts to understand mechanisms driving the mild cognitive impairment often seen in cancer survivors that have undergone chemotherapy, the first author has extensively collaborated with an analytical chemist skilled in measuring the dynamics of neurotransmitter function (Jarmolowicz et al., 2019; Kaplan et al., 2016; Sofis et al., 2017).

While this step away from pure behavior analysis is jarring to many, it is neither new nor unusual. In his earliest attempts to demonstrate the applicability of his science of behavior, Skinner was instrumental in the efforts to establish behavioral pharmacology laboratories at several pharmaceutical companies (Laties, 2003). Similarly, behavior analysts such as Joe Brady were pioneers in biopsychology and neuroscience (Barrett, 2008; Thompson, 2012). More contemporarily, many basic researchers conduct research that is closely aligned with pharmacology and/or neuroscience. With all things considered, it is likely that the orthodoxy taught in graduate training programs is the exception rather than the rule.

From a unit price perspective, mission creep likely times into the model multiple ways. If being a behavior analyst is a major part of the investigator's identity, the value (V) of the research products produced may be somewhat diminished by their divergence from the products generated by mainstream behavior analytic research—decreasing the research's benefit for the investigator. Moreover, the effort (E) entailed in acquiring the knowledge needed to be a successful collaborator may be cumbersome—representing considerable costs. The extent to which these additional costs/and diminished benefits impact the individual will depend upon the extent to which the individual values the purity of behavior analytic research and the extent to which the investigator enjoys learning new things.

This mission creep can also impact others. For example, if researchers allocate their attention away from studying core behavioral processes, the amount (A) of research for students to consume when searching for literature on those core processes is decreased. Similarly, the research that is found may be of lower value (V) because it is less directly oriented toward the processes prioritized.

Methodological creep. Behavior analysts are often taught that single case designs are central to behavior analysis. In fact, many cannot disentangle the two when describing our science. Research grant applications, however, are generally reviewed by researchers with little to no experience with single case designs. Some of these reviewers even have strong biases against them. Unfortunately, with the stiff competition that grant applications face, failing to win over a single reviewer almost assures that your application will go unfunded. As such, researchers are often faced with an uncomfortable choice. They can (1) use their limited page space to explain single case designs to this skeptical audience, or (2) they could use a design that will be more comfortable to this critical audience. In my experience, many basic researchers use the group designs with which their audience is comfortable while retaining important elements of the single case design tradition (e.g., repeated measures, stable baselines, analysis of within subject change).

This methodological creep can be uncomfortable for those who feel that it makes their work less behavior analytic and who markedly value their behavior analytic identity. It is, however, a natural outgrowth of the prevailing social contingencies—yielding much reinforcement—which is likely a good thing (Skinner, 1971). Although behavior analytic training programs often emphasize single case designs, the use of single case designs is neither necessary nor sufficient to identify a study as behavior analytic. For example, although top basic research outlets such as the *Journal of the Experimental Analysis of Behavior* traditionally have emphasized single case designs, traditional group design research is becoming increasingly common within the outlet. Moreover, while behavior analysts frequently use single-case designs—they are not alone in doing so. In 2016, a panel of distinguished scientists assembled to determine a consensus for what should be reported in single-case designs. The outcomes of the panel discussion were simultaneously published in numerous journals (e.g., *Journal of Physical Therapy, Journal of Clinical Epidemiology, Archives of Scientific Psychology, Journal of School Psychology, Canadian Journal of Occupational Therapy, The American Journal of Occupational Therapy, Physical Therapy, Aphasiology, Neuropsychological Rehabilitation, Evidence Based Communication Assessment and Interventions*) representing a wide range of scientific disciplines and theoretical orientations.

All things considered; methodological creep associated with seeking funding for basic research may be a real phenomenon. For researchers that prioritize being a behavior analyst—and cannot disentangle behavior analysis from the research methods commonly associated with it—this methodological creep may decrease the value (V) of the research they produce because they see the findings as less definitive. This decrease in value (V) would be experienced by similarly minded research consumers within the field. For those that are less tied to a single methodology and view dissemination as a goal, research that be understood by a wider audience may be associated with a greater amount (A) of reinforcement.

Questionable research practices. The pressure to acquire grant funds can be notable. Behavior analysts working at research institutes, for example, often must bring in enough grant funds to cover their salary. Similarly, many researchers in academic positions leverage these funds to support graduate students and/or cover the operating expenses of their laboratories.

One key component of many successful grant applications is pilot data. Simply put, funders want to see that you can do the study that you are proposing. This is reasonable, the funders are charged with being good stewards of the resources they are allotted and providing funds to researchers that cannot do what they propose is a waste.

Accumulating pilot data can be challenging. You are proposing studies for which you will need considerable resources. Conducting a smaller version of that study also requires resources. Often, the resources can be hobbled together from other sources—but they are typically finite. Research budgets for funded projects are often padded to allow for sessions to be rerun if errors occur, or if a larger dose of the independent variable is needed, or to tweak your dependent variable if it is insensitive, etc. This cushion is typically not available for pilot studies. As such, the pressure to produce the first time is very high. Faced with all the pressures described above, and with underwhelming pilot data, the researcher is faced with a dilemma. Some of the options are defensible. The researcher could change course, finding a new direction for your research. They could hobble together the resources to try again. They could look at the data in a different way (e.g., % change). Other options are less defensible. The researcher could exclude data that are problematic for their hypothesis. They could "find" data that better fit the narrative, etc. These potential ethical lapses and the factors that drive them are a considerable ethical cost of running a program of grant-funded research.

As with every other factor considered, questionable research practices surely impact the cost/benefits ratio of research. First, although it may seem simple, coming up with creative ways to convincingly lie is quite effortful (E), and if the researcher retains any inkling of integrity surely dampens the value (V) of the research product. But the bigger costs are to others. Every time that a research consumer finds out that they have been lied to, it decreases their faith in the entire endeavor, markedly decreasing the amount (A) and value (V) of rewards for consuming research. Moreover, the number of responses (R) required to sift through the literature is increased in that they bare an additional burden of determining the trustworthiness of the researcher. This step is particularly important, because those that are dishonest in their research once, can typically be relied upon to repeat that performance—especially because the effort in doing so decreases with each infraction.

Opportunity costs. Research time and funds are finite. When a researcher commits to completing a lengthy research project, completing that project can displace the time desired to complete other research projects. The end result can be labs with research agendas set up to 5 years in advance. In itself, this is not an ethical cost. But if this prevents the researcher from following up on interesting findings, or conducting time-sensitive research in areas important to public health (e.g., decision-making associated with COVID-19), ethical costs (i.e., changes in P) appear.

Relatedly, each research dollar you secure is a research dollar that could have been used to fund a different project. Although we all view our research as the most important and innovative out there, this is not "Lake Wobegon, where all the women are strong, all the men are good looking, and all the children are above average" (About a Prarie Home Companion: A brief history). A researcher may have a great idea, many do. Unfortunately, most of those great ideas sit in a proverbial file drawer of unfunded projects. If that researcher's great idea is funded, congrats. But remember others were not, and those others may have yielded an important step forward in our efforts to improve the human condition. While there is no way to remedy this situation, it is a cost to consider. This very cost has led the NIH to provide special consideration for the ideas of newer researchers—out of concern that the ideas of older and more experienced researchers may crowd out the ideas of those getting started, yielding a dearth of researchers as the older generation retires.

Even success can entail ethical costs. Successful lines of research can crowd out other lines—potentially impacting the amount (A) and value (V) of reinforcement a researcher may experience if their research endeavors were to vary more freely. Moreover, with research funds being finite, one researcher's success may be markedly decrease the amount (A) of research other researchers can obtain. From a research consumers stand point, this decreases the amount (A) of topics with sufficient empirical coverage.

Benefits. While there are ethical costs associated with seeking research funds, the process also has its ethical benefits. As a counterweight to the costs described above, these benefits should be considered whenever weighing the ethics of seeking funding for basic research. As with the costs, the degree to which these benefits apply to any given situation will vary.

Social validity. As behavior analysts, we are often concerned with social validity. This concern does not check itself at the laboratory door. It is not a stretch to note that strongest check on the social validity of basic research may be the willingness of entities such as the National Institutes of Health (NIH) or other health related foundations (e.g., the American Cancer Society, National Multiple Sclerosis Society) to pay for such research. The mission of these entities is to promote health—an unquestionably socially valid goal (Baer et al., 1968; Wolf, 1978). As such, research that these funders support must be aimed toward that socially valid goal.

Ironically, the social validity of funded basic behavior analytic research may preclude its categorization as basic research. Recall, the label applied is not determined by the research procedures but by the interest that society shows in the problems being studied (Baer et al., 1968, p. 92). Perhaps it would be best to take the basic versus applied monikers with a grain of salt.

The social validity of basic research often favorably factors into the ethical cost/benefit ratio of basic research. By being pushed toward issues of societal importance, the amount (A) and value (V) of rewards for conducting the research can be markedly facilitated. Importantly, these selection pressures push research toward having greater value (V) for a wider range of individuals.

Innovation. As behavior analytic researcher, it is easy to find questions. Behavior is everywhere and seems to touch nearly every important aspect of life. As an applied researcher, there is always some behavior to fix. As a basic researcher, behavior is rife with puzzles, and the more that you learn about our science, the more holes can be found in our empirical net. Demonstrating these applications and plugging these holes is satisfying, and further cements the footing of our behavioral science—but is it innovative?

The contingencies of grant funding push innovation. Agencies such as the NIH explicitly score applications on their innovation, and many foundations favor work that will be able to be sustained by federal funding after the life of their support. As such, basic behavior analytic researchers are obligated to keep their research innovative. This is good for the field. Innovative research adds more to our basic behavior analytic cannon than research filling interesting holes in our empirical foundation. If one takes the stance that new applications come from the translation of basic behavior analytic findings to better the human condition, a broader set of findings to pull from a net positive.

Related to innovation, grant-funded research contributes to the field's much needed variability. While the innovation pushed by funding agencies certainly drives research and contributes to the variability in the behavior analytic cannon, this is not the variability of which I am speaking. Instead, I would like to focus on the variability in scientists and settings that result.

Innovation is a good thing. From a researcher's standpoint, the novelty of findings can be a great contributor to their being a valuable (V) reinforcer. The same can be said for consumers of research.

Summation and summary

In the example provided above, the costs and benefits of seeking funding to complete basic research were considered. Some of the potential costs associated with seeking this research funding are highly dependent on perspective. For example, for some moving away from the traditional topics and/or methods used by behavior analysts may markedly decrease the value of the research product. Other researchers, however, may not see this as much of a cost. Other potential costs are more straightforward. For example, if the pressure to produce leads to questionable research practices, this would surely dampen the value of the research produced and increase the effort of research consumers. Lastly, one necessary point of structure in behavior is that it cannot all occur at the same time (Baer, 1982). Thus, engaging in efforts to secure funding can crowd out other research efforts. This can impact the amount and value of the reinforcers that the researchers and other derive from their research efforts.

There are also marked benefits of seeking research funding. Funders are typically only willing to fund research that society finds interesting—a robust check on social validity that can markedly increase the value of the research produced. Similarly, these constraints encourage innovation—yielding a greater variety of interesting behavioral findings—which may have an important role in assuring the long-term viability of behavior analytic research (Madden, 2013).

References

About a Prarie Home Companion: A brief history. Minnesota Public Radio. Retrieved 1/7/22 from https://www.prairiehome.org/about/history.html.

Baer, D. M. (1982). The imposition of structure on behavior and the demolition of behavioral structure. *Nebraska Symposium on Motivation, 29*, 217–254.

Baer, D. M., Wolf, M. M., & Risley, T. R. (1968). Some current dimensions of applied behavior analysis. *Journal of Applied Behavior Analysis, 1*, 91–97.

Bailey, J. S., & Burch, M. R. (2016). *Ethics for behavior analysts* (3 ed.). Routledge.

Barrett, J. E. (2008). Pioneer in behavioral pharmacology: A tribute to Joseph V. Brady. *Journal of the Experimental Analysis of Behavior, 90*, 405–415.

Bruce, J. M., Bruce, A. S., Catley, D., Lynch, S., Goggin, K., Reed, D. D., Lim, S. L., Strober, L., Glusman, M., Ness, A. R., & Jarmolowicz, D. P. (2016). Being kind to your future self: Probability discounting of health decision-making. *Annals of Behavioral Medicine, 50*, 297–309.

Bruce, J. M., Bruce, A. S., Lynch, S., Thelen, J., Lim, S. L., Smith, J., Catley, D., Reed, D. D., & Jarmolowicz, D. P. (2018). Probability discounting of treatment decisions in multiple sclerosis: Associations with disease knowledge, neuropsychiatric status, and adherence. *Psychopharmacology, 235*, 3303–3313.

Bruce, J. M., Jarmolowicz, D. P., Lynch, S., Thelen, J., Lim, S. L., Smith, A. K., Catley, D., & Bruce, A. S. (2018). How patients with multiple sclerosis weigh treatment risks and benefits. *Health Psychology, 37*, 680–690.

Burger, J. M. (2009). Replicating Milgram: Would people still obey today? *American Psychologist, 64*, 1–11.

Chiesa, M. (2003). Sobre la meta-ética, la ética normativa y el conductismo. *Revista Latinoamericana de Psicología, 35*, 289–297.

Cooper, J. O., Heron, T. E., & Heward, W. L. (2020). *Applied behavior analysis* (3 ed.). Pearson.

Day, W. (1977). Ethical philosophy and the thought of B. F. Skinner. In J. E. Krapfl, & E. A. Vargasrapfl (Eds.), *Behaviorism and ethics* (pp. 7–23). Behaviordelia.

Dewey, J., & Tufts, J. H. (1908). *Ethics*. Henry Holt & Company.

Garrett, R. (1979). Value conflict in a Skinnerian analysis. *Behaviorism, 7*, 917.

Garrett, R. (1987). Practical reason and a science of morals. In S. Modgil, & C. Modgil (Eds.), *B. F. Skinner: Consensus and controversy* (pp. 319–327). Falmar Press.

Graham, g. (1977). On what is good: A study of B. F. Skinner's operant behaviorist view. *Behaviorism, 5*, 97–112.

Hake, D. F., Vukelich, R., & Olvera, D. (1975). The measurement of sharing and cooperation as equity effects and some relationships between them. *Journal of the Experimental Analysis of Behavior, 23*, 63–79.

Hart, C. L. (2021). *Drug use for grown ups*. Penguin Press.

Hayes, L. J., & Tarbox, J. (2007). Ethics and values in behavior analytic perspective. In J. A. Jacobson, J. A. Mulick, & J. Rojahn (Eds.), *Handbook of intellectual and developmental disabilities* (pp. 691−717). Springer Publishing Co.

Hinde, R. A. (2002). *Why good is good: The sources of morality*. Wiley.

Hinnman, L. M. (1979). How not to naturalize ethics: The untenability of a Skinnerian naturalistic ethic. *Ethics, 89*, 292−297.

Hocutt, M. (1977). Skinner on the word "good": A naturalistic semantics for ethics. *Ethics, 87*, 319−338.

Hocutt, M. (2009). Values: A reply to Staddon's "faith and goodness". *Behavior and Philosophy, 37*, 187−194.

Hume, D. (1739-1740/2001). *A treatise of human nature*. Oxford University Press.

Hursh, S. R. (September 1980). Economic concepts for the analysis of behavior. *Journal of the Experimental Analysis of Behavior, 34*(2), 219−238. http://www.ncbi.nlm.nih.gov/entrez/query.fcgi?cmd=Retrieve&db=PubMed&dopt=Citation&list_uids=16812188.

Hursh, S. R., Raslear, T. G., Shurtleff, D., Bauman, R., & Simmons, L. (November 1988). A cost-benefit analysis of demand for food. *Journal of the Experimental Analysis of Behavior, 50*(3), 419−440. https://doi.org/10.1901/jeab.1988.50-419

James, W. (1896). *The will to believe*. New World. Retrieved May 3, 2011 from http://educ.jmu.edu/~omearawm/ph101willtobelieve.html.

Jarmolowicz, D. P. (2018). EAB is fine, thanks for asking. *Behavior Analysis: Research and Practice, 18*, 169−173.

Jarmolowicz, D. P., Bruce, A. S., Glusman, M., Lim, S. L., Lynch, S., Thelen, J., Catley, D., Zieber, B., Reed, D. D., & Bruce, J. M. (2017). On how patients with multiple sclerosis weigh side effect severity and treatment efficacy when making treatment decisions. *Experimental and Clinical Psychopharmacology, 25*, 479−484.

Jarmolowicz, D. P., Gehringer, R. C., Lemley, S. M., Sofis, M. J., Kaplan, S. V., & Johnson, M. A. (2019). 5-Fluorouracil impairs attention and dopamine release in rats. *Behavioural Brain Research, 362*, 319−322.

Jarmolowicz, D. P., Reed, D. D., Bruce, A. S., Catley, D., Lynch, S., Goggin, K., Lim, S. L., Strober, L., Glusman, M., Norouzinia, A. N., & Bruce, J. M. (2016). Using EP50 to forecast treatment adherence in individuals with multiple sclerosis. *Behavioural Processes, 132*, 94−99.

Jarmolowicz, D. P., Reed, D. D., Bruce, A. S., Lynch, S., Smith, J., & Bruce, J. M. (2018). Modeling effects of side-effect probability, side-effect severity, and medication efficacy on patients with multiple sclerosis medication choice. *Experimental and Clinical Psychopharmacology, 26*, 599−607.

Jarmolowicz, D. P., Reed, D. D., Schneider, T. D., Smith, J., Thelen, J., Lynch, S., Bruce, A. S., & Bruce, J. M. (2020). Behavioral economic demand for medications and its relation to clinical measures in multiple sclerosis. *Experimental and Clinical Psychopharmacology, 28*(3), 258−264.

Kaplan, S. V., Limbocker, R. A., Divis, J. L., Osterhaus, G. L., Newby, M. D., Sofis, M. J., Jarmolowicz, D. P., Newman, B. D., Mathews, T. A., & Johnson, M. A. (2016). Impaired brain dopamine and serotonin release and uptake in Wistar rats following treatment with carboplatin. *ACS Chemical Neuroscience, 7*, 689−699. https://doi.org/10.1021/acschemneuro.5b00029

Kuhn, T. S. (1962). *The structure of scientific revolution*. University of Chicago Press.

Laties, V. (2003). Behavior analysis and the growth of behavioral pharmacology. *The Behavior Analyst, 26*, 235−252.

Lattal, A. D., & Clark, R. W. (2007). *A good day's work: Sustaining ethical behavior and business success*. McGraw-Hill.

Lea, S. E. G., & Roper, T. J. (1977). Demand for food on fixed-ratio schedules as a function of the quality of concurrently available reinforcement. *Journal of the Experimental Analysis of Behavior, 27*, 371–380.

Madden, G. J. (2013). Go forth and be variable. *The Behavior Analyst, 36*, 137–143.

Milgram, S. (1963). Behavioral study of obedience. *Journal of Abnormal and Social Psychology, 67*, 371–378.

Mill, J. S. (1863/1906). *Utilitarianism*. Chicago University Press.

Moore, G. E. (1903/1993). *Principia ethica* (Revised Edition). Cambridge University Press.

Popper, K. R. (1945/1966). *The open society and its enemies* (Vol. I). Princeton University Press.

Rand, A. (1982). *Signet*.

Rice, G. E., & Gainer, P. (1962). "Altruism" in the albino rat. *Journal of Comparative and Physiological Psychology, 55*, 123–125.

Rottschaefer, W. A. (1980). Skinner's science of values. *Behaviourism, 8*, 99–112.

Ruiz, M. R., & Roche, B. (2007). Values and the scientific cultura of behavior analysis. *The Behavior Analyst, 30*, 1–16.

Schnaitter, R. (1977). Behaviorism and ethical responsibility. In J. E. Krapfl, & E. A. Vargas (Eds.), *Behaviorism and ethics* (pp. 29–43). Behvaiordelia.

Searle, J. R. (1964). How to derive "ought" from "is". *The Philosophical Review, 73*, 43–58.

Sidman, M. (1960). *Tactics of scientific research: Evaluating experimental data in psychology*. Basic Books, Inc.

Skinner, B. F. (1957). *Verbal behavior*. Prentice-Hall.

Skinner, B. F. (1969). *Contingencies of reinforcement*. Appleton Century Crofts.

Skinner, B. F. (1971). *Beyond freedom and dignity*. Knopf.

Sofis, M. J., Jarmolowicz, D. P., Kaplan, S. V., Gehringer, R. C., Lemley, S. M., Garg, G., Blagg, B. S., & Johnson, M. A. (2017). KU32 prevents 5-fluorouracil induced cognitive impairment. *Behavioural Brain Research, 329*, 186–190.

Staddon, J. E. R. (2004). Scientific imperialism and behaviorist epistemology. *Behavior and Philosophy, 32*, 231–242.

Staddon, J. E. R. (2009). Faith and goodness: A reply to Hocutt. *Behavior and Philosophy, 37*, 181–185.

Thompson, T. (2012). Joseph V. Brady: Synthesis reunites what analysis has divided. *The Behavior Analyst, 35*, 197–208.

Vargas, E. A. (1977). Rights: A behavioristic analysis. In J. E. Krapfl, & E. A. Vargas (Eds.), *Behaviorism and ethics*. Behaviordelia.

Vogeltanz, N. D., & Plaud, J. J. (1992). On the goodness of Skinner's system of naturalistic ethics in solving basic value conflicts. *The Psychological Record, 42*, 457–468.

Waller, B. (1982). Skinner's two stage value theory. *Behaviorism, 10*, 515–528.

Weiner, H. (1977). An operant analysis of human altruistic responding. *Journal of the Experimental Analysis of Behavior, 27*, 515–528.

Wolf, M. M. (1978). Social validity: The case for subjective measurement or how applied behavior analysis is finding its heart. *Journal of Applied Behavior Analysis, 11*, 203–214.

Zimbardo, P. G. (2007). *The Lucifer effect: Understanding how good people turn evil*. Random House.

Zuriff, G. (1987). Naturalistic ethics. In S. Modgil, & C. Modgil (Eds.), *B. F. Skinner: Consensus and controversy* (pp. 309–381). Falmer.

Chapter 5

Obtaining resources to support research in applied clinical settings

Amber L. Valentino and Olivia M. Onofrio
Trumpet Behavioral Health, Lakewood, CO, United States

Many professions, including the profession of applied behavior analysis, have acknowledged a gap between research and practice (Valentino & Juanico, 2020). This gap can be seen through practitioners failing to implement the latest research findings into their practice or implementing treatments without empirical support. Although practitioners may implement novel treatment strategies, it is less common for them to systematically evaluate these interventions for research purposes (Valentino & Juanico, 2020; Wandersman et al., 2008). The research-to-practice gap can produce several challenges related to scholarly literature. First, the research literature will consist of ideas and studies from a relatively small group of individuals, working on specific and systematic lines of research. Second, practitioners may implement out-of-date behavioral strategies because the research literature does not keep pace with modern issues prevalent in daily practice. Third, research produced by a small group of people may not represent the myriad of applied research questions that remain unanswered and are of practical relevance. Additionally, this small group may not fully reflect the range of diversity and perspectives of practitioners.

One way to overcome the abovementioned challenges is for behavior analytic practitioners to conduct and publish research. Historically, behavior analyst professionals may have had to choose between research and practice; however, this is no longer the case. New resources and new perspectives (e.g., Valentino, 2022) have made it possible for practitioners to conduct research in the context of their clinical practice. Some of these resources include clarity on

Research Ethics in Behavior Analysis. https://doi.org/10.1016/B978-0-323-90969-3.00009-8

the role of a research review committee in private organizations (LeBlanc et al., 2018), a newly released ethics code for behavior analysts that specifically addresses research with consumers (BACB, 2020),[1] and implementation guides for practitioners to conduct research and to manage scholarly tasks atop full-time clinical work. Recent research suggests practitioners are indeed motivated to conduct applied research, with nearly 84% of respondents in a survey reporting they would conduct research if no barriers existed (Valentino & Juanico, 2020). Though some barriers are certainly present when conducting any type of applied research, they can be overcome with proper planning, oversight, research competence, and ethical considerations.

Indeed, the very nature of conducting applied research creates ethical issues that are different than one might face in practice alone or in research alone. Examples of ethical issues at the forefront of applied research include client protection (Normand & Donohue, in press), navigating conflicts of interest (Bottema-Beutel et al., 2021), and obtaining and using physical and human resources appropriately. The *Ethics Code for Behavior Analysts* (BACB Code) (Behavior Analyst Certification Board, 2020) Standard 6.0 includes eleven sections focused on topics such as research committee review, informed consent, confidentiality, and research credit.

Resources available to guide practitioner researchers through ethical considerations and dilemmas are sparse. Understanding the ethical issues in conducting applied research has several benefits including protecting clients, protecting staff, collecting data with integrity, and disseminating science that is considerate of the practical environment. This chapter is designed to address common ethical issues practitioners may face in conducting applied research in clinical settings and how to overcome them. We focus specifically on obtaining resources, and we propose sustainable ways to align the contingencies surrounding organizational support and researcher behavior around a primary research purpose. We discuss how to choose research questions that align with the organization's mission; and we discuss the nuances of obtaining and sustaining research support in settings where research is not a primary component of the organization's mission, and where the goals of research and application may not always align. Throughout, we consider the factors involved in ethically obtaining resources for research support in applied settings, facilitate further discussion, and promote professional development.

Identifying resources to conduct applied research

Resources needed for applied research are often nonconventional and may not resemble the resources required by those who conduct research in university

---

[1]The Behavior Analyst Certification Board code of ethics is often referred to throughout this chapter, as an example of one code of ethics that behavior analysts are drawn to. Some readers with other professional credentials may be bound to additional codes.

settings. Resources can consist of time, people, participants, knowledge and expertise, leadership, mentoring, ongoing education, technology, training, organizational systems and processes, organizational support, location, supplies, time, and money. These serve as just a few in the long list of resources necessary to conduct high-quality research. However, arguably, the first most important step is to establish organizational values that can drive applied research.

Values

The notion of adopting and acting according to values in applied research is not new. In 1991, Fawcett discussed that behavioral research was shifting from very controlled experiments in lab settings to less controlled research in community settings. This trend in the type of applied research has continued through today (Kelley et al., 2015). Although Fawcett did not explicitly discuss how to ethically obtain resources to conduct applied research, they proposed several values that should guide applied research, given the work is often conducted with vulnerable populations. These values include creating collaborative relationships with participants; providing the correct information for the setting and audience; choosing participants and measures that align with the therapeutic setting; identifying interventions that are sustainable and replicable; disseminating research findings; and choosing research questions that lead to change and understanding. In addition, Jacobs (1991) encouraged thoughtful reflection around applied research, suggesting that applied researchers conduct cost−benefit analyses, are aware of the multiple and often competing sources of stimulus control, and that they consider the multiple roles the behavior analyst may play, such as the roles of a researcher, advocate, and innovator.

While Fawcett's (1991) suggestions for and Jacob's (1991) ideas about broad values focus on research conducted in the community (broadly defined as anywhere outside the lab), behavior analysts in applied settings may wish to establish their own set of broad values focused on the applied setting in which they work. As a hypothetical example, an organization chooses to support applied research and establishes core values that will lead those conducting research to always act in the best interest of their clients. Thus, one core value is "clients first" with a specific focus on creating collaborative relationships with each other and with clients. A BCBA at this organization wishes to conduct research at her clinic and shares the organization's value of prioritizing client welfare. She identifies interest in an intervention that she learned about at a recently attended conference. She truly believes that the intervention could solve a common clinical problem. Although pursuing this line of research will take some extra time, she wants to conduct the study to help clients overcome this clinical issue. She focuses on identifying clients who struggle in the area targeted by the intervention and proceeds by working directly with clients on her caseload as well as two other BCBAs to support the families who have agreed to participate. With organizational support and an organization that prioritizes client protections, she can pursue this research endeavor while still meeting the needs of her clients and adhering to her and her organization's core values.

Ethical values and principles are relevant to both good research practices and good clinical decision-making. Despite this overlap, some ethical conflicts may arise for the practitioner researcher that seem to make research and clinical work at odds with one another. For example, most services for individuals with autism spectrum disorder are paid for by managed care companies. A practitioner conducting research needs to decide if a research project aligns with clinical goals such that it is appropriate to conduct a study during session time that is then billed to a third-party payer, or if study sessions should be conducted outside of scheduled session time because the research question is not aligned with clinical goals for the client. Another example of an ethical conflict between research and clinical work may be unexpected destructive behavior that occurs because of study procedures. In a controlled lab setting, destructive behavior might be easily managed, but in an applied setting may take more time and require more highly trained staff to support the individual fully. A final example exists when resources are needed to conduct an applied study, but those resources are needed elsewhere. For example, a therapist may be scheduled to collect interobserver agreement for a research study, but due to a staff callout that therapist needs to conduct clinical sessions with a different client. In each of these situations, the applied researcher may act in accordance with their own values and their organization's values, but still experience conflict between ethical clinical practice and ethical researcher conduct. Once those conflicts are identified and planned for, the solutions will require systems of support.

Systems of support

Although general recommendations for creating organizational structure to teach people to conduct applied research exist (e.g., LeBlanc et al., 2018), comprehensive systems and processes for conducting applied research have not been published. Previously published literature in ethics and behavior analysis provides a framework for establishing processes of ethical research training and oversight. Below, we highlight examples in the published literature.

Example #1: Ethics Coordinators. Brodhead and Higbee (2012) discuss several recommendations for how organizations can create a system of ethical research practices. Ethics coordinators can oversee these research practices involving supervision and management, customized training on topics and processes such as informed consent, research review committees, team member consent, and utilizing resources for research purposes. Systems can also be flexible in that they promote a process of ethical decision-making and participant protection and align researcher goals with the organization's mission and values (Rosenberg & Schwartz, 2019). For example, an ethics coordinator might establish a competency-based training on obtaining informed consent for research that utilizes a behavioral skills training model. The coordinator would ensure all team members complete the training upon hire and at regular intervals and demonstrate competence in the skills needed to obtain informed consent responsibly and in line with the organization's mission and values.

Example #2: Ethical Review Committee. Cox (2020) discusses how different learning histories and experiences will likely lead to variation in the application of ethical codes. This idea also applies to obtaining resources for research—organizations must not only have written rules about how to ethically approach this task, but also provide guidance and modeling on how to apply those rules. Of note, Cox discusses the benefits of creating an institutional ethics committee (not specific to research, but the guidelines here apply) and provides recommendations for organizations with limited resources. One specific recommendation offered by Cox includes splitting work on the ethical review committee among volunteers. Since many of the resources needed to conduct applied research involve people, this guidance is useful for considering research infrastructure and support in an organization where the goals of research and application may not always align.

Cox (2020) also provides direct guidance on utilizing a general ethics committee to review research activities, which may serve as an efficient way to leverage team members' time and meet multiple needs within an organization. LeBlanc et al. (2020) expanded upon Cox's framework and described strategies for establishing an ethics committee in a large human service setting. Specifically, LeBlanc et al. discuss creating ethics leaders across an organization and facilitating a culture of ethical decision-making. This culture of ethical decision-making can be created by defining ethical behavior, monitoring, and incentivizing its occurrence.

Relatedly, the BACB Code describes that research projects must be approved by a research review committee (BACB Code Standard 6.02). The way in which the committee is constructed may vary depending on people available and the committee's primary focus. Here, the research committee can review requests to conduct research, monitor ongoing research activities and risks, and ensure balance of resource use in alignment with organizational needs and standards.

Example #3: Incentivize Research. In 2018, Hayes published an article discussing the contingencies in place for some academics conducting research in certain university settings (Hayes, 2018). For tenure-track academic positions, these contingencies include publishing articles in peer-reviewed journals and chapters in edited books all of which lead to promotion with tenure and advancement in rank (e.g., promotion from assistant to associate professor). In applied settings, research behavior is less likely to be connected to these types of contingences. That is, in an organization focused on service delivery, a behavior analyst is unlikely to be promoted or offered monetary bonuses for conducting research. Therefore, an example of an organizational system to support applied research is to incentivize applied research with the primary focus remaining on consumer protection. For example, an organization may provide reimbursement for conference registration and financial support for attending to employees who successfully conduct an applied study at that organization. These incentives should be provided for research activity (e.g., collecting data, calculating IOA, graphing, helping to edit), regardless of specific outcome (e.g., publication). By making incentives based on research activity, the ethical dilemmas associated with conducting research will be minimized (e.g., undue influences exerted because conference attendance is only contingent on publishing study results). It is in an organizations' best interest to minimize the pressure to publish research and instead reinforce behavior associated with conducting research.

Example #4: Develop and Foster Research Leadership. It is entirely possible to integrate ethical research practices into daily activities of clinicians. This can be accomplished through asking applied questions that have clinical value, utilizing existing resources, and developing a strong culture of communication and ethical oversight, to name a few. Applied research should be conducted to further the service mission of the agency. Organizations should be led by a senior staff member. An organization may choose to have a specific "research director" but the designation of a formal "research director" role is not necessary. Whether the research director job is solely focused on research or has additional clinical responsibilities, it is important for the person to be connected to clinical practice and able to integrate themselves into applied research with staff. A leader in the organization who has another primary function could take the role of research director—providing oversight to projects across the organization, leading the research review (or general ethics) committee, and creating processes and systems to support ethical decision-making. This leader can be well versed in appropriate and ethical behavior surrounding use of resources and guide the efforts of the organization accordingly.

Practice recommendations

Above, we provided descriptions of literature that emphasized two common themes: establishing values that drive applied research and creating systems to support that applied research. Below, we provide practice recommendations, which are specific examples of how to begin and continue to conduct high-quality research in applied settings. It is important to note that our recommendations are designed to serve as a starting point and should not be considered all inclusive. Each practitioner and organization will have its own needs and competing contingencies. Therefore, readers should consider our recommendations in the context in which they may be applied and consider ways to improve upon, or modify, our recommendations so they can be appropriately and ethically executed.

Practice 1: establish values and connect them to research

Most organizations have a mission statement, as well as an established set of core values by which they operate. Examples of these core values may include teamwork, integrity, clients first, excellence, and fun. In an organization where research is not a primary goal, the organization's established core values likely guide business and clinical practices. In organizations where core values are established, these values should be connected to the research endeavors. In the unlikely scenario that an organization does not have an established set of core values, the research team should write their own, connecting them to research practices as well as the larger organization's mission.

As an example of connecting values to research initiatives, a core value for an organization may be "clients first," which emphasizes protecting the client and doing what is best for them above all else. The research team should use this specific value when making decisions about research resource allocation. For example, if a team member wishes to conduct a research study during a client's regular session (therapy) time, the research team should assess if the project is directly connected to that client's clinical goals and is of upmost clinical benefit. If it does not benefit the client clinically, using session time to conduct the study is likely not aligned with the value of putting clients first. Any organizational values structure created should ultimately guide decision-making and lead to ethical practices in obtaining resources for research.

Ethical considerations. There are several ethical considerations to make when establishing core values and connecting them to research. Organizations will need to be sure to conform with laws and regulations, arrange research activities such that client services and client welfare are prioritized, maintain confidentiality, and the committee will need to ensure those conducting research demonstrate competence in doing so. In addition to these research ethical implications, values might conflict, resulting in an ethical dilemma and leaving individuals involved in research to make critical decisions. For example, an individual might find they have personal values that compete with organizational values. An individual might value scientific contributions to the literature, and this value at times may conflict with the clinical mission of the organization. As another example, the applied researcher should consider the broader context of the client's values (e.g., family's values), some of which may conflict with research. Perhaps a family does not wish to prioritize a particular goal that the clinician believes important to prioritize clinically and for an applied research study. In these scenarios, the applied researcher should always make the decision that prioritizes client welfare, which may mean valuing the client's or organization's values over their own.

Practice 2: obtain leadership buy-in

Obtaining leadership buy-in is important because applied researchers will need to ask organizational leaders for resources and support to conduct that research. If resources and support are not available, it will be difficult to conduct applied research and sustain that research over time. An organization may choose to assign a high-level leader to take on the role of research oversight in addition to their primary role. The research leader will need to enlist organizational support to conduct research. This support can be accomplished through working directly with an organization's key leadership team such as the Chief Executive Officer or President of the company and any other invested parties (e.g., Chief Operating Officer, Human Resources Executive, Chief Financial Officer). Working with this leadership team can include discussing the goals of applied research and providing training on how research fits into the organization, including how the organization can conduct research ethically. We recommend explaining the advantages that research can have to the organization, including positive impact on retention, recruitment, reputation, marketing, connections in the profession, and employee morale (Valentino & Juanico, 2020).

Ethical considerations. As with all practice recommendations, the applied researcher will need to work with the leadership team to arrange research activities such that client services and client welfare are prioritized. Perhaps the most salient ethical consideration when obtaining leadership buy-in is conflicts of interest. There may be multiple scenarios when the interests of key leadership do not align with the interests of research endeavors. These conflicts are inevitable and not entirely negative—if the leadership team acts in accordance with its mission and values, the leadership team and key researchers can make decisions that are aligned with those values. As an example of this type of conflict of interest, an organization needs to be profitable and any research positions that are not directly connected to profit may be seen as excessive or unhelpful. In this situation, the leadership may feel a conflict between investing in a nonbillable position to support research versus maintaining long-term profitability. In these situations, the organization can work closely with the research team to connect the research positions to factors that influence profitability of the company. For example, participation in research may attract team members and retain them, and recruitment and retention are key drivers in creating and sustaining profitably over time. Here additional conflicts of interest arise, because conducting and publishing research can be of benefit (including financial) to the organization. Therefore, it is important for applied researchers to disclose any conflicts of interest in any research presentations or articles that arise from their work (see, any published research should still take care to disclose any conflicts of interest) (see Bottema-Beutel et al., 2021).

Practice 3: establish an ethics committee/RRC

If there is one strong conclusion that can be drawn from related literature, it is that organizations should establish a governing body to oversee research practices—either a general ethics committee that manages research requests and resource use or a specific research review committee. LeBlanc et al. (2018) outline how organizations can establish their own internal Research Review Committee (RRC). The committee must be arranged to include individuals not employed at the same organization to reduce the risks or potential risks associated with conflicts of interest that may occur without an external representation. Having a committee in place focused on ethical issues specific to research can help practitioners use resources appropriately and effectively. For example, a team member may be unsure about whether a project needs a specific informed consent document in addition to the organization's informed consent process. Writing the informed consent and reviewing it with the participant will take time from the researcher. The ethics or research review committee can help the researcher understand when it would be appropriate to create additional informed consent documents and how to obtain consent appropriately (e.g., not within billable session time). Such a committee can be the main source of checks and balances on resource use, provided the committee has been given decision-making authority by organizational leadership to use and allocate organizational resources.

We recommend specific training for the RRC on the resources available (and their ethical use) to conduct applied work. Through training, committee members should become familiar with the organization's structure, mission and values, and how research fits into the organization so they can appropriately assess projects and ethical use of the organization's resources for research purposes. Recommendations for topics that can be a focus of committee member training include: (1) the structure of the organization (size, clients, primary funding sources, etc.); (2) the profile of the research lead and how the position is structured to support research; (3) the positions the organization anticipates will be involved in research and any benefits or compensation associated with involvement in those positions; (4) the organization's primary clinical and/or research missions; (5) the organization's core values; (6) how the core values are exercised throughout the organizations' daily activities; (7) the organization's history with research; (8) the organization's goals for research; (9) the organization's leadership and their involvement in research; (10) resources that are available to support research (making special mention of any resources that have been specifically allotted to research goals); (9) how the organization leadership views research endeavors and their ability to meet multiple goals (e.g., marketing, recruiting, etc.); (10) any anticipated ethical issues that might arise around using resources for research (e.g., funder restrictions or requirements, clinician capacity and performance expectations, scheduling issues).

Organize resources categorically and have research team members identify which resources will be used prior to the study commencing. For example, an organization might divide its resources into the following categories: human, financial, physical, and organizational. Committee members can review and approve resource use for any given study. Examples of resources that might be categorized under each of these areas included in Table 5.1.

Ethical consideration. A key ethical consideration in establishing an ethics committee or research review committee is that members of the committee may need to navigate multiple relationships. Multiple relationships are most likely to occur for those internal committee review members. It is important that the committee be comprised of individuals from outside of the organization who will not have these same multiple relationships and internal individuals who are not directly involved in the research project. The existence of multiple relationships does not necessarily constitute a problem. Instead, multiple relationships should be disclosed and recognized, and steps should be taken to mitigate their potential negative impacts on decision-making (see Normand & Donahue, in press). Ethics committee members will need to conform with laws and regulations in research and so, it is helpful to have a team member who is knowledgeable about staff requirements, regulations and laws, such as someone representing the human resources profession.

Practice 4: create opportunities

A major resource needed to conduct research in an applied setting is people (and their time). While integration of research questions into one's daily activities is critical for research success, team members will still need time outside of their primary role to fully engage with the research process. Time can be obtained either through creating volunteer opportunities or providing some extra monetary support for efforts. As we have identified, some ABA

TABLE 5.1 Examples of categories and resources necessary to conduct applied research.

Category	Resources
Human	Time, people, participants, knowledge and expertise, leadership, mentoring, institutional review board/research review committee
Financial	Money, time
Physical	Location, supplies, protective equipment
Organizational	Ongoing education, technology, training, organizational systems and processes, organizational support, access to literature

practitioners might be highly motivated to conduct research, so establishing opportunities for them to work beyond their primary job expectations can provide cost-effective resources to an organization's research mission. Volunteer opportunities can be designed in several ways and their makeup will be at least partially affected by the size of the organization, research leadership, and their own scholarly goals.

It is important for the organization to consider the ethical issues involved in asking people to volunteer their own time to further the agency's mission through research. For example, team members may have competing activities that need to be completed within any given client session—some related to a research project, some unrelated. In this situation, the team member will need to prioritize tasks according to the client's greatest needs and recognize that some research related tasks may not get accomplished if other activities take priority. If the individual is already donating a lot of their own time to research related activity, they may be tempted to always prioritize research to minimize time spent conducting clinical duties. They will need to be aware of this conflict and always make the decision that is focused on client welfare. Here, a potential solution is to develop a systematic way to track time spent on research activities that can be reviewed by supervisors (or the Research Director if such a role exists) to ensure proper allocation of time.

As another example of an ethical issue related to volunteer time—some state laws indicate that employees cannot volunteer to do a task that someone else in the organization who is paid to do does—the volunteer must be paid. In these situations, allowing a team member to volunteer may be impossible. Some ways an organization can create an environment where people's research contributions are acknowledged and supported are to (1) offer stipends for research activity, (2) ensure the research opportunity is completely voluntary and that team members can stop research activity at any time with no impact on their performance, (3) offer a reduction in caseload to give team members time for conducting research, (4) provide additional performance review acknowledgment or scores for contributing to the research culture at the organization, (5) monitor the research contributions of each team member to be sure the hours stay below a certain predetermined manageable level, (6) give extra professional development funds for presenting at conferences, (7) create paid research assistant opportunities for additional support on research-related tasks.

The specific opportunities offered by an organization can vary depending on the goals of the research team. Not all activities need to be specifically focused on a project, some activities can be peripherally related to research and focus on creating an environment where practitioners are connected to the literature, thinking about applied research questions and engaged in other scholarly activities. For example, organizations can:

- Design a reading group where interested team members can read articles and generate research ideas;

- Create a research lab where ideas are presented and participation in various projects is welcomed;
- Encourage attending continuing education events as a group and have a "debrief" session afterward to generate novel ideas for research questions relate to the event;
- Partner with an academic institution and give the organization's team members access to mentorship and projects through that institution;
- Have the research leaders initiate and direct specific projects and connect high-performing team members with volunteer opportunities to participate in those specific projects;
- Create opportunities for individuals seeking extra experience as part of their supervised fieldwork experience to contribute to research. These activities could involve data entry, interobserver agreement tasks, training on protocols, shadowing data analysis, summarizing literature, or conducting literature searches;
- Create and manage a journal club, where external researchers come to present their research to the organization.

The more people who volunteer for research activities, the less burdensome it will be on a small group of people in the organization. We encourage you to get creative. Further, we encourage you to work collaboratively with colleagues in a moderately sized group of people as it has been our collective experiences that collaborative group efforts greatly facilitate research initiatives. Additionally, giving team members opportunities to rotate off volunteer events will keep the research group motivated and fresh and help to avoid research burnout.

Ethical considerations. The primary ethical issues associated with creating opportunities to conduct research are that an organization might create inequity, favoring people who choose to conduct research over those who do not. Organizations can address this issue by creating equity for other tasks for which the organization values such as workplace culture, training, staff morale, or social activities. An organization can make stipends available for other nonresearch related tasks, providing other opportunities to volunteer so that doing research is not the only way to go above and beyond and earn added recognition within the company, therefore providing additional opportunities outside of research for career advancement and professional development. The organization will need to be considerate of any work that is completed that is considered voluntary in nature. To address this ethical dilemma, it may be ideal for the organization to make research activities a part of an individual's job description and pay them for their time. If payment is not possible, the organization should make it explicitly clear that individuals can stop volunteering to conduct research activities at any time without risk to their primary role. An identified leader (e.g., Research Director) can plan to pick up responsibilities if a volunteer team member ceases participation. Here, the Research Director is critical to continuing research progress while protecting team members from exploitative relationships.

Practice 5: create systems for efficiently accessing resources

To conduct research responsibly, individuals will need access to recent scientific research. Recently, Briggs and Mitteer (2021) published an article that described strategies for overcoming barriers related to searching the literature, accessing journal content, and contacting the contemporary literature. Some of these strategies include contacting members from special interest groups, purchasing PsychInfo access, and organizing bookmarks to journal sites in your web browser. Indeed, peer-reviewed scientific literature is an important resource for practitioners to utilize in their applied work. Implementing strategies such as those recommended by Briggs and Mitteer will enable individuals to minimize the costs associated with accessing resources.

It is important to use resources efficiently by aligning research initiatives with organization's mission. In addition to volunteer time, consider resources such as ongoing education, technology, training, supplies, and money and then consider ways that those resources can serve a dual purpose and be used for both research and another business function. As an example of how an organization can align resources and have them serve both research and another business function, an organization may offer a monthly continuing education unit (CEU) event that is typically attended by most clinicians. The Research Director, for example, could provide training on research ethics and decide to choose to have two of the monthly CEU events dedicated to this purpose. This could be an event that would be held regardless of research initiatives, so overlapping the goals creates efficiency.

As a second example, scholarly literature needs to be made available to an organization to support clinical standards and stay up to date with current practices in the field of applied behavior analysis. Scholarly literature is also an important resource for conducting research. An organization should choose to purchase its own literature search engine subscription and subscriptions to several behavior analytic journals and create a system in which team members can submit requests for literature, for any purpose. This system makes one subscription available to the entire organization for multiple purposes.

As another example, a project management software, or other research related software such as Qualtrics or PRISM could be used by an organization's department for project-based work. The Research Director (or whoever is in charge of the research efforts) may use the project management software to plan research projects and use the remaining user subscriptions for research team members (if available).

As a final example, an organization could look to evaluate how effective its' training and supervision programs are on implementation of various clinical protocols. The organization could put great effort into specifically training its staff on verbal behavior and specific mand training protocols. Several research questions can then be developed to test the efficacy of this training. These questions involve creation of procedural integrity checks to determine if staff are implementing the mand training protocols correctly. Answering these questions helps the organization assess the effectiveness of existing training, while simultaneously answering research questions about training and supervision.

As an applied example of a published project that was integrated into clinical services and utilized minimal extra resources, Sleeper et al. (2017) sought to change a company's data collection system from paper and pencil to electronic data collection. Sleeper et al. were interested in return on investment (ROI), a common performance measure used to evaluate the efficiency or profitability of an investment or compare the efficiency of several different investments. Sleeper et al. examined the impact of electronic data collection on clinician productivity with certain tasks (e.g., updating graphs). The results of this study revealed that clinicians increased their percentage of updated graphs from 0% to 100% with the use of the new software and the ROI was 59% positive over 5 years. The company later confidently switched to electronic data collection and published the paper in the *Journal of Organizational Behavior Management (JOBM)*.

If an organization can minimize the number of resources that are solely dedicated to research by utilizing resources for both applied research and practice, the research initiatives are likely to be well supported and maintain over time. Studies that focus on organizational behavior management (OBM), secondary analyses of already collected data, evaluation of existing human resource or training programs, or evaluation of existing business practices are likely to support both research and practice efforts. In each of these situations, the notable cost is in time needed to complete the project. If an organization is faced with financial hardship and needs to make cuts to resources, it is unlikely to do so for something that is critical to the business. Therefore, it is ideal if a resource is simply being used by the research team for no additional cost to the organization. There will be times when it is necessary to obtain a resource for research only, but efforts should be made to minimize those situations.

Ethical considerations. Conducting research in the context of service delivery requires balancing the research agenda with a sincere focus on prioritizing client welfare. These two considerations must be made while maintaining an infrastructure of high-quality care. Careful ongoing oversight of research goals and objectives will be necessary to propel research initiatives along while prioritizing client welfare. When conflicts regarding use of resources arise, client welfare should always be prioritized. The presence of conflict also presents another example as to when the RRC may be of value to an organization. Here, the RRC can work to resolve conflict (if at all possible) or present potential pathways for resolution or further action.

Practice 6: create a decision-making model for research resource use

Organizations should create a decision-making model for prioritizing the use of resources and to ensure the organization is systematic in how it allocates those resources. This decision-making model should describe how research activities can be integrated into existing organizational infrastructure and how additional resources should be used above and beyond what is typically needed.

The list below presents questions organizations can ask (and answer) to build such a model. In this decision-making process, the team member walks through a series of questions to determine if resources should be allocated to a research project. We provide additional guidance on considering each of the questions for your organization.

- *Does the project fit into an existing organizational need?* The team member should assess whether the project represents a question or need that the organization already has. This question should only be answered in the affirmative if nothing extra is needed to conduct the study and the organization would not change its practices or questions in any way to conduct the study. If extra resources are needed solely for the research study or the organization would be required to proceed differently the answer should be "no."
- *Are any additional resources needed to conduct the study?* The team member should ask if there are additional resources needed to conduct the study. They should consider all resources including time, people, participants, knowledge, expertise, leadership, mentoring, ongoing education, technology, training, organizational systems and processes, organizational support, location, supplies, and money. In most cases, the project will require some of these additional resources, even if not extensive.
- *Has an ethics/research review committee approved the study?* This question simply prompts the team member to identify if an ethics or research review committee has approved the study. The level of review needed (e.g., expedited vs. full) will vary depending on the extent of resources needed and the research question.
- *Is the research question applied?* Team members should consider whether the findings from the study will result in meaningful change to the organization and/or specific clients. Though the term "applied" can be interpreted differently depending on the context in which the word is used, in this case, the research study should meet a current organizational or clinical need and result in direct application of a strategy or other intervention. While translational studies could also be conducted, extra care should be taken to conduct them outside of formal clinical service delivery unless there is a way to specifically connect research activities to clinical questions during paid intervention time.
- *Can you adapt the study to better fit an applied need?* If it is deemed the research study does not result in a direct application of a strategy or other intervention (i.e., it is not applied), the team member should assess whether it is possible to adapt the study to fit with an existing applied need. Perhaps

slight protocol modifications, different participant characteristics, or a specific type of research design would yield a study that is applied.

The possible results of asking and answering these questions include:

- *Proceed with the study*—this result indicates that any resources used are appropriate for the research study, are integrated with the organizations' service delivery model, and present minimal ethical concerns.
- *Adapt the project to better fit (an applied need), adapt research structure for translational studies, or do not proceed*—these three options are available for studies that do not meet an applied need—either they need to be adapted to fit an applied need, the structure for a translational study should be changed (e.g., research sessions conducted outside of traditional service delivery times), or the team members should not proceed.
- *Do not proceed*—the project is not applied and cannot be adapted to meet an organizational need, so team members should not proceed.

This is a sample model for how an organization might process resources allocation for a research study. Organizations can create their own model tailored to their company's mission statement, values, investment in research, and overall infrastructure. Regardless of the form the model takes, having a systematic process in place will support ethical decision-making when utilizing resources for applied research.

Ethical considerations. All research studies should be approved by a formal research review committee. Once a study is approved, there are several ethical considerations to be made about resource allocation. It is quite possible that a resource needed for research is also one that is needed clinically. For example, collecting interobserver agreement takes time, but it is not only important for publishing research, it is important for ensuring the integrity of the clinical intervention. When making decisions about resource allocation, applied researchers should take special note of this overlap and be able to clearly distinguish between resources needed solely for one purpose and those that can serve multiple purposes. Further, because an applied researcher likely has multiple roles within the organization, they should be clear to identify the capacity they are working in. For example, they may indicate, "Right now, I am collecting data in my capacity as a researcher" so others may better discriminate between that person's research and clinical responsibilities. This distinction should also be made to clients and families, whenever possible, so they, too, are clear in what capacity that person is operating (see Normand & Donahue, in press).

Practice 7: build community connections

Partnering with external institutions can bolster research creativity, create professional development opportunities for staff, and support efficient use of resources. This practice recommendation may be particularly relevant to organizations that are not large enough to support a research infrastructure themselves, but still want to contribute to research in a meaningful way. For example, partnering with a university may be an efficient way to utilize the university's IRB so a small organization does not have to independently utilize its own time and people to provide this type of oversight. Having a representative at the organization who can provide oversight through guidance from the IRB is ideal. In addition, academics or other university researchers may be willing to offer their expertise, mentorship, and their own time in exchange for resources such as access to a participant pool or writing grants to support the research. It is best if all the parties involved are aligned on important topics such as:

- Research interests
- Values and ethics
- Missions of each organization
- Available resources and how they will be used
- Opportunities to benefit from shared resources
- Barriers to research that may exist given the size and mission of the organization (s) and the university
- Opportunities such as conference presentation, authorship, and research representation/affiliation in public formats such as publications

Both organizations and academic institutions have much to gain through these partnerships, and they can minimize the overall use of resources by sharing them across organizations. It is recommended that if two organizations or institutions can share at least one resource, it is worth forming a connection. As an example of sharing resources, one organization may choose to purchase a statistical software program for data analysis that can be shared across both companies. Another example might include rotation of leadership to lead research events such as labs or journal clubs for both organizations and institutions. If there are two research leaders representing different organizations, sharing the responsibility of conducting meetings and facilitating discussions can lessen the overall burden on any one leader. These types of connections do not need to be formalized; we recommend outlining the terms of the agreement in a formal document such as a memorandum of understanding (MOU).

Ethical considerations. Applied researchers should be aware of the possibility of coercive exploitive relationships and multiple relationships that can arise when building community connections. For example, a community partner may ask for more work from an organizations' employees than is agreed upon in the initial partnership, possibly exploiting the individuals' willingness to volunteer and the organization's desire to contribute to applied research. Organizations can navigate these ethical issues by having a large, diverse group of individuals providing oversight to research initiatives and communicating clearly with community partners about expectations, responsibilities, and overall commitment.

Practice 8: obtain outside consultation and mentorship

Not every organization employs a team member with the knowledge and expertise to lead the organizations' research efforts. Particularly in organizations where research is not a priority, the ability to independently conduct research may not be a skill that is desired or sought after in the recruiting process. Seeking outside consultation and mentorship is one way for an organization to develop research skills of its employees. An organization may wish to obtain outside consultation and mentorship through utilizing the skills of an advisory board (Courtney et al., 2021). Many organizations already have an advisory board and those who do not, can follow the recommendations of these authors to establish one, using the skills of the board for research consultation and mentorship. Use of an advisory board can be a low-cost, effective way to bring expertise into the organization on a variety of topics, not just research. Organizations can also obtain outside consultation and mentorship by utilizing the expertise from community connections. For example, if you have established a relationship with a local university as outlined in practice 6, you can ask that person if they would be willing to provide guidance on research design, writing, and other research-related tasks. This expertise could be in exchange for other support that you have established as part of that partnership, and so the requests will be expected. Finally, an organization could choose to connect with someone with an established record and positive reputation, or someone who is interested in the same topics as your organization and ask if they would be willing to support a project or two. We recommend asking the person to commit either to one project or for a specific time (e.g., 3 months). Making a smaller request with a limited time commitment may increase the likelihood someone would be willing to provide support. As the organization designs various research projects over time, this arrangement can be made with other professionals in the profession of behavior analysis. After consultation with experts on various topics, a research lead or group of team members may find that they have they eventually have enough knowledge to begin developing and working on projects independently. Obtaining outside consultation and support can increase the likelihood research activities will be productive, particularly in organizations where this type of research expertise may not exist, and in organizations where research is not a primary objective.

   Ethical considerations. When obtaining outside consultation and mentorship, parties should outline the relationship between mentors and the organization clearly at the outset. Sometimes, mentors may not play a formal supervisory role and will need to be knowledgeable of the organizations values and mission to help support team members conducting applied research. It is important to consider the role of multiple relationships that could develop and to work to minimize their influence if possible. For example, a team member at an organization may choose to complete their Ph.D. under the guidance of one of the research mentors at a local university while maintaining employment at the organization. The outside research mentor may find themselves in a multiple relationship—both providing research mentorship to the team ember through their organization and becoming their formal advisory. In these situations, the research mentor may excuse themselves from evaluating any projects the team member is actively involved in or may decide that continuing to serve as a research mentor to the organization is not sustainable given the team member's new status as a Ph.D. student.

Practice 9: provide education and training

As several authors of papers focused on ethics (e.g., Brodhead & Higbee, 2012; Cox, 2020; LeBlanc et al., 2020) have noted, one way to create ongoing ethical decision-making and culture is to provide training. It is important to create ongoing knowledge through education and training related to ethical research and research practices. Training or continuing education opportunities can support research activities and are also valuable to the organization in that individuals are taught to engage in continuous quality improvement evaluation that can be used to improve everyday practice. Training or continuing education can be provided via several mechanisms including simple presentations with research related content, readings, company blogs, guest speakers, publishing, or "fun facts" (bits of information that are provided via email or chat rooms). Some organizations may wish to create a post-doctoral fellowship or internship program to support research efforts. These roles can be split between clinical and research time. Having continuous dialogue and information about the research practices in an organization will raise awareness about how resources are utilized.

Ethical considerations. A primary ethical consideration in considering the education and training needed to conduct research is that applied researchers should conduct research only if they are appropriately trained to do so. Training should be provided at the organizational level either by internal experts or by enlisting the help of outside expert trainers. Organizations should delineate the training needed to conduct high-quality clinical work from that needed to conduct research and understand that overlap is likely to occur (however, skill transfer from one category to the other should never be assumed). For example, training a team to graph data in a specific way may be applicable for a research project but also help the clinical team make effective decisions about the effectiveness of a clinical intervention.

Create organizational culture and awareness

Related to education of staff, an organization should work to create a culture of research ethics and awareness of projects. Like with education and training, having awareness of ethical research practices will ensure checks and balances—that any resources used for research purposes are done so in consideration of the ethical code of conduct. Organizations that begin conducting research should focus on continuous dialogue about the purpose of the RRC and policies, decision-making for the utilization of resources, current projects, the resources being used, upcoming projects and considerations of resources that will be utilized for them. We recommend researchers make weekly and monthly goals to share data, systems, and processes even if simply via email or a quick "FYI" at the beginning of a meeting. In the event a project drifts and the research goals and clinical goals of the organization do not align, having a wide net of people to identify this disconnect is imperative to ongoing ethical decision-making.

Ethical considerations. The applied researcher will need to continue to balance clinical and research objectives and to be sure activities do not drift from their original intent. Creating regular project check-ins by a regulatory body (committee.g., an RRC) will help the applied researcher maintain this balance. Researchers should maintain awareness of any new conflicts of interest that arise and report those to the organizations' review committee for support in navigating them. Creating organizational awareness of ethical considerations when conducting applied research may not boil down to one specific activity, but rather creation of a knowledgeable workforce of individuals who feel comfortable being transparent when a question arises and a team who encourages thoughtful dialogue about ethical conduct.

Conclusion

The profession of applied behavior analysis is evolving and growing, with more practitioners entering the profession each day. With this growth comes the opportunity to further develop the way we think about applied research and the role of the practitioner in contributing to the literature. There are gaps in the published literature that cannot be filled by researchers working in academic settings. We also know that many practitioners are motivated to conduct research and more organizations are offering research opportunities to their team members, even if research is not one of the organization's primary areas of focus. As organizations create infrastructure for practitioners to be productive applied researchers, many questions will arise about how to access and allocate resources ethically such that team members continue meeting the expectations of their primary role and the research is of high quality.

Each of the practice recommendations in this chapter has yet to be empirically tested and validated, leaving many questions for future researchers to ask an answer. For example, a researcher could quantify and find an objective way to measure leadership buy in, assess it across several organizations, and match the level of "buy in" with the organizations' research productivity to determine a connection. Finally, a simple return on investment

(ROI) analysis could yield interesting results to determine if the resources invested in research result in positive outcomes and which topics lead to higher ROI. Some of these outcomes may be in the form of longer employment of key team members, lower business costs for marketing and recruiting, and improved overall retention.

In this chapter, we have discussed the nuances of obtaining and sustaining research support in settings where research is not a primary component of the organization's mission and in applied settings where the goals of research and application may not always align. We have provided practice recommendations and highlighted areas for future researchers to explore. Following these best practices and continuing to support the growth on this topic will enable behavior analysts to integrate research successfully and ethically into their practice while continuing to contribute to an organization's primary mission while simultaneously minimizing harm and maximizing client outcomes.

References

Behavior Analyst Certification Board. (2020). *Ethics code for behavior analysts.* Littleton, CO: Author. https://bacb.com/wp-content/ethics-code-for-behavior-analysts/.

Behavior Analyst Certification Board. (n.d). BACB certificant data. Retrieved from https://www.bacb.com/BACB-certificant-data.

Bottema-Beutel, K., Crowley, S., Sandbank, M., & Woynaroski, T. G. (2021). Research review: Conflicts of interest (COIs), in autism early intervention research—a meta-analysis of COI influences on early intervention effects. *The Journal of Child Psychology and Psychiatry, 62*(1), 5—15. https://doi.org/10.0000/jcpp.13249

Briggs, A. M., & Mitteer, D. R. (2021). Updated strategies for making contact with the scholarly literature. *Behavior Analysis in Practice.* https://doi.org/10.1007/s40617-021-00590-8

Brodhead, M. T., & Higbee, T. S. (2012). Teaching and maintaining ethical behavior in a professional organization. *Behavior Analysis in Practice, 5*(2), 82—88. https://doi.org/10.1007/BF03391827

Courtney, W. T., Hartley, B. K., Rosswurm, M., Leblanc, L. A., & Lund, C. J. (2021). Establishing and leveraging the expertise of advisory boards. *Behavior Analysis Practice, 14*, 253—263. https://doi.org/10.1007/s40617-020-00503-1

Cox, D. J. (2020). A guide to establishing ethics committees in behavioral health settings. *Behavior Analysis in Practice, 13*, 939—949. https://doi.org/10.1007/s40617-020-00455-6

Fawcett, S. B. (1991). Some values guiding community research and action. *Journal of Applied Behavior Analysis, 24*(4), 621—636. https://doi.org/10.1901/jaba.1991.24-621

Hayes, L. J. (2018). Research, etc. *Behavior Analysis in Practice, 11*(3), 187—188. https://doi.org/10.1007/s40617-018-0231-2

Jacobs, H. E. (1991). Ya shoulda, oughta, wanna, or laws of behavior and behavioral community research. *Journal of Applied Behavior Analysis, 24*(4), 641—644. https://doi.org/10.1901/jaba.1991.24-641

Kelley, D. P., 3rd, Wilder, D. A., Carr, J. E., Rey, C., Green, N., & Lipschultz, J. (2015). Research productivity among practitioners in behavior analysis: Recommendations from the prolific. *Behavior Analysis in Practice, 8*(2), 201—206. https://doi.org/10.1007/s40617-015-0064-1

LeBlanc, L. A., Nosik, M. R., & Petursdottir, A. (2018). Establishing consumer protections for research in human service agencies. *Behavior Analysis in Practice, 11*(4), 445—455. https://doi.org/10.1007/s40617-018-0206-3

LeBlanc, L. A., Onofrio, O. M., Valentino, A. L., & Sleeper, J. D. (2020). Promoting ethical discussions and decision making in a human service agency. *Behavior Analysis in Practice, 13*, 905—913. https://doi.org/10.1007/s40617-020-00454-7

Normand, M. P., & Donohue, H. E. (in press). Research ethics for behavior analysts in practice. Behavior Analysis in Practice. https://link.springer.com/article/10.1007/s40617-022-00698-5.

Rosenberg, N. E., & Schwartz, I. S. (2019). Guidance or compliance: What makes an ethical behavior analyst? *Behavior Analysis in Practice, 12*(2), 473—482. https://doi.org/10.1007/s40617-018-00287-5

Sleeper, J. D., LeBlanc, L. A., Mueller, J., Valentino, A. L., Fazzio, D., & Raetz, P. B. (2017). The effects of electronic data collection on the percentage of current clinician graphs and organizational return on investment. *Journal of Organizational Behavior Management, 37*, 83—95. https://doi.org/10.1080/01608061.2016.1267065

Valentino, A. L. (2022). *Applied Behavior Analysis Research Made Easy: A Handbook for Practitioners Conducting Research Post-Certification*. Foreword written by Dr. Patrick Friman. Oakland, CA: New Harbinger Publications.

Valentino, A. L., & Juanico, J. F. (2020). Overcoming barriers to applied research: A guide for practitioners. *Behavior Analysis in Practice, 13*, 894—904. https://doi.org/10.1007/s40617-020-00479-y

Wandersman, A., Duffy, J., Flaspohler, P., Noonan, R., Lubell, K., Stillman, L., & Saul, J. (2008). Bridging the gap between prevention research and practice: The interactive systems framework for dissemination and implementation. *American Journal of Community Psychology, 41*, 171—181. https://doi.org/10.1007/s10464-008-9174-z

Further reading

Brodhead, M. T., Quigley, S. P., & Cox, D. J. (2018). How to identify ethical practices in organizations prior to employment. *Behavior Analysis in Practice, 11*(2), 165—173. https://doi.org/10.1007/s40617-018-0235-y

Guest, G., Namey, E., & Mitchell, M. (2013). *Collecting qualitative data: A field manual for applied research*. Thousand Oaks, CA: Sage Publishing.

Thyer, B. A. (1989). The art of clinical research. *Journal of Applied Behavior Analysis, 22*(4), 449—450. https://doi.org/10.1901/jaba.1989.22-449

Chapter 6

Subject recruitment, consent, and assent

Allison N. White[1], Jessica L. Herrod[2], Holly M. Long[1] and Matthew T. Brodhead[1]

[1]Department of Counseling, Educational Psychology, and Special Education, Michigan State University, East Lansing, MI, United States; [2]Department of Communication Sciences and Special Education at the University of Georgia, Athens, GA, United States

Introduction

Though research can take many forms, the US Government has defined human subjects research as consisting of two categories. The first category of human subjects research is defined as obtaining "information or biospecimens through intervention or interaction with the individual, and uses, studies, or analyzes the information or biospecimens" (National Institute of Health, 2020). The US Government defines the second category of human subjects research as a study where the investigator "obtains, uses, studies, analyzes, or generates identifiable private information or identifiable biospecimens" (National Institute of Health, 2020). It is important to note that, under the second category, even though a behavior analyst may not interact with a participant, if the behavior analyst analyzes identifiable information, the research includes human subjects (Spellecy & Busse, 2021).

Behavior analysts often conduct research that satisfies both categories of human subjects research. For example, a behavior analyst may expose participants to experimental conditions and observe behavior over the passage of time in an autism preschool, satisfying category one (e.g., Brodhead et al., 2014), and due to the nature of the experiment and setting, the researchers may have access to identifiable information (e.g., participant name and age), therefore satisfying the second category. In other cases, behavior analysts may conduct research that satisfies only one category of the above definition. For example, behavior analysts may measure participant responses to survey questions (e.g., Sellers et al., 2019), and though this research involves interaction between the behavior analyst and participant (i.e., category one), no identifiable private information is collected. In another example, research may take the form of a secondary data analysis, where behavior analysts

Research Ethics in Behavior Analysis. https://doi.org/10.1016/B978-0-323-90969-3.00002-5

125

retroactively review previously collected data to answer new research questions (e.g., Bourque & Goldstein, 2020). In this case, identifiable private information is collected (i.e., category two), but there is no active intervention or researcher—participant interaction taking place. The National Institute of Health developed a decision-making tool designed to assist researchers in determining if and how their research involves human subjects (see https:// grants.nih.gov/policy/humansubjects/hs-decision.html).

The above examples represent just a few ways behavior analysts may approach human subjects research to answer important and socially significant research questions. Whatever form the research study may take, human subjects do not appear out of thin air, and their protections are not immediately guaranteed without deliberate, institutional action. Instead, participants are recruited, and protections afforded and honored, in accordance with ethical guidelines espoused in the Nuremberg Code, the Declaration of Helsinki, and the Belmont Report. Further, institutional review boards (IRB) exist to protect human subjects in all aspects of research and to ensure the researcher is fulfilling their ethical and legal obligations to reduce harm (see Nichols, 2016 for an in-depth overview of IRB). In addition, relevant federal, state, and local laws or policies (e.g., those imposed by a public school district) may also demand additional safeguards in order to further protect human subject research participants. Therefore, proper safeguard of human subject research participants must include consideration of a range of factors, not just federal laws (though federal laws are no less important).

General ethical oversight

Ethical guidelines in behavior analysis have evolved over time in response to changes in the field of behavior analysis and societal norms. Behavior analysts in the mid to late 1900s began to use multiple forms of punishment to treat engagement of severe problem behavior (e.g., self-injury). For example, behavior analysts used contingent electric shock (Lovaas & Simmons, 1969) and sensory consequences (Durand, 1982) to decrease inappropriate behavior. In addition, exclusionary practices (e.g., suspension) and corporal punishment were common consequences to challenging behaviors in school settings (Sugai & Horner, 2008). Further, a study by Rekers and Lovaas (1974) evaluated the behavior of a young participant and used reinforcement-based strategies to change behavior based on dated gender norms. The unethical consent and intervention practices described in the study had devastating outcomes, including the loss of life of the participant and later justification for conversion therapy based on experimental methods (Society for the Experimental Analysis of Behavior & LeBlanc, 2020). These exploitative practices are a result of many procedural and ethical downfalls, one of which being lack of informed consent from both residents and residents' caregivers.

Though the ethical obligation for the researcher to protect human subject research participants may seem straightforward, its interpretation and application are far from easy. Instead, human subjects' protection during the recruitment, consent, and assent processes requires continuous evaluation of the ethical standards in the context of the research question and the relative risks to participants. The Behavior Analyst Certification Board (BACB) (2020) (hereafter referred to as the BACB Code) provides an example of such guidelines for behavior analysts who may be conducting research. Standard 6.04 specifies that behavior analysts must obtain informed consent or assent from all research participants. The BACB Code defines informed consent as "permission given by an individual with the legal right to consent before participating in services or research" (BACB Code, 2020, p. 7). Additionally, behavior analytic researchers must also obtain informed consent before disseminating any data or information obtained from a research study. Though the BACB requirements provide specific guidelines for acquiring research participants and consent for Board Certified Behavior Analysts (BCBA), behavior analysts need to consider how to incorporate these considerations in the most appropriate and ethical way for their specific research participants. Further, not all behavior analysts are certified by the BACB, but may instead adhere to ethical codes for related professions or moral values that are ubiquitous across cultures (see Rachels, 2012). Though students of behavior analysis may not be bound to any specific ethical code, they are one of the most frequent contributors to the scientific research process. Therefore, guidance for behavior analysts recruiting human subject participants, along with the consent and assent process, is warranted and incredibly timely.

The purpose of this chapter is to discuss the ethical recruitment of human subject research participants and the process for gaining consent and assent. Below, we will describe recommendations for conducting research in the context of behavioral practice and discuss ethical issues surrounding informed consent when adults, parents, or caregivers decide to participate in research, and when they decide their child or loved one will participate in research. Furthermore, we discuss ethical issues around informed assent, where people without decisional capacity are asked to about their preference for participating in research, and its implications. Along the way, we provided examples to help illustrate the complexities and nuances required during the recruitment, consent, and assent process, in hopes of helping to inspire better research practices for today and tomorrow's generations of human subject researchers.

Human subjects recruitment

Behavior analysts aiming to conduct research in human service settings are often working with vulnerable populations of individuals (e.g., adolescents) and should consider the implications of their solicitations for participants. Though there are multiple factors that could weigh into ethical decision-making during the recruitment process, the three core principles from the Belmont report, *respect for persons, beneficence,* and *justice,* are worth highlighting. The principles of *respect for persons, beneficence,* and *justice* should inform a behavior analyst's plan and activity during human subjects recruitment. As Spellecy and Busse (2021) note, the three principles from the Belmont report are all equally important; no one principle stands before the other. Below, we describe each of these principles in more detail, along with examples of ethical considerations pertaining to each.

Respect for persons

Respect for persons is based on two ethical principles: autonomy and protection of vulnerable persons. People are autonomous beings[1] and, when given correct and sufficient information about the research, have the right to decide for themselves whether to participate in a research project. Further, vulnerable populations require even more protections but still require the same autonomy and respect as all other participants (Miracle, 2016). Respect for persons recognizes that consenting adults can make their own decisions, and the researcher is obligated to facilitate and respect those decisions (Spellecy & Busse, 2021). We will discuss autonomy and respect for persons in the context of ethical recruitment in more detail below.

Autonomy

Participants have the right to consent or not consent when asked to participate in a research project. Behavior analysts have the ethical requirement to respect potential participants' autonomous decisions. In order to ensure an autonomous decision of whether to participate or not, researchers are required to provide and make potential participants aware of that choice. Online survey research is an example of research in which participants can be provided with two explicit choices: "I have read the informed consent and agree to participate in the survey," and "I have read the informed consent and do not agree to participate on the survey." Based on the individual's response, they can either begin to complete the survey or do something else (they are also able to close their browser tab without answering either question). It is also critical to be transparent about everything that will be asked of the participant. For example, if a behavior analyst is recruiting individuals for a parent training program that includes individualized one-on-one coaching and weekly focus group meetings, the behavior analyst should inform potential participants of requirements for both the one-on-one coaching and group meetings.

Further, consent is considered an ongoing process and should be treated as such throughout the duration of a research project (Gupta, 2013). Any

---

1. See Skinner (1971) for a discussion of the autonomous human.

participant can choose to withdraw from the research study at any time, without penalty. It is also a researcher's responsibility to obtain consent regularly and inform participants of any new information or changes on an ongoing basis (Gupta, 2013). The principle of autonomy is critical to ensuring the participant is making decisions on their own behalf and that undue influence, whether intentional or not, from the behavior analyst is not affecting the participant's willingness to engage in research throughout the entirety of the research project.

Participants' choices to engage in research must be *voluntary*. Simply providing individuals with a choice to participate or not does not ensure the decision was voluntary. For example, prior relationships may place undue influence on the potential research participant where they may feel "obligated" or "required" to participate, due to a preexisting relationship.

Multiple Relationships. The BACB Code defines a multiple relationship as, "a comingling of two or more behavior analyst's roles (e.g., behavioral and personal) with a client, stakeholder, supervisee, trainee, research participant, or someone closely associated with or related to the client." Multiple relationships can easily develop, for example, when a behavior analyst is in the role of the practitioner and researcher. The practitioner–researcher relationship can impact a client's willingness to participate in the proposed research due to obligation or fear of losing services (LaBlanc et al., 2018). As another example, consider a scenario where a behavior analyst is recruiting adults at a local management office to participate in a group-contingency study in a small town where the behavior analyst is recognized by most of the office staff. The primary researcher may send an unknown colleague into the office to explain the study and recruit participants. Additionally, the behavior analyst may consider conducting the study "masked" so that they do not know who is and who is not a participant in the study. Communicating the nature of the masked study to participants may also help to ensure their decisions to agree to participate were voluntary.

Not all multiple relationships are avoidable, but undue influence must be mitigated and reduced to the greatest extent possible to protect the potential participant's right to voluntarily participate in research. Conducting research in small communities may be a setting in which behavior analysts have personal relationships with possible research participants, such as family members serving as schoolteachers. Recruiting research participants in small or tightknit community settings may blur the lines of voluntary recruitment, and the behavior analyst must explain that there is no penalty for not agreeing to participate in the research and take additional measures to ensure participation remains completely voluntary.

Protection of vulnerable persons

Research conducted with vulnerable populations warrants additional recruitment considerations. As defined by the Belmont Report, vulnerable populations include but are not limited to children, prisoners, women who are pregnant, individuals of disadvantaged socioeconomic status, and individuals with intellectual or cognitive impairments. In order to protect vulnerable populations, behavior analysts need to acknowledge that some people cannot make an informed decision on their own, and it is the researchers' responsibility to protect the dignity of these populations (Spellecy & Busse, 2021). Later in this chapter, we discuss the importance of assent and the role it plays in protecting vulnerable persons in research. We encourage the reader to visit that section, where more detail is provided on consent and assent with vulnerable populations. However, we would be remiss to not at least briefly mention it in this section.

Additional considerations in respect for persons

Additionally, the right to privacy and confidentiality are fundamental to the value of respect for persons, and any recruitment activities should support these rights. Participation in all human subjects research involves at least some level of risk, and often that risk involves loss of privacy and loss of confidentiality. Therefore, the behavior analyst must develop recruitment processes where participants are recruited in such a way where at least privacy and confidentiality are maintained (Gyure et al., 2014).

Recruiting participants online for survey research is an example of a context in which behavior analysts may inadvertently violate the principle of respect for persons. For example, a behavior analyst may be conducting a survey to understand the extent to which risky drug use occurs within a professional community. The behavior analyst may distribute the recruitment flyer via mass email to all potential participants using an organization's database of e-mail addresses; however, the individuals on that list had not provided consent for their e-mail address to be used for the purpose of research recruitment. In this case, recruiting through email would likely violate the respect for persons' principle because the e-mail addresses were obtained in a manner in which the owners of those e-mail addresses did not consent to. However, if that organization had received consent from its constituents to share their e-mail addresses for the purpose of research recruitment (with the option to "opt out" of recruitment requests), the behavior analyst's behavior would likely not have violated the respect for persons' principle.

Consider another example where a behavior analyst is recruiting high school students receiving special education services to participate in a self-monitoring study. In this scenario, the behavior analyst must develop ways to recruit students privately in order to protect their status of receiving special education services as this is considered private information. The behavior analyst may consider posting recruitment fliers in the entire school with instructions for students who receive special education services to contact the researcher if they are interested in participating. Here the behavior analyst has protected the dignity of the participants by allowing them to initiate contact with the researcher.

Conflicts of Interest Disclosures. There is an emerging, yet incredibly important, discussion about conflicts of interest (COI) in research conducted in practice-related settings. Though this body of work has been critical of autism-related research, it is relevant well beyond this area. In short, Bottema-Beutel et al. (2020) found that only 6% of nonpharmacological group design autism intervention studies published between 1970 and 2018 had COI disclosures. Relatedly, a review of research conducted by clinical providers in behavior-analytic journals found that only 2% of authors disclosed a COI, even though 84% of authors were identified as having at least one COI (see Bottema-Beutel & Crowley, 2021, February 3).

What may be an example of a COI? For one, if you work in a practice setting and you produce research that suggests positive outcomes occur at your practice setting, you stand to benefit financially from those outcomes (and perhaps socially as well). In another example, say you develop and name a particular type of intervention, and that intervention performs well in research, again you stand to benefit financially from those positive outcomes. The benefits you may receive as a result to positive outcomes, either direct or indirect, may impair your ability to be impartial and therefore require disclosure. It is important to note that having a COI does not make you a greedy and horrible person. Instead, it means you are being transparent, and that you are letting the readers come to their own conclusions about the extent to which that COI may affect their interpretation of your study.

It is also important to note that it may be best to err on the side of caution when deciding whether or not something may actually constitute a COI. For example, the last author on this paper conducted a review of a book that was written by a person who had featured the last author on two of his podcast episodes. Though he made all efforts in that book review to remain impartial, he concluded the potential COI was worth disclosing. And by not disclosing that COI, he may then be giving the appearance of providing partial treatment to the authors of the book he reviewed (see Sipila-Thomas & Brodhead, 2020, for the example of this specific COI disclosure).

Beneficence

Beneficence colloquially refers to "the principle of doing good." Aligning with this principle, behavior analysts (1) do no harm and (2) increase potential benefits and decrease possible adverse events or harm (Miracle, 2016). Beneficence requires that the behavior analyst weigh all possible risks and benefits of the research and ensure that the benefits always outweigh the risks (Spellecy & Busse, 2021). Below, we describe both components in more detail.

Do no harm

When behavior analysts *do no harm,* it means they reduce or minimize any harm that the individual may experience while participating in research. Harm can come in many ways, and harm does not simply represent physical harm (though it could). Harm could come in the form of psychological, legal, social, and economic harm. Further, as behavior analysts plan and develop their research, they must consider all possible harm to participants and create a plan to mitigate potential harm. Harm mitigation can be conceptualized as preventative, in the moment, ongoing, and system altering. Below, we will discuss harm mitigation through the four previously mentioned actions.

Preventative. Preventative harm mitigation occurs during research planning and before recruitment of participants. In order to do no harm, the behavior analyst needs to consider the safety of the environment where the research will take place (e.g., items in the research space), the availability of resources in the environment (e.g., number of support staff), and participant characteristics (e.g., severity of the behavior) (Pollard et al., 2017). It is important to note that this is not an exhaustive list of preventative considerations; they are instead a starting point. Consider an example where a potential participant may be recruited to participate in a study where behavior analysts interview them about their experiences with alcohol abuse. A participant's prior experience with alcohol may set the occasion for them to experience moments of psychological distress during the interview, and therefore the behavior analysts would need to consider active measures they may take to proactively reduce risk of harm from occurring such as working with psychologists or mental health professionals to discuss best practice for preparing individuals for questions regarding alcohol abuse as well as how the interview questions are worded to ensure they are less harmful. Here, it is not that such research on alcohol abuse should not be conducted because of the potential harms it poses. Instead, harms need to be considered and preventative measures need to be taken to reduce the likelihood of harms or reduce the impact of harms if they occur.

In the Moment. In the moment harm mitigation occurs at the onset of potential harm as the study takes place. Aligning with the previous example, the behavior analysts may need to respond to actual moments of psychological distress that may occur during the interview itself (e.g., offering a break from the interview). Because of the threat of psychological distress, behavior analysts may consider having a mental health professional on their team to assist with in the moment mitigation of harm.

Ongoing. Ongoing harm mitigation involves providing supports to participants that experience harm during the research. An example of ongoing harm mitigation may be providing on-site counseling and support to participants in the previous example, free of charge. Ongoing harm mitigation can occur throughout the research study to ensure any psychological distress is addressed during each session and behavior analyst can be aware of any harm that may take place.

System Altering. System altering is a process of analyzing any possible or previous exposures of harm to modify research studies to minimize future harm (often referred to as *Continuous Quality Improvement* in behavioral systems analysis) As an example, a participant may experience an unforeseen harm (e.g., increase in alcohol consumption) and the behavior analyst alters the current protocol to include risk mitigation of increased alcohol consumption for future participants. Researchers must carefully monitor all short- and long-term study outcomes to address any potential avenues of harm and make systematic changes accordingly.

Increase potential benefits and decrease possible adverse events or harm

Before consenting to participate in a research project, all consenting parties must be made aware of any known potential adverse events or harm—not all harm is known, but once identified, steps to mitigate the harm must be initiated. One example of such protection is through providing written informed consent documentation (see Fig. 6.1).

Consider an example where a behavior analyst is recruiting elementary-aged students with low preforming math scores to participate in individualized math instruction. One potential risk of recruiting students in school settings is time away from instruction. In this scenario, it is reasonable to assume that the individualized math instruction outweighs the harm of time away from instruction. The behavior analyst could mitigate time away from instruction by planning sessions during leisure time in order for the study's benefits to outweigh any potential causes of harm (e.g., time away from instruction).

Justice

The principle of justice is meant to ensure that human subject participants are recruited and treated in a fair and equitable manner. As described in the Belmont Report, justice (1) ensures a fair distribution of the risks and benefits associated with the research and (2) ensures that no one group sought for research participation is burdened by being the sole target of recruitment nor that groups of individuals are excluded from recruitment or from the benefits of participating in the research (Spellecy & Busse, 2021). Furthermore, justice implies that fair and equitable recruitment efforts cover the demographics of individuals who may meet the study's inclusion criteria (Gyure et al., 2014; Miracle, 2016). We will discuss this principle in more detail below.

Equitable recruitment

Equitable recruitment can be broken into two parts: individual justice and social justice (National Commission for the Protection of Human Subjects of Biomedical and Behavioral Research, 1979). *Individual justice* ensures that

Research Participant Information and Consent Form

You are being asked to participate in a research study. Researchers are required to provide a consent form to inform you about the research study, to convey that participation is voluntary, to explain risks and benefits of participation, and to empower you to make an informed decision. You should feel free to ask the researchers any questions you may have.

Study Title:
Researcher and Title:
Department and Institution:
Address and Contact Information:
Sponsor:

1. PURPOSE OF RESEARCH
[provide a brief study description and goal(s) of the study]

You are being asked to participate in a research study on strategies to help you learn to remotely conduct an assessment. You have been selected as a possible participant for this study because you are 18 years or older. From this study, the researchers hope to learn about ways to better teach people to conduct assessments remotely, which in turn should help to better support recipients of future assessments. Your participation in this study will take about 4 to 6 weeks to complete.

2. WHAT YOU WILL DO
[describe what the participant will be asked to do]

In this study, all interactions between you and the researcher will be remote and will not require any face to face contact. First, you will be asked to watch a 30 video about an assessment. Then, you will be asked to meet with a trained research assistant through a secure, online platform (e.g., Zoom) who will ask you to show them how to conduct the assessment. Each interaction should take about 10 minutes to complete, and following that interaction, the research assistant will send you an e-mail to indicate how well you did. We anticipate we may ask you to complete up to 15 individual sessions with the research assistant. Then, we will ask you to complete a brief survey about your opinions of participating in the study. Following the completion of the study, we will provide you with the findings obtained from you. In addition, following the completion of the study, we will provide you with a $100 gift card to Amazon.com.

3. POTENTIAL BENEFITS
[describe potential benefits for agreeing to participate]

The potential benefits to you in this study are that you may learn how to better conduct an assessment. In addition, your participation in this study may contribute to the understanding of how professionals can better teach individuals to conduct an assessment, which in turn benefits the recipients of assessments in the future.

4. POTENTIAL RISKS
[describe potential risks for agreeing to participate]

The potential risks of participating in this study are loss of confidentiality. However, we intend to minimize this risk by storing all collected information on a secure server that is password protected by two-factor identification. We will de-identify all information prior to any analysis we conduct. We will refer to you using pseudonyms in any discussions as well as in any published reports we may render.

FIGURE 6.1   Example informed consent documentation.

researchers are recruiting participants fairly. That is, behavior analysts offer potentially beneficial research to the same class of individuals that would be offered risky research (e.g., high SES groups and low SES groups). Injustice would arise if the behavior analyst recruited participants based on social, racial, sexual, and/or cultural biases. However, consider a scenario where a behavior analyst is only interested in evaluating vocal communication in females with autism. The inclusion criteria (i.e., females with autism) automatically create a bias. In order to ensure justice, the behavior analyst must provide equal opportunity to participate in the research to the pool of potential participants.

5. PRIVACY AND CONFIDENTIALITY
[describe how you will ensure client privacy and confidentiality]

All information we collect will be stored on a server that is password protected by two-factor identification; only the researchers will have access to this information. We will assign pseudonyms to you and use those pseudonyms during private conversations directly related to the research study. If we ever publicly share our research results, we will refer to you using pseudonyms and will not provide or share any identifiable information. Information about you will be kept confidential to the maximum extent allowable by law. Any information you provide or we collect will not be shared with anyone else, including any professor, instructor, or other person in your life. Although we will make every effort to keep your data confidential there are certain times, such as a court order, where we may have to disclose your data. In addition, [University] researchers are mandated reporters and are required to disclose some or all identifiable information to [University] and relevant authorities in the event a mandated reporting requirement is met.

6. YOUR RIGHTS TO PARTICIPATE, SAY NO, OR WITHDRAW
[describe participant's rights to participate, say no, or withdraw]

Participation is voluntary. Refusal to participate will involve no penalty or loss of benefits to which you are otherwise entitled. You may discontinue participation at any time without penalty or loss of benefits to which you are otherwise entitled. You have the right to say no. You may change your mind at any time and withdraw. You may choose not to answer specific questions or to stop participating at any time. Choosing not to participate or withdrawing from this study will not make any difference in your standing in any group or organization, including any group or organization affiliated with [University]. If you withdraw from the study prior to completion, you will not be eligible to receive financial compensation in the form of a $ 100 gift card to Amazon.com.

7. COMPENSATION FOR BEING IN THE STUDY
[describe compensation for participation if applicable]

If you complete the requirements of the study, you will be compensated in the form of a $ 100 gift card to Amazon.com. The gift card will be provided to you electronically to an e-mail address with 60 days of the completion of the study.

10. CONTACT INFORMATION
[provide contact information of the primary researcher]

If you have concerns or questions about this study, such as scientific issues, how to do any part of it, or to report an injury, please contact the researcher [name, address, email, phone].

If you have questions or concerns about your role and rights as a research participant, would like to obtain information or offer input, or would like to register a complaint about this study, you may contact, anonymously if you wish, the [University's Human Research Protection Program] [University Human protection Program Contact].

12. DOCUMENTATION OF INFORMED CONSENT.
Your signature below means that you have voluntarily agree to participate in this research study.

_____   _____
Adult Signature   Date
You will be given a copy of this form to keep.

FIGURE 6.1   cont'd

Social justice acknowledges that some classes of individuals should and should not participate in certain research (e.g., adults before children), and some classes of individuals already bear burdens (e.g., economic) and should not be recruited for research as research may place additional burdens on the individual. Protections such as these are put in place following exploitative research practices, such as in The Tuskegee Syphilis Experiment. In the study, doctors studied the effects of untreated syphilis in over 400 black males by purposefully withholding medical treatment (Jones & TuskegeeInstitute, 1981). Due to pervasive societal racism, southern black individuals were targeted as vulnerable participants whose consent to participate in the research study was not afforded.

The principle of justice should not be interpreted to suggest that every single person who may qualify for the study should always be considered for study recruitment. Contextual factors, such as availability of resources, also play a role in what is likely a "fair and equitable" recruitment process. Consider an example where a behavior analyst is in the beginning phases of their research and has limited funds to conduct the study. Here, a fair and equitable recruitment process may be to recruit all eligible participants, stop study enrollment once a predetermined number (e.g., 5) of participants are identified, and use a waitlist to enroll additional participants if attrition occurs or initial participants do not qualify for the study. In this situation, the behavior analyst would identify all possible participants and randomly select five participants. An unfair and inequitable recruitment process may include the behavior analyst hand-picking participants from a list because they recognize certain names based on prior interactions.

Additional considerations for equitable recruitment

It is impossible to describe every ethical consideration that needs to be considered during the participant recruitment process. Research takes place in many different environments, which can lead to unlimited context-specific considerations for equitable recruitment. However, we present the following recruitment examples of additional factors to consider, in order to help illustrate the nuance required to ensure equitable participant recruitment.

Consideration of the research setting and availability of resources in the surrounding community is vital when planning to recruitment research participants. For example, community-based settings (e.g., schools) in low-income districts may not have access to the necessary resources such as consistent reliable internet connection or may not have well-established organizations that are frequently used as a method of recruitment (e.g., recruiting parents of children with autism via a support group for parents of children with autism). Failing to consider the community you wish to work in can create barriers to accessibility of services for families, which can in turn result in lifelong consequences for participants and their families (Pollard et al., 2017). Additionally, individuals may be more likely to engage in research when participation involves compensation, especially financial or resource compensation (e.g., buying resources for a study that the school can keep afterward). In this situation, the Office for Human Research Protections specifies that compensation for participation must be disclosed to prospective participants during the recruitment process (Protection of Human Subjects, 2009).

Recruitment in Virtual Settings. With the increased use of and access to technology, behavior analysts have begun seeking research participants in virtual settings. Advantages to recruiting in a virtual environment may include an increased participant pool as in many virtual studies, proximity is not as great of a concern. Participants are not meeting face to face, so they do not need to live in close proximity. This can allow for increased participant interest as it removes barriers that may prevent individuals from participating in research (e.g., lack of transportation, long travel time, scheduling issues, physical limitations) (Schneider et al., 2011; Walker et al., 2020).

However, access to the resources necessary to participate in virtual research can pose additional challenges. Studies involving virtual components such as video calls and online surveys require families to have a device with internet capabilities as well as access to the internet either in their home or in an accessible public space. Requiring internet access immediately excludes participants who do not have access to internet. Specifically, those who are of advanced age, Latinx, African American, low-income, and less educated are less likely to have access to internet (Schneider et al., 2011; Walker et al., 2020). If participants do not have the proper resources and researchers cannot provide them, participation in the study may not be possible.

There may be instances in which a behavior analyst seeks to conduct a study in person but intends to recruit virtually. Instead of solely relying on recruiting virtually, the behavior analyst may also consider mailing recruitment fliers, posting fliers in public spaces frequently accessed by the target population when allowed, and encourage active participants and their families to spread recruitment fliers to their already established networks. Additionally, individuals in low-resource areas may be more likely to engage in research when participation involves financial compensation. In this situation, the Office for Human Research Protections specifies that compensation for participation must be disclosed to prospective participants during the recruitment process (Protection of Human Subjects, 2009).

Informed consent and assent

Informed consent and assent protect consumers' autonomy and well-being by providing a thorough description of the research project as well as the potential risks and benefits of participating in the research project, thereby allowing the consumer to make an informed decision about their participation (Pollard et al., 2017). Informed consent and assent are critical processes of participant protection in human subjects research and are considered core ethical and legal obligations for human subjects researchers (Shah et al., 2020). Further, the Belmont Report states that *information, comprehension, and voluntariness* are key components of informed consent (Spellecy & Busse, 2021). As Manti and Licari (2018) astutely note, the consent process is much more than signing a form or acknowledging a willingness to participate in research. Consent is "a *process* in which the subject has an understanding of the research and its risks" (p. 145, emphasis added). Below, we describe the underlying ethical principles for the consent process and discuss the importance and implications of assent in behavioral research. We also discuss three core elements that should be present in the consent process.

Core principles underlying consent

Before a behavior analyst can begin the consent process, they first must determine the consenting party. While definitions of consenting party are different across states, typically, the consenting party is defined as a person 18 years or older who has the capacity to make informed decisions for themselves. However, when conducting research with minors or individuals from vulnerable populations, legal guardians are the consenting party for the protection of the minor or vulnerable person involved (Liu et al., 2017). Here, the legal guardian (e.g., a parent) would provide informed consent and the minor would provide assent. When conducting research with minors, behavior analyst should be considerate of varying state laws in relation to capacity to consent as many states have differing laws for the age of adulthood, guidelines for guardianship, and who has the capacity to legally consent (LeBlanc et al., 2018).

In situations where the participant is not of legal age or does not have the ability to give informed consent, the participant should still provide assent to participate (Al-Sheyab et al., 2019). Assent is the agreement of someone who is not legally allowed to provide consent and is often provided in the form of a verbal agreement. For example, if a behavior analyst is interested in conducting a study exploring the effects of a class-wide mathematics intervention on a skill acquisition task with fourth grade students, the fourth graders are not legally allowed to provide consent. However, once their legal guardian has provided consent, the behavior analyst should obtain assent from the students to participate in the study. In this example, the behavior analyst may explain the study to the students and ask each of them if they would like to participate. Alternatively, they can distribute a handout that explains the study, written in a way that fourth grade students can comprehend, and have each child sign their name as a form of assent.

Assent is just as important as consent, as forcing a student to participate in a research study simply because their legal guardian consented may cause increased harm to the participant. Assent ensures the participant is informed of how they will participate in the research and allows them to decide if they would like to participate. Further, similar to consent, it is important to communicate that assent can be terminated at any time without penalty. If a participant is no longer willing to participate in the study, they can revoke their assent without penalty.

Researchers often refer to two forms of consent: active and passive. In active consent, caregivers are informed of the research and provide their permission for a minor to participate in the research project. In passive consent, requirement of written permission for a minor to participate is waived (e.g., parental nonresponse to consent documentation; Liu et al., 2017). As an example, passive consent may be enacted in a situation where all sixth grade students in a school are enrolled in a study evaluating the effects of a homework self-monitoring strategy. Here, caregivers would be sent a letter explaining the study with the option to unenroll in the study; parental nonresponse would indicate passive consent. Passive consent has many advantages, especially in studies with large numbers of participants. Some advantages include lower cost, less labor required, and an increased rate of participation (Liu et al., 2017). However, this should not be taken advantage of to ensure high numbers of participants, behavior analysts should be sure to continue adhering to the ethical principles discussed in this chapter and should only use passive consent when appropriate (Liu et al., 2017).

The behavior analyst's role in the informed consent process is to inform participants of the true nature, aims, and intent of the research project, explain any potential risks, benefits, and expected outcomes of the study, to answer any and all questions the participant(s) may have, and to respect consent, assent, or dissent decisions (Plasek et al., 2011). Shah et al. (2020) described that the informed consent process contains three primary elements: (1) *disclosure of information*; (2) *competency of the patient (or surrogate) to make a decision*; and (3) *voluntary nature of the decision*. Below, we describe these concepts in more detail.

Disclosure of information

Behavior analytic researchers should disclose all factors of proposed research that may influence a participant's willingness to take part in the study. This includes a description of (a) intended goals of the research, (b) requirements of participation, and (c) all possible benefits and risks of participation (Protection of Human Subjects, 2009). Here, the behavior analysts are agents for sharing information—a key component of informed consent established by the Belmont Report. Further, it is recommended that behavior analysts (1) use understandable language when explaining the research project and consent information (i.e., remove scientific jargon, include documentation in the participant's first language), (2) obtain informed consent at all stages of the research study (e.g., initial planning, prior to assessment, prior to intervention implementation), (3) clarify the participant's right to withdraw at any stage of the project without penalty, and (4) disclose all possible risks and benefits of participating in the research study. Safeguards like the ones mentioned previously are put in place to protect the potential research participant, caregivers, researchers, and any stakeholders.

An adequate description of research components involves explanation of research procedures in a manner that allows a participant to make a voluntary decision of consent or assent by a behavior analyst with the competency to communicate effectively and respond to questions about the research process (LeBlanc et al., 2018; Peterson et al., 2019). At a minimum, consent should include written documentation (see Fig. 6.1) as well as a conversation between the behavior analyst and participant (Agre & Rapkin, 2003; Plasek et al., 2011). Research descriptions should also include the study purpose and how confidentiality will be maintained.

Consider an example of a randomized controlled trial (RCT) where you have a treatment group receiving a treatment to increase time-on-task and a control group receiving no treatment. Here, it is imperative that the participant and/or consenting party understand that they are randomly assigned to one group, and they may not know to which group they have been assigned. For instance, if the participant is assigned to the control group, they will not receive the possible benefits of the treatment and their behavior may not change. If this study was not explained in detail or if the consent information was not explained in an understandable manner, the participant and/or consenting party of the control group may be confused as to why the participant is not displaying a behavior change. The lack of disclosure can lead to many problems such as attrition, emotional distress, and loss of trust with the research team (Plasek et al., 2011; Purcaru et al., 2014). One way to ensure all participants receive access to the intervention is to provide that treatment to participants in the control condition after the original treatment-control comparison is complete (often, this group of participants would be referred to as a "waitlist control group").

All research involves some risk. It is incredibly important that individuals consenting to participate in research understand the relative risks involved in participating in that research. Often, new applied researchers will contend that their research is strictly beneficial to their participants and therefore involves no risk. This is utterly incorrect, as all research involves at least some level of risk. At the very least, loss of confidentiality is a risk to participating in research. It is for this very reason that we have devoted a special subheader to emphasize this critical point. Potential risks associated with research participation should be inclusive of direct risks to the participants during the research (e.g., emotional distress) as well as indirect risks (e.g., time away from instruction). Emotional distress and time away from instruction are explicitly noted, because emotional distress is one of the most common risks associated with human subjects research, and participants' involvement in research in school settings often results in time away from academic instruction.

Competency of the patient or surrogate

The increasing complexity of research questions and designs has created more complicated, and at times more confusing, consent processes (Purcaru et al., 2014). From an ethics perspective, it is essential that the participant and/or the consenting party comprehend and understand what their participation in the research entails (Purcaru et al., 2014). Competency should be considered as the ability of the participant to understand the information provided about the research study and make an informed decision based on the provided information. As noted in the Belmont Report, comprehension and competency are critical for securing informed consent. Behavior analyst should be aware of each participant's ability to comprehend documents/audio and should provide further explanations and simplified or translated texts/audio to ensure the highest level of comprehension (Kadam, 2017).

A standardized method of acquiring informed consent may not be effective for all participants (Plasek et al., 2011). Agre and Rapkin (2003) suggest that the process of acquiring informed consent must include at least one written component, one verbal component, and a method of assessing participant comprehension of research procedures. To ensure the information that is presented is more accessible to participants with a range of comprehension skills, behavior analyst can provide clear simplified consent documents, assess comprehension abilities, use printed information sheets and brochures, use multiple medias (e.g., print information along with video and audio presentations), engage in discussions with participants about the research, and provide supplemental aids to support participant decision-making (Kadam, 2017). By using the abovementioned comprehension strategies, behavior analyst can enhance participant comprehension of the consent process and in turn be confident their participants are competent to give consent to participate in the study. Plasek et al. (2011) evaluated the effects of various communication styles, including vocal speech and various gestures, on participant behavior during the consent process. Their findings suggest that researchers' use of gestures throughout the consent process may positively affect participant consenting behavior. Based on the Plasek et al. study, face-to-face consent discussion may be more effective in conveying consent information compared to only distributing textual documentation. Their findings support the notion that simply giving consent documents to a potential participant does not necessarily ensure informed consent (Purcaru et al., 2014).

In addition, behavior analysts should be considerate of cultural differences (e.g., language use, religious affiliations, clothing, gender roles; see Beaulieu et al., 2019 for a discussion of becoming a culturally competent behavior analyst) and how those differences may affect the potential participant during the informed consent process, as well as the behavior analyst's ability to confidently maintain that informed consent has been adequately obtained. One way to ensure participants comprehend the consent process is to improve the accessibility of consent documents and other information presented during the consent process. For example, behavior analysts may present consent information through printed copy, electronic copy, audio recording, or video recording. We recommend that behavior analysts ask potential participants their preferred mode of communication (e.g., written or audio) as well as their preferred language to receive consent information. When providing consent documentation via written word, it can be beneficial to (1) simplify the language to short, familiar, simple word; (2) use headings and subtitles to reduce the density of the text; (3) avoid medical terminology or other terminology that would be considered jargon; (4) keep sentences under 12 words and paragraphs under seven lines; (5) ensure each paragraph conveys only one main idea; (6) and use active voice and personal pronouns (Kadam, 2017). To assist with readability, Microsoft Word editor provides a score of 0−100 indicating the level of a documents' *readability*; the higher the score, the easier it is to read the document. We recommend using the readability function (found under review > editor > insights) to evaluate how easy it will be for potential participants to understand written consent documentation.

Voluntary nature of the decision

Voluntariness means that the participant's decision to participate in the research is made without coercion or persuasion. For instance, participants and their families may feel inclined to consent even if they have concerns about the research (LeBlanc et al., 2018); providing consent while still having concerns regarding the research is uninformed consent. Further, a signature on the consent document does not guarantee the participant and their guardian understand what they are consenting for (Purcaru et al., 2014). We recommend beginning the consent process with a detailed conversation between the behavior analyst and participants. The conversation should include an explanation of the research goals, procedures, risks, benefits, and participant rights (Purcaru et al., 2014). The risks and benefits discussed in the consent conversation may include a detailed description of evidence-based benefits and detriments associated with the research procedures. Conducting thorough consent conversations prior to a study can help to ensure understanding of consent as well as allow participants a low stakes environment in which to ask questions and seek clarification.

Additional considerations for vulnerable populations

Behavior analysts have a storied history executing research aimed to support and improve the lives of vulnerable populations. However, behavior analytic researchers must consider their own ability to identify considerations that may influence the livelihoods of vulnerable populations. One way to ensure that research goals are aligned with the target population is to conduct participatory research. Participatory research refers to research methods and methodologies that include the community. Through participatory research, the community that is affected by the research works with the researchers in order to make decisions about the research (den Houting at al., 2020). Participatory research involves research partners collaborating with community partners (e.g., teachers, caregivers, and service providers) at any and all stages of the research. This collaborative community can benefit all stakeholders in the recruitment, consent, and assent processes. Partnerships should be developed between relevant stakeholder groups, and there needs to be greater engagement between academic/research members and community members during the research process (Pellicano et al., 2014), considerations that may be necessary if conducting research with vulnerable populations.

Stringent requirements for consent continue to be enforced in order to help protect human subjects. The U.S. Department of Education, IRBs, and local school boards have increasingly added additional levels of scrutiny to the consent process (Liu et al., 2017). For example, there is now a greater push to obtain active caregiver consent for any research or research-related activity (e.g., assessment data). However, overly stringent requirements for consent may be hindering the progress of research (Liu et al., 2017). Liu et al. (2017) concluded that in studies with active consent, overall participation was lower. Additionally, the demographics of participants consenting via active consent and passive consent varied greatly. For example, female students, Caucasian students, and students with high academic achievement were overrepresented in active consent procedures. Active consent procedures underrepresented African American students, Asian American students, Hispanic students, students identified as low academic achievers, and students whose caregivers were less educated. These results suggest that overly stringent consent processes may be creating a research bias regarding representation of vulnerable populations in research literature. As a result, critical information about ways to better support already underserved and supported populations may not be obtained. Behavior analyst must balance consent regulations along with their pursuit for knowledge and ethical responsibilities. This is one of the many examples of structural inequities that exist in the research process that researchers must overcome.

The BACB reports that 77.76% of behavior analysts serve primarily individuals with autism or other developmental disability. Based on the data, we can assume the majority of behavior analytic researchers are also conducting research with vulnerable populations. Therefore, behavior analysts must find ways to modify the consent and assent processes that protect the dignity of potential participants. Morris et al. (2021) recently conducted a review of behavior analytic journals for specific description of consent and assent processes for participants with autism and/or developmental disabilities. Of their 187 included articles, only 28 (15%) gave what met qualifications for "detailed" descriptions of the assent process. One example of a study with a detailed description was Slaton and Hanley's (2016) evaluation of schedules of reinforcement on stereotypy and item engagement. In this study, participants gave consent to participate by vocalizing "yes," "okay," or by coming to the designated location of the study. Additionally, participants could give assent using a variety of communication modalities (e.g., vocal communication or speech generating devices) to say "no" or "all done."

Consent to share research findings

Usually, informed consent documents will detail the information the individual consents to be released. For example, the document may describe that data will be deidentified in any research reports that are presented or published. However, through the course of research, the behavior analyst may realize that videos, for example, of research sessions would help to illustrate the concept being studied. In this case, the behavior analyst would need to obtain additional consent from that participant to share those videos. When behavior analysts wish to disseminate the data obtained though research, the BACB Code (Standard 6.04) states that behavior analysts must (1) obtain informed consent for the use of the data before dissemination, (2) clarify that services will not be impacted by consent or dissent of the distribution of data, and (3) clarify that the participant has the right to withdraw from the research at any point without penalty. If the participant, caregivers, or stakeholders have any questions about the dissemination of data collected during research, it is up to the behavior analyst to clarify any questions and error on the side of caution in the best interest of the participant.

Considerations regarding the ability to share research findings to the public may also be much more situation specific and nuanced than the ability to obtain videos of research sessions. Consider an example where a behavior analyst is surveying caregivers of individuals with autism in a specific community. The behavior analyst wants to disseminate the information gained through interviews to the scientific community. Here, the behavior analyst would obtain informed consent from each participant to include their deidentifiable information in a research manuscript. Now, consider a caregiver who has disclosed that because they have multiple children with autism and are active in their community, they are concerned that the information provided in their interviews may be identifiable to people in their community. In this situation, the behavior analyst must honor the participant's request for anonymity and omit their data from public display and analysis.

Conclusion

Understanding the complexities of recruitment, consent, and assent is essential to conducting successful and ethical research with human subjects. We cannot emphasize, enough, how important it is for you to understand the relevant local, state, and federal laws that regulate research activity, as well as your own ethical standards outlined by your credentialing or licensing bodies. The growth in the field of behavior analysis presents opportunities to develop and evaluate recruitment, consent, and assent procedures (LeBlanc et al., 2018). Developing and evaluating these procedures will improve the quality and effectiveness of behavior analytic research will assist researchers in making recruitment, consent, and assent decisions (LeBlanc et al., 2018). We call for systematic evaluations of recruitment, consent, and assent procedures in order to help in assuring best research practice (Pollard et al., 2017) while also identifying successes and pitfalls in current recruitment, consent, and assent procedures (Pollard et al., 2017). Systematic evaluations can also help promote suitable procedures and correct failures (Menendez et al., 2017).

References

Agre, P., & Rapkin, B. (2003). Improving informed consent: A comparison of four consent tools. *IRB: Ethics & Human Research, 25*(6), 1–7. https://doi.org/10.2307/3564285

Al-Sheyab, N. A., Alomari, M. A., Khabour, O. F., Shattnawi, K. K., & Alzoubi, K. H. (2019). Assent and consent in pediatric and adolescent research: School children's perspectives. *Adolescent Health, Medicine and Therapeutics, 10*, 7–14.

Beaulieu, L., Addington, J., & Almeida, D. (2019). Behavior analysts' training and practices regarding cultural diversity: The case for culturally competent care. *Behavior Analysis in Practice, 12*(3), 557–575. https://doi.org/10.1007/s40617-018-00313-6

Behavior Analyst Certification Board. (2020). *Ethics code for behavior analysts.* https://bacb.com/wp-content/ethics-code-for-behavior-analysts/.

Bottema-Beutel, K., & Crowley, S. (February 3, 2021). *Pervasive undisclosed conflicts of interest in applied behavior analysis autism literature.* https://doi.org/10.31234/osf.io/zh64e

Bottema-Beutel, K., Crowley, S., Sandback, M., & Woynaroski, T. G. (2020). Research review: Conflicts of interest (COIs) in autism early intervention research—a meta-analysis of COI influences on intervention effects. *Journal of Childhood Psychology and Psychiatry, 62*(1), 5–15. https://doi.org/10.1111/jcpp.13315

Bourque, K. S., & Goldstein, H. (2020). Expanding communication modalities and functions for preschoolers with autism spectrum disorder: Secondary analysis of a peer partner speech-generating device intervention. *Journal of Speech, Language, and Hearing Research, 63*, 190–205. https://doi.org/10.1044/2019_JSLHR-19-00202

Durand, V. M. (1982). Analysis and intervention of self-injurious behavior. *Research and Practice for Persons with Severe Disabilities, 7*(4), 44–53.

Gupta, U. C. (2013). Informed consent in clinical research: Revisiting few concepts and areas. *Perspectives in Clinical Research, 4*(1), 26–32. https://doi.org/10.4103/2229-3485.106373

Gyure, M. E., Quillin, J. M., Rodríguez, V. M., Markowitz, M. S., Corona, R., Borzelleca, J., Jr., Bowen, D. J., Krist, A. H., & Bodurtha, J. N. (2014). Practical considerations for implementing research recruitment etiquette. *IRB, 36*(6), 7–12.

Brodhead, M. T., Higbee, T. S., Pollard, J. S., Akers, J. S., & Gerencser, K. R. (2014). The use of linked activity schedules to teach children with ASD to play hide-and-seek. *Journal of Applied Behavior Analysis, 47*, 645–650. https://doi.org/10.1002/jaba.145

den Houting, J., Higgins, J., Isaacs, K., Mahony, J., & Pellicano, E. (2020). "I'm not just a Guinea pig": Academic and community perceptions of participatory autism research. *Autism*, 1–16. https://doi.org/10.1177/1362361320951696

Jones, J. H., & Tuskegee Institute. (1981). *Bad blood: The Tuskegee syphilis experiment.* New York: Free Press.

Kadam, R. A. (2017). Informed consent process: A step towards making it more meaningful. *Perspectives in Clinical Research, 8*(3), 107–112. https://doi.org/10.4103/picr.PICR_147_16

LeBlanc, L. A., Nosik, M. R., & Petursdottir, A. (2018). Establishing consumer protections for research in human service agencies. *Behavior Analysis in Practice, 11*, 444–455. https://doi.org/10.1007/s40617-018-0206-3

Liu, C., Cox, R. B., Jr., Washburn, I. J., Croff, J. M., & Crethar, H. C. (2017). The effects of requiring parental consent for research on adolescents' risk behaviors: A meta-analysis. *Journal of Adolescent Health, 61*(1), 45–52. https://doi.org/10.1016/j.jadohealth.2017.01.015

Lovaas, I. O., & Simmons, J. Q. (1969). Manipulation of self-destruction in three retarded children. *Journal of Applied Behavior Analysis, 2*, 143–157.

Manti, S., & Licari, A. (2018). How to obtain informed consent for research. *Breathe, 14*(2), 145−152. https://doi.org/10.1183/20734735.001918

Menendez, A. L., Mayton, M. R., & Yurick, A. L. (2017). Board Certified Behavior Analysts and related ethical and professional practice considerations for rural schools. *Rural Special Education Quarterly, 36*, 31−37. https://doi.org/10.1177/8756870517703397

Miracle, V. A. (2016). The Belmont report: The triple crown of research ethics. *Educational Dimension, 35*(4), 223−228. https://doi.org/10.1097/DCC.0000000000000186

Morris, C., Detrick, J. J., & Peterson, S. M. (2021). Participant assent in behavior analytic research: Considerations for participants with autism and developmental disabilities. *Journal of Applied Behavior Analysis, 54*(4), 1300−1316. https://doi.org/10.1002/jaba.859

National Commission for the Protection of Human Subjects of Biomedical and Behavioral Research. (1979). *The Belmont report: Ethical principles and guidelines for the protection of human subjects of research.* U.S. Department of Health and Human Services. https://www.hhs.gov/ohrp/regulations-and-policy/belmont-report/read-the-belmont-report/index.html.

National Institute of Health. (January 13, 2020). *Definition of human subjects research.* https://grants.nih.gov/policy/humansubjects/research.htm.

Nichols, A. S. (2016). Research ethics committees (recs)/institutional review boards (irbs) and the globalization of clinical research: Can ethical oversight of human subjects research be standardized? *Washington University Global Studies Law Review, 15*(2), 352−380.

Pellicano, E., Dinsmore, A., & Charman, T. (2014). What should autism research focus upon? Community views and priorities from the United Kingdom. *Autism, 18*(7), 756−770. https://doi.org/10.1177/1362361314529627

Peterson, S. M., Eldridge, R. R., Rios, D., & Schenk, Y. A. (2019). Ethical challenges encountered in delivering behavior analytic services through teleconsultation. *Behavior Analysis: Research and Practice, 19*(2), 190. https://doi.org/10.1037/bar0000111

Plasek, J. M., Pieczkiewicz, D. S., Mahnke, A. N., McCarty, C. A., Starren, J. B., & Westra, B. L. (2011). The role of nonverbal and verbal communication in a multimedia informed consent process. *Applied Clinical Informatics, 2*(2), 240.

Pollard, J. S., Karimi, K. A., & Ficcaglia, M. B. (2017). Ethical considerations in the design and implementation of a telehealth service delivery model. *Behavior Analysis: Research and Practice, 17*(2), 298−311. https://doi.org/10.1037/bar0000053

Protection of Human Subjects. (2009). *45 C.F.R.* § *46.101−46.505.*

Purcaru, D., Preda, A., Popa, D., Moga, M. A., & Rogozea, L. (2014). Informed consent: How much awareness is there? *PLoS ONE, 9*(10).

Rachels, S. (2012). *The elements of moral philosophy* (7th ed.). McGraw Hill.

Rekers, G. A., & Lovaas, O. I. (1974). Behavioral treatment of deviant sex-role behaviors in a male child. *Journal of Applied Behavior Analysis, 7*(2), 173−190. https://doi.org/10.1901/jaba.1974.7-173

Schneider, J., Makelarski, J. A., Van Haitsma, M., Lipton, R. B., Abramsohn, E., Lauderdale, D. S., & Lindau, S. T. (2011). Differential access to digital communication technology: Association with health and health survey recruitment within an African-American underserviced urban population. *Journal of Urban Health: Bulletin of the New York Academy of Medicine, 88*(3), 479−492. https://doi.org/10.1007/s11524-010-9533-6

Sellers, T. P., Clay, C. J., Hoffmann, A. N., & Collins, S. D. (2019). Evaluation of a performance management intervention to increase use of trial-based functional analysis by clinicians in a residential setting for adults with intellectual disabilities. *Behavior Analysis in Practice, 12*, 412−417.

Shah, P., Thornton, I., Turrin, D., & Hipskind, J. E. (August 22, 2020). *Informed consent.* updated. StatPearls Publishing.

Sipila-Thomas, E. S., & Brodhead, M. T. (2020). A review of remote fieldwork supervision for BABA trainees by Lisa N. Britton and Matthew J. Cicoria. *Behavior Analysis in Practice, 13*(4), 992–999. https://doi.org/10.1007/s40617-019-00407-9

Skinner, B. F. (1971). *Beyond freedom and dignity.* Hackett Publishing.

Slaton, J. D., & Hanley, G. P. (2016). Effects of multiple versus chained schedules on stereotypy and item engagement. *Journal of Applied Behavior Analysis, 49*(4), 927–946. https://doi.org/10.1002/jaba.345

Society for the Experimental Analysis of Behavior, & LeBlanc, L. A. (2020). Editor's note: Societal changes and expression of concern about Rekers and Lovaas' (1974) behavioral treatment of deviant sex-role behaviors in a male child. *Journal of Applied Behavior Analysis, 53*(4), 1830–1836. https://doi.org/10.1002/jaba.768

Spellecy, R., & Busse, K. (2021). The history of human subjects research and rationale for institutional review board oversight. *Nutrition and Clinical Practice, 36*(3), 560–567. https://doi.org/10.1002/ncp.10623

Sugai, G., & Horner, R. H. (2008). What we know and need to know about preventing problem behavior in schools. *Exceptionality, 16*(2), 67–77. https://doi.org/10.1080/09362830801981138

Walker, D. M., Hefner, J. L., Fareed, N., Huerta, T. R., & McAlearney, A. S. (2020). Exploring the digital divide: Age and race disparities in use of an inpatient portal. *Telemedicine Journal and E-Health, 26*(5), 603–613. https://doi.org/10.1089/tmj.2019.0065

Chapter 7

Ethical considerations with balancing clinical effectiveness with research design*

Wayne W. Fisher[1,2], Ashley M. Fuhrman[1,2], Brian D. Greer[1,2], Vivian F. Ibañez[1,2,4], Kathryn M. Peterson[1,2] and Cathleen C. Piazza[1,3]

[1]*Children's Specialized Hospital—Rutgers University Center for Autism Research, Education, and Services, Somerset, NJ, United States;* [2]*Department of Pediatrics, Rutgers Robert Wood Johnson Medical School, New Brunswick, NJ, United States;* [3]*Graudate School of Applied and Professional Psychology, Rutgers University, New Brunswick, NJ, United States;* [4]*University of Florida, Gainesville, FL, United States*

Most clinicians in routine clinical practice use informal methods of evaluating the efficacy of their interventions. For example, the clinician might ask the patient periodically whether the target behavior has improved, worsened, or remained unchanged. Even if the patient reports that the target behavior has improved, the clinician cannot be certain whether the intervention produced the improvement. *Experimentation* is necessary to evaluate whether the intervention caused the change and to rule out extraneous causes for the change (Kazdin, 2011), which is important for purposes of accountability and preventing treatment recidivism.

Single-case design is the form of experimentation most behavior analysts use to evaluate the effects of intervention both in research and in clinical practice. Nevertheless, experimentation is a word many associate with research but not clinical practice. For some, the word experimentation equates human participants with laboratory nonhuman animals and separates research from clinical practice. We would argue that this dichotomy is false and may create a barrier that prevents behavior analysts in clinical practice from evaluating the effects of their interventions.

---

*Author Note: The authors are listed in alphabetical order, which was selected over reverse alphabetical order by a coin flip. Address correspondence to Ashley M. Fuhrman, 888 Easton Ave., Somerset, NJ 08873 (E-mail: ashley.fuhrman@rutgers.edu).

Research Ethics in Behavior Analysis. https://doi.org/10.1016/B978-0-323-90969-3.00007-4
149

Consider the term experimentation as it relates to single-case design. Single-case design provides the framework for the behavior analyst to systematically manipulate an independent variable, such as an intervention, to determine its effects on a dependent variable, such as a target behavior. As the term implies, single-case design is a form of experimentation that evaluates the relation between independent and dependent variables on an individual's behavior, making it uniquely suited for use in research *and* clinical practice. Given that the goal of behavior analysis is to make meaningful changes in socially significant behavior, single-case design is the method by which behavior analysts ascertain whether behavior has changed and whether those changes are meaningful. As such, single-case design is the gold standard for evaluating the efficacy of interventions in behavior analysis.

One way to consider the so-called dichotomy between research and clinical practice relative to single-case design is to ask why behavior analysts would use their best tool for evaluating the effects of intervention with their research participants and not with their clinical patients. Why do our research participants deserve the gold standard,[1] but our clinical patients do not? Do they not both deserve the same high quality of care? This chapter will address these questions by describing the overlap between research and clinical practice, highlight the points where research and clinical practice diverge, and provide recommendations for addressing ethical issues that arise at these points.

Evaluating effectiveness in research and clinical practice

A critical feature of single-case design is its data-based approach to assessment and treatment. Critical features include identifying the target behavior, operationally defining the target behavior, selecting a measurement procedure, and assessing the reliability of the data. In fact, behavior analysts have an ethical obligation to collect data, graphically display it, and interpret it (Behavior Analyst Certification Board, 2020b). Behavior analysts most often collect direct-observation data in part because it may be less prone to bias, such as whether the patient likes or dislikes the treatment goals, procedures, and personnel (Schwartz & Baer, 1991). The repeated measurement inherent in single-case design is critical for determining the level, stability, and trend of the target behavior, which we discuss later in the chapter.

Behavior analysts should be mindful of the purpose of data collection. The data are important because they represent the patient's behavior, they tell us what the patient is doing, and they help us to identify what variables affect what the patient will do. For example, we use single-case designs to conduct

---

1. The term "good standard" is commonly used metaphorically in healthcare to denote an established or best standard of care for a particular type of assessment or treatment. The term was originally used in economics to provide a standardized way of setting the value of difference currencies for the purpose of international trade.

functional analyses of target behavior. Data from the functional analysis can identify the environmental conditions that affect the probability of the target behavior. The behavior analyst can use the data from the functional analysis to inform an intervention for the target behavior and test the effects of intervention with a single-case design.

As the example above illustrates, single-case design involves the systematic manipulation of variables. The behavior analyst describes a procedure and ensures that implementers execute it with high levels of fidelity. The behavior analyst selects the single-case design best suited to the evaluation at hand and uses the logic of the selected design to test the effects of the intervention. Single-case designs are flexible, and the behavior analyst can refine, add, or remove intervention components based on incoming data. Without the experimentation inherent in single-case design, such as data collection and systematic manipulation of variables, the behavior analyst is left with a trial-and-error approach for evaluating what works. Even then, without data, the behavior analyst would not know whether the target behavior has actually changed or be able to identify variables that affected any apparent change in the target behavior. Analyzing behavior using single-case designs and describing and implementing procedures with precision represent two foundational dimensions of applied behavior analysis (analytic and technological, respectively; Baer et al., 1968).

Another important advantage of using single-case design is that it provides feedback to the behavior analyst about the quality of their work. The data tell the behavior analyst whether the interventions they selected are effective for a given patient's target behavior. Thus, the behavior analyst can use the data to improve their clinical skills. The behavior analyst also can aggregate data from multiple patients to evaluate outcomes programmatically. For example, a behavior analyst in private practice might calculate the percentage reduction in self-injurious behavior for patients who received intervention to determine whether the practice was producing meaningful changes in behavior.

Using such systematic methods to evaluate clinical interventions often leads to better outcomes. For example, in a meta-analysis of behavioral and psychotherapeutic treatments for problem behavior in individuals with intellectual disability, Didden et al. (2006) found that conducting functional analyses; assessing the reliability of recording; evaluating generalization; and implementing internally valid, single-case designs (e.g., ABAB) produced larger treatment effects than when those characteristics were not present.

Hayes (1981) pointed out the striking parallels between good clinical decision making and single-case experimental designs. Both typically involve the collection of accurate data before initiating treatment. That is, clinicians and researchers treating or studying problem behavior seek to determine how often problem behavior occurs, and under what environmental conditions, to develop hypotheses about behavioral function(s), which they test using single-case designs in a functional analysis. In addition, repeated measurement is critical for determining variability in the problem behavior prior to initiating treatment in both clinical practice and single-case experiments. After the initiation of treatment, single-case designs test whether observed treatment effects can be replicated using reversals or other experimental control techniques, and such replications are essential for clinical accountability (e.g., showing that the treatment produced the observed change in behavior as opposed to a "honeymoon effect" resulting from another change). Finally, single-case designs are flexible and allow the addition or replacement of treatment components based on the data collected up to a given point in time (e.g., changing an ABAB to an ABCBC design after no observed treatment effect in the first B phase), and such flexibility lends itself to evaluating treatment components sequentially in a research study, as well as during effective, data-based clinical decision making. For example, a clinician might add treatment components sequentially (e.g., differential reinforcement, then prompting, then response blocking) until clinically meaningful reductions in problem behavior are observed and then withdraw the entire treatment package (i.e., return to baseline) and then reintroduce the entire package to show its effectiveness. It should be noted that behavior analysts are not required to use single-case designs to demonstrate functional relations between their interventions and patient outcomes by patients, third-party payers, or licensing or accrediting agencies. Nevertheless, implementing such rigorous evaluative procedures can provide clear and convincing evidence regarding the effectiveness of a given intervention or treatment program.

In our clinical programs, we use single-case designs to (a) evaluate the effects of intervention on individual patient behavior, (b) produce excellent clinical outcomes for each patient (e.g., 90% reduction in aggression), and (c) advance our understanding of the variables that improve outcomes for future patients. We refer to this approach as *patient-oriented research*. The goal is to improve outcomes for both current and future patients, but the clinical goals of the current patients are always the priority, because they come to us as patients seeking treatment for their socially important problems rather than as volunteer participants for a study that may benefit others in the future. Single-case designs allow us to achieve each of the three aims listed above.

For example, two patients in Bowman et al. (1997) emitted destructive behavior after emitting a mand that did not produce the reinforcer it specified. The functional analysis showed that destructive behavior functioned as a precurrent response that increased the probability that adults would comply with and deliver the reinforcers specified by the patients' subsequent mands. Systematically analyzing this unique function of destructive behavior led to a specific and effective treatment not only for these two patients but also for many subsequent patients (e.g., Owen et al., 2020). This example illustrates how behavior analysts can integrate research and practice to meet the immediate needs of the current patients while advancing our understanding of a clinical phenomenon, which then benefits future patients.

Behavior analysts should be mindful, however, when integrating research and practice, because situations can arise in which the goals of research and clinical practice diverge. This is most likely to occur when the behavior analyst is conducting a clinical trial with an overarching hypothesis, and the primary goal of the research is to collect data that either supports or refutes that hypothesis. The National Institutes of Health (2021) defines a clinical trial as, "A research study in which one or more human subjects are prospectively assigned to one or more interventions (which may include placebo or other control) to evaluate the effects of those interventions on health-related biomedical or behavioral outcomes." By contrast, with patient-oriented research, the participant is first and foremost a patient. The patient comes to us seeking help with a problem, and we select an intervention that we believe will appropriately address the problem rather than assigning the patient to a predetermined intervention we wish to study.

With clinical trials, the behavior analyst may face decision points in which the research protocol specifies one course (e.g., continue with Intervention A for 12 weeks) and the behavior analyst's clinical judgment indicates a different course (e.g., switch to Intervention B earlier). In such cases, having clear, a-priori criteria for when to continue the research protocol and when to withdraw the patient from the protocol and switch to the alternative treatment should be the standard to which clinical researchers adhere. However, in the absence of such a-priori criteria, the behavior analyst should err generally on the side of clinical judgment about the best course for their patient. Seeking input from peers who are not involved in the research or with the specific patient may be helpful in such cases for obtaining clinical guidance that is not biased. In addition, the patient or caregiver (whoever provided informed consent) should be consulted whenever such decision points occur.

In the sections that follow, we discuss similar choice points that behavior analysts may face when integrating research with clinical practice, including during recruitment and retention of research participants, when selecting specific single-case designs, when deviating from research protocols due to the clinical needs of the patient, when monitoring and reporting adverse events, and when determining whether to bill for clinical services an individual receives while participating in a research study.

Recruitment and retention

An important element of research design is participant recruitment and retention. Researchers often aim to recruit only those participants well suited for the research question at hand. For example, if the research question involves an intervention for negatively reinforced problem behavior, enrolled participants should engage in negatively reinforced problem behavior. Retention is similarly important in research design. Participant attrition can negatively impact the study's findings and may have implications for the practicality of the independent variable under consideration. For instance, if half the participants withdraw from a study, the resulting data may be insufficient for producing generalizable results. If the reason for participant attrition is that problem behavior increased to unsafe levels, the target intervention may be impractical, even if the dataset is publishable. Balancing the aims of a research study with the clinical goals of individual patients can be challenging for researchers who also are clinicians, and conflict between the two can begin during participant recruitment. There are several considerations for recruiting patients as participants, which we discuss. We then discuss potential issues surrounding participant retention.

Institutional review boards (IRBs) tasked with ensuring safe and ethical research practices often balance the risks of each prospective research project with its potential for therapeutic benefit, especially when patients serve as participants. Institutional review boards consider whether the risks of research participation are *greater than minimal,* which they usually determine by considering what the patient would otherwise experience and what other, nonpatients typically experience. When the risk is greater than minimal, institutional review boards generally require the prospect of direct therapeutic benefit and rarely approve research projects without it.

Factors that might increase study risk are the population, such as patients who engage in severe destructive behavior (e.g., self-injurious eye poking); the experimental procedures (e.g., exposing patients to the establishing operation for destructive behavior for extended periods; Fisher et al., 2018); or both. Behavior analysts who conduct research that has greater than minimal risk must consider each prospective participant carefully and weigh the relative risks and potential benefits of including the patient in the study. Some variables that might impact enrollment include whether (a) the research-specific risks will be more or less likely to occur with the patient, (b) those risks will affect the patient in worse ways than other prospective participants if they do occur, (c) the potential for therapeutic benefit exists for the patient, and (d) those therapeutic benefits will be more or less beneficial than for other prospective participants if they do occur.

Clinical research that does not involve greater than minimal risk does not require the prospect of therapeutic benefit. Such studies often proceed with relatively relaxed oversight from IRBs. Note, however, that *low risk* studies rarely have no risk, and the behavior analyst should still consider the relative risks and potential benefits of including each patient in the study. Considerations include lost therapy time for the patient if the behavior analyst substitutes the patient's therapy time with participation in a research study that is not likely to produce therapeutic benefit. Enrolling participants from nonclinical populations may be an alternative in this case. This example highlights that the risks associated with research are relative to the study and to the population it enrolls. The same research may be low risk for one population but higher risk for another population. Considering what is in the best interest of each patient is always best practice when conducting clinical research.

If the data support patient enrollment, the behavior analyst should conduct ongoing evaluation of whether continued enrollment is warranted. Ongoing evaluation of the relative risks and benefits is especially important when conducting research of greater than minimal risk. Research participation must halt if the risk−benefit ratio changes such that the potential therapeutic benefits of continued enrollment no longer justify the risks. Note that a change in the risk−benefit ratio can result from increased risk, decreased prospect of therapeutic benefit, or both.

Consent is another consideration for continued research enrollment. Most think of the consent process as the first step of research participation, a step that ends once the participant or legal guardian signs the consent document. On the contrary, patient participation in clinical research requires ongoing consent throughout the study. At any point, research participants or their guardians may revoke their consent for participation. Best practice is to treat consent as a continual process throughout the study. Likewise, continual dialogue between the researchers and the participants, legal guardians, or both is necessary to help ensure that participants understand the aims of the study and the individual participant's progress through it. Frequent check-ins and updates can help to ensure there are no surprises when it comes to research participation.

Considerations of single-case designs for research and clinical practice

Behavior analysts have multiple single-case-design options for evaluating the effects of intervention in research and clinical practice. Common designs behavior analysts use include the ABAB (reversal) design, the multiple baseline design, and the multielement design. Each design has its own unique strengths and weaknesses, which the behavior analyst should consider before selecting a design option. Factors that might affect selection of a specific single-case design include whether the design will (a) be the best fit for the specific research or clinical question(s); (b) provide internal validity and confirmation that the independent variable alone is responsible for behavior change (Sidman, 1960); (c) allow the behavior analyst to control and eliminate extraneous or confounding variables (Kazdin, 2011); and (d) reliably produce the effects with the application or withdrawal of the independent variable. The following section will describe the logic of common single-case designs, the considerations for selecting each design, and the ethical issues that might arise with each design.

Reversal designs

The logic of the ABAB or reversal design is that systematic introduction and withdrawal of an independent variable demonstrates its effects on the dependent variable. For this discussion, a *baseline* phase (A) is followed by introduction of an intervention (B), withdrawal of the intervention and return to baseline (second A phase), and reintroduction of the intervention (second B phase). The purpose of the baseline phase is to establish the level, stability, and trend of target behavior and predict its future level, stability, and trend without intervention. The level of target behavior can reflect the extent of the problem. The stability and trend of target behavior during baseline are factors that determine whether the behavior analyst should implement intervention. Stable levels or rates of target behavior that trend in the direction of worsening behavior, such as an increasing rate of inappropriate mealtime behavior, suggest that no improvement will occur without intervention. Demonstration of functional control relies on clear changes in the level or rate of target behavior as the behavior analyst introduces and withdraws the intervention. We use the terms improvement and worsening of behavior rather than increases and decreases because whether levels or rate of behavior should increase or decrease during intervention depends on the target behavior. For example, improvement might entail increasing levels of acceptance of a target food but decreasing rates of inappropriate mealtime behavior.

Concerns that arise with the ABAB design typically relate to withdrawal and reintroduction of the intervention. However, demonstration of functional control depends on replication. Levels or rates of target behavior should be equivalent during the first baseline A phase and after the withdrawal of intervention and return to the second baseline A phase. Similarly, levels or rates of target behavior should be equivalent during the initial introduction of intervention in the first B phase and during the reintroduction of the intervention in the second B phase. Conclusions about the effects of intervention will be limited if replication does not occur in either A or B phases.

The ABAB design is most appropriate when the intervention is likely to produce an unambiguous change in the level or rate of target behavior, and that effect occurs only when the intervention is present. The ABAB design may not be suited for interventions that produce persistent behavior change as level or rate of behavior may not return to baseline during the reversal. For example, an ABAB design likely would not be the best choice to demonstrate the effects of an intervention to teach a child to read the word "dog." Instances of reading the word "dog" might increase during the first B phase of intervention but might persist during the withdrawal of intervention and return to the baseline A phase. Additional threats to the internal validity of the ABAB design include time and other extraneous variables that might affect behavior differentially during baseline or intervention phases. For example, rates of self-injurious behavior might be high in a baseline A phase when self-injurious behavior produces escape from demands, decrease in the B phase with an escape-extinction intervention, but not increase during the withdrawal of the escape-extinction intervention because the evocative effects of the demand decreased with repeated exposure.

Some stakeholders have questioned whether withdrawing intervention is ethical. To address this question, behavior analysts should weigh the advantages of demonstrating the effects of the intervention on target behavior with the risks related to withdrawing the intervention. Brief reversals may be of minimal risk for patients whose target behavior has not caused self-harm, harm to others or property, or a combination. In these cases, the advantage of identifying an effective intervention may outweigh the potential increase in the level or rate of behavior during a reversal. By contrast, a reversal design might not be appropriate for a patient whose target behavior caused serious harm during the original baseline phase. In this case, carefully considering other design options that minimize the risk to the patient would be the appropriate alternative relative to abandoning attempts to demonstrate functional control of the intervention.

Another factor that should be considered when determining whether to use a reversal design is whether or not establishing functional control of the selected intervention might increase the long-term benefits versus risks to the patient. For example, a child who displays severe self-injurious behavior might show a large improvement the first time an intervention is introduced not because it is effective but because everyone in the child's environment is conscientiously avoiding the establishing operation that evokes the child's self-injurious behavior. Conducting reversals using an ABAB design in such a case would help to determine whether the intervention actually produced the observed improvement in the child's behavior, which would be important to the long-term outcome of the case because everyone in the child's environment is not likely to continue avoiding the establishing operation for self-injurious behavior forever.

Multiple baseline design

The logic of the multiple baseline design is that staggering the introduction of an independent variable across baselines of different lengths demonstrates its effects on the dependent variable. Behavior analysts use multiple baseline designs to evaluate the effects of an independent variable across different responses or conditions (e.g., participants, settings, therapists; e.g., Crowley et al., 2020). Each response or condition across which the behavior analyst will introduce the intervention is called a *leg* of the multiple baseline. The purpose of the baseline for each leg is the same as for the ABAB design, to establish the level, stability, and trend of target behavior. The demonstration of functional control relies on (a) an unambiguous change in the level or rate of target behavior concomitant with the introduction of the intervention in each leg of the multiple baseline, (b) sustained improvement in the level or rate of target behavior in each leg of the multiple baseline during the intervention, and (c) no improvement in the level or rate of target behavior during the baselines of each leg of the multiple baseline. The premise of this design is to control for history and the passage of time by implementing the intervention sequentially across targeted dependent variables, individuals, or stimulus contexts. Conclusions about the effects of intervention will be limited if levels or rates of target behavior (a) do not change concomitant with the implementation of intervention in one or more legs of the multiple baseline, (b) do not maintain at the changed level or rate during intervention in one or more legs of the multiple baseline, or (c) improve before the behavior analyst implements the intervention in one or more legs of the multiple baseline.

Like the ABAB design, the multiple baseline design is appropriate when improvements in the level or rate of target behavior are likely to occur concomitant with the introduction of the intervention and are likely to sustain during intervention. Unlike the ABAB design, the multiple baseline design may be appropriate for interventions that produce persistent behavior change given that a reversal of the intervention is unnecessary.

Some stakeholders have questioned whether allowing baseline contingencies to continue during one or more legs of the design while applying the independent variable sequentially across others is ethical. For example, with a multiple-baseline-across-participants design consisting of four legs, the participants in the last two legs of the design could easily remain in baseline for nine and 12 sessions (or days), respectively. Such delays may be reasonable for an intervention targeting increases in the variability of social greetings (e.g., variably saying "Hello," "Good day," or "Nice to see you" rather than always saying "Hi"), but not when the intervention is targeting elopement into busy streets. As with the ABAB design, behavior analysts should weigh the advantages of demonstrating the effects of the intervention on target behavior with the risks associated with extending the baselines.

The behavior analyst should also consider the risks associated with concluding that an intervention is effective based on incomplete information (e.g., based on an observed improvement relative to a single baseline following the initial introduction of the intervention). For example, if a patient has displayed chronic, severe destructive behavior that varies in frequency over time, the behavior analyst may falsely conclude that an intervention is effective based on the results of an AB design, when in fact, the observed improvement occurred for reasons other than the introduction of the treatment. In this case, the behavior analyst may discharge the patient with an ineffective treatment, thereby extending the health risks associated with the patient's severe destructive behavior, whereas introducing the treatment across multiple settings according to a multiple baseline design probably would have detected the deficient intervention and led to the evaluation of an alternative and potentially effective intervention.

Multielement design

Multielement designs involve rapid alternation between independent-variable manipulations. The logic of the design is that levels or rates of target behavior during each independent-variable manipulation demonstrate the effects of those manipulations on the dependent variable. The demonstration of functional control relies on differential levels or rates of target behavior during one independent-variable manipulation relative to the others (e.g., Amari et al., 1995). Conclusions about the effects of intervention will be limited if levels or rates of target behavior are not differentiated in one or more conditions.

The multielement design is appropriate for comparing one intervention with one or more other interventions, and it is a particularly useful design when rapidly identifying an effective intervention is important. The multielement design does not require inclusion of an extended baseline condition, which may be another advantage for patients whose target behavior has caused harm during baseline conditions in the past. A disadvantage of the design is that rapid alternation between conditions can result in carryover or interaction effects where the effects of one condition spill over and effect responding in another condition (Kennedy, 2005). Such carry-over effects can obscure the results and limit the conclusions about the functional relations between independent and dependent variables or sometimes prolong the analysis. Programming discriminative stimuli, reducing the number of alternating conditions, or using the multielement design with another design (e.g., reversal or multiple baseline) might be alternatives to improve the demonstration of functional control.

Other experimental design features

Randomization and counterbalancing provide another set of critical techniques to control for interference from extraneous variables. In randomized clinical trials, participants are often assigned to the intervention and control groups according to a randomization strategy (e.g., simple randomization, randomization with minimization; Fisher et al., 2014, 2020). The major ethical issue raised by this practice has to do with assigning half of the participants to an inactive control group (e.g., such as a waitlist control group; e.g., Fisher et al., 2014). Individuals assigned to a control group may wait weeks or even months before they receive intervention. Another disadvantage is that this particular design may result in a masking of effects for individual participants if the data are analyzed at the group level (i.e., determining whether the average participant improved but not whether any specific individual improved). By contrast, when treatments are evaluated using single-case designs, the individuals typically receive intervention sooner and the results are directly relevant to each individual (e.g., Tiger et al., 2009).

Recently, researchers have increasingly recommended the use of randomization and counterbalancing strategies for use with single-case designs (cf. Kratochwill & Levin, 2014). That is, researchers can randomize and counterbalance the sequencing of conditions, participants, or settings when using single-case designs. The primary advantages of including randomization strategies in single-case designs are that they help to control for experimenter bias and add scientific credibility to the research. However, from an ethical perspective, such randomization procedures can extend the length of an intervention evaluation, which may delay implementation of an effective intervention in the natural environment. In addition, such randomization strategies typically reduce the flexibility and individualization of single-case designs, which are important features of single-case designs when they are used in clinical settings.

Protocol deviations due to clinical need

A systematic and data-based approach as part of routine service provision can be critical for improving individual patient outcomes and the quality of behavior-analytic services. Therefore, behavior analysts who conduct or supervise research in their clinical work must navigate this systematic approach in a way that fluidly integrates research and practice. For example, factors such as ensuring that everyone follows the research plan exactly and making one change at a time are crucial parts of this systematic approach. At some point, however, there might be conditions that warrant deviations from the original research plan. A continuum of clinical and administrative obligations might require behavior analysts to make decisions that do not align directly with a given research protocol. In this section, we discuss a few scenarios to highlight the type of competencies that we should expect of behavior analysts who intend to be scientist-practitioners in their daily clinical practice.

It is important to recognize the skill and dedication that behavior analysts must exert to bridge the gap between research and practice in a clinical setting. There is a myriad of variables that a clinical team must simultaneously evaluate such as the physical environment, number of staff, organizational policies, and caregiver or stakeholder priorities. From a practical standpoint, one overarching consideration is the time allocated for behavior analysts to render services according to requirements of a third-party payor. In some cases, a client's period of authorization might expire, or a family reports an upcoming change with insurance, which often requires a new authorization process. If a client's hours or services will be reduced or discontinued, and an active research protocol is in place, clinicians should be ready to make amendments, particularly if the research plan had been to replicate the effects of an intervention over time with the same individual. In these cases, it might be useful for the clinical team to consider changes related to the duration of a baseline phase or perhaps shift to a multiple-baseline-across-subjects design

(Crowley et al., 2020). Above all, providing stakeholders and caregivers with the level of support they need to be successful in the face of challenges with continuity of services should guide deviations from research protocols.

If certain features of single-case design are not considered a luxury in a given applied setting (e.g., number of baseline days), behavior analysts should prepare a clinical research program accordingly. For example, Kazdin (2011) highlighted how most school settings already arrange students by group (i.e., classroom), which promotes between-group studies. Relatedly, Roane, Fisher, and Carr (2016) noted that clinicians should determine whether a client's availability will be sufficient for specific designs (e.g., reversal). Although unforeseen events like those mentioned above are, by definition, unpredictable, being able to assess whether the design and data collection can change as events unfold should be a critical consideration when planning clinical research.

Competing contingencies (e.g., percentage of time allocated for nonbillable activities) for organizations that deliver behavior-analytic services might raise considerations that are unique to clinical research in specific areas like staff training. For example, Erath et al. (2020) indicated that clinicians might not carry out ideal training procedures as a result of variables like time and organizational resources. Results of their study demonstrated an example of arranging training for a clinical research protocol that could be completed in 1 day to mitigate some of these concerns. However, the ability for clinicians to meet in a group as they did in Erath et al. (2020) might be challenging in certain organizations. Therefore, clinicians might consider a deviation such as repeated AB designs across subjects to obtain some evidence about the efficacy of training procedures when the organization cannot accommodate removing staff from clinical activities at the same time. Although aspects of certain demonstrations of experimental control might seem alternative and unfamiliar, Johnston and Pennypacker (1993) caution against rigidity with experimental design to the point of preventing flexibility in a dynamic environment.

Special considerations for certain populations also require an understanding of the conditions under which deviations from the original research plan are necessary. Importantly, humans often have unknown histories that interact with contingencies in ways that might change how clinicians intend to carry out experimental procedures (Branch, 2021). Kazdin et al. (2011) provides an example of how clinicians might need to change the length of baseline if dangerous behavior emerges and warrants intervention sooner rather than later. For example, studies by Joslyn et al. (2014) and Joslyn et al. (2017) included high-school classrooms of students who exhibited severe disruptive, dangerous, or illegal behavior and residential treatment facilities for criminal offenders with intellectual disabilities, respectively. In these cases, keeping the participants and those around them safe should guide decisions related to whether the potential therapeutic benefits of research participation no longer justify the risks. The school setting might also be associated with external pressures, such as funding from the Department of Education (Leachman, Masterson, & Figueroa, 2017), making it more difficult to justify running baseline phases for an extended period of time. Fortunately, a hallmark of behavior-analytic research is making ongoing data-based decisions for each subject, which should aid researchers in detecting problems as they emerge and allow them to adjust the research plan accordingly. For example, data that show an increase in problem behavior during a critical experimental condition (e.g., problem behavior during a test for resurgence) might present a safety concern for the client or therapists. To this end, ensuring the clinical team has a mastered understanding of inclusion and exclusion criteria is critical. For example, Peterson et al. (2016) included children with food selectivity who had a weight-for-height at or greater than the fifth percentile. Therefore, it would be important for the clinical study team to have a way to monitor changes in a participant's growth throughout study participation to make informed decisions in the best interest of the child.

According to recent data from the Behavior Analysis Certification Board (BACB), about 74% of credentialed clinicians (e.g., BCBA, RBT) identify autism spectrum disorder as their primary area of professional emphasis. In a study the BACB commissioned in 2015, about 85% of job postings for behavior analysts were in the health care, educational services, or social-assistance industries between 2012 and 2014 (Burning Glass Technologies, 2015). Combined, these statistics suggest that many BCBAs are performing jobs that require at least some face-to-face interactions with patients, clients, students, supervisees, or a combination. However, restrictions on face-to-face interactions (e.g., due to a pandemic) might require some behavior analysts to transition to a telehealth service-delivery model (Peterson et al., 2021; Schieltz & Wacker, 2020). Although service delivery via telehealth is not new to behavior analysis (e.g., telehealth model at the University of Iowa, Wacker, 2016), for some behavior analysts, this transition might be unexpected, which raises important considerations in the context of clinical research protocols. From an ethical standpoint, behavior analysts are tasked with conducting research only within the boundaries of their competence. For example, the BACB posted guidelines on their website during the COVID-19 pandemic to remind certificants that transition-to-telehealth plans should not sacrifice clinical quality and should be delivered in a safe manner. Therefore, a change in the method of service delivery should invite a conversation among the clinical team related to the necessary knowledge and practical training to safely manage the client's behavior remotely. It might be the case that client participation via telehealth requires a change in the research question or experimental design and provision of caregiver training to determine whether the team can accurately and safely implement the research protocol. The behavior analyst also should consider whether a change from in-person to telehealth delivery of the intervention under study warrants reobtaining informed consent from the participant or guardian.

Ultimately, implementing research in daily clinical practice should support the delivery of evidence-based and cost-effective care. The ability to maintain the effects of interventions over time after a research study has ended remains another challenge that requires additional research. In general, behavior-analytic organizations would likely benefit from advisory boards that can help establish parameters of a clinical research program in an applied setting. For example, Courtney et al. (2020) described a knowledge of ethics as one domain from which an advisory board assists behavior-analytic organizations. Presumably, this would help clinicians navigate ethical dilemmas related to research protocols in active and fast-paced applied settings. For example, clinicians need to recognize when the programmed therapeutic goals of a client shift in a way that no longer aligns with the aims of the research protocol. In any case, organizations that carry out research with participants should carefully consider how they seek a review of their research practices. For example, if the organization is not part of a university or hospital that already has an established IRB, the organization could arrange for an "outside" review. Part of this process might also result in the development of a standing committee that forms a research review board, defined as a group that provides feedback on "research proposals to ensure the ethical treatment of human research participants" (Behavior Analyst Certification Board, 2014).

Participant safety

Researchers must carefully consider numerous variables related to participant safety when designing and implementing research protocols. In the case of experimental design, researchers should review the prescribed procedures and assess the implications for the safety of individual participants. An initial step in this risk analysis is to consider the projected population of participants and the target behavior that will be the focus of the study. Then, researchers must consider how that population may be more vulnerable to certain safety risks that may be associated with specific target behavior and experimental designs. For example, if the inclusion criteria include severe self-injurious behavior (e.g., head banging), researchers should consider using an experimental design that does not include excessive exposure to baseline conditions or repeated withdrawals of an effective treatment. Clinicians should also consider whether inclusion in their study warrants input from other professionals or a multidisciplinary team. For example, one of the inclusion criteria in the study by Peterson et al. (2019) was that participants were identified by either a physician or speech and language pathologist as safe oral feeders.

Along the same lines, researchers should develop strict exclusion criteria if they are measuring dangerous behavior and using procedures (e.g., extinction) that might result in an increase in responding. For instance, when we conduct research on the resurgence of problem behavior, we do not enroll patients who engage in self-injurious behavior at unsafe levels. We also conduct the Destructive Behavior Severity Scale (Fisher et al., 2013) to allow us to better determine whether a participant is appropriate for a research protocol and what precautions we need to take to minimize risk to participants. For example, if the severity scale reveals that a patient engages in high-intensity and high-frequency head banging that regularly results in tissue damage, we would exclude that individual from a resurgence evaluation. Whereas if the severity scale revealed that the patient engages in high-frequency but low-intensity head banging, we may include them in a resurgence evaluation and develop specific procedural guidelines to maintain safety (e.g., establish criteria for blocking).

Relatedly, researchers must keep safety in mind as they design research protocols and throughout the course of the study. Doing so allows them to determine (a) what specific procedures will be the safest to use to answer the experimental question and (b) how to modify them if needed. Researchers should always consider if they need to develop session termination criteria such that therapists have clear conditions under which they should end a research session prematurely to maintain participant safety.

It is important to note that researchers should always be aware of clinic polices and IRB requirements (if the research requires an IRB application) surrounding patient safety. Research protocols must always align with these requirements as well as the ethical guidelines provided by their respective credentialing agencies. Similarly, researchers should follow the policies on reporting incidents that occur during research. That is, if a patient experiences an adverse event during a research study, researchers may need to file a report both with the IRB and with the clinic agency where the research is conducted.

Billing practices

When integrating research with clinical practice, clinicians must determine the conditions under which certain activities constitute billable services. At the outset, clinicians should decide the specific research procedures they will bill for in relation to the design of a research protocol. In general, clinicians should bill only for research procedures that are considered current standard of care or routine clinical practice. That is, if there are any procedures in a research protocol that will be conducted solely for research purposes, clinicians should have clear guidelines for ensuring that such research procedures are not billed to third-party payors. Similarly, it is important that clinicians bill consistently across participants in a research protocol. That is, they should not charge insurance for procedures that they did not bill for with other participants.

Although several applied-behavior-analysis organizations have issued general practice guidelines (e.g., Behavior Analyst Certification Board, 2020a), such guidelines typically do not provide detailed information on what specific behavior-analytic procedures are considered current standard of care. Thus, we recommend that clinicians reference the literature (e.g., reviews and meta-analyses), consult with colleagues, and use other resources (e.g., university IRBs or clinical research offices) as needed to determine whether they should bill for the procedures that they plan to use in a research protocol. After clinicians determine whether they will bill for all, none, or some of the research procedures, they should develop a system to track research participation in accordance with regulations put forth by their employer, IRB, and other key stakeholders. Designing a precise way to track research participation is especially important when clinicians have research protocols that include both billable and non-billable procedures. For example, if clinicians determine that the specific baseline procedures that they plan to conduct are not current standard of care, but the treatment procedures are, they will need to precisely track the amount of time that each participant spends in baseline and treatment phases such that insurance is billed accurately (i.e., only for the time spent in standard-of-care procedures).

Although we suggest that clinicians determine what research procedures they will bill for during the initial designing of a research protocol, it is important that they monitor and re-evaluate the billing procedures on an ongoing basis. There may be scenarios that arise that require clinicians to change the billing procedures they developed before the start of the study. For example, new literature or regulations that come out during the course of a study might change billing procedures for clinical research. If clinicians encounter scenarios in which they are unsure of how to ethically bill for research procedures, they should consult with relevant stakeholders such as their employer, compliance officers, the IRB, and insurance companies. Finally, we recommend that clinicians who have questions about billing for such procedures seek continuing education on appropriate billing practices (e.g., Association of Professional Behavior Analysts, 2021).

Concluding comments

Conducting research on existing and novel behavior-analytic assessments and treatments is critical to the growth of applied behavior analysis and to the continual refinement of the clinical services we develop and deliver. As the preceding sections have illustrated, behavior analyst who conduct research with their clients must be cognizant of the situations in which the goals of research and patient care converge and diverge. Those goals more often align when the behavior analyst is engaged in patient-oriented research to improve outcomes for both current and future clients, but the clinical goals of the current client always take priority. These goals may align less often when the behavior analyst is conducting programmatic research with the primary goal of supporting or refuting the study's hypotheses. When the goals of research and clinical practice diverge, behavior analysts should take the path that leads to the best clinical care of their clients. When behavior analysts are uncertain with regard to the best course of action, they should seek consultation and advice from peers, regulatory bodies, and other relevant stakeholders.

References

Amari, A., Grace, N. C., & Fisher, W. W. (1995). Achieving and maintaining compliance with the ketogenic diet. *Journal of Applied Behavior Analysis, 28*(3), 341−342. https://doi.org/10.1901/jaba.1995.28-341

Association of Professional Behavior Analysts. (December 2021). *Recorded webinar on "audits, recoupments, and fraud allegations".* https://www.apbahome.net/store/viewproduct.aspx?id=16132125.

Baer, D. M., Wolf, M. M., & Risley, T. R. (1968). Some current dimensions of applied behavior analysis. *Journal of Applied Behavior Analysis, 1*(1), 91. https://doi.org/10.1901/jaba.1968.1-91

Behavior Analysis Certification Board. (2020a). *Applied behavior analysis treatment of autism spectrum disorder: Practice guidelines for healthcare funders and managers* (2nd ed.) https://www.bacb.com/team-view/applied-behavior-analysis-treatment-of-autism-spectrum-disorder-practice-guidelines-for-healthcare-funders-and-managers-2nd-ed/.

Behavior Analyst Certification Board. (2014). *Professional and ethical compliance code for behavior analysts.* Littleton, CO: Author. https://www.bacb.com/wp-content/uploads/2020/05/BACB-Compliance-Code-english_190318.pdf.

Behavior Analyst Certification Board. (2020b). *Professional and ethical compliance code for behavior analysts.* Littleton, CO: Author. https://www.bacb.com/wp-content/uploads/2020/11/Ethics-Code-for-Behavior-Analysts-210902.pdf.

Bowman, L. G., Fisher, W. W., Thompson, R. H., & Piazza, C. C. (1997). On the relation of mands and the function of destructive behavior. *Journal of Applied Behavior Analysis, 30*(2), 251−265. https://doi.org/10.1901/jaba.1997.30-251

Branch, M. (2021). Lessons worth repeating: Sidman's Tactics of scientific research. *Journal of the Experimental Analysis of Behavior, 115*(1), 44−55. https://doi.org/10.1002/jeab.643

Burning Glass Technologies. (2015). *US behavior analyst workforce: Understanding the national demand for behavior analysts.* Retrieved from https://www.bacb.com/wp-content/uploads/2017/09/151009-burning-glass-report.pdf.

Courtney, W. T., Hartley, B. K., Rosswurm, M., LeBlanc, L. A., & Lund, C. J. (2020). Establishing and leveraging the expertise of advisory boards. *Behavior Analysis in Practice.* https://doi.org/10.1007/s40617-020-00503-1

Crowley, J. G., Peterson, K. M., Fisher, W. W., & Piazza, C. C. (2020). Treating food selectivity as resistance to change in children with autism spectrum disorder. *Journal of Applied Behavior Analysis, 53*(4), 2002−2023. https://doi.org/10.1002/jaba.711

Didden, R., Korzilius, H., van Oorsouw, W., & Sturmey, P. (2006). Behavioral treatment of challenging behaviors in individuals with mild mental retardation: Meta-analysis of single-subject research. *American Journal on Mental Retardation, 111*(4), 290−298. https://doi.org/10.1352/0895-8017(2006)111[290:BTOCBI]2.0.CO;2

Erath, T. G., DiGennaro Reed, F. D., Sundermeyer, H. W., Brand, D., Novak, M. D., Harbison, M. J., & Shears, R. (2020). Enhancing the training integrity of human service staff using pyramidal behavioral skills training. *Journal of Applied Behavior Analysis, 53*(1), 449−464. https://doi.org/10.1002/jaba.608

Fisher, W. W., Greer, B. D., Mitteer, D. R., Fuhrman, A. M., Romani, P. W., & Zangrillo, A. N. (2018). Further evaluation of differential exposure to establishing operations during functional communication training. *Journal of Applied Behavior Analysis, 51*(2), 360−373. https://doi.org/10.1002/jaba.451

Fisher, W. W., Luczynski, K. C., Blowers, A. P., Vosters, M. E., Pisman, M. D., Craig, A. R., Hood, S. A., Machado, M. A., Lesser, A. D., & Piazza, C. C. (2020). A randomized clinical trial of a virtual-training program for teaching applied-behavior-analysis skills to parents of children with autism spectrum disorder. *Journal of Applied Behavior Analysis, 53*(4), 1856−1875. https://doi.org/10.1002/jaba.778

Fisher, W. W., Luczynski, K. C., Hood, S. A., Lesser, A. D., Machado, M. A., & Piazza, C. C. (2014). Preliminary findings of a randomized clinical trial of a virtual training program for applied behavior analysis technicians. *Research in Autism Spectrum Disorders, 8*(9), 1044−1054. https://doi.org/10.1016/j.rasd.2014.005.002

Fisher, W. W., Rodriguez, N. M., Luczynski, K. C., & Kelley, M. E. (2013). The use of protective equipment in the management of severe behavior disorders. In D. Reed, F. DiGennaro Reed, & J. Luiselli (Eds.), *Handbook of crisis intervention for individuals with developmental disabilities* (pp. 87−105). New York, NY: Springer.

Hayes, S. C. (1981). Single case experimental design and empirical clinical practice. *Journal of Consulting and Clinical Psychology, 49*(2), 193−211. https://doi.org/10.1037/0022-006X.49.2.193

Johnston, J. M., & Pennypacker, H. S. (1993). *Strategies and tactics of behavioral research* (2nd ed.). Hillsdale, NJ: Erlbaum.

Joslyn, P. R., Vollmer, T. R., Dickens, E. N., & Walker, S. F. (2017). Direct assessment of quality of care in secure residential treatment facilities for criminal offenders with intellectual disabilities. *Behavioral Interventions, 33*(1), 13−25. https://doi.org/10.1002/bin.1501

Joslyn, P. R., Vollmer, T. R., & Hernández, V. (2014). Implementation of the good behavior game in classrooms for children with delinquent behavior. *Acta de Investigación Psicológica, 4*(3), 1673−1682. https://doi.org/10.1016/s2007-4719(14)70973-1

Kazdin, A. E. (2011). *Single-case research designs: Methods for clinical and applied settings* (2nd ed.). Oxford University Press.

Kennedy, C. H. (2005). *Single-case designs for educational research.* Boston: Allyn and Bacon.

Kratochwill, T. R., & Levin, J. R. (2014). *Single-case intervention research: Methodological and statistical advances.* American Psychological Association. https://doi.org/10.1037/14376-003

Leachman, M., Masterson, K., & Figueroa, E. (November 29, 2017). A punishing decade for school funding. In *Center on Budget and Policy Priorities.* https://www.cbpp.org/sites/default/files/atoms/files/11-29-17sfp.pdf.

National Institutes of Health. (December 2021). *NIH's Definition of a clinical trial.* https://grants.nih.gov/policy/clinical-trials/definition.htm.

Owen, T. M., Fisher, W. W., Akers, J. S., Sullivan, W. E., Falcomata, T. S., Greer, B. D., … Zangrillo, A. N. (2020). Treating destructive behavior reinforced by increased caregiver compliance with the participant's mands. *Journal of Applied Behavior Analysis, 53*(3), 1494−1513. https://doi.org/10.1002/jaba.674

Peterson, K. M., Ibañez, V. F., Volkert, V. M., Zeleny, J. R., Engler, C. W., & Piazza, C. C. (2021). Using telehealth to provide outpatient follow-up to children with avoidant/restrictive food intake disorder. *Journal of Applied Behavior Analysis, 54*(1), 6−24. https://doi.org/10.1002/jaba.794

Peterson, K. M., Piazza, C. C., Ibañez, V. F., & Fisher, W. W. (2019). Randomized controlled trial of an applied behavior-analytic intervention versus wait-list control for food selectivity in participants with autism spectrum disorder. *Journal of Applied Behavior Analysis, 52*(4), 895−917. https://doi.org/10.1002/jaba.650

Peterson, K. M., Piazza, C. C., & Volkert, V. M. (2016). A comparison of a modified sequential oral sensory approach to an applied behavior-analytic approach in the treatment of food selectivity in children with autism spectrum disorder. *Journal of Applied Behavior Analysis, 49*(3), 485−511. https://doiorg/10.1002/jaba.332.

Roane, H. S., Fisher, W. W., & Carr, J. E. (2016). Applied behavior analysis as treatment for Autism spectrum disorder. *The Journal of Pediatrics, 175*, 27−32. https://doi.org/10.1016/j.jpeds.2016.04.023

Schieltz, K. M., & Wacker, D. P. (2020). Functional assessment and function-based treatment delivered via telehealth: A brief summary. *Journal of Applied Behavior Analysis, 53*(3), 1242−1258. https://doi.org/10.1002/jaba.742

Schwartz, I. S., & Baer, D. M. (1991). Social validity assessments: Is current practice state of the art? *Journal of Applied Behavior Analysis, 24*(2), 189−204. https://doi.org/10.1901/jaba.1991.24-189

Sidman, M. (1960). *Tactics of scientific research: Evaluating experimental data in psychology.* Basic Books.

Tiger, J. H., Fisher, W. W., & Bouxsein, K. J. (2009). Therapist-and self-monitored DRO contingencies as a treatment for the self-injurious skin picking of a young man with Asperger syndrome. *Journal of Applied Behavior Analysis, 42*(2), 315−319. https://doi.org/10.1901/jaba.2009.42-315

Wacker, D. P. (2016). Telehealth. In N. Singh (Ed.), Handbook of evidence-based practices in intellectual and developmental disabilities (pp. 585−613). Cham: Springer. https://doi.org/10.1007/978-3-319-26583-4_22

Chapter 8

Conducting research in applied settings: Aligning research and applied goals

Jill M. Harper
Melmark New England, Andover, MA, United States

Conducting research in applied settings: aligning research with applied goals

Behavior analysis is both a science and a professional practice with a shared foundation of theory and methodology. As a science, behavior analytic research focuses on the study of principles of learning though interactions between the environment and behavior. Research in behavior analysis exists on a continuum from basic to applied, with each domain lending to the evolution of the science and practice (Epling & Pierce, 1986). Behavior analytic research is categorized as basic or applied not by the location in which it is conducted (e.g., laboratory vs. applied setting) but rather by the way in which the specific variables under study are selected (Baer et al., 1968). In an oversimplification, basic research helps to answer questions derived from theories of learning through carefully selected variables while applied research is defined by the application (or extension) and analysis of the science to socially significant variables.

Applied research is the foundation of the field of applied behavior analysis (ABA). In the formative article "Some Current Dimensions of Applied Behavior Analysis," Baer et al. (1968) set forth the defining features of ABA. ABA maintains its roots in the science (e.g., behavioral, analytic, and conceptually systematic) while focusing on areas of social significance, or of immediate importance to stakeholders (e.g., consumer, society). Take, for example, the first publication to exemplify applied research in behavior analysis, "The Psychiatric Nurse as a Behavior Engineer" by Ayllon and Michael (1959). Ayllon and Michael applied behavioral principles (e.g., extinction, reinforcement) to the assessment and treatment of disruptive behavior (e.g., hoarding, wandering) in a hospital setting. This study not only

Research Ethics in Behavior Analysis. https://doi.org/10.1016/B978-0-323-90969-3.00005-0

169

provided simple yet powerful demonstrations of the application of the science of the behavior to areas of social significance, but also systematically adapted research methodology to the applied setting through (1) selection of precise target behaviors with complete operational definitions, (2) systematic data collection, and (3) identification of controlling variables through the demonstration of experimental control (Bailey & Burch, 2017).

In fact, applied research and clinical practice have often been described on a continuum (National Commission for the Protection of Human Subjects of Biomedical and Behavioral Research [NCPHSBBR], 1979). The extent to which the science and clinical practice of behavior analysis should and do overlap is both an area of question and an area of debate (e.g., Johnson, 1992; Malott, 2018; Pritchard & Wine, 2015; Reid, 1992). Some members of the ABA community have expressed the view that practitioners should focus on the application of the science to produce meaningful change and that research methodology is not necessary to accomplish clinical goals (e.g., Malott, 1992). Other members of the community have noted that training in and application of research methodology are an essential component of good clinical practice as it allows practitioners to solve clinical problems through the extension of the current literature (e.g., Reid, 1992). With shared methodology across research and clinical practice, research-oriented practice is inherent to the field of ABA (e.g., Baer et al., 1968; LeBlanc et al., 2018; Norman, 2008).

Thus, the question is not so much should the science and clinical practice overlap, they already do. What needs to be clarified is how the clinical practice of behavior analysis fundamentally differs from that of the application of behavior analysis for scientific purposes (Baer et al., 1968; Barlow et al., 1984; Cooper et al., 2020; Johnston, 1996). The defining feature of clinical practice is the application of the principles of the science of behavior to *produce socially significant change for the individual client* (Johnson, 1996; Pierce & Epling, 1980) while the defining feature of research often includes the objective to extend *generalizable knowledge*. For example, research is defined in the Belmont Report (1979) to include any activity designed to *develop or contribute to generalizable knowledge* through hypothesis testing, which permits conclusions to be made. Similarly, the BACB defines research as, "Any data-based activity, including analysis of preexisting data, designed to *generate generalizable knowledge for the discipline* [emphasis added]" (BACB, 2020, p. 8).

Often times, the intersection of these two activities, research and practice, is the origin of applied research. Therefore, the fundamental distinction between research and practice is necessary to identify under what conditions research requirements should be applied. The aforementioned definitions highlight the functional difference between the two—the purpose of the activity itself. If the purpose of the activity is to produce meaningful change for the individual served *and nothing else*, the activity is best categorized as clinical practice. But, when the purpose of the activity extends to, "*generate generalizable knowledge,*" the activity must be categorized as research (e.g., LeBlanc et al., 2018; NCPHSBBR, 1979).

Ethical guidelines provide general rules of conduct. Professionals are tasked with applying these general rules to the specific situations encountered in research (basic and applied) and clinical practice alike (Cox, 2020; NCPHSBBR, 1979). For example, one general ethical guideline (beneficence) states that benefits should out weight risks; however, there is no one formula that allows the evaluation of benefits and risks to each specific situation that may be encountered. This example demonstrates the complexity of navigating the generality of ethical guidelines, which often requires the evaluation of multiple variables within specific situations and at times, may require the consideration of multiple ethical guidelines (Cox, 2020). Thus, the outcomes of ethical situations similar in nature (e.g., risks vs. benefits) may be different depending on the context in which the situation arises. To behave ethically in research and practice is more than simply following a set of rules or guidelines. Ethical research requires continuous and careful consideration of how the general ethical principles and codes of professional conduct are best applied to the situation at hand, throughout the research process from inception to dissemination (Lindoff, 2010).

This chapter discusses how to ethically conduct research in applied settings and develop ethical systems for creating sustainable research practices in nonacademic organizations. The chapter provides an organizational perspective for establishing effective collaborations of clinical practice and research. Consideration is given to the contingencies of external researchers (e.g., sustained access to applied settings) and organizations (e.g., research directly targets the organization's mission; minimal noncompensated cost). Examples of organizational research practices are included throughout.

Ethics of conducting research in applied settings: general principles and specific codes

Behavior analysts must take many factors into consideration (e.g., general ethical principles, specific professional ethics code) well before they embark on the journey of conducting research within an applied setting. One critical area of consideration is the protection of research participants. Research conducted within applied settings involves human participants, and thus, requires the protection of the rights and welfare of those participants (e.g., American Psychological Association (APA), 2017; Behavior Analysis Certification Board (BCBA), 2020; NCPHSBBR, 1979). Ethical guidelines and federal regulations for the protection of human participants (e.g., Nuremberg Code, Declaration of Helsinki, Belmont Report, and the Protection of Human Subjects) arose form a series of unfortunate, and unethical research-related events throughout the 1900s (e.g., Mandal et al., 2011; Miracle, 2016).

Together, these guidelines and regulations provide the basis of research ethics today including the ethics of research in behavior analysis.

The Belmont Report (1979) summarizes three general ethical principles that guide research involving human participants (1) respect for persons, (2) beneficence, and (3) justice.

The principles set forth in the Belmont Report are intended to be used as a framework for ethical decision-making and problem-solving in the context of research activities and as such, have been incorporated into many professional codes of ethics, including the Ethics Code for Behavior Analysts (hereafter referred to as the BACB Code) published by the Behavior Analysis Certification Board (BACB, 2020). Within this section of the chapter, the ethics of conducting research with an applied setting will be discussed in terms of the general ethical principles and application of the principles as outlined in the Belmont Report (NCPHSBBR, 1979), and specific examples will be described using the BACB Code.

Respect for persons. The principle of respect for persons highlights two areas of ethical considerations when planning and conducting research activities with human participants. First, respect for persons holds that individuals are autonomous and, therefore, should maintain the right to participate or decline the request to participate in research. Second, some individuals may have a reduced capacity as it relates to autonomy, and additional safeguards should be put into place to ensure the protection of these individuals. Respect for persons aligns with requirements of informed consent required by federal regulation (Protection of Human Subjects, 2009) and by the BACB Code (2020). Behavior analyst conducting research within applied settings must be familiar with the conditions under which and the process by which informed consent is obtained across both research (BACB Code 6.04) and practice (BACB Code 2.11).

Many individuals served in applied behavior analytic settings are considered members of vulnerable populations such as children and individuals with cognitive impairments (e.g., intellectual and development disabilities) and, as such, additional safeguards are needed when seeking informed consent for participation in research. Because of the vulnerable nature of individuals served in applied settings, informed consent is often obtained through parents or other legal guardians. Careful attention must be paid to the way in which informed consent is presented to ensure the necessary information is included in a way that can be comprehended and that consent remains voluntary, without coercion and undue influence (U.S. Department of Health and Human Services Office of Human Research Protections [USDHHSOHRP], 2016b).

Because clinical services are also provided within applied contexts, the delineation of research and practice must be clear when obtaining informed consent (LeBlanc et al., 2018). Parents or guardians must be provided with, and understand what will be involved as part of the research and how, if at all, participation in the research will affect clinical services. For example, let's say that a research-oriented practitioner has obtained consent for a study that compares the effects of two different interventions for self-injurious behavior. In this case, it would be important to discuss both when each intervention will be implemented (e.g., only during research sessions), what will occur outside of research sessions (e.g., what intervention will be implemented when the individual is not participating), and at what point what point the results of the research will be incorporated into the behavior intervention plan, if at all. Only with a comprehensive understanding of the interaction between research and clinical service such as these will the guardian be able to make a choice about informed consent in the best interest of the participant.

The voluntary requirement of informed consent requires consideration around the relationship between those seeking consent and the individual providing consent (Greaney et al., 2012). Several areas of the BACB Code are relevant here, including conflicts of interest (BACB Code 6.07) and multiple (BABC Code 1.11) or coercive and exploitive relationships (BACB Code 1.13). Services provided within applied settings often involve ongoing, collaborative relationships between practitioners and families. Through this collaborative relationship, families may begin to feel a sense of commitment to practitioner and organization providing care for their loved ones. With this sense of commitment may come a sense of obligation to consent to participate in research despite remaining concerns or for fear that services will be impacted if consent is not provided, even if explicitly told otherwise (LeBlanc et al., 2018). Researchers in applied settings should take precaution when seeking informed consent in the context of multiple roles (e.g., practitioner and researcher). One precaution might include a clear definition of the role under which consent is being requested and explicit statement around the independence of the consent for research and clinical services. It is the burden of the research to ensure informed consent is obtained without undue influence.

Another related are of ethical concern when informed consent is obtained through a parent or guardian is that of assent from the participant themselves. Assent is defined as, "Affirmative agreement to participate in research" (USDHHSOHRP, 2016b). Assent, when required, should involve an active affirmative response on the part of the participant (Morris et al., 2021). Obtaining assent may prove difficult when working with individuals with reduced cognitive capacities, like those often served in applied behavior analytic settings. Consider a child diagnosed with Autism who does not yet reliably answer "yes" or "no" when offered known preferred items. How should the researcher go about defining assent for such an individual? Assent should be defined based on the abilities of the individual participant. Assent does not always mean a vocal-verbal affirmation, but should demonstrate respect of the person (participant) through the careful selection of responses that demonstrate affirmation and refusal to participate (e.g., showing displeasure or lack of interest in participating). In the above example, assent might be defined as accepting the researchers hand when offered and physically transitioning to the location of research sessions independently. Operationally defined active assent responses allow for the protection of the individual participant though differential consequences (e.g., continuing or terminating research sessions).

Beneficence. When referencing the principle of beneficence, it is common to see the phrase, "do no harm" (NCPHSBBR, 1979). "Do no harm" is an essential part of the principle of beneficence, but this principle extends to maximizing benefits while minimizing the risks of participation. All research likely involves some level of actual or potential risk. Risks can take several forms including physical, psychological, financial, or social (e.g., Fujii, 2012; Greaney et al., 2012; Lindoff, 2010; NCPHSBBR, 1979). The principle of beneficence requires researchers to balance the probability and magnitude of each potential risk with direct and indirect benefits not only at the onset but throughout the research process. In essence, the principle of beneficence ensures well-being of participants (Greaney et al., 2012).

When conducting research, the risk–benefit analysis should include considerations across research participants, the organization, and the larger community. There is no one magical formula that aids researchers in the systematic analysis of risks and benefits. Risks are not always actual risks, but may be potential risks at the initiation of the research or may arise as actual or potential risks as the research progresses. For example, a change in the experimental design from a multiple baseline design to a reversal design might increase the risk of harm or frustration upon returning to the baseline condition. Another unanticipated risk might involve negative peer interactions when examining social contingencies. Risks are not always predictable at the onset of the study and often require researchers to evaluate risks and benefits at various points throughout the project.

Research in the context of service delivery (BACB Code 6.03) requires behavior analysts to, "… Arrange research activities such that the client services and client welfare are prioritized" (BACB, 2020, p. 17). A simple example of this might involve the way in which research sessions are scheduled. Let's say that an individual has consented or assented to participate in a research study and that upon scheduling sessions the researcher has requested to remove the individual from the classroom environment during a regularly scheduled social skills group, which happens to also be a target on the individualized education plan. In alignment with BACB Code 6.03, the researcher should consider alternative times to conduct research sessions, thereby minimizing the effects of the research on the individual's clinical and educational services. This is just one example of the way in which clinical services and client welfare can be prioritized when conducting research in applied settings. The point here is that as researchers, we must continually examine the way in which the research we conduct both directly and indirectly impacts individuals involved across risks and benefits alike.

Justice. Justice requires that the burdens and benefits of research are balanced (Lindorff, 2010; Miracle, 2016). While the Belmont Report discussed justice in terms of participant selection, the principle of justice also seems applicable to other areas of research in applied settings such as competing contingencies of different persons involved in the research (e.g., researchers, participants), as well as individuals or groups who may be indirectly impacted by the research (e.g., related populations, organizations) and the balance between contingencies controlling the behavior of research-oriented practitioners.

As it relates to participant selection, justice must be considered in terms of both the specific individuals selected for participation and the greater social groups relevant to the research at hand (NCPHSBBR, 1979). Justice requires the burden of research participation such as time, effort, and resources to be balanced across potential individual participants and groups rather than selection of participation based on variables such as availability (Lindoff, 2010). Two considerations around justice and participant selection are particularly relevant to research in applied settings. First, applied settings that support applied research may, by default, place additional burden on the individuals they serve clinically. Individuals who received clinical services within organizations that support research are more likely to be asked to participate than those who are served within organizations who do not support research. It is also possible, however, that individuals who participate in research may also access greater benefits, or at least more immediate benefits of the research in which they participate. Second, and more broadly speaking, specific populations (e.g., Autism) are typically served in applied settings that offer behavior analytic services. Thus, these populations as a whole may bear more burden in terms of research participation then other populations (e.g., neurotypical individuals) who may also benefit from ABA research outcomes. For example, outcomes from research in areas such as behavior analytic teaching procedures or strategies for behavior management established in applied settings with a neurodiverse population might then be extended to general education practices. There may not be an immediate solution to the potential ethical concerns around justice as it relates to participant selection; however, researchers should continue conversations of the need to balance the burdens and benefits when conducting research in applied settings.

The contingencies controlling the behavior of the researcher likely differ depending on the reason or context under which the research is conducted (Lindoff, 2010; Reid, 1992). The behavior of any researcher may be under the control of multiple variables such as recognition of work through awards, professional development opportunities such as presentation and publication, or job advancement (LeBlanc et al., 2018). For example, student research conducted as part of a degree requirement (e.g., master's thesis or doctoral dissertation) is likely controlled by contingencies around graduation and publication (e.g., Malott, 2002) while research conducted by university faculty is likely controlled by contingencies around job security (e.g., tenure) or grant funding. Organizational leaders may be motivated by obtaining positive outcomes of research examining the effectiveness of provided services (e.g., assessment and intervention) and organizational practices (e.g., integrity). Lindoff (2010) discussed competing contingencies (e.g., potential conflicts of interest—BACB Code 1.11) that must be balanced when different types of research are conducted within applied settings. For example, an organization may be more likely to consent to research proposed by a university researcher if the area of research is likely to provide direct benefits to the organization or individual participants. The university researcher may in turn be motivated to propose research in an area supported by the organization to access ongoing resources provided through such a collaboration (e.g., participants). In the above example, the researcher's interests in the selection of the experimental question and the need for access to participants may be in conflict.

The contingencies that control the behavior of the researcher, the organization, and even the larger community are complex and may be difficult to change, but as researchers it is our responsibility to try. Malot (2002) proposed several ways in which the balance of burden and benefit might be established between university researchers and the applied organizations within which their research is conducted. For example, researchers could be required to ensure that outcomes are incorporated into clinical practice through direct service and training and student and faculty researchers might be required to complete service hours within the research setting through practicum placements or consultative services. What is important is the ongoing discussion of how different and sometimes competing contingencies can be balanced to ensure justice through the shared burden and benefit to all involved.

Competing contingencies can also occur when practitioners take on the role of researcher. As discussed in the context of informed consent, multiple relationships (BACB Code 6.07) and potential conflicts of interest (BACB Code 1.11) are inherent when practitioners conduct research within the framework of research-oriented practice (e.g., LeBlanc et al., 2018; Malott, 2018). The roles of both researcher and practitioner are at play and the contingencies influencing behavior are at times competing. Thus, the research-oriented practitioner should take proactive steps to well define each role (BACB Code 1.04) and to identify when the role of researcher and the role of practitioner may be in conflict. One way to help manage multiple relationships and to better define roles may be to limit the extent to which a practitioner can also serve as the lead researcher for individuals on their caseload. Providing distance between the role of practitioner and the role of research may avoid the potential conflict between motivation of maintaining experimental control (as a researcher) and motivation for positive treatment effects (as a practitioner).

It is the responsibility of each member of a professional field (e.g., behavior analysis) to be familiar with and apply the general ethical principles of respect for persons, justice, and beneficence, as well as the specific code of

TABLE 8.1 Ethical principles and corresponding applications set forth in the Belmont Report (1979).

Ethical principle	Principle in application
Respect for persons - Individuals are autonomous - Individuals with decreased autonomy should be protected	Informed consent and assent - Information - Comprehension - Voluntariness
Beneficence - Do no harm - Maximize benefits and minimize potential harm	Risk-benefit analysis - Initial analysis - Ongoing monitoring
Justice - Even distribution of burden and benefits	Recruitment and selection of participants - Individuals selected - Social groups included

ethics adopted by that profession (e.g., BACB Code) to their research practices. In addition to describing the ethical principles of research, the Belmont Report (1979) also outlined ways in which the ethical principles can be applied during the research process (informed consent, risk—benefit analysis, selection of participants) (Table 8.1). Notwithstanding the responsibility of the individual researcher, organizations can uphold the integrity of research ethics within their setting by establishing ethical systems with respect to the general principles described in the Belmont report. The next section of this chapter will provide recommendations on ways in which organizations can promote ethical and sustainable research practices through the establishment of effective collaborations of research and clinical practice. But first, a discussion on the distinction of research and clinical practice is warranted.

Ethical systems for creating sustainable research practices

Research within applied settings requires a complex skill set that extends beyond research methodology. Reid (1992) proposed that the success of applied research is dependent on how the research is conducted in relation to the resources and routine practices of the setting in which it is conducted. Reid provides examples of how conducting applied research may be enhanced by practices such as balancing the specific topics of research between the interests of the organization and the interests of the researcher (the principle of justice), planning experimental methods that support clinical services (e.g., day-to-day operations), and collaborating with staff at the organization. Other authors have also examined the conditions under which research in applied settings is either accelerated or hindered (e.g., Kelly et al., 2015; Valentino & Juanico, 2020).

Kelley et al. (2015) conducted an indirect assessment on the practices of productive applied researchers. The authors conducted a literature review to identify the most "prolific" applied researchers in the field based on the total number of publications over a 14-year span and then identified potential controlling variables of research productivity through interviews. From these interviews, Kelley et al. provided the following recommendations to increase or maintain research productivity within applied settings, (1) meet regularly with research community including peers, collaborators, and supervises; (2) use data collection methods that are economical, reliable, and when possible use current resources (e.g., staff) to collect data; (3) employ a collaborative writing approach; (4) establish dedicated time to research activities; and (5) remain intimate with your project from inception to publication.

Valentino and Juanico (2020) took a different approach to the extension of the work of Kelley et al. (2015) when they asked participants of their survey to identify common barriers to conducting applied research. Four prominent barriers were identified in the areas of, (1) access to an institutional review board (IRB)/research review committee (RRC), (2) dedicated time, (3) mentorship, and (4) research community. Valentino and Juanico offer recommendations to overcoming each identified barrier that included behavior change at the level of the practitioner, as well as organizational changes to support the behavior of the individual practitioners employed.

Kelly et al. (2015) and Valentino and Juanico (2020) provided some descriptive data on variables that may prevent (barriers) or facilitate (solutions) conducting research within applied settings. The examination of barriers to conducting research in applied settings must continue through careful consideration of the environmental variables (e.g., contingencies) that establish and maintain research activities, clinical practice, and the integration of research and practice goals both at the individual and organizational levels. Essential to the analysis is the consideration of ethical practices across both research and clinical systems alike.

Establish Culture that Supports Research. As it relates to research, the behavior of the organization and its individual members is driven by mission, vision, and commitment as designed by the leadership team. Both the organization as whole and its individual members benefit when an organization makes a commitment to the integration of applied research and clinical practice. Reid (1992) summarized the indirect benefits of commitment to a research-focused mission to include avoidance of the adoption of unfounded research and clinical practices through informed consumption and evaluation of the current literature, improvement of clinical systems through the integration of research practices lending to the incorporation of current best practice, and professional development opportunities and service provisions related to research activities such as consultation and presentations.

Commitment to applied research at the organizational level may take many forms, several of which could address the barriers of and solutions to conducting research in applied settings such as the dedication of organizational resources to research and the establishment of collaborative research communities (Kelley et al., 2015; Valentino & Juanico, 2020). Resources dedicated to research might include positions, materials (e.g., computers, software), space, and time. Research takes time. Dedicated time was identified as a way to facilitate (e.g., Kelley et al., 2015) research productivity in applied settings. An organization will fall short in its support of research without the dedication of time to research activities.

With its commitment to time, an organization may provide organizational support through the personnel. Organizations could dedicate entire positions to research activities (e.g., director of research, postdoctoral internships) or include research activities in aspects of different job positions (e.g., research-oriented practitioner, director of training and research). While a dedicated research position would limit competing priorities, funding a dedicated position may be difficult in some cases. Many applied settings receive funding though federal, state, or local agencies based on the services provided under which a dedicated research position may not be covered. On the other hand, the inclusion of research activities across different job positions may decrease the burden of funding but could increase the probability that competing priorities could delay or disrupt research activities.

Another way in which organizations can support research is through the establishment of research teams or groups to facilitate the development of a research community. The inclusion of research groups would not only provide dedicated time for research activities, but also provide opportunities for collaboration and mentorship. Research groups may meet on some regular schedule to complete activities such as review current literature (e.g., Parsons & Reid, 2011), prepare research proposals, and monitor ongoing research projects. Research meetings would provide a mentorship and collaboration during which theoretical, technical, and ethical considerations of research in applied settings can be discussed.

Organizations may demonstrate commitment to applied research through the development of organizational research agendas informed by systematic data and supplemented by individual case studies. Organizational agendas might address broad topic areas such as assessment methodology, staff training, or skill acquisition while providing specific examples through independent studies. This avenue of organizational research practice likely requires fewer dedicated resources and less dedicated time as compared to research groups, but still allows for the mentorship and collaboration throughout the data analysis and dissemination processes. For example, key organizational personnel (or collaborators across smaller practice organizations and research institutions) might meet for a few hours per quarter to discuss research projects, provide research mentorship, and review organizational research agendas.

The above examples are just that, examples of ways in which organizations can create the foundations of culture that integrate applied research and clinical practice. Each organization, with its unique structure, will need to evaluate how best to create a culture supportive of research within the applied setting. Although the structure of organizational systems that support research in applied settings may differ, each should emphasize the ethical principles that guide research activity.

Align Methodology Across Research and Clinical Practice. Methodological and procedural similarities are evident across research and practice within the field of ABA (Barlow et al., 1984; Kazdin, 2011). The basic steps are similar, a question is formulated, participants are selected, a protocol is designed and implemented, and results are shared (Bailey & Burch, 2016; Barlow et al., 1984; Cooper et al., 2020). A summary of the methodological steps across research and practice is provided in Table 8.2.

Closer examination of the procedural similarities across research and clinical practice can help to identify systems that ease the alignment of these two activities within applied settings. Some procedural components such as data collection, reliability, and integrity measures can be shared across research and clinical systems. For example, data collection systems and the collection of reliability and integrity data are critical components of both

TABLE 8.2 Comparison of applied research and clinical evaluation components.

Applied research	Clinical evaluation
1. Question to understand functional relations between socially significant behavior and environmental variables	1. Question determined by clinical needs of client(s)
2. Participation based on variables under study	2. Participation based clinical need
3. Design specific to experimental question	3. Design specific to clinical environment
4. Systematic data collected	4. Systematic data collected
5. Intervention selection specific to experimental question	5. Intervention selection based on clinical environment
6. Professional dissemination may result	6. Socially significant outcomes may result in professional dissemination

Adapted from Cooper, J. O., Heron, T. E., & Heward, W. L. (2020). Applied behavior analysis (3rd ed.). Hoboken, NJ: Pearson Education; Barlow, D. H., Hayes, S. C., & Nelson, R. O. (1984). The scientist practitioner: Research and accountability in clinical and educational settings (No. 128). Pergamon.

research and practice (e.g., Doucette et al., 2012; Kratochwill & Wetzel, 1977; Vollmer et al., 2008). That is, data need to be collected as means to evaluate research and clinical interventions alike, and the inclusion of interobserver agreement and procedural or treatment integrity measures strengthens the demonstrated effects whether in research or practice. Therefore, to the extent possible, organizations might consider using the same general practices to collect data, ensure data are reliable, and ensure procedures (e.g., research protocol, clinical intervention) are implemented with accuracy.

In a recent study, Hartz et al. (2021) successfully increased the integrity with which staff in an applied setting collected interobserver reliability data through a brief, behavioral skills training (BST) session. This study demonstrated a system within clinical practice that also meets the standards for research practice—reliability data collection by two, simultaneous but independent observers. There are several benefits to the alignment of research and clinical systems such as the one demonstrated by Hartz et al. (2021). First, alignment of research and clinical practices might minimize the need for additional organizational resources to conduct research. Second, the integration of research and clinical systems promotes research-oriented practice through contribution to the *generalizable knowledge* when warranted and research informed by clinical practices within the context of ongoing service delivery. To maintain ethical practices, organizations should ask *what actions should be taken by the researcher or practitioner when research informs clinical practice and clinical practice guides research activity?*

Research-oriented practice. At times, activities fall distinctively into the category of research *or* practice but at other times, the lines between research and practice become blurred. Organizations can align ethical research practice through systems that include clear delineations of research and practice as previously described in this chapter. Recall, clinical practice is designed to meet the needs of the individual client *and* does not include prior plans to increase general knowledge. Clinical activity that meets both of these criteria (and therefore not defined as research) would follow the policies and procedures outlined within the organization's clinical systems and abide by ethical codes directly related to practice (e.g., BACB Code Section 2—Responsibility in Practice). An example of clinical practice might involve the systematic replication of published literature to reduce attention maintained aggression across settings (e.g., school, home, community) using a multiple baseline design. Although in this example, the behavior analyst used previous literature to inform the intervention and demonstrated experimental control, the data will not be shared with the larger community and therefore, would not be considered an example of research.

Research, on the other hand, is designed to answer an empirical question and often includes prior plans of dissemination to increase generalizable knowledge. The previous example would quickly become an example of research if, upon completing the literature review, the behavior analyst planned to share the results of the proposed treatment analysis with the larger community through presentation or publication. In this case, the behavior analyst should follow the policies and procedures outlined within the organizations research systems and abide by ethical codes directly related to research (e.g., BACB Code Section 6—Responsibility in Research).

At times a behavior analyst might decide retrospectively that the outcome of a clinical assessment or intervention should be shared to contribute to generalizable knowledge either as a single case study or replicated with additional individuals. In both of these cases, the activity would transition from clinical practice to research at the point at which the behavior analyst planned to share the data in an effort to contribute to generalizable knowledge. And at this point, ethical research practices would require peer review of the proposed research and consent to share the data (Protection of Human Subjects, 2009).

Establish System of Peer Review. Once the organization has defined how research and clinical practices will be categorized and the systems under which each will be carried out, processes and procedures for peer review should be established to ensure ethical practices and the protection of all persons involved. The first step in accomplishing this goal is to set up a committee whose primary function is to ensure that proposed research projects follow federal regulation (The Protection of Human Subjects, 2009) and ethical guidelines (APA, 2017; BACB, 2020). And above all, to protect the rights, welfare, safety, and dignity of the participant(s) and the researcher(s) alike.

The BACB Code 6.02 (Research Review) requires that all research conducted by behavior analysts must be reviewed by a "formal research review committee" (BACB, 2020, p. 17) prior to implementation and provides a broad definition of an RRC to include,

> A group of professionals whose stated purpose is to review research proposals to ensure the ethical treatment of human research participants. This committee might be an official entity of a government or university (e.g., IRB), Research Ethics Board, an independent committee within a service organization, or an independent organization created for this purpose (p. 8).

The BACB's definition maintains the requirement of review to ensure federal and ethical compliance while allowing for flexibility in format. Although this flexibility allows for the contribution of research from organizations in the absence of affiliation with formal entities, independent RRCs must be carefully established to ensure compliance with laws, regulations, and ethical guidelines. Several authors have provided insight and recommendations that organizations can use when establishing a formal system of ethical review within applied settings (Cox, 2020; LeBlanc et al., 2018).

LeBlanc et al. (2018) provided guidelines for the establishment and ongoing processes of RRC within the context of human service organizations.

The guidelines ensure compliance with both federal regulations and professional codes to cover the areas of committee membership and training, as well as protocols and procedures for submission, review, revision, and monitoring. While you can refer to the LeBlanc et al. (2018) publication for a more detailed description, the main points will be summarized here.

The RRC serves as the gatekeeper to the integrity of ethical research systems within an organization. Memberships of the RRC must consist of varied members including individuals that are not affiliated with the organization to minimize bias during the review process. The organizational research systems should maintain a detailed outline of processes and procedures specific to applied research proposals to ensure integrity of the review system itself. And finally, members of the RRC should receive explicit training in the protection of human research and requirements of review process (e.g., review, revision, acceptance or rejection, and monitoring). One way to complete this training is through The Collaborative Institutional Training Initiative (https://www.citiprogram.org/), which offers an online training on the previously mentioned components of research review (LeBlanc et al., 2018; Miracle, 2016).

While some RRCs may be the sole review of research conducted within a particular organization, other RRCs may be affiliated with a more formal review process such as university IRB. For example, organizations affiliated with university programs often require an initial review and subsequent letter of support from the affiliate program prior to submission of the proposal to the university IRB. Another model of review employed may involve an organizational proposal to an affiliate IRB for consent to conduct research in a particular area (e.g., educational assessment, treatment of problem behavior). In this case, the RRC may review and make a decision on research proposals within specific areas of research but may request that the proposal be directly reviewed by the university IRB if the research proposal falls outside of the particular research area. These examples provide a number of models from which organizations can establish a peer review process of research proposed within a clinical setting.

The principal function of RRC is to review the ethical basis of the research proposal to ensure that it aligns with federal and ethical standards including the ethical principles of respect of persons (informed consent and assent), beneficence (risk—benefit analysis), and justice (fair procedures around participant selection). Although organizations may establish systems to promote alignment of research and clinical practices, it is through the establishment an RRC that organizations commit to ethical research practices by all of its individual members. Through the review process, areas of needed development around ethical research practices will be identified (e.g., assent procedures may be lacking across proposals). Organizations can use such information to modify systems related to areas of deficit and provide additional training and resources to researchers within the applied setting.

Align Training and Supervision Systems. Although students of behavior analysis are required to complete coursework in research methodology, there is no performance competency requirement; therefore, some practitioners enter the applied setting with no previous research experience. And even when practitioners gain some level of supervised research experience during their training program, the degree to which these experiences demonstrate competence in the specific area of applied research is likely to vary (Shawler et al., 2018). Master's degree requirements may range from no formal experience to capstone projects or formal thesis requirements. A capstone project typically demonstrates the application of behavior principles without demonstration of experimental control. Thesis requirements may include demonstration of skills for assessing literature (i.e., formulating the research question), selection of research methodology, implementing the research protocol, analyzing the data, and some method of communicating the results (e.g., oral presentation, written presentation). Although there may be some similarities between the degree research requirements and research within an applied setting such as the selection of experimental design, measurement, and visual display of the data, conducting research within an applied setting often requires additional pragmatic considerations (e.g., Critchfield, 2015; Reid, 1992; Valentino & Juanico, 2020) and will often require further training to some standard of competence.

Just as clinical practice must remain with the practitioner's scope of competence (BACB Code 1.06), the behavior analyst must also remain within their scope of competence as it relates to research activity (BACB Code 6.06). The applied researcher must limit *independent* activities to those on which they have been trained and demonstrated competency, otherwise the applied researcher must seek additional training and ongoing supervision until competence has been demonstrated. As pointed out by Cox (2020), a standard definition of competence cannot be found as competence is often defined by an individual's learning history. Therefore, it is important for organizations to determine set criteria for competence in research practices. And because of the complex nature of conducting research, specifically within applied settings, requirements of competence should involve the demonstration across a number of component skills extending from selection the research question and specific procedures (e.g., experimental design, measurement) to the application of ethical principles throughout the research process. Organizations may be tasked not only with defining and measuring competence in research practices but also providing training and ongoing mentorship when skills are not yet demonstrated.

Competency- and performance-based methods such as BST (e.g., Parsons et al., 2012) have been established as effective training procedures. BST involves providing a written description and verbal of the skill including the rationale followed by modeling of the skill by the trainer and practice session with feedback until some criterion of competency is met. Examples of training on many of the essential components of an applied research repertoire have already been demonstrated within the literature including, collecting data (Dempsey et al., 2012; Mayer & DiGennaro Reed, 2013), implementing protocols (e.g., Hogan et al., 2015; Love et al., 2013), completing procedural integrity checks (Doucette et al., 2012; Hartz et al., 2021), and creating graphs (Kranak et al., 2019). While other component skills necessary to carry out applied research have not necessarily been demonstrated through empirical studies, discussion articles can be used to guide practitioner behavior around these skills such contacting (Briggs & Mitteer, 2021; Carr & Briggs, 2010), reviewing (Parsons & Reid, 2011), and evaluating (Green, 2010) the literature. Organizations could offer such component trainings to practitioners who have expressed interest in conducting applied research but are lacking the necessary training and experience.

While previous research focused on training of one specific component skills of applied research, Love et al. (2013) examined the effects of a modified BST on the repertoire of applied research across 24 clinical staff. The BST curriculum consisted of knowledge competencies assessed through pre- and posttests following didactic lectures and practice opportunities across skills (e.g., measurement, single-subject design, research ethics, and protocol development and implementation) The modified BST curriculum was effective in establishing competency in the targeted research skills within an applied setting. Organizations and universities might also consider using a systematic training curriculum such as that described by Love et al. (2013) when training practitioners to conduct research within applied settings. Although training may produce competence as it relates to conducting research, training alone will not necessarily maintain research productivity. Recall that one of the barriers to conducting applied research noted by Valentino and Juanico (2020) was lack of a mentorship. Thus, ongoing supervision and mentorship should be established to maintain productive organizational research systems.

Conclusions: fitting ethical principles into applied research practices

The three ethical principles set forth by the Belmont Report (1979)—respect for persons, beneficence, and justice—provide general guidance around the ethics of research practices alongside professional codes of conduct (e.g., APA, 2017; BACB, 2020). The generality of ethical principles (e.g., NCPHSBBR, 1979) and codes (e.g., BACB, 2020) allows them to be applied to a variety of unique situations (Cox, 2020; Kelly et al., 2021). The application of the ethical principles facilitates the protection of participants through research review, informed consent, risk—benefit analysis, and fairness in participant selection (NCPHSBBR, 1979). Organizational systems can establish sustainable research practices that align research and practice goals within applied settings such as setting up research communities, establishing consistent methodology across research and practice, creating models of research review, and training and mentoring other in research practice. Such organizational systems not only align research and practice goals but can also contribute to research ethics in applied settings through the application general principles and codes in several ways.

Organizational systems can provide a platform for the discussion of ethical considerations across research activities. For example, systems that support organizational research such as the establishment of research communities can provide a platform for discussion around ethical considerations as they pertain to the research process. Discussions within such a platform may be enhanced through a standard meeting agenda that includes activities such as contacting current literature on research ethics or reviewing of case scenarios with guided practice on the application of ethical principles and codes. Another example of how organizational systems can actively engage researchers in discussion of ethical considerations is through the interaction between researchers and RRCs (Lindoff, 2010). The review of research by RRCs is often a passive process by which researchers and reviewers communicate asynchronously. Instead, organizations require synchronous reviews during which researchers orally present the research proposal to include rationale and justification for decisions pertaining to research ethics. Active dialogue would help to better understand the ways in which researchers integrate general ethical principles and codes into their research practice.

Some organizational systems directly contribute to the application of research ethics in practice. The alignment of research and clinical methodology directly relates to both the principle of beneficence and the principle of justice. In terms of beneficence, methodology itself can impact the probability of risk or benefit of the research to both the immediate participant and the greater community (Greaney et al., 2012). For example, research with poor experimental control may falsely identify an "effective" intervention. Risk of harm then follows if that intervention is incorporated into the clinical services for the immediate participants or informs clinical practice for similar populations. As it relates to justice, alignment of research and clinical practice can reduce the burden of those involved in research by reducing the need for dedicated resources to conduct research in applied settings and by increasing the feasibility of conducting research in the context of ongoing daily activities, thus allowing participants to may remain within the educational/clinical setting. Researchers within applied settings should be aware of the ways in which organizational systems directly contribute to research ethics and provide such information with research applications.

Organizational systems such as those described in this chapter set the foundation for ethical practice of research conducted within applied settings. The success of these systems is evaluated by the outcomes produced: the ethical behavior of the applied researcher. Researchers must evaluate the current situation and then apply relevant codes and principles of ethics to determine the best course of action (BACB, 2020; Kelly et al., 2021). To analyze the ethical behavior of the researcher is to directly observe the ways in which they apply these general ethical principles and codes to ensure the protection of research participants. The results of such analyses will in turn identify necessary refinements to organizational systems that will further promote ethical behavior of the applied researcher.

References

American Psychological Association. (2017). *Ethical principles of psychologists and code of conduct,* 2002, amended effective June 1, 2010, and January 1, 2017 https://www.apa.org/ethics/code/.

Ayllon, T., & Michael, J. (1959). The psychiatric nurse as a behavioral engineer 1. *Journal of the Experimental Analysis of Behavior,* 2(4), 323−334. https://doi.org/10.1901/jeab.1959.2-323

Baer, D. M., Wolf, M. M., & Risley, T. R. (1968). Some current dimensions of applied behavior analysis. *Journal of Applied Behavior Analysis, 1*(1), 91. https://doi.org/10.1901/jaba.1968.1-91

Bailey, J. S., & Burch, M. R. (2016). Ethics for behavior analysts. Routledge. In J. S. Bailey, & M. R. Burch (Eds.), *Research methods in applied behavior analysis.* Routledge, 2017.

Bailey, J. S., & Burch, M. R. (2017). *Research methods in applied behavior analysis.* Routledge.

Barlow, D. H., Hayes, S. C., & Nelson, R. O. (1984). *The scientist practitioner: Research and accountability in clinical and educational settings (No. 128).* Pergamon.

Behavior Analyst Certification Board. (2020). *Ethics code for behavior analysts.* Littleton, CO: Author.

Briggs, A. M., & Mitteer, D. R. (2021). Updated strategies for making regular contact with the scholarly literature. *Behavior Analysis in Practice,* 1−12. https://doi.org/10.1007/s40617-021-00590-8

Carr, J. E., & Briggs, A. M. (2010). Strategies for making regular contact with the scholarly literature. *Behavior Analysis in Practice, 3*(2), 12−18. https://doi.org/10.1007/BF03391760

Cooper, J. O., Heron, T. E., & Heward, W. L. (2020). *Applied behavior analysis* (3rd ed.). Hoboken, NJ: Pearson Education.

Cox, D. J. (2020). A guide to establishing ethics committees in behavioral health settings. *Behavior Analysis in Practice, 13*(4), 939−949.

Critchfield, T. M. (2015). What counts as high-quality practitioner training in applied behavior analysis? *Behavior Analysis in Practice, 8*(1), 3−6. https://doi.org/10.1007/s40617-015-0049-0

Dempsey, C. M., Iwata, B. A., Fritz, J. N., & Rolider, N. U. (2012). Observer training revisited: A comparison of in vivo and video instruction. *Journal of Applied Behavior Analysis, 45*(4), 827−832. https://doi.org/10.1901/jaba.2012.45-827

Doucette, S., DiGennaro Reed, F. D., Reed, D. D., Maguire, H., & Marquardt, H. (2012). Implementation of a posted schedule to increase class-wide interobserver agreement assessment. *Journal of Organizational Behavior Management, 32*(3), 263−269. https://doi.org/10.1080/01608061.2012.698187

Epling, W. F., & Pierce, W. D. (1986). The basic importance of applied behavior analysis. *The Behavior Analyst, 9*(1), 89−99. https://doi.org/10.1007/BF03391932

Fujii, L. A. (2012). Research ethics 101: Dilemmas and responsibilities. *PS: Political Science & Politics, 45*(4), 717−723. https://doi.org/10.1017/S1049096512000819

Greaney, A. M., Sheehy, A., Heffernan, C., Murphy, J., Mhaolrúnaigh, S. N., Heffernan, E., & Brown, G. (2012). Research ethics application: A guide for the novice researcher. *British Journal of Nursing, 21*(1), 38−43.

Green, G. (2010). Training practitioners to evaluate evidence about interventions. *European Journal of Behavior Analysis, 11*(2), 223–228. https://doi.org/10.1080/15021149.2010.11434346

Hartz, R. M., Gould, K., Harper, J. M., & Luiselli, J. K. (2021). Assessing interobserver agreement (IOA) with procedural integrity: Evaluation of training methods among classroom instructors. *Child & Family Behavior Therapy, 43*(1), 1–12. https://doi.org/10.1080/00168890.2020.1848404

Hogan, A., Knez, N., & Kahng, S. (2015). Evaluating the use of behavioral skills training to improve school staffs' implementation of behavior intervention plans. *Journal of Behavioral Education, 24*(2), 242–254. https://doi.org/10.1007/s10864-014-9213-9

Johnston, J. M. (1992). Managing our own behavior: Some hidden issues. *Journal of Applied Behavior Analysis, 25*(1), 93. https://doi.org/10.1901/jaba.1992.25-93

Johnston, J. M. (1996). Distinguishing between applied research and practice. *The Behavior Analyst, 19*(1), 35–47. https://doi.org/10.1007/BF03392737

Kazdin, A. E. (2011). *Single case research design in clinical and applied settings.* New York: Oxford University Press.

Kelley, D. P., Wilder, D. A., Carr, J. E., Rey, C., Green, N., & Lipschultz, J. (2015). Research productivity among practitioners in behavior analysis: Recommendations from the prolific. *Behavior Analysis in Practice, 8*(2), 201–206. https://doi.org/10.1007/s40617-015-0064-1

Kelly, E. M., Greeny, K., Rosenberg, N., & Schwartz, I. (2021). When rules are not enough: Developing principles to guide ethical conduct. *Behavior Analysis in Practice, 14*(2), 491–498. https://doi.org/10.1007/s40617-020-00515-x

Kranak, M. P., Shapiro, M. N., Sawyer, M. R., Deochand, N., & Neef, N. A. (2019). Using behavioral skills training to improve graduate students' graphing skills. *Behavior Analysis: Research and Practice, 19*(3), 247–260. https://doi.org/10.1037/bar0000131

Kratochwill, T. R., & Wetzel, R. J. (1977). Observer agreement, credibility, and judgement: Some considerations in presenting observer agreement data. *Journal of Applied Behavior Analysis, 10*(1), 133–139. https://doi.org/10.1901/jaba.1977.10-133

LeBlanc, L. A., Nosik, M. R., & Petursdottir, A. (2018). Establishing consumer protections for research in human service agencies. *Behavior Analysis in Practice, 11*(4), 445–455. https://doi.org/10.1007/s40617-018-0206-3

Lindorff, M. (2010). Ethics, ethical human research and human research ethics committees. *Australian Universities' Review, The, 52*(1), 51–59. https://search.informit.org/doi/10.3316/ielapa.938474897728995.

Love, J. R., Carr, J. E., LeBlanc, L. A., & Kisamore, A. N. (2013). Training behavioral research methods to staff in an early and intensive behavioral intervention setting: A program description and preliminary evaluation. *Education and Treatment of Children, 3*(1), 139–160. https://doi.org/10.1353/etc.2013.0003

Malott, R. W. (1992). Should we train applied behavior analysts to be researchers? *Journal of Applied Behavior Analysis, 25*(1), 83. https://doi.org/10.1901/jaba.1992.25-83

Malott, R. W. (2002). Is it morally defensible to use the developmentally disabled as Guinea pigs. *Behavior and Social Issues, 11*(2), 105–106. https://doi.org/10.5210/bsi.v11i2.90

Malott, R. W. (2018). A model for training science-based practitioners in behavior analysis. *Behavior Analysis in Practice, 11*(3), 196–203. https://doi.org/10.1007/s40617-018-0230-3

Mandal, J., Acharya, S., & Parija, S. C. (2011). Ethics in human research. *Trop Parasitol, 1*(1), 2–3. https://doi.org/10.4103/2229-5070.72105

Mayer, K. L., & DiGennaro Reed, F. D. (2013). Effects of a training package to improve the accuracy of descriptive analysis data recording. *Journal of Organizational Behavior Management, 33*(4), 226–243. https://doi.org/10.1080/01608061.2013.843431

Miracle, V. A. (2016). The Belmont Report: The triple crown of research ethics. *Dimensions of Critical Care Nursing, 35*(4), 223−228. https://doi.org/10.1097/DCC.0000000000000186

Morris, C., Detrick, J. J., & Peterson, S. M. (2021). Participant assent in behavior analytic research: Considerations for participants with autism and developmental disabilities. *Journal of Applied Behavior Analysis, 54*(4), 1300−1316. https://doi.org/10.1002/jaba.859

National Commission for the Protection of Human Subjects of Biomedical and Behavioral Research. (1979). *The Belmont report: Ethical principles and guidelines for the protection of human subjects of research.* U.S. Department of Health and Human Services. https://www.hhs. gov/ohrp/regulations-and-policy/belmont-report/read-the-belmont-report/index.html.

Normand, M. P. (2008). Science, skepticism, and applied behavior analysis. *Behavior Analysis in Practice, 1*(2), 42−49. https://doi.org/10.1007/BF03391727

Parsons, M. B., & Reid, D. H. (2011). Reading groups: A practical means of enhancing professional knowledge among human service practitioners. *Behavior Analysis in Practice, 4*(2), 53−60. https://doi.org/10.1007/BF03391827

Parsons, M. B., Rollyson, J. H., & Reid, D. H. (2012). Evidence-based staff training: A guide for practitioners. *Behavior Analysis in Practice, 5*(2), 2−11. https://doi.org/10.1007/bf03391819

Pierce, W. D., & Epling, W. F. (1980). What happened to analysis in applied behavior analysis? *The Behavior Analyst, 3*(1), 1−9. https://doi.org/10.1007/BF03392373

Pritchard, J. K., & Wine, B. (2015). Icing on the cake: The role of research in practitioner training. *Behavior Analysis in Practice, 8*(2), 140−141.

Protection of Human Subjects. (2009). *45 C.F.R. § 46.101−46.505.*

Reid, D. H. (1992). The need to train more behavior analysts to be better applied researchers. *Journal of Applied Behavior Analysis, 25*(1), 97. https://doi.org/10.1901/jaba.1992.25-97

Shawler, L. A., Blair, B. J., Harper, J. M., & Dorsey, M. F. (2018). A survey of the current state of the scientist-practitioner model in applied behavior analysis. *Education and Treatment of Children, 41*(3), 277−297. https://doi.org/10.1353/etc.2018.0014

U.S. Department of Health and Human Services Office of Human Research Protections. (2016b). *Informed consent FAQs.* Retrieved from https://www.hhs.gov/ohrp/regulations-and-policy/ guidance/faq/informed-consent/index.html.

Valentino, A. L., & Juanico, J. F. (2020). Overcoming barriers to applied research: A guide for practitioners. *Behavior Analysis in Practice, 13*(4), 894−904. https://psycnet.apa.org/doi/10. 1007/s40617-020-00479-y.

Vollmer, T. R., Sloman, K. N., & Pipkin, C. S. P. (2008). Practical implications of data reliability and treatment integrity monitoring. *Behavior Analysis in Practice, 1*(2), 4−11. https://doi.org/ 10.1007/BF03391722

Chapter 9

Data handling: ethical principles, guidelines, and recommended practices

Brent A. Kaplan, Shawn P. Gilroy, W. Brady DeHart, Jeremiah M. Brown and Mikahil N. Koffarnus

Department of Family and Community Medicine, University of Kentucky College of Medicine, Lexington, KY, United States; Department of Psychology, Louisiana State University, Baton Rouge, LA, United States; Optum Labs, Eden Prairie, MN, United States; Department of Human Nutrition, Foods, and Exercise, Fralin Biomedical Research Institute at VTC, Virginia Tech, Blacksburg, VA, United States

Data are encountered at nearly every step of the clinical and research process. The organization and management of data are important starting from the initial recruitment of a potential participant through dissemination of the research. Managing data may often be overlooked during the day-to-day activities of a productive laboratory or clinic, and established practices that "just work" might be assumed to preclude the need for direct training on data management and data handling. However, consistent and ethical systems for data handling are of the utmost importance given the many areas where data may be compromised, altered, or otherwise mishandled (e.g., human error). Specific trainings and established guidelines for the management of data help to protect the anonymity and confidentiality of individuals, reduce the chance of human error, minimize bias and conflicts of interest, and enhance reproducibility efforts, including dissemination and research synthesis endeavors (e.g., meta-analyses; Haidich, 2010; Lipsey & Wilson, 2001). With the ever-increasing quantity of research studies being conducted and disseminated, data need to be more quickly collected, organized, and synthesized. If data are not properly managed, the available data may be incomplete or contain bias, and this may limit the generality of subsequent analyses.

The overarching goal of this chapter is to provide considerations, practices, and suggestions to enhance the integrity of data handling throughout behavior analytic research and, to a lesser degree, clinical process. We (the authors of this chapter) have worked in various settings and have managed various types

Research Ethics in Behavior Analysis. https://doi.org/10.1016/B978-0-323-90969-3.00006-2

of data in behavior analysis, including applied clinical work, nonhuman animal laboratory, human experiential research, crowdsourced survey data, and archival medical record data. To accomplish our overarching goal, we first discuss various types of data commonly encountered in behavior analysis ranging from highly sensitive data (e.g., personally identifiable) to anonymized data. We then discuss the various stages of the data handling process, from initial data collection and storage, to data validation, to data analysis, and ultimately to dissemination. At each stage, we will discuss aspects of data handling across the different domains relevant to behavior analysts including applied clinical work, human and nonhuman experimental work, largely anonymized or survey data (i.e., data gathered is initially anonymized, not after the fact that can be done with clinical and experimental data), and archival data (e.g., medical records).

A theme we will weave throughout the discussion of this chapter is the integration of open-source tools in the process of data handling. Open-source software is software where the underlying code is distributed and can be modified for free or with at least some recognition of the developers. Many open-source tools are free to use, which can reduce barriers to sharing, inspecting changes/revisions, and reproducibility. Because open-source tools typically rely on code that is open for inspection, the code can be "vetted" to determine the extent to which the code does what it was intended to do (for example, open-source encryption software may be routinely audited to ensure vulnerabilities are fixed). We believe that understanding and utilizing open-source tools wherever possible and appropriate enhance the ethical handling of data, including protecting confidentiality, promoting transparency and responsibility (e.g., using audit trails), and aid in reproducibility.

Legal and regulatory landscape of data handling

There are a number of legal considerations of which behavior analysis should be aware with regards to data handling. The General Data Protection Regulation (GDPR; European Parliament and Council, 2016) is a regulation of the European Union that addresses the handling of personal data of individuals, giving European Union citizens rights over their personal data and limiting the actions of companies using personal data for marketing. The California Consumer Privacy Act (CCPA) and the California Privacy Rights Act (CPRA) are laws in the US state of California that regulate businesses' ability to sell or share customer's personal data without consent (for more information on the GDPR and the CPRA, see Mueller et al., 2022, pp. 267–288). Relatedly, cybersecurity standards have been outlined by the National Institute of Standards and Technology (NIST; a nonregulatory agency of the U.S. Department of Commerce) to protect digital data. The Health Insurance Portability and Accountability Act (HIPAA; United States, 1996) stipulates how personally identifiable information should be protected from involuntary disclosure; the

Health Information Technology for Economic and Clinical Health Act (HITECH; United States, 2009) regulates certain aspects of privacy and data security, including health information exchange standards. Additionally, the Family Education Rights and Privacy Act (FERPA; United States, 1974) specifies the rights of parents to access, amend, and disclose certain components of their child's educational records. While an in-depth review of these laws and regulations is beyond the scope of this chapter, it should be noted that researchers and clinicians would likely benefit from collaborating with individuals with knowledge of relevant legal or cybersecurity concerns.

Types of data in behavior analysis

As mentioned earlier, data exist in various forms. Data can include things such as video recordings, products of behavior monitoring systems (both physical and digital including physiological measurements), electronic surveys, and more. Data range on a continuum from highly personal and identifiable to completely anonymized. Data containing sensitive or identifiable information need to be stored confidentially (e.g., video recordings), especially those including protected health information (PHI), whereas other data require minimal safeguards (e.g., anonymized survey responses). As a result, we will discuss data handling along a continuum ranging from highly sensitive data to not very sensitive data (e.g., anonymized, archival, nonhuman data). Here, we will briefly discuss and highlight some of the different types of data encountered in various behavior analytic settings.

Highly sensitive data

Research and practice in behavior analysis emphasize the role of information and data. Various dimensions of data and aspects of the environment are recorded and interpreted to inform ecologically based research and treatment. Broadly, this follows a sequence of participant characterization (i.e., identifying individual, diagnostic profile, demographics), treatment development (e.g., defining behavior, evaluating functional relations), and treatment evaluation (i.e., determining if treatment meaningfully influences behavior). Each of these steps is driven by different forms of information that must be organized and maintained to either inform treatment or answer specific research questions.

Data related to the characterization of participants are particularly sensitive because this information most closely associates individuals with their recorded data. For example, individual identification numbers (e.g., social security number) and dates of birth are (largely) unique and easily cross-referenced (cf., year of birth). Furthermore, certain forms of information (if made publicly available) have the potential to expose participants to negative social consequences or outright discrimination. For example, individuals may be treated differently by their coworkers or community if it were known that they participated in mental health treatment (Sickel et al., 2014). It is for this reason that such highly sensitive data are protected (i.e., PHI) under the US HIPAA (https://www.hhs.gov/hipaa/) when related to healthcare. This act requires healthcare providers to avoid disclosing any identifiable information related to healthcare to any third party without explicit permission, including information that could be reasonably used to identify a patient. Although not always required for research studies outside healthcare settings, the information sharing systems developed for HIPAA compliance are often useful for managing participant information flows in research. For example, HIPAA compliance refers, but is not limited, to ensuring the confidentiality, integrity, and availability of PHI, identification and protection against reasonably anticipated threats to security, and protection against unauthorized disclosure. If dealing with PHI, researchers and clinicians should familiarize themselves with current guidelines regarding HIPAA (https://www.hhs.gov/hipaa/for-professionals/index.html) and in the context of schools and student records, the Family Educational Rights and Privacy Act (FERPA; https://studentprivacy.ed.gov/faq/what-ferpa).

Data collected for the purpose of treatment development and evaluation can be highly sensitive as well. These data often consist of interviews, open-ended surveys designed to support the definition of targeted behavior (along with respective deficits) and direct observations of behavior in context. For example, clinical interviews and reviews of family histories reveal a wealth of clinically relevant, but sensitive, information (e.g., history of medical, behavioral disorders). Once behavior is well-characterized and defined, behavior can be sampled to explore possible functional relations (e.g., structural analysis) as well as determine baseline levels (e.g., rate, duration) as they pertain to treatment. This may be extended to experimental manipulations as well (e.g., functional analysis), toward the same ends. Further, the preferences and perspectives of participants and their families may also be captured to support the social validity of programmed supports.

The specific types of data collected during treatment development and evaluation can vary significantly between cases. For example, the types of behavior being recorded could range from disruptive child behavior, to substance use, and to nonsuicidal self-injury. In such a situation, data may be collected using a range of formats (e.g., pencil/paper behavior data sheets, video-recorded interviews, electronic data monitoring) because there is considerable variability in the types of behavior observed and how those are tracked. Researchers should consider how each of these mediums of data collection is handled. For example, after data are collected on paper/pencil sheets, they should be placed in a binder and not left unattended. The binder with data sheets should be moved to the secure location (e.g., locked filing cabinet) when data collection is complete. Likewise, for electronic data entry, the researcher should ensure the browser is closed and the computer is locked (or shut down) after collection is complete. Task analyses or a checklist for the steps required when completing a session may aid in ensuring data are properly transmitted and stored.

Several types of data are collected in human research studies. For example, these data may consist of those considered to be PHI (e.g., name, physical address, meeting appointment dates and times) while others, in combination, could be used to potentially identify someone (e.g., sex, age, zip code). These types of data are distinct from others that do not have as much of a possibility of identifying individuals (e.g., deidentified data; questionnaires, response times). According to the U.S. Department of Health and Human Services (The Office for Civil Rights (OCR) & Malin, 2012), the following pieces of information are considered identifiers of or related (relatives, employers) to the individual: names; geographic subdivisions smaller than a state; elements of a date (except year); telephone numbers; vehicle identification numbers (including license plates); fax numbers; device identifiers and serial numbers; email addresses; URLs that are explicitly associated with an individual; social security numbers; internet protocol (IP) addresses; medical record numbers; finger and voice prints; health plan beneficiary numbers; full-face photographs and comparable images (e.g., images that contain any unique characteristic related to the individual that could lead to identification such as a tattoo, a unique setting, a birthmark; Nettrour et al., 2018); account numbers; other unique identifying number (e.g., a subject identification number); or certificate and license numbers. In essence, these data can be directly used to identify the individual. As such, they are highly sensitive and should be handled and stored with the highest precautions. In later sections, we will consider certain safeguards and data handling techniques to maximize security and protection. For now, we mention that, depending on the scope of the human experiential studies, researchers may collect a relatively large or small amount of PHI.

Potentially sensitive data

Additional data gathered in the clinic or research lab may be considered potentially sensitive but, in and of themselves, are not sensitive. Certain types of demographic information may enable others to identify an individual when combined with other data. For example, when conducting research among diverse populations, uncommon cultural, linguistic, ethnic, racial, gender, ability, or other demographic characteristics may be identifying if few members of the community share those characteristics. While there may not be a general test to determine whether any of these demographic characters may be considered identifying information, the researcher or clinician should rely on their expert domain knowledge to assess whether there is a likely chance information may be identifiable. In instances where there may be a chance certain demographics are identifiable, researchers or clinicians should rely on a board such as an Institutional Review Board to determine whether to classify the information as identifiable.

Similarly, 5-digit ZIP codes may have a relatively small number of residents and—combined with other information such as a person's sex and age—their identity could be ascertained. A common strategy when handling with ZIP codes in public reporting of results or other contexts where divulging of PHI is unwarranted is to omit the final two numbers of the ZIP code, retaining only the first three. This provides a broader, but still useful, characterization of location without increasing the likelihood of being personally identifiable. In sparsely populated areas, even the first three digits are too specific, so the US Department of Health and Human Services maintains a list of 3-digit ZIP codes that contain a small enough number of individuals that they could be considered identifying information (The Office for Civil Rights (OCR) & Malin, 2012). For example, as of the 2000 census data, there are currently 17 three-digit restricted ZIP codes that contain 20,000 or fewer persons. Some of these ZIP codes include 036 (Bellows Falls, VT), 692 (Valentine, NE), 878 (Socorro, NM), and 063 (New London, CT). Researchers wanting to deidentify datasets including zip codes should consult the most recent census data available to determine whether the first three digits of a ZIP code may be restricted. In order to avoid ZIP code ambiguity completely, researchers and clinicians should determine whether they need to collect the information in the first place. Some studies or projects may not need ZIP codes and explicitly not collecting these data may be preferred.

Archival data are commonly collected for other purposes (e.g., healthcare, quality, and organizational improvement, treatment efficacy) and are retrospectively gathered and analyzed from various sources after the initial reason for the data collection is completed. Sometimes the archival data may be from previous research in the laboratory, or they can be from publicly available repositories (e.g., data.gov, census.gov, Panel Study of Income Dynamics), or they may be available upon request for specific purposes or analyses. For data collected previously in, for example, a laboratory, researchers and clinicians should ensure they have the appropriate permissions to access the data if the data contain identifiable information or otherwise have someone who has existing permissions deidentify the data. Archival data can exist in many forms including surveys, medical records, behavioral metrics such as web browser activity, and patient data logs. Archival data often include identifying information and PHI and steps should be taken to ensure PHI, if included, are protected. If the research can be accomplished without the PHI, then this may be the best approach as the data then may be classified as not very sensitive. Ultimately, researchers and clinicians working with existing and archival data sources should work directly with the custodians of those data to ensure privacy, if applicable, is maintained (e.g., understanding the scope of access to the data, if data can only be accessed on the server on which it is stored).

Not very sensitive data

Finally, various other types of data collected can be considered less sensitive (i.e., less than what is necessary to identify individuals). We make the distinction here that these data are still sensitive and thus, should be handled with care regardless. These data, however, do not necessarily warrant the multiple safeguards that more sensitive information require. For example, nonhuman animal data do not require the same protections as human participant data. Additionally, data gathered in human experimental studies wherein that data are comprised of response times or choice responses or infusions of a drug are often deidentified, and as such, cannot be used to link back to the participant without identifying data. Not very sensitive data may include response times, responses to behavioral tasks, and other data (e.g., comments, general ratings of behavior). Although these data may not allow someone to directly identify individuals, they should be handled with care similar to other data, and researchers should ensure that these data are not located in the same place as PHI (i.e., digitally or otherwise), as this might allow one to link the responses.

Deidentification removes all identifying information that can be possibly linked to a given individual. Some of these identifying pieces of information have been discussed already (e.g., name, age, medical record numbers). There are two ways in which deidentifying data can occur. They include the Safe Harbor method and Expert Determination approach (Kayaalp, 2018, pp. 1044−1050). To meet the Safe Harbor method, all identifiers must be removed from the dataset. For the Expert Determination approach, certain statistical or scientific principles are applied to the data (e.g., adding random amounts to values but retaining the underlying distribution) that make it unlikely the data can be linked back to any specific individual.

Crowdsourcing is increasingly being used for collecting behavioral data (Chandler et al., 2019; Peer et al., 2017; Strickland & Stoops, 2019). Crowdsourcing services such as Amazon Mechanical Turk, Prolific, and Qualtrics Panels provide researchers additional or alternative avenues for collecting data for certain types of research questions. The type of data collected from these sites are often anonymous but need not be depending on the types of questions being asked. Researchers should be aware of the data being collected (e.g., IP address, other identifiable information) and take proper precautions and steps to ensure participants are being fully informed of the data being collected as well as proper mechanisms by which to transmit and store the data, which will be overviewed in later sections. For example, these mechanisms may include encrypted transmission, user-defined role access through a secured database, and how long any PHI will be stored. These safeguards should be in place to minimize risk and harm to the participant and protect confidential information.

Data collection

One of the core aspects of data handling is data collection. Planning for the data collection strategy (e.g., electronic, physical) occurs at the very beginning of the clinical or research process, and data collection begins the moment anything related to the potential participant or client is obtained and stored. We will highlight and discuss several themes and key aspects to increase the likelihood that data will be collected with high integrity, free of bias, and such that confidentiality is maintained. These considerations include proper training of research personnel, clear definitions related to what and how data are to be collected, and tools to support the ethical collection of complete data.

Training and Clear Definitions. First, research personnel should have sufficient and adequate training in the handling of data. Those who are collecting the data should have an intimate understanding of the different types of data being collected. For example, research staff should be able to identify data considered PHI compared to deidentified or anonymized data that cannot be directly linked to the participant. Valuable training resources include hands-on experiential training from others in the laboratory and courses provided in services such as the Collaborative Institutional Training Initiative (also known as CITI Program; https://about.citiprogram.org/en/homepage/). For example, the CITI program has courses entitled "Mobile Apps and Human Subjects Research" and "Good Laboratory Practice," which cover aspects of data collection and PHI. Whereas individuals who are not associated with a specific institution can sign up for these trainings as an independent learner and pay for courses, for individuals seeking alternatives to fee-based training, the Office for Human Research Protections offers free human research protection training (https://www.hhs.gov/ohrp/education-and-outreach/online-education/human-research-protection-training/index.html). Data not considered PHI should still be handled with care. With the increased availability of tools to find individuals online and the proliferation of social media and other public repositories of data, it is increasingly possible to use combinations of seemingly arbitrary data to identify a participant. Researchers should consider the volume and combination of data collected as a potential identifier when determining the extent to which different types of research data are confidential.

Proper training of research personnel can also reduce the likelihood of bias. This bias may manifest itself in the form of screening and/or deciding whether a potential participant meets inclusion criteria for the study. The need for clear and definable inclusion and exclusion criteria is important here, as well as for research personnel to identify whether someone meets those criteria. For example, in a study looking at a population of cigarette smokers, an inadequate criterion for inclusion may be "Currently smokes cigarettes." This criterion may be inadequate by virtue of being overly nonspecific because "currently" is not well defined and cigarette smoking does not correspond with a quantitative level. Consider the example of an individual who smokes a single cigarette

1 day before volunteering for the research study. Would this behavior count for inclusion and importantly, would this individual's data be reflective of other "current cigarette smokers"? A better inclusion criterion may be "Smokes at least five cigarettes per day on average during the past 30 days." Here, there is a clear window of time as well as frequency of behavior.

Tools can also minimize the risk of human error and bias. These tools may be in paper format, or they may be used electronically. One such tool is the use of a tracker (physical or electronic) along with physical (paper) research materials. A tracker can most easily be thought of as similar to a task analysis or checklist that breaks down every step the researcher must take to conduct the session according to the procedure defined by the IRB approved protocol or the behavioral support plan. In other words, the tracker tries to maximize the extent to which procedures are implemented as they are intended (e.g., treatment fidelity). In our studies, we have used trackers successfully to ensure enrollment logs are updated and data are checked for completeness after a participant completes a task. For example, a tracker created for the purposes of an informed consent session might have the following components: (a) date, (b) participant ID, (c) research assistant consenting the participant, (d) checkboxes for individual inclusionary/exclusionary criteria, (e) checkboxes associated with discussing the consent form with the participant, answering any questions, and obtaining participant and researcher signatures, and (f) a checkbox associated with payment delivered to the participant. Whereas this type of tracker is no replacement for proper training in effectively executing the protocol as written and approved, utilizing a tracker will help increase the likelihood all steps of the research protocol are implemented with high fidelity and adherence.

The degree to which trackers support the goals of high fidelity, close adherence, and minimizing errors and bias can be enhanced by integrating several safeguards. Two safeguards include validating data entry fields (among electronic trackers) and requiring double entry for important values or other values that may be easily transposed or misread. For data validation, the electronic tracker should be programmed and tailored to the expected data type. For example, if an entry field should include a date, then with most electronic software (e.g., Qualtrics Research Suite), a rule can be implemented whereby an error will display and the page will not advance until the entry field contains text in a date format (see Fig. 9.1 for an illustrative example). Double entry requires that an important value (e.g., a participant's assigned condition) is entered in twice and that both fields contain the exact same characters. Depending on the software this could be accomplished on the same page or on separate pages (e.g., on an initial intake page and a few pages later so as to identify the error quickly). Although double entry like this would be preferred with two different researchers or clinicians independently entering data in to the fields, this is not necessary and sometimes not feasible. This safeguard is highly useful for ensuring the correct value is implemented. For

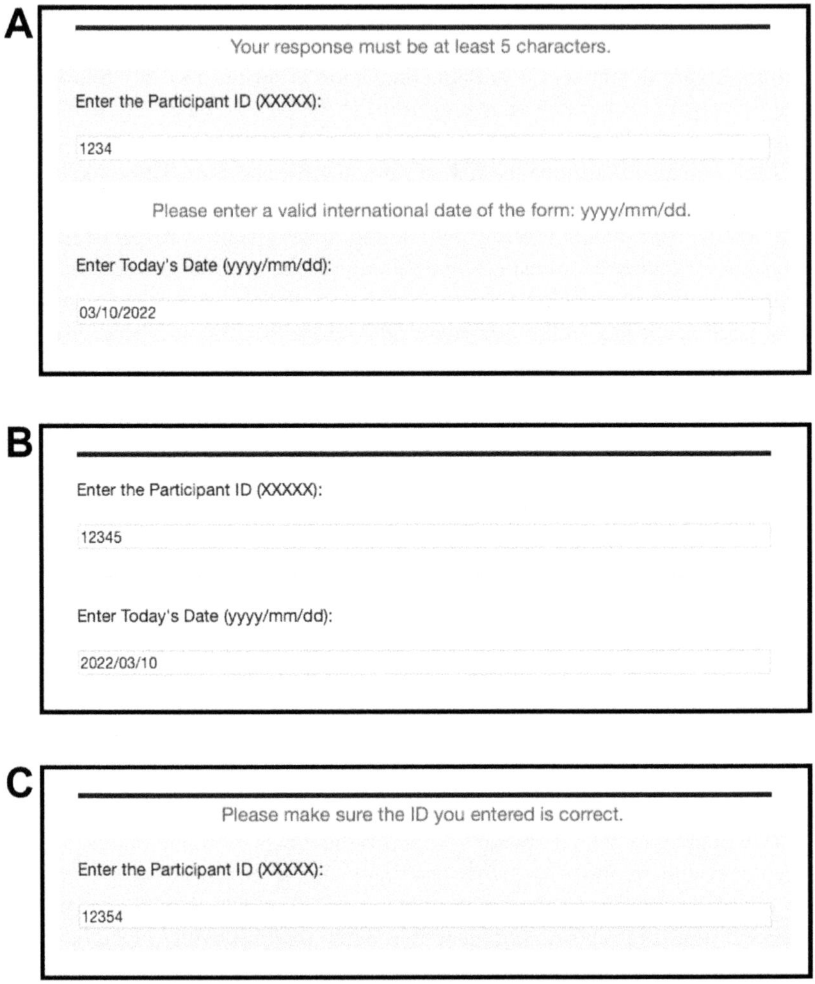

A

Your response must be at least 5 characters.

Enter the Participant ID (XXXXX):

1234

Please enter a valid international date of the form: yyyy/mm/dd.

Enter Today's Date (yyyy/mm/dd):

03/10/2022

B

Enter the Participant ID (XXXXX):

12345

Enter Today's Date (yyyy/mm/dd):

2022/03/10

C

Please make sure the ID you entered is correct.

Enter the Participant ID (XXXXX):

12354

FIGURE 9.1   An illustration of content validation in a tracker. **Panel A** shows the validation error codes when an invalid response is provided. In the first case, the ID is not long enough and doesn't meet the five character requirements. In the second case, the date is entered incorrectly and any date other than in the format "yyyy/mm/dd" will not be accepted. **Panel B** shows correct responses that do not trigger validation errors. **Panel C** shows double entry validation. Notice the transposition of "5" and "4" at the end. The required text is "12,345."

example, a participant's identification code may be prone to transposition errors (e.g., correct: 12,345; transposed: 12,354; see Fig. 9.1 for an example), and so requiring entry twice should minimize such errors. We note, however, this is no guarantee and that those collecting data should understand where and when errors might be more likely to occur. An excellent way to determine where errors might occur is to have someone who is not familiar with the study follow and complete the steps (e.g., complete the tracker, complete the study questions, conduct a "mock" session). When at all possible, extensive testing should occur prior to conducting actual sessions.

Paper data collection

Due to limitations in using physical paper to collect data, safe handling techniques are relatively limited in scope compared to electronic data collection. Clear, understandable instructions should be provided, as well as a sufficient range of possible answers. To decrease the likelihood of missing responses, instructions should remind participants to answer all questions and each question should be distinct as to not be easily missed or skipped. All paper data associated with a given participant should be kept together. If paper data contain highly sensitive data, they should be stored in accordance with those data (see Storage section below).

Electronic data collection

Many types of data are collected electronically to streamline the process of entering and saving information. Furthermore, not all types of studies require physical, in-person interaction. Data can be collected electronically regardless of whether the research occurs in the laboratory (e.g., linked to specific apparatus), in a clinical or educational setting (e.g., via direct observation), or electronically over the Internet (e.g., via survey software). These collection practices carry their own set of considerations and safeguards compared to traditional in-person research. Likewise, electronic data collection can range from highly sensitive to not very sensitive data.

Researchers often strive to minimize the proportion of missing responses during data collection, as missing responses can present difficulties when analyzing the data. However, in practice, requiring participants to answer every question may not be ethical as individuals may not wish to share certain types of information (e.g., trauma, legal, drug use history). In the case of electronic survey tools, this type of situation requires thought and planning. For instance, rather than making questions optional to answer, researchers often utilize "forced" response questions (whereby the participant must select some response before advancing) while including a specific "Do not wish to answer" option. This setup is preferred over optional answers as a non (or missing) answer does not distinguish whether the participant simply skipped the question or whether the participant was not comfortable answering that question. A high proportion of "Do not wish to answer" responses may be indicative of a poorly worded or unnecessarily intrusive question, and the researcher may wish to investigate the question.

Missing data may also occur in applied and educational settings. A therapist or teacher may be working with a client or student and may inadvertently fail to record a behavior within an interval. Alternatively, school teachers may incorrectly enter an unrealistic achievement scores into a database such that the value is flagged and removed when validating the data. These cases are often outside the control of the researcher analyzing the data and statistical techniques (e.g., imputation) may be required to provide a "best guess" of what the data *ought* to be. When possible, frequent intermittent data checks should occur so that identifying missing or implausible data can lead to fixes or other solutions specific to the situation at hand.

Another feature of data collection that can enhance data integrity and collection is using attending questions. These questions may be used to evaluate whether the respondent is attending to the relevant stimuli and responding accordingly. For example, attending questions may be used after a vignette outlining a hypothetical scenario or for ensuring that the participant understands the operational definition of a term. Participants may be provided feedback on the spot; if they answer incorrectly, they may be told to reread the section and asked another similar attending question related to the content until comprehension is achieved. We have used attending-like questions in our studies in the form of a "consent teachback" (Talevski et al., 2020). After reading an informed consent form, potential participants will complete an electronic survey where portions of the consent forms are displayed. Potential participants then answer multiple choice questions related to that portion of the consent form. If answered incorrectly, potential participants are provided feedback on the wrongly answered questions and are provided additional chances to answer correctly (e.g., programmed instruction).

Data handling and integrity can be maximized when using electronic survey software to collect data. Several features of these surveys can be implemented to ensure compliance, and we have discussed these features previously in the context of an electronic tracker. The first feature is data type validation whereby entries must match a predefined data type. Relevant to collecting data from participants, researchers may restrict an entry to numbers only. This would avoid a situation in which a participant might be inclined to respond with a range (e.g., 2–4) and would be forced to provide a specific number (e.g., 3). The second feature is one of double entry. Researchers may want to reduce any ambiguity or error in the participant's response by requiring them to enter the response identically in two separate places.

In addition to tools that organize the collection of data, various types of software exist to perform the actual measurement of behavioral data. Historical methods of measuring behavior, in both research and practice, relied on manual data recording (e.g., long-form descriptions, completing data sheets) or physical products (e.g., tape audio/video recordings). These methods have good utility; however, there is considerable administration necessary when using these materials and may be inefficient and limit analytic options. For example, these methods require human interaction to score, evaluate for interrater reliability, and physically save the data for long-term archiving and backup. Each of these steps is expensive in terms of staffing and resources, and this is a barrier to reliably implementing good data management processes. Multiple tools have been developed to address such barriers, largely concerning data collection (e.g., BDataPro—Bullock et al., 2017; DataTracker—https://github.com/miyamot0/DataTracker3). These electronic data collection tools have been designed to minimize the burden of proactive data management practices. For instance, the programs listed here automate the process of calculating interrater agreement and related indicators of data quality. Further, programs such as DataTracker store both human- and computer-readable data as an added layer of redundancy and layer of data validation. Having multiple layers of data allows for automated checks for the consistency of data records and auditing.

Various open-source tools and programming languages exist and can be used to automate different types of data collection. For example, we have used Integrated Development Environments (IDE) such as Visual Studio (https://visualstudio.microsoft.com) and modern programming languages such as Python (https://www.python.org) to collect different types of behavioral data. However, there are many alternatives for IDEs (e.g., Visual Studio Code) and languages (e.g., C#, F#, Go). Of course, the researcher will need to weigh the costs in terms of time, money, and training to implement such systems within their laboratory or clinical work. For instance, these tools have the potential to run highly specialized tasks and streamline data collection (i.e., limiting the potential for human error) but may require considerable expertise to effectively design and manage these systems.

Data storage

Information and data can be collected using different platforms and various platforms differ in how they are secured. We will separate storage methods by whether storage is physical (i.e., secured location) or electronic (i.e., stored via remote or local media). Sensitive data such as PHI should be collected and stored in locations where only approved study personnel can access the information. Physically, this may be in a locked cabinet in a locked office (i.e., double-locked and secured location). Only authorized personnel should have access to these files, and these files should be kept in secured storage except for when the data are actively being used (e.g., data validation, data analysis). Electronically, data should be stored using services that are not accessible to third parties and that offer robust encryption and rights management capabilities. Encryption means that the data are transmitted and stored in such a way as to hide the actual information and are only accessible by individuals who have the rights and methods to unhide the information. For particularly sensitive information, data collection tools such as RedCap (Harris et al., 2019) can be installed on local servers and provide additional security compared to "cloud"-based services that store data on the servers of private companies (e.g., https://www.dropbox.com/). Nonetheless, data stored on cloud-based servers should still be protected via passwords and only authorized users should have access to the data. Two-factor authentication methods (e.g., use of a one-time code via an authenticator application) should be used whenever possible to reduce the likelihood of unauthorized personnel gaining access to the service. When data are locally stored on a computer, users should ensure the computer is password protected and locked whenever unattended, even for a short duration. When in doubt, researchers and clinicians should discuss storage options with their team and any governing body (e.g., Institutional Review Board) to ensure compliance.

Services used to collect and store the information should allow the ability to specify rights management, meaning users can be assigned roles and their roles dictate the extent to which they can interact with the data (see Fig. 9.2). For example, the principal investigator or primary project lead may have the right to read and edit all data, whereas a research assistant may only be able to read a subset (e.g., no sensitive information) of the data. Furthermore, raw data collected should be saved in a "read-only" manner whenever possible. Read-only refers to the permissions of a file whereby once saved, the data cannot be changed. These raw data files may be duplicated so that analyses can be conducted. Saving and storing raw data in this state greatly increase the chances that the original data do not get tampered with or altered. Analyses and data manipulations can be conducted on copies of the data, but a read-only copy of the original data ensures that an unaltered version is always available. This does not guarantee subsequent manipulations of the data will be free from error or other issues, but does allow reanalysis and external validation of the data if needed.

Retrospective archival data researchers often have little control over how data were collected. That is, these researchers typically do not have input on how the data were originally collected and can only deal with the data now. For example, patient data collected in the hospital may have billing codes instead of diagnoses codes. This may be due to other individuals having originally collected data or the data were collected for different purposes. When possible, researchers should collaborate with the teams collecting the data to encourage systems that maximize both the practical utility and the research potential of the data. To extend the example, billing codes may not provide the necessary specificity a research question necessitates (e.g., a billing code related to "high blood pressure" may be insufficient when actual values are needed). Nonetheless, researchers should work with the entities or other researchers who originally collected the data to understand the scope of the data available.

Depending on how securely the data are stored, researchers may not have direct access to the data. Frequently, organizations employ data analysts/extractors who are skilled in extracting data from archival sources. There are positives and negatives to such situations. On the one hand, this can cause delays in acquiring the data, and miscommunications between the research

FIGURE 9.2 An example of user permissions in the RedCap interface. Different roles can be assigned and those roles can have prepopulated access to different permissions (e.g., renaming records, lock/unlock records). Notice how different users can have access to the full data set or the deidentified data.

team and the data analysts may lead to the incorrect type or level of data being attained. On the other hand, relying on another individual to extract the data can help increase HIPAA compliance and can allow access to complex database systems. The research analyst can deidentify the data and remove sensitive information to be in line with Safe Harbor guidelines discussed above (e.g., recode ages over 90, mask zip codes). However, despite this extra step of deidentification, the research team is under the same expectations to safeguard delivered datasets as other data types.

Some data may contain or be derived from highly sensitive information and medical records. These data are especially sensitive and must be protected. Failure to properly protect medical records could violate established HIPAA laws and expose the research team and sponsoring facility to legal action including fines and lawsuits. Archival data are best stored on local servers that are user restricted or password-protected (see Storage section above). This ensures that only approved researchers can access the data. Archival data should never be stored on personal devices or personal cloud storage sites and should never be shared via email.

A final note about data storage and optimal conditions regards the concept of redundancy. Redundancy of data can help in the event something catastrophic should affect the data. In general, best practice suggests a "3-2-1" rule. Keep at least three copies or versions of the data; one copy serving as the primary copy and two as backups. These copies are distributed across at least two different locations, with at least one of the locations being "off-site" (for example, secure and encrypted data could be stored on a server or literally at another physical building). This rule, of course, means that each version or copy of the data (especially highly sensitive data) at each location would need to be protected with similar safeguards. While this rule may not be feasible in all laboratories and clinics, researchers should understand and be aware of the general concept and apply it accordingly in their settings. Further, given we live in the era of big data, many database vendors offer solutions that meet the "3-2-1" rule at a reasonable cost.

Data validation

Data validation refers to efforts to characterize the available data and ensure that the data record reflects what the instrument was designed to measure. During the research process, there are several opportunities to validate data: data collection, post data collection, and post data analyses. Data validation is a vitally important step to ensure the data collected are complete, error-free, and unaltered. Here, we will discuss considerations for validating data, including auditing of data for integrity, completeness, and replicability.

Modern data storage resources are inexpensive and plentiful, allowing for a full data auditing trail to be maintained. An easy and automatic way to increase the integrity of data auditing capabilities is to use versioning software that stores old versions of data files indefinitely. Common office software such as Microsoft Office 365 (https://www.office.com) now supports versioning to automatically save old copies of files, and services such as GitHub (https://github.com) and the Open Science Framework (OSF; https://www.osf.io) support similar functionality for any type of file including research data files. If an error is made in a data cleaning or analysis step that compromises the integrity of the data, a copy of the original data or earlier versions of data files allow for auditing analysis steps and recovering uncompromised data. Whether or not versioning software is being used, naming conventions should be thoughtful. For example, a file's name may include the date it was downloaded (e.g., "20220310"; March 10th, 2022) and an indicator of whether the file contains original, raw data or manipulated data (e.g., ResearchStudy-20220310-raw.csv).

GitHub is a public platform supporting the Git version control language and supports the open science initiative (Gilroy & Kaplan, 2019). Version control software such as Git allow for detailed record keeping of changes in documents (working best with text-based files such as .txt, .csv, or other text-based coding files, e.g., .R) and allow for collaboration. Fig. 9.3 is an example from a GitHub repository (a project composed of many different files) maintained by the first author (Kaplan) showing collaboration with the second author (Gilroy). The second author copied the repository and made changes that he felt would be useful for the repository (in this specific case, an R package). The second author then made a "pull request" so that the first author could integrate the changes. A full description of Git and GitHub is beyond the scope of this chapter, but interested readers are directed to Gilroy and Kaplan (2019) for an introductory tutorial.

Collaborative research is the norm, and most research studies now involve individuals with varying needs to access sensitive data. Additionally, research collaborations are often complex across multiple studies such that each specific collaborator may have unique access requirements for components of the data. Data storage and sharing tools such as Microsoft Sharepoint or RedCap allow for sophisticated permission systems to control these data access hierarchies (see Fig. 9.2). The planning stages of any research project that includes highly sensitive data should include data permission charts and strategies to limit the dissemination of such data as much as possible. Data should be stored in locations that allow for access permissions to be dynamically modified as necessary and should not be shared with mechanisms such as email that do not allow for access permissions to be modified.

Archived data, because it is commonly collected for other purposes, may contain two levels of information: individual raw data and individual summary data. For example, a healthcare dataset may include both lab and vital values (collected at different time points) and diagnosis codes derived from those labs and vitals. As another example, behavior analysts may be analyzing previously collected data obtained from a clinic related to the effects of certain

FIGURE 9.3 Snapshot from GitHub showing collaboration and version control benefits. The second author made a pull request wherein he made additions and deletions that would be useful for the repository. The first author accepted these changes and incorporated them (i.e., merge pull request) into the repository. Notice how the version control language documents each addition and subtraction from each of the different files.

interventions. Though the summary data can be useful because others have created those summary values, the researchers may consider re-creating their summary values based on the raw data available. In this sense, the researcher gains additional confidence in the validity of the summary data and can be more comfortable moving forward analyzing that summary data.

Data analysis and dissemination

The act of analyzing data involves numerous different ethical considerations, especially when statistical methods are applied. We will focus broadly on considerations related to conflicts of interest among those overseeing the data analysis, the use of preregistration prior to conducting the research, and utilizing software that minimizes errors and enhances replicability.

First, anyone who is handling data and oversees carrying out the primary duties related to data analysis should ensure they are free from conflicts of interest. Conflicts of interest are situations in which financial or personal considerations may interfere with or otherwise influence the decisions made regarding or interpretations of the data (Brody, 2011). Even perceived conflicts of interest may inadvertently inject bias in how decisions are made or influence the extent to which the consumer of the analytics trusts the purported results. To deter these potential sources of bias, the individuals tasked with analyzing and validating the data must be free from any conflicts of interest. Many colleges and universities have departments or offices (e.g., Office of Research Integrity and Compliance) that specialize in overseeing and advising potential conflicts of interest, as well as developing management plans for such instances.

Another consideration to minimize ethical complications related to data analysis is to preregister the study (https://www.cos.io/initiatives/prereg). Preregistration can fall on a continuum from precommitting an analytical plan to a time-stamped site (e.g., GitHub) to writing various aspects of the research process including methods, data collection, and data analytic plans and getting the preregistered report reviewed by peers. By preregistering the study and obtaining expert feedback prior to analyzing the data, sources of bias may be identified beforehand, or sources of bias may be minimized or eliminated completely by adhering to the prespecified research plan (Simmons et al., 2021).

Finally, using certain types of software that produce a reproducible record will enhance the ability to verify the data were analyzed in ethical, appropriate, and scientifically defensible ways. For example, open-source statistical programs (or software that support specific statistical packages) such as R (Jamovi is a graphical user interface for easier use of R; see also RStudio, an IDE (RStudio Team, 2020)), SAS, and Python (see SciPy package) provide the ability to document the entire data analytic strategy from the unaltered, raw data to the final products (statistical results, graphs, tables). Different software packages, tools, and tutorials are being created by behavior analysts for behavior analysts (e.g., Gilroy & Kaplan, 2019; Gilroy et al., 2018, 2017; Kaplan et al., 2019), making use of these open-source tools more accessible and appealing.

Considerations in Archival Datasets. Archival datasets can present unique analytic challenges. Multiple steps can be necessary to organize the data for statistical analyses because data were collected from different sources, stored in different locations, and compiled by an analyst who is not part of the research team. Indeed, many archival data researchers report that the bulk of their interaction with the dataset is spent on data "cleaning" or "normalizing."

Data cleaning refers to screening, identifying, and correcting missing or implausible values, and ensuring the data are valid (e.g., data fall within a certain range for a given response), accurate, complete, consistent, and uniform as possible. Data normalizing refers to bringing the variables of interest in proportion to one another so that different variables can be compared (e.g., data can be centered such that the mean is zero and the standard deviation is one). Because archival data often require these complex preparations, proficiency in software that records these analytic steps is essential. These programs often allow for data to be combined and manipulated without altering the original datasets. These programs also document the steps taken and allow for analyses audits (e.g., the ability to trace the steps of the analyses starting from the raw data all the way to the final result) and replications.

Analyzing archival data can require a flexibility that may not be necessary in personally collected datasets, meaning the tools to analyzing these types of data will be largely dependent on the types of data available (as mentioned before, one may have billing codes instead of diagnoses codes). Miscoded values, institutional labeling differences, and missing data are common challenges that the research team may face. Fortunately, archival datasets can be very large (on the order of thousands of entries), which allows the researcher to remove individual data based on a priori exclusionary criteria. However, such large datasets present additional challenges. Because of the possible large sample sizes, obtaining statistical significance (e.g., $P < .05$) but not clinical significance (e.g., a "real-world" outcome that would encourage implantation or intervention; effect size) is a common possibility. Therefore, the calculating and reporting of effect size (e.g., how large the change or effect is, not simply the probability of observing the effect as large or larger if the null hypothesis is correct) are essential to provide the information necessary to evaluate the strength of your findings.

Sharing data with other researchers and the public can accelerate the pace of scientific discoveries by allowing individuals with diverse skills to access valuable datasets and by providing an opportunity for research conclusions to be verified by others. Many funding agencies and journals encourage or require data to be shared publicly or upon request when a manuscript is published in the scientific literature. Typically, an Informed Consent Form wherein the potential participant is informed of their rights, benefits, costs, and other aspects of the study will outline under what conditions participant's data will be used. Potential participants are typically informed as to what happens to their data if they withdraw. Furthermore, Institutional Review Boards (IRB) or other governing boards require researchers to follow guidelines requiring all data to be stored for a specific period of time, after which identifying information should be destroyed. This regulation is outlined in the US Department of Health and Human Services' Code of Federal Regulations Title 45 Part 46 (45CFR46), also known as the "Common Rule." Simultaneously meeting all these requirements and best practices can be greatly facilitated by avoiding the mixing of highly sensitive data with other study data during the data collection phase, which makes it much easier to create a deidentified dataset.

Depending on the type of information requested and transmitted, the parties may need to engage in a Data Use Agreement (see Appendix for a template Data Use Agreement provided by the National Institutes on Health; https://www.niaid.nih.gov/research/sample-data-sharing-plan). These Data Use Agreements broadly specify the scope of use of the data, who will access the data, safeguards in place to protect the data, etc. However, in cases where only deidentified data are shared, once this dataset is created sharing raw data with other researchers is quick and easy, and the IRB required data management steps years after a study concludes are also straightforward to complete. However, we stress that researchers should ensure the deidentified dataset is truly considered deidentified. In academic institutions, there is often someone in the Office of Research Integrity who may help assist and verify the data are truly deidentified. As we discussed previously, the combination of certain demographic information (e.g., certain full zip codes, specific ages) may be linked together to identify the individual. When sharing datasets that may contain these types of linking information, researchers may use strategies such as binning values (e.g., instead of age 32, this dataset could be coded as between 30 and 34) or perturbing values (e.g., instead of age 32, this dataset could be coded as 34) whereby the qualities of the data (e.g., variance) are maintained.

Finally, researchers and clinicians should be aware of data ownership when considering disseminating results from a study. In academic institutions, research funding is typically awarded to the institution, and so it is the institution that has responsibilities of overseeing activities related to the research, including ensuring the researcher is maintaining records and proper storage. Although institutions differ in their ownership policies, researchers should not assume that they may take the data as they wish when they transfer institutions. Ownership should be clearly articulated prior to data collection, and this is often conveyed either by the funding institution or company or through discussions with the fundee.

Conclusions

In this chapter, we have overviewed different links in the research process—all of which require considerations of proper and ethical data management. We have overviewed different types of data behavior analysts might encounter across a range of settings and disciplines, ranging from clinical work to large, archival datasets. We have discussed considerations in the data collection phase for minimizing errors, and ensuring bias is minimized among those who handle the data. We then discussed considerations and recommendations for ensuring data are analyzed with integrity and that data are valid, such as recognizing potential conflicts of interest and using replicable software. Finally, we discussed how dissemination efforts can meet the goals of accelerating scientific discoveries while ensuring participant protection. While integrating all the aforementioned recommendations may not be viable for researchers, we encourage researchers to consider the gaps in their research process with respect to data handling. Ensuring policies and procedures are in place for maintaining confidentiality, minimizing errors and bias, and enhancing reproducibility should be a priority in any research laboratory and clinic, and these procedures should be audited and evaluated as frequently as necessary.

Appendix

Example Plan addressing Key Elements for a Data Sharing Plan under NIH Extramural Support

(For questions, contact the NIH Office of Extramural Research (OER), Email Sharing@nih.gov)

Example Data Sharing Plan for FOA-XX-XXXX
What data that will be shared:

I will share phenotypic data associated with the collected samples by depositing these data at _____, which is an NIH-funded repository. Genotype data will be shared by depositing these data at _____. Additional data documentation and deidentified data will be deposited for sharing along with phenotypic data, which includes demographics, family history of XXXXXX disease, and diagnosis, consistent with applicable laws and regulations. I will comply with the NIH GWAS Policy and the funding IC's existing policies on sharing data on XXXXXX disease genetics to include secondary analysis of data resulting from a genome-wide association study through the repository. Meta-analysis data and associated phenotypic data, along with data content, format, and organization, will be available at _____. Submitted data will confirm with relevant data and terminology standards.

Who will have access to the data:

I agree that data will be deposited and made available through _____, which is an NIH-funded repository, and that these data will be shared with investigators working under an institution with a Federal Wide Assurance (FWA) and could be used for secondary study purposes such as finding genes that contribute to process of XXXXXX. I agree that the names and Institutions of persons either given or denied access to the data, and the bases for such decisions will be summarized in the annual progress report. Meta-analysis data and associated phenotypic data, along with data content, format, and organization, will be made available to investigators through _____.

Where will the data be available:

I agree to deposit and maintain the phenotypic data and secondary analysis of data (if any) at _____, which is an NIH-funded repository and that the repository has data access policies and procedures consistent with NIH data sharing policies.

When will the data be shared:

I agree to deposit genetic outcome data into _____ repository as soon as possible but no later than within 1 year of the completion of the funded project period for the parent award or upon acceptance of the data for publication, or public disclosure of a submitted patent application, whichever is earlier.

How will researchers locate and access the data:

I agree that I will identify where the data will be available and how to access the data in any publications and presentations that I author or coauthor about these data, as well as acknowledge the repository and funding source in any publications and presentations. As I will be using _____, which is an NIH-funded repository, this repository has policies and procedures in place that will provide data access to qualified researchers, fully consistent with NIH data sharing policies and applicable laws and regulations.

Rev. 20100831

References

Brody, H. (2011). Clarifying conflict of interest. *The American Journal of Bioethics, 11*(1), 23−28. https://doi.org/10.1080/15265161.2010.534530

Bullock, C. E., Fisher, W. W., & Hagopian, L. P. (2017). Description and validation of a computerized behavioral data program: "bDataPro.". *The Behavior Analyst, 40*(1), 275−285. https://doi.org/10.1007/s40614-016-0079-0

Chandler, J., Rosenzweig, C., Moss, A. J., Robinson, J., & Litman, L. (2019). Online panels in social science research: Expanding sampling methods beyond mechanical turk. *Behavior Research Methods, 51*, 2022−2038. https://doi.org/10.3758/s13428-019-01273-7

European Parliament and Council. (2016). *Regulation (EU) 2016/679 of the European Parliament and of the Council of 27 April 2016 on the protection of natural persons with regard to the processing of personal data and on the free movement of such data, and repealing Directive 95/46/EC*. Retrieved from https://eur-lex.europa.eu/legal-content/EN/TXT/?uri%BCCELEX: 02016R0679-20160504.

Gilroy, S. P., Franck, C. T., & Hantula, D. A. (2017). The discounting model selector: Statistical software for delay discounting applications. *Journal of the Experimental Analysis of Behavior, 107*(3), 388−401. https://doi.org/10.1002/jeab.257

Gilroy, S. P., & Kaplan, B. A. (2019). Furthering open science in behavior analysis: An introduction and tutorial for using GitHub in research. *Perspectives on Behavior Science, 42*(3), 565−581. https://doi.org/10.1007/s40614-019-00202-5

Gilroy, S. P., Kaplan, B. A., Reed, D. D., Koffarnus, M. N., & Hantula, D. A. (2018). The demand curve analyzer: Behavioral economic software for applied research. *Journal of the Experimental Analysis of Behavior, 110*(3), 553−568. https://doi.org/10.1002/jeab.479

Haidich, A. B. (2010). Meta-analysis in medical research. *Hippokratia, 14*(Suppl. 1), 29−37.

Harris, P. A., Taylor, R., Minor, B. L., Elliott, V., Fernandez, M., O'Neal, L., McLeod, L., Delacqua, G., Delacqua, F., Kirby, J., & Duda, S. N. (2019). The REDCap consortium:

Building an international community of software platform partners. *Journal of Biomedical Informatics, 95*, 103208. https://doi.org/10.1016/j.jbi.2019.103208

Kaplan, B. A., Gilroy, S. P., Reed, D. D., Koffarnus, M. N., & Hursh, S. R. (2019). The R package beezdemand: Behavioral economic easy demand. *Perspectives on Behavior Science, 42*(1), 163–180. https://doi.org/10.1007/s40614-018-00187-7

Kayaalp, M. (2018). Modes of de-identification. In , *2017. AMIA annual symposium proceedings*. American Medical Informatics Association.

Lipsey, M. W., & Wilson, D. B. (2001). Practical meta-analysis. In *Applied social research methods series*. SAGE Publications.

Mueller, S., Taylor, C. R., & Mueller, B. (2022). Managing change related to consumer privacy laws: Targeting and personal data use in a more regulated environment. In M. Karmasin, S. Diehl, & I. Koinig (Eds.), *Media and change management: Creating a path for new content formats, business models, consumer roles, and business responsibility*. Springer International Publishing. https://doi.org/10.1007/978-3-030-86680-8_15

Nettrour, J. F., Burch, M. B., & Bal, B. S. (2018). Patients, pictures, and privacy: Managing clinical photographs in the smartphone era. *Arthroplasty Today, 5*(1), 57–60. https://doi.org/10.1016/j.artd.2018.10.001

Peer, E., Brandimarte, L., Samat, S., & Acquisti, A. (2017). Beyond the turk: Alternative platforms for crowdsourcing behavioral research. *Journal of Experimental Social Psychology, 70*, 153–163. https://doi.org/10.1016/j.jesp.2017.01.006

RStudio Team. (2020). *RStudio*. Boston, MA: Integrated Development for R. RStudio, PBC. URL http://www.rstudio.com/.

Sickel, A. E., Seacat, J. D., & Nabors, N. A. (2014). Mental health stigma update: A review of consequences. *Advances in Mental Health, 12*(3), 202–215. https://doi.org/10.1080/18374905.2014.11081898

Simmons, J. P., Nelson, L. D., & Simonsohn, U. (2021). Pre-registration: Why and how. *Journal of Consumer Psychology, 31*(1), 151–162. https://doi.org/10.1002/jcpy.1208

Strickland, J. C., & Stoops, W. W. (2019). The use of crowdsourcing in addiction science research: Amazon mechanical turk. *Experimental and Clinical Psychopharmacology, 27*, 1–18. https://doi.org/10.1037/pha0000235

Talevski, J., Wong Shee, A., Rasmussen, B., Kemp, G., & Beauchamp, A. (2020). Teach-back: A systematic review of implementation and impacts. *PLOS ONE, 15*(4), e0231350. https://doi.org/10.1371/journal.pone.0231350

The Office for Civil Rights (OCR), & Malin, B. (2012). *Guidance regarding methods for de-identification of protected health information in accordance with the Health Insurance Portability and Accountability Act (HIPAA) privacy rule*. Health Information Privacy.

United States. (1974). *Family Education Rights and Privacy Act (FERPA)*, 20 U.S.C. § 1232g; 34 CFR Part 99.

United States. (1996). *The Health Insurance Portability and Accountability Act (HIPAA)*. Washington, DC: U.S. Department of Labor, Employee Benefits Security Administration.

United States. (2009). *Health Information Technology for Economic and Clinical Health Act. TITLE XIII—Health Information Technology. American Recovery and Reinvestment Act of 2009* (ARRA) (Pub.L. 111-5). Retrieved from https://www.congress.gov/bill/111th-congress/house-bill/1.

Chapter 10

Ethically Communicating Research Findings

Fernanda S. Oda[1], James K. Luiselli[2] and Derek D. Reed[1]
[1]*Department of Applied Behavioral Science, University of Kansas, Lawrence, KS, United States;*
[2]*Melmark New England, Andover, MA, United States*

Introduction

Communicating research findings is behavior. As operant behavior, the communication of research findings can be analyzed in terms of its controlling variables. We can also engage in verbal behavior about behavior. Was that an *ethical way* to present data? Were there any *unethical behaviors* observed when reporting information in the manuscript submission process? When we interpret behavior as "ethical" or "unethical," we tact the conditions under which behavior is emitted, as well as its effects on other individuals.

Disseminating findings is behavior that has an effect on groups of people. When information is delivered and is publicly available—in conferences, workshops, articles, books, and social media—information can serve as a stimulus for the behavior of listeners. If findings are presented in the oral medium (e.g., presentations at conferences or workshops), they can have an effect on the immediate audience and listeners. If findings are presented in the written medium (e.g., articles, books, and social media), they can serve as a verbal stimulus to readers. Both oral and written verbal behavior can produce permanent products such as audio/video recording of a presentation and published articles available online that can affect the behavior of individuals in a larger temporal scale. In all these examples, it is safe to assume that communicating scientific findings is behavior that bears a huge responsibility for the behavior of the communicator, who should be sensitive to the potential effects of their behavior on the behavior of listeners and readers.

As listeners or readers of the behavior of individuals, scientific communities of diverse fields have been describing ethical and unethical behaviors. For example, the American Psychological Association (APA) *Ethics Code* (2017) and the APA *Publication Manual* (2020) describe ethical conduct for professionals. Important guidelines to avoid misconducts, to report scientific

Research Ethics in Behavior Analysis. https://doi.org/10.1016/B978-0-323-90969-3.00001-3

findings, and to consider conflicts of interests and authorship are described in these documents and are summarized in this chapter.

Another influential scientific and practice community is the Behavior Analyst Certification Board (BACB). The BACB *Ethics Code for Behavior Analysts* (2020) describes ethical behaviors for the profession. Regarding providing public statements, Standard 5.03 states that behavior analysts "take reasonable precautions to ensure that the statements are truthful and do not mislead or exaggerate either because of what they state, convey, suggest, or omit." (BACB, 2020, p. 16). The Code also describes how behavior analysts should respect intellectual property (Standard 5.05), avoid plagiarism (Standard 6.09), and report accurate data (Standard 6.11). Thus, behavior analysts should be knowledgeable of the conduct prescribed by their scientific communities. Ethical aspects of disseminating including intellectual property and plagiarism are discussed later in the chapter.

To disseminate ethically, you need material to disseminate. Once you have material, you should take into consideration ethical aspects of your writing. Thus, the first step to disseminate is to discover what you have to say (Reed, 2014; Skinner, 1981). This process of discovering is behavior that should be taught and shaped during academic training. Programs should offer well-rounded education and teach students to critically think about concepts and principles of behavior analysis (Schlinger, 2014), allowing them to become "ambassadors" for the field (Reed, 2014; Schlinger, 2014). One could consider publishing outside of the field as well. To do so, Reed (2014) recommends identifying the field's interests and considering professional and personal contingencies to decide whether publishing outside of the field should be a priority.

Once you decide what you have to say, it is time to start writing. When writing for publication, you may face some challenges that include lack of knowledge about editorial guidelines and limited time to write (Luiselli, 2010). While writing itself is hard work, writing ethically involves additional effort. Disseminators should be aware of guidelines prescribed by communities and engage in behaviors that produce socially desirable outcomes for listeners and readers.

The purpose of this chapter is to describe and prescribe ethical conduct related to disseminating research findings. First, we begin by presenting an overview of discussions related to writing and publishing within the field of behavior analysis. An emphasis is given to communicating findings in the written medium, including writing a manuscript or article for peer review. Next, the chapter covers common unethical practices, including issues such as inaccurate reports, plagiarism, self-plagiarism, and piecemeal publication; we subsequently provide a guide on prescribed practices that could help communicators to navigate common ethical dilemmas, such as conflicts of interest and authorship. We then describe other guidelines related to the editorial process. Finally, we conclude with brief discussions on the considerations on disseminating findings in presentations and social media.

Review of pertinent literature

The behaviors of writing and publishing have been studied by some behavior analysts. The literature is not extensive, and publications fall under these three categories: (a) nonempirical on writing or teaching writing, (b) empirical study on teaching writing, and (c) bibliographical research on publishing productively. Specific guidelines for writing ethically are discussed outside of the field and are described in subsequent sections of this chapter.

In an article addressed to students, Skinner (1981) described some controlling variables that influence the behavior of writing. These can include both antecedent environmental variables and motivating operations. As operant behavior, writing can be determined by immediate antecedent stimuli or events and motivating operations. He detailed how arranging the context to engage in writing can be important (e.g., setting, materials, time of the day, etc.) to evoke good writing. For example, Skinner describes potential influences on writing, such as feeling rested and not sleep deprived as potential motivating operations. In another behavioral account, Wallace and Pear (1977) analyzed the behavior of writing novels by famous novelists. Self-control techniques to promote productive writing were described. Although the emphasis of the article is not on scientific writing, similarities between this article and Skinner's report (1981) can be found. For example, they both described self-management strategies to promote writing and described writing as an activity under a fixed-ratio schedule of reinforcement.

There are two anecdotal report articles that focus on describing strategies to teach writing from a behavior-analytic perspective. One is Vargas (1978), who described writing in terms of verbal operants. By analyzing the mand, Vargas (1978) interpreted that writers may specify directions by engaging in mands, which could enable readers to be successful at performing the task the writer specified. In other words, a mand is effective when the reader does what the writer wants. Another important verbal operant is the tact, and a writer should engage in good descriptions to enable readers to experience what the writer experienced. Thus, according to Vargas (1978), teaching writing involves training students to write directions and to engage in descriptive writing. Another report is Welsch (1987), who reviewed a book by Peter Elbow on writing. Strategies described put an emphasis on natural contingencies of writing by recognizing aversive control and shaping of this skill.

Empirical articles on teaching writing include applied studies with typically developing children (e.g., Ballard & Glynn, 1975; Fawcett & Fletcher, 1977; Glover & Gary, 1976; Hanna et al., 2004; Hansen & Wills, 2014) and adults (e.g., Luna & Rapp, 2019; Pennington et al., 2014; Porritt et al., 2006; Ramey et al., 1978) or individuals with developmental disabilities (e.g., Delano, 2007; Stromer et al., 1998). The writing modalities targeted in these studies included creative writing (Glover & Gary, 1976), academic essays

(Delano, 2007), journal reviews (Ramey et al., 1978), cover letters (Pennington et al., 2014), lists (Stromer et al., 1998), fictions (Porritt et al., 2006), instructional packages (Fawcett & Fletcher, 1977), and notes (Luna & Rapp, 2019).

A last group of publications focuses on writing productivity in the field. These articles are bibliographical studies on authorship trends in behavior-analytic journals. Dixon et al. (2015) ranked the top 10 most productive behavior-analytic training BACB-approved graduate programs and faculty members. They suggested faculty productivity (i.e., peer-reviewed publications) could be used as a possible metric of program quality. Research productivity was measured by counting publications that appeared in behavior-analytic journals published by the Society of the Experimental Analysis of Behavior (SEAB) and the Association for Behavior Analysis International (ABAI). An adapted follow-up of this study with similar goals was published by Alligood et al. (2019), who identified productivity during the 2000–15 period. They included an expanded database criterion and focused their analysis in 715 peer-reviewed journals indexed by the PsycINFO database. Another study is Kelley et al. (2015), who identified prolific practitioners in the field of applied behavior analysis and described recommended practices for research productivity. Finally, Kranak et al. (2020) identified publication trends in the *Journal of Applied Behavior Analysis* (*JABA*) and analyzed the results based on the authors' gender, years of publishing in the field (i.e., new vs. veteran authors), and authorship order.

Synthesis of literature and implications

To date, the extant literature on dissemination in behavior analysis has primarily focused on dissemination via the writing medium (e.g., peer-reviewed publications). In the preceding section, we reviewed how published accounts of dissemination via writing falls into the categories of nonempirical writing or teaching writing, empirical study on teaching writing, and bibliographical research on publishing productively. Nonempirical accounts discuss the importance of approaching dissemination—and, generally, writing—as a form of verbal behavior and thereby subject to the same environmental influences as most operant behavior. Empirical studies on teaching cover a range of populations and writing products, with little empirical work on using the science of behavior to improve writing for dissemination. Finally, bibliographical research sheds light on productivity metrics and publication trends.

Collectively, the synthesized literature provides several implications that we will use as the basis for practice recommendations in the subsequent section. First, using principles of behavior science, prospective authors can emit a variety of responses to directly improve their writing repertoire (e.g., Luiselli, 2010). Second, understanding the processes involved in dissemination can inform expectations and other choices, such as dissemination outlets, authorship, and promoting one's work. Third, through these recommendations, many unethical issues may be circumvented, but other potential pitfalls exist that warrant further discussion.

Practice recommendations

Writing for dissemination

Antecedents to publishing. Behavior analysts must read the research literature in order to stay current with the most contemporary evidence-based practices (BACB, 2020), and this activity is also a prerequisite to writing for publication. One reason is that authors have to be knowledgeable about publication trends such as the range of topics appearing in peer-reviewed journals, direction of research inquiry, and research recommendations that can guide potentially publishable projects. A second purpose of dedicated reading is to be familiar with the research subject matter and research methodologies that specific journals publish. A manuscript describing a well-executed and heuristic (i.e., hypothesis-generating) case study as an example will not be reviewed favorably by journals that only publish rigorous experimental research. Finally, much can be learned about writing style and exposition by carefully reading multiple journals and, in particular, articles published by highly visible and respected authors—in effect, there are many exemplary models to emulate!

Mattson (2017) presented several tips for accessing the peer-reviewed literature. Searching for relevant content begins by reading the dominant ABA journals, notably, *Behavior Analysis in Practice, Behavior Analysis: Research and Practice, Behavioral Interventions, Behavior Modification, Child & Family Behavior Therapy, Journal of Applied Behavior Analysis, Journal of Behavioral Education, Perspectives on Behavior Science, The Analysis of Verbal Behavior, Journal of Organizational Behavior Management, and Education and Treatment of Children.* Many other multidisciplinary journals also publish behavioral research and should be read with regularity. Both hardcopy and electronic versions of journals are available through personal and institutional subscriptions and literature access can be gained as well from library accounts, internet databases such as PsycINFO and ERIC, and open-access repositories (e.g., Google Scholar, ResearchGate, Academia.edu). Further, most journals offer contents alert emails, which list all articles published in the most recent issue, some freely available, with corresponding author information to request copies (see Carr and Briggs (2010) for specific strategies on accessing published literature). Additional recommendations from Mattson (2017) are for professionals to prepare reading lists generated from career development goals, bookmark journal websites, plan formal "reading time" within a work schedule, and assemble journal clubs with colleagues (Parsons & Reid, 2011).

We noted earlier that Skinner (1981) offered writing advice, specifically to accumulate ideas in a writing notebook, work from an outline, start small, put words on paper you can revise later, write at the same time each day, and compose at a location set up exclusively for writing. Of note, only limited ABA research has focused on procedures to improve writing as evaluated with college students (Johnson et al., 2016), faculty (Boice, 1983), and professional authors (McDougall, 2006; Porritt et al., 2006), and concentrating on productivity, time devoted to writing, and meeting deadlines. Described below, several learning principles can be applied to build and maintain writing skills (Luiselli, 2010, 2017), and there is a wealth of writing advice presented in user-friendly guidebooks (King, 2010; Lamott, 2007; Silvia, 2018; Zinsser, 2012).

Building writing for dissemination into one's repertoire. The starting point for the following practice recommendations is to integrate writing for publication among the many responsibilities of busy ABA professionals. By putting a publication lens on clinical activities, performance improvement projects, consultations, and the like, you will produce data and service descriptions that can be molded into quality manuscripts suitable for journal submission.

1. Establish and adhere to a writing schedule in the same way you would plan staff meetings, supervision sessions, observations, and similar duties. Pick a day of the week (including weekends!) that is most conducive to maintaining a writing schedule, for example, a 60-minute period without interruption every Wednesday. Try to avoid a missed writing session but if encountered, make it up the following week.
2. Choose a writing location that is comfortable, eliminates distractions, and allows you to write productively. This degree of stimulus control may be exerted in your work office or at home, a library, or community café while enjoying a cup of coffee.
3. The benefits of scheduled writing sessions in a preferred location notwithstanding take advantage of "opportunistic writing" that arises outside of your planned day and time. Situations such as canceled meetings and arriving to your office an hour before the work day begins can be devoted to additional writing that will quickly increase output.
4. The best writing occurs when you are clear about what you want to say in the context of a case report, experimental study, discussion article, or systematic review. Consider how the manuscript contributes to the existing literature and identify several journals that publish on your topic and that publish your methodology.
5. Preparing an outline is a valuable prewriting task that will help organize your ideas, sequence sections of a manuscript, highlight critical narratives, and reference publication citations. Organize any notes that pertain to

manuscript preparation and arrange hardcopy or electronic versions of articles that are featured prominently in your writing.

6. Writing a publication-worthy manuscript takes time and patience. Successful writers are motivated by small gains, which add up gradually into a completed manuscript. There are several tactics that apply.

   - "Write for time" instead of number of words or pages produced. That is, focus on conscientiously adhering to your writing schedule and capitalizing on unanticipated writing opportunities independent of what ultimately appears on paper or the computer screen.
   - Another approach to successive approximation is to write the easiest sections of a manuscript first and compose short segments that capture main ideas but do not represent a final product.
   - Your first draft manuscript is just that an approximation that will be shaped into a journal submission through editing and rewriting. "Sloppy" first drafts are better than perfection-induced blank pages.
   - Use behavioral momentum to promote writing that sometimes stalls because the words just won't come. For example, you could write, "I am trying to start this manuscript about a study we completed on behavioral intervention for motor stereotypy. I am going to briefly describe some of the prior research that guided our work …"

7. Goal setting is a recommended tactic when beginning a manuscript as long as objectives can be achieved with respect to other responsibilities involved in the writing process. Designating deadlines for completion of a first-draft manuscript and journal submission are reasonable performance goals.

8. Build pleasurable activities into your writing schedule so that you contact reinforcers. In illustration, take a rest break or consume a favorite snack following a productive writing session, inform coauthors about positive advances in manuscript preparation, and celebrate eventual publication of your work. However, never use "not writing" as a programmed consequence, as this disrupts the habit formation afforded by the other tactics.

9. Be sure your manuscript meets all of the style and preparation guidelines of selected journals before submission, especially formatting, word count, page limits, and declarations of informed consent, funding, conflicts of interest, and compliance with ethical standards. Failure to attend to these matters will result in the manuscript being returned, more of your time correcting the errors and omissions, and delayed editorial review by the journal. Information for submission is usually described in the journal website under an "Author Guidelines" section.

Keep in mind that the preceding recommendations allow professionals to design an individually tailored writing program. Persons will differ on the time of day that optimizes attention and energy level (e.g., morning or afternoon writing sessions), writing-contingent pleasurable activities, preferred writing medium, and the most facilitative writing environment (see, for example,

Epstein, 1997). Performance monitoring of writing progress will confirm whether your chosen tactics are effective or need to be modified.

Finally, most journal publications are written collaboratively by two or more authors, and this process requires additional elements to a writing program. A writing group is a strong support for persons who have limited experience disseminating research, sets mutual accountability for writing projects, and offers a collaborative learning opportunity for improving writing skills (Drotar, 2000). Community writing demands a group leader who is responsible for coordinating assignments among and communicating with participants, tracking manuscript preparation, and supervising publication success including responses to editorial reviews that lead to manuscript revision and resubmission. Another challenge to collaborative efforts is ensuring that all participants understand and follow the ethical principles and practices of research dissemination detailed in this chapter.

Identifying Authorship. Authorship recognizes scientific contribution and identifies to the public who is responsible for the work (McGue, 2000). Unethical practices regarding authorship are prevalent (Smith & Master, 2017), including ghost authorship (i.e., exclusion of an important contributor) and gift authorship (i.e., inclusion of person who made little to no contribution). Scientists should reserve authorship for those who made a "substantial contribution" (APA, 2020, p. 46). According to the APA Manual, examples of substantial contribution may include formulating hypotheses, structuring the experiment design, conducting data analysis, or interpreting findings and results. Examples of nonsubstantial contributions could include designing apparatus, advising about analysis, collecting or entering data, and recruiting participants. In general, contributions that are technical in nature do not warrant authorship (McGue, 2000). A way to recognize contributors is by acknowledging their contributions in an author note. In addition, combinations of these tasks may justify authorship. Proper identification of authorship allows readers to easily contact who was responsible for the work. As a cumulative enterprise, science benefits from collaboration between peers, easy access to information that can allow replication of studies by scientists. Correct deidentification of authorship also allows editors to contact authors and request additional information of clarification. By accepting authorship, an author indicates that they are willing to publicly defend the information and its interpretation (McGue, 2000).

Collaboration and transparency are encouraged to avoid unethical conduct related to authorship. To mitigate these issues, some journals request "contributorship" information, asking self-report from each author's contribution (Smith & Master, 2017). The APA Manual (2020) recommends that collaborators should decide which tasks are necessary and how they will be divided, and which tasks or combinations of tasks merit authorship credit. This process can be dynamic, reassessing authorship may be necessary, and agreements should be documented in written form (McGue, 2020).

Regarding authorship order, collaborators are responsible for determining it, and it should reflect the relative contributions of all involved. The APA Manual (2020) mentioned that, in general, first author is the principal contributor, followed by names of contributors in order of decreasing contribution. It also notes that these conventions can vary from fields and journals (for a review of differing practices across discipline, see Marušić et al., 2011). Also, if authors played equal roles, this could be included in the author note (see Custer et al., 2021, or Fong et al., 2016, for an example of note).

Misconduct

Writing can be considered "problem behavior" if it produces undesirable outcomes. For example, unethical writing could mislead a reader, appropriate another writer's idea, and disrespect a participant's right to confidentiality. Table 10.1 depicts common problem behaviors discussed in the literature and recommendations to avoid misconduct.

Inaccurate Reporting consists of fabricating or falsifying data (McGue, 2000), presenting deceptive data, or omitting relevant information (APA, 2020; BACB, 2020). Researchers should report data in a way that "allows readers to draw reasonable conclusions about the validity and generalizability of research findings" (McGue, 2000, p. 82). Regarding data omission when reporting results, the APA Manual (2020) describes examples of this conduct, which include selectively failing to report observations to "present a more convincing story" or "representing data-generated hypothesis (post hoc) as if they were preplanned" (APA, 2020, p. 39). Possible controlling variables for inaccurate reports could be lack of time or attention when writing. Authors should reserve time to write carefully and revise their writings before submitting for publication.

Other controlling variables could be personal or professional biases and motivation of the writer. For example, if a researcher discovers that data do not support, or even contradict, their initial hypothesis, this could be aversive, and they could selectively report only data that suggest that their hypothesis was right. Engaging in this behavior could be negatively reinforced by avoiding social disapproval or positively reinforced by receiving recognition for presenting a more appealing story.

Another relevant variable is publication bias (Joober et al., 2012; Simundić, 2013), which is related to the relative higher likelihood to accept a manuscript for publication by a journal for a "positive result" study (e.g., treatment produced desirable outcome) in comparison with "negative results" (e.g., treatment produced no effect, opposite effect, or exploratory data). Being aware of this type of bias can influence the behavior of the writer to omit important information.

Bias related to research can occur even before publishing or reporting data. For example, errors related to bias can occur during the study design, selecting

TABLE 10.1 Writing misconducts.

Types	Description	Recommendations
Inaccurate Reporting	Fabricating or falsifying data, presenting deceptive data, or omitting important information.	- Report all relevant data and discuss them; - Acknowledge personal and professional biases and engage in intellectual honesty - Describe any missing data - If errors are discovered in published data, take steps to correct them by publishing a retraction or erratum; - Reserve time to write carefully and revise your writing.
Plagiarism	Presenting ideas, words, contributions, or images of others without proper citation or acknowledgment.	- Paraphrase and provide citation; - Directly quote the words of others and provide citation; - Reprint or adapt a table/figure or commercially copyrighted test item; - Reserve time to write carefully and revise your writing.
Self-Plagiarism	Misrepresenting information as original when it has been published before.	- Publish original work only; - If mentioning previous work, provide citation; - Reserve time to write carefully and revise your writing.
Piecemeal or *Fragmented Publication*	Unnecessary splitting of findings from one study into multiple works.	- Publish original work only; - If publication is part of a larger project, describe how these publications interrelate; - Reserve time to write carefully and revise your writing.

participants, and selecting measurement system (Pannucci & Wilkins, 2010). Being aware of types of research biases can be the first step to identify biases when disseminating information. Scientists should acknowledge personal and professional biases and motivation and engage in intellectual honesty when reporting information. Data should speak for science, not the scientist's biases or motivation. Scientists should report all relevant data. If a datum contradicts their initial hypothesis, it should be reported and discussed. If there are missing data, these should also be described. In addition, if errors are discovered after publication, a retraction or erratum should correct them by informing the community about these errors (APA, 2017).

Plagiarism consists of presenting ideas, words (APA, 2020; McGue, 2000), contributions (McGue, 2000), or images (APA, 2020) of another without proper citation or acknowledgment. This form of misconduct may be deliberate or unintentional. Possible controlling variables for plagiarism could be receiving credit from the scientific community for an "original" idea. Also, writers may engage in plagiarism due to response effort—it can be easier to simply "copy-paste" a sentence instead of writing it in their own words. Writers should directly quote the words of others and provide citation, paraphrase, reprint, or adapt a table/figure or a commercially copyrighted test item (APA, 2020). To avoid plagiarism of ideas, search the literature to find sources of ideas or facts that you are writing about. Also, when describing your own idea, use frames such as "I believe that" to distinguish between your idea and other's point of view. Finally, it is important to note that inappropriate citation can be problematic too, and researchers need to make sure that the source cited supports the claim being made (McGue, 2000). For example, attributing intellectual credit inappropriately can misrepresent the original work or give the reader misleading information that can lead to poor or inaccurate interpretation.

Researchers can be pressured by grant and academic institutions to increase the number of publications. This could be a controlling variable for misconduct writing, including *self-plagiarism* and *piecemeal publications*. *Self-Plagiarism* consists of misrepresenting information as original when it has been published before (APA, 2020). In other words, an author reuses parts of their previously published work in another publication without properly citing it (Debnath, 2016). For example, if a researcher publishes a previously published study in a new journal, it could be misleading to readers, who could expect that more information is available than actually exists. In addition, it could suggest replicability or lead to violations in copyright (APA, 2020). *Piecemeal* or *Fragmented Publication* consists of unnecessary splitting of the findings from one research effort into multiple works (APA, 2020, p. 42). Writers should avoid engaging in these behaviors. A new publication should consist of original work and should add new contributions to the literature. Scientists are expected to expand previous work but should cite and refer to it appropriately. To avoid piecemeal publication when there are multiple studies from the same project, authors should describe the project and how the other works interrelate. For example, if publication of a preliminary study precedes the publication of a subsequent study from the same project, the latter publication should explain how the samples relate (McGue, 2000).

Other types of misconduct when communicating findings consist of not protecting participants' confidentiality and not respecting agreements described in the informed consent for the study regarding data release (APA, 2020). The BACB (2020) also prescribes that behavior analysts should make efforts to prevent accidental or inadvertent sharing of confidential or identifying information when disseminating research data. An important discussion related participants' demographic information is the inclusion of individuals who are members of underrepresented populations (e.g., ethnicity, race, gender, gender identity, socioeconomic status, nationality, etc.) in the research process—from the recruitment to data report in publications Benefits of reporting more demographic data include broader dissemination of studies and development of culturally sensitive interventions (Jones et al., 2020). Considering that underrepresented populations could also be underserved and not have easy access to behavior-analytic services, behavior analysts should carefully consider which type of demographic information should be reported in publications in order to protect confidentiality and balance it with the need of inclusion of more demographic data of these populations.

Students, researchers, and writers should know that misconducts can have profound harmful effects in the world. Individuals who engage in these unethical behaviors can face publication rejection, long-term community rejection, and academic/employment censure. Thus, to avoid inaccurate reporting, plagiarism, self-plagiarism, and piecemeal publications, authors should attribute intellectual credit and reserve time to write carefully and revise their writing. In addition, editorial practices include mechanisms for correcting the literature and maintaining trust in scientific data. For example, if data are no longer considered trustworthy due to misconduct, publications may be retracted (Fang & Casadevall, 2011). Analyses of retracted articles are also reported in the "Retraction Watch" database, where retracted articles can be found (Collier, 2011).

Table 10.2 depicts a summary of recommendations for writing, writing for publication, and writing ethically for publication described in previous sections of this chapter. These guidelines mention appropriate and alternative behaviors that can prevent or replace unethical writing. Finally, when submitting a manuscript for publication, authors must disclose activities or relationships that might be perceived as potential conflicts of interest. If there are no conflicts of interests, this should be stated too.

Research direction

Navigating the dissemination process

Disseminating in peer-reviewed journals is the most typical form of scholarship in the sciences, but also the most difficult, with only about 30% of papers in our field being accepted for publication (see Reed, 2014). As described earlier, the process begins by identifying a journal that is a good outlet for the kind of work being submitted. Across all sciences, there is a continuum of journal outlets, spanning basic/conceptual concerns to frontline practical guides. Ethical dissemination requires speaking to the appropriate audience so the information being shared actually gets consumed. Audience control of the work thereby becomes imperative.

Basic journals in behavior analysis (e.g., *Journal of the Experimental Analysis of Behavior*) require precise documentation of research technicalities,

TABLE 10.2 Summary of recommendations.

Task	Barrier	Recommendations
Writing	*Lack of knowledge or Difficulty to know what to say*	- Receive academic training; - Discover what motivates you; - Read the research literature; - Identify gaps in the literature and potential contributions; - Emulate exemplary models of writing.
	Lack of time	- Schedule time to write; - Set writing goals for writing time; - Reschedule missed writing sessions; - Take advantage of "opportunistic writing".
	Lack of motivation to start and/or to continue writing	- Arrange antecedent events (e.g., setting, materials, remove distractions); - Manipulate motivating operations (e.g., avoid sleep deprivation); - Prepare an outline; - Write the easiest sections first; - Write a draft first and shape it after; - Use behavioral momentum; - Set goals and deadlines; - Include pleasurable activities into your writing schedule.
Writing for publication	*Lack of knowledge about journal guidelines*	- Read guidelines for submission and instructions for authors; - Reading recommendation: Luiselli (2010).
	Lack of knowledge on purpose of writing	- Discover types of publications and modalities (e.g., review, report, empirical study); - Decide if publishing inside or outside the field.
Writing ethically for publication	*Lack of knowledge on what is ethical/unethical*	- Consult scientific communities' guidelines including conflicts of interests, authorship, inaccurate reporting, plagiarism, self-plagiarism, and piecemeal publication; - Reading recommendation: APA *Manual for Publication* 7th edition (2020).

with explicit discussion of how the work contributes to fundamental knowledge of behavioral principles. Conceptual journals in behavior analysis (e.g., *Perspectives on Behavior Science*) do not require original data but demand strong contributions to conceptual issues of contemporary importance; these journals typically publish articles related to defining—or challenging existing definitions of—existing concepts, proposing new interpretations of existing research findings, or translating work from outside behavior analysis to advance foundational knowledge of behavioral concepts. Translational journals in behavior analysis span a wide continuum, in and of themselves (e.g., *The Analysis of Verbal Behavior, The Psychological Record, Behavior Analysis: Research & Practice, Journal of Applied Behavior Analysis*); the common thread of each of these journal outlets is a high degree of experimental rigor that is typically beyond what would naturally be present in actual service delivery) and generates information directly improving practice-related behavior or intervention development. Finally, practice-focused journals exist (e.g., *Behavioral Interventions, Behavior Analysis in Practice*) that publish applied research that mirrors the kinds of methods and control procedures that one would expect to be readily present in clinical settings. Practice-focused journals often share results of empirical evaluations of applied work (in nonlaboratory/controlled settings) or tutorials on using the extant scientific literature in behavior analysis to directly improve one's practical skillsets.

As one final note, readers should be advised of the nuances of open-access journals and predatory journals. Open-access journals typically require a substantial financial fee for payment, since the journals are open to the public and do not require library access or journal subscription to access it; these journals are often ideal outlets for grant-funded work, since grant funding agencies often require public access to the findings and because grant dollars can be used to pay the fee. Predatory journals disguise themselves as open access, but really exist to simply profit from authors—these journals often accept any work (so long as the author pays) and are not reputable in scientific communities (for more, see Grudniewicz et al., 2019; a curated list of *potential* predatory journals is provided by https://beallslist.net/). Submitting work to the wrong outlet may provide lengthy delays to dissemination, due to the publication process itself (see below).

Ethical dissemination of work to a peer-reviewed journal officially begins with manuscript submission. Most journals now use online portals to systematize the submission process and workflow (e.g., Editorial Manager, ScholarOne). A corresponding author must be identified from the author list—this person is the one who will receive all formal communications from the journal and must provide attestation to ethical concerns. The corresponding author need not be the lead (first) author in the author list (or, for that matter, they need not be in any particular sequence in the list); senior clinicians, laboratory directors, research/practical supervisors, or academic mentors often serve as the corresponding author. For example, graduate students may be a lead author, but the mentor may serve as corresponding author because the student will eventually graduate and lose their university email and address. Similarly, practitioners may move out of positions or across agencies, so a senior clinician or supervisor may serve as corresponding author because their contact information is more likely to remain static. The corresponding author will be asked to provide a statement that all ethical concerns of the work were appropriately managed. For example, research journals may ask for confirmation that an institutional review board approved the procedures, a human subjects committee endorsed the methods as having minimal risk of harm, and/ or an agency's clinical peer review committee approved intervention/treatment procedures (Luiselli & Russo, 2005). Moreover, the corresponding author must typically certify that all authors deserve authorship (see above) and all listed authors have approved of the manuscript submission. The corresponding author must be aware of these requirements and must truthfully answer those questions. Note that smaller clinical agencies often do not have internal review committees for research, but that does not preclude the work from needing such approvals (for more on this topic, see Mechling et al., 2014)—in those cases, identifying external review committees or collaborating with academic researchers who have access to such committees is advisable.

Upon submission, the manuscript and its paperwork of attestations are reviewed by the journal's Editor-in-Chief (EIC; typically only one or two persons serve in this capacity and oversee all operational and procedures processes). The EIC determines whether the manuscript is suitable for consideration, and if so, identifies which Associate Editor (AE; typically three or more individuals serve in this capacity—these AEs report to the EIC) directly handle the manuscript review process. The EIC will pick an AE with expertise most closely related to the work presented in the manuscript. The AE then selects and invites two to five reviewers from the journal's editorial board (an invited group of scholars with subject matter expertise directly relevant to the journal's mission) to provide peer review. Most often, journals employ a double-blind review process, wherein neither the authors of the submitted manuscript nor the journal reviewers know the identity of each other, to reduce bias. During the submission process, the corresponding author is typically instructed to disclose potential conflicts of interest with respect to the editorial board members of the journal. Doing so circumvents ethical dilemmas wherein a reviewer's judgment may be influenced by existing relationships or experiences with the author.

When reviewers receive a manuscript for peer review, they are typically given 2—5 weeks to return their comments. The reviewers critique all aspects of the manuscript: quality of writing, structure, grammar, thoroughness of the literature review/summary, rigor of the methods used, adequacy of analytic techniques, accuracy of results and their interpretation, discussion of limitations, implications for future work, and overall contribution to the literature (for a general checklist for peer reviewers of scientific manuscripts, see Parker et al., 2018). Reviewers are often instructed to provide an editorial recommendation (but also, maybe not; the AE ultimately makes the actual editorial decision). Editorial recommendations range from Reject (i.e., the manuscript is not adequate for publication and even moderate revision is unlikely to make it acceptable), Revision (i.e., additional work is necessary before it can be deemed acceptable; this may mean more data collection/analyses, clarifying results or data displays/tables, editing the writing, improving the discussion of existing research, etc.), to Accept (i.e., the manuscript is near-publication ready). Manuscripts with a Revision decision often undergo additional peer review, and the AE provides a decision letter instructing the authors on what revisions are necessary for the manuscript to be sent to reviewers. Manuscript with an Accept decision does not typically get sent back to reviewers, but the AE or EIC may have some additional minor revision requests (e.g., citation errors, formatting concerns, typographical mistakes) for the authors to handle before the manuscript is sent into production. Each round of peer review (from submission to decision letter) can range from as quickly at 2 weeks, to as long as several months, depending on the number of reviewers. Thus, if a manuscript is submitted to a journal in which it is not a good fit, it may take upward of 2 months to simply find out that it is rejected after review. It is important, then, to ensure that the manuscript is in good shape and matches the journal's mission, before ever submitting. A 2017 paper by Huisman and Smits suggests that, on the average, accepted manuscripts in Psychology or the Social Sciences required around 23 weeks from submission to acceptance, with approximately two rounds of review. And, as stated at the start of this section, only about 30% of submissions are accepted for publication (see Reed, 2014).

Once a manuscript is accepted, the corresponding author works with the journal's production team to handle all remaining copyedits, permissions to publish figures, and approves the page proofs before the manuscript will be printed. Most journals also require a copyright transfer from the author to the publishing house—thus, in these cases, the journals will own the copyright on the information printed. Clinical researchers should take careful note, as agency-specific materials such as datasheets, protocols, or resource tables will become copyrighted by the journal; if such proprietary information is intended to remain agency-owned, the corresponding author should ensure the copyright permissions account for that, or ensure that this information is not directly printed in the copyrighted article. Similarly, authors should be aware that images (stock photos, data figures, etc.) and reprinted material (e.g., figures or tables from another publication) must have copyright clearance or permissions granted from the copyright holder before the target journal will permit production of the article.

Postpublication conduct

Following publication, authors' ethical dissemination responsibilities for that work do not end. Authors have ethical obligations to respect the journal's copyright of the work and to respond to readers' inquiries. Many science promotion services now exist (e.g., ResearchGate) that enable authors to post their works. Authors who post the published version of articles may be violating the copyright standards of the journal in which their work was published. Journal publishers often permit some form of public dissemination, such as a preprint of the article (i.e., an earlier draft or an accepted version in manuscript form before typeset into article format), on social media or in digital archives designed for open access to scientific materials. Moreover, authors are obligated to respond to readers' requests for information related to the published product. For instance, the APA (Ethics Code 8.14; 2017) requires that authors "do not withhold the data on which their conclusions are based from other competent professionals who seek to verify the substantive claims through reanalysis and who intend to use such data only for that purpose, provided that the confidentiality of the participants can be protected and unless legal rights concerning proprietary data preclude their release." (APA, 2017, p. 12). Finally, if any portion of the manuscript is found to be inaccurate or misrepresented after publication, the authors should contact the journal's EIC and inquire about the best path forward, which typically entails a published erratum to correct for the inaccurate information—such errata are linked to the original publication so readers accessing the original work can also see the correction accompanying it.

Other considerations

While the focus of content in this chapter was on the ethics of dissemination in written form, we believe the considerations we raised apply to other forms of dissemination as well, whether it be conference presentations, invited talks/ workshops, or social media posts. However, we acknowledge unique ethical nuances associated with those forms of dissemination and will briefly convey some considerations here. When disseminating research outside of published works, it is important to recognize that the communicator is thereby making public statements, and this form of communication is subject to BACB Code 8.0. For example, presentations/posters and social media posts can be put out to the public without going through the gatekeeping safeguards afforded by peer review. These forms of dissemination may thereby be more prove to mistakenly (or, worse: intentionally) speaking beyond data (which could result in false or deceptive statements), sharing trademarked information in slides or images (which could violate intellectual property concerns), informal "storytelling" about the work that could inadvertently violate confidentiality of clients or participants, and/or providing testimonials or implicit advertising of one's employer/agency—all of which are violations of section 8.0 in the BACB Code. For specific guidance on properly approaching conference-based dissemination and social media use, we recommend readers consult Feldman and Silvia (2010) and O'Leary et al. (2017), respectively.

Across all forms of dissemination—publications, presentations, social media, or otherwise—certified behavior analysts are obliged to promote behavior-analytic methods and findings to the public (BACB, 2020) but too often, communicate in words that are confusing and off-putting to general audiences (Becirevic et al., 2016; Critchfield et al., 2017). In commenting about ABA language nearly 30 years ago, Bailey (1991) wrote, "Somehow we neglected to develop socially acceptable terminology for presenting our concepts to consumers" (p. 447). Similarly, Lindsley (1991) advised behavior analysts to drop the technical jargon in favor of plain English words that have accurate meaning, were learned at an early age, and most persons understand. But these issues of yesteryears remain issues today. For example, Critchfield et al. (2017) lamented behavior analysts' insistence on jargon, which often involves terms that mean something different in traditional parlance than in the field—they termed these uses of jargon: "*functionally abrasive repurposed terms* (FRTs)." They added that when behavior analysts emit FRTs, they "cast an unproductive haze over the interactions between behavior analysts and the nonexperts they hope to recruit as clients (or students, or colleagues, or professional allies)" (p. 103); moreover, "People who emit too many FRTs find themselves alone in the room—in view of which, we suggest that solitude is a poor vantage point from which to accomplish good in the everyday world" (p. 103). To avoid these missteps, we paraphrase Skinner (1957): select words for their effect on the reader/listener and not their effects on the writer/speaker. If behavior analysts desire to present ABA research accurately to other disciplines, potential consumers, and society-at-large, ethics demand that our language is welcoming and easy to comprehend. We recommend that readers consult Friman (2017) for a primer on research dissemination through public speaking, and Critchfield et al. (2017) for a discussion on the general public's view of "behaviorese" language and ways to circumvent associated pitfalls in dissemination.

In summary, behavior analysts are ethically obligated to serve as stewards of the field, and do so "by making information about it available to the public through presentations, discussions, and other media" (BACB Code 6.02). Ethical dissemination begins with effective dissemination—we hope the information disseminated in this chapter is effective in promoting both ethical and effective research dissemination.

References

Alligood, C., Anderson, C., & McGee, H. (2019). Casting a wider net: An analysis of scholarly contributions of behavior analysis graduate program faculty. *Behavior Analysis in Practice*, 12(2), 466–472. https://doi.org/10.1007/s40617-018-00281-x

American Psychological Association. (2017). http://www.apa.org/ethics/code/index.html [Accessed 27 June 2022].

American Psychological Association. (2020). *Publication manual of the American Psychological Association* (7th ed.). American Psychological Association.

Bailey, J. S. (1991). Marketing behavior analysis requires different talk. *Journal of Applied Behavior Analysis*, 24, 445–448. https://doi.org/10.1901/jaba.1991.24-445

Ballard, K. D., & Glynn, T. (1975). Behavioral self-management in story writing with elementary school children. *Journal of Applied Behavior Analysis, 8*(4), 387−398.

Becirevic, A., Critchfield, T. S., & Reed, D. D. (2016). On the social accessibility of behavior-analytic terms: Crowdsourced comparisons of lay and technical language. *The Behavior Analyst, 39*, 305−317. https://doi.org/10.1007/s40614-016-0067-4

Behavior Analyst Certification Board. (2020). *Ethics code for behavior analysts.* Retrieved from https://www.bacb.com/wp-content/uploads/2020/11/Ethics-Code-for-Behavior-Analysts-2109 02.pdf.

Boice, R. (1983). Contingency management in writing and the appearance of new ideas: Implications for the treatment of writing blocks. *Behavior Research and Therapy, 5*, 537−543. https://doi.org/10.1016/0005-7967(83)90045-1

Carr, J. E., & Briggs, A. M. (2010). Strategies for making regular contact with the scholarly literature. *Behavior Analysis in Practice, 3*, 13−18. https://doi.org/10.1007/BF03391760

Collier, R. (2011). Shedding light on retractions. *CMAJ: Canadian Medical Association Journal, 183*(7), E385−E386. https://doi.org/10.1503/cmaj.109-3827

Critchfield, T. S., Doepke, K. J., Kimberly Epting, L., Becirevic, A., Reed, D. D., Fienup, D. M., ... & Ecott, C. L. (2017). Normative emotional responses to behavior analysis jargon or how not to use words to win friends and influence people. *Behavior Analysis in Practice, 10*(2), 97−106. https://doi.org/10.1007/s40617-016-0161-9

Custer, T. N., Stiehl, C. M., & Lerman, D. C. (2021). Outcomes of a practical approach for improving conversation skills in adults with autism. *Journal of Applied Behavior Analysis, 54*(1), 309−333. https://doi.org/10.1002/jaba.752

Debnath, J. (2016). Plagiarism: A silent epidemic in scientific writing−Reasons, recognition and remedies. *Medical Journal Armed Forces India, 72*(2), 164−167. https://doi.org/10.1016/j.mjafi.2016.03.010

Delano, M. E. (2007). Improving written language performance of adolescents with asperger syndrome. *Journal of Applied Behavior Analysis, 40*(2), 345−351. https://doi.org/10.1901/jaba.2007.50-06

Dixon, M. R., Reed, D. D., Smith, T., Belisle, J., & Jackson, R. E. (2015). Research rankings of behavior analytic graduate training programs and their faculty. *Behavior Analysis in Practice, 8*(1), 7−15. https://doi.org/10.1007/s40617-015-0057-0

Drotar, D. (2000). Training professional psychologists to write and publish: The utility of a writer's workshop seminar. *Professional Psychology: Research and Practice, 31*, 453−457. https://psycnet.apa.org/doi/10.1037/0735-7028.31.4.453.

Epstein, R. (1997). Skinner as self-manager. *Journal of Applied Behavior Analysis, 30*, 545−568. https://psycnet.apa.org/doi/10.1901/jaba.1997.30-545.

Fang, F. C., & Casadevall, A. (2011). Retracted science and the retraction index. *Infection and Immunity, 79*(10), 3855−3859. https://doi.org/10.1128/IAI.05661-11

Fawcett, S. B., & Fletcher, R. K. (1977). Community applications of instructional technology: Training writers of instructional packages. *Journal of Applied Behavior Analysis, 10*(4), 739−746. https://doi.org/10.1901/jaba.1977.10-739

Feldman, D. B., & Silvia, P. J. (2010). *Public speaking for psychologists: A lighthearted guide to research presentations, job talks, and other opportunities to embarrass yourself.* Washington, D.C.: American Psychological Association.

Fong, E. H., Catagnus, R. M., Brodhead, M. T., Quigley, S., & Field, S. (2016). Developing the cultural awareness skills of behavior analysts. *Behavior Analysis in Practice, 9*(1), 84−94. https://doi.org/10.1007/s40617-016-0111-6

Friman, P. C. (2017). Practice dissemination: Public speaking. In J. K. Luiselli (Ed.), *Applied behavior analysis advanced guidebook: A manual for professional practice* (pp. 349–365). Elsevier/Academic Press.

Hanna, E. S., Souza, D. G., Rose, J. C., & Fonseca, M. (2004). Effects of delayed constructed-response identity matching on spelling of dictated words. *Journal of Applied Behavior Analysis, 37*(2), 223–227. https://doi.org/10.1901/jaba.2004.37-223

Glover, J., & Gary, A. L. (1976). Procedures to increase some aspects of creativity. *Journal of Applied Behavior Analysis, 9*(1), 79–84. https://doi.org/10.1901/jaba.1976.9-79

Grudniewicz, A., Moher, D., Cobey, K. D., Bryson, G. L., Cukier, S., Allen, K., ... & Lalu, M. M. (2019). Predatory journals: no definition, no defence. *Nature, 576*, 210–212. https://www.nature.com/articles/d41586-019-03759-y.

Hansen, B. D., & Wills, H. P. (2014). The effects of goal setting, contingent reward, and instruction on writing skills. *Journal of Applied Behavior Analysis, 47*(1), 171–175. https://doi.org/10.1002/jaba.92

Johnson, P. E., Perris, C. J., Salo, A., Deschaine, E., & Johnson, B. (2016). Use of an explicit rule decreases procrastination of university students. *Journal of Applied Behavior Analysis, 49*, 1–13. https://doi.org/10.1002/jaba.287

Jones, S. H., St Peter, C. C., & Ruckle, M. M. (2020). Reporting of demographic variables in the journal of applied behavior analysis. *Journal of Applied Behavior Analysis, 53*(3), 1304–1315. https://doi.org/10.1002/jaba.722

Joober, R., Schmitz, N., Annable, L., & Boksa, P. (2012). Publication bias: What are the challenges and can they be overcome? *Journal of Psychiatry & Neuroscience: JPN, 37*(3), 149–152. https://doi.org/10.1503/jpn.120065

Kelley, D. P., Wilder, D. A., Carr, J. E., Rey, C., Green, N., & Lipschultz, J. (2015). Research productivity among practitioners in behavior analysis: Recommendations from the prolific. *Behavior Analysis in Practice, 8*(2), 201–206. https://doi.org/10.1007/s40617-015-0064-1

King, S. (2010). *On writing: A memoir of the craft.* Scribner.

Kranak, M. P., Falligant, J. M., Bradtke, P., Hausman, N. L., & Rooker, G. W. (2020). Authorship trends in the journal of applied behavior analysis: An update. *Journal of Applied Behavior Analysis, 53*(4), 2376–2384. https://doi.org/10.1002/jaba.726

Lamott, A. (2007). *Bird by bird: Some instructions on writing and life.* Anchor.

Lindsley, O. R. (1991). From technical jargon to plain English for application. *Journal of Applied Behavior Analysis, 24*, 449–458. https://doi.org/10.1901/jaba.1991.24-449

Luiselli, J. K. (2010). Writing for publication: A performance enhancement guide for the human services professional. *Behavior Modification, 34*(5), 459–473. https://doi.org/10.1177/0145445510383529

Luiselli, J. K. (2017). Practice dissemination: Writing for publication. In J. K. Luiselli (Ed.), *Applied behavior analysis advanced guidebook: A manual for professional practice* (pp. 325–347). Elsevier/Academic Press.

Luiselli, J. K., & Russo, D. C. (2005). Clinical peer review: Description of a comprehensive model in behavioral healthcare. *Behavior Modification, 29*(3), 470–487. https://doi.org/10.1177/0145445504273279

Luna, O., & Rapp, J. T. (2019). Using a checklist to increase objective session note writing: Preliminary results. *Behavior Analysis in Practice, 12*, 622–626. https://doi.org/10.1007/s40617-018-00315-4

Marušić, A., Bošnjak, L., & Jeronćić, A. (2011). A systematic review of research on the meaning, ethics and practices of authorship across scholarly disciplines. *PloS ONE, 6*(9), e23477.

Mattson, J. G. (2017). Continuing education: Accessing the peer-reviewed literature. In J. K. Luiselli (Ed.), *Applied behavior analysis advanced guidebook: A manual for professional practice* (pp. 309–324). Elsevier/Academic Press.

McDougall, D. (2006). The distributed changing criterion design. *Journal of Behavioral Education, 15,* 237–247.

McGue, M. (2000). Authorship and intellectual property. In B. D. Sales, & S. Folkman (Eds.), *Ethics in research with human participants* (pp. 75–95). American Psychological Association.

Mechling, L., Gast, D. L., & Lane, J. D. (2014). Ethical principles and practices in research. In D. L. Gast, & J. R. Ledford (Eds.), *Single case research methodology: Applications in special education and behavioral sciences* (pp. 31–49). New York: Routledge.

O'Leary, P. N., Miller, M. M., Olive, M. L., & Kelly, A. N. (2017). Blurred lines: Ethical implications of social media for behavior analysts. *Behavior Analysis in Practice, 10,* 45–51. https://doi.org/10.1007/s40617-014-0033-0

Pannucci, C. J., & Wilkins, E. G. (2010). Identifying and avoiding bias in research. *Plastic and Reconstructive Surgery, 126*(2), 619–625. https://doi.org/10.1097/PRS.0b013e3181de24bc

Parker, T. H., Griffith, S. C., Bronstein, J. L., Fidler, F., Foster, S., Fraser, H., … Nakagawa, S. (2018). Empowering peer reviewers with a checklist to improve transparency. *Nature Ecology & Evolution, 2*(6), 929–935. https://doi.org/10.1038/s41559-018-0545-z

Parsons, M. B., & Reid, D. H. (2011). A practical means of enhancing professional knowledge among human services practitioners. *Behavior Analysis in Practice, 4,* 53–58. https://doi.org/10.1007/BF03391784

Pennington, R., Delano, M., & Scott, R. (2014). Improving cover-letter writing skills of individuals with intellectual disabilities. *Journal of Applied Behavior Analysis, 47*(1), 204–208. https://doi.org/10.1002/jaba.96

Porritt, M., Burt, A., & Poling, A. (2006). Increasing fiction writers' productivity through an internet-based intervention. *Journal of Applied Behavior Analysis, 39*(3), 393–397. https://doi.org/10.1901/jaba.2006.134-05

Ramey, G., Peters, J., Souweine, J., & Sulzer-Azaroff, B. (1978). Effect of the manuscript task analysis on evaluating applied behavior analysis research: A technical report. *Journal of Applied Behavior Analysis, 11*(4), 528. https://doi.org/10.1901/jaba.1978.11-528

Reed, D. D. (2014). Determining how, when, and whether you should publish outside the box: Sober advice for early career behavior analysts. *The Behavior Analyst, 37*(2), 83–86. https://doi.org/10.1007/s40614-014-0012-3

Schlinger, H. D., Jr. (2014). Training graduate students to effectively disseminate behavior analysis and to counter misrepresentations. *Behavior Analysis in Practice, 8*(1), 110–112. https://doi.org/10.1007/s40617-014-0028-x

Silvia, P. J. (2018). *How to write a lot: A practical guide to productive academic writing.* American Psychological Press.

Simundić, A. M. (2013). Bias in research. *Biochemia Medica, 23*(1), 12–15. https://doi.org/10.11613/bm.2013.003

Skinner, B. F. (1957). *Verbal behavior.* Appleton-Century-Crofts.

Skinner, B. F. (1981). How to discover what you have to say: Talk to students. *Behavior Analyst, 4,* 1–7. https://doi.org/10.1007/BF03391847

Smith, E., & Master, Z. (2017). Best practice to order authors in multi/interdisciplinary health sciences research publications. *Accountability in Research, 24*(4), 243–267.

Stromer, R., Mackay, H. A., McVay, A. A., & Fowler, T. (1998). Written lists as mediating stimuli in the matching-to-sample performances of individuals with mental retardation. *Journal of Applied Behavior Analysis, 31*(1), 1–19. https://doi.org/10.1901/jaba.1998.31-1

Vargas, J. S. (1978). A behavioral approach to the teaching of composition. *The Behavior Analyst, 1,* 1624.

Wallace, I., & Pear, J. J. (1977). Self-control techniques of famous novelists. *Journal of Applied Behavior Analysis, 10,* 515–525.

Welsh, T. M. (1987). Teaching writing functionally: A review of Peter Elbow's writing with power. *The Behavior Analyst, 10,* 109110.

Zinsser, W. (2012). *On writing well: An informal guide to writing nonfiction.* Harper Perennial.

Chapter 11

Supporting the replication of your research

Heather J. Forbes[1], Jason C. Travers[2] and Jenee Vickers Johnson[3]

[1]*West Virginia University, Morgantown, WV, United States;* [2]*Temple University, Philadelphia, PA, United States;* [3]*University of Kansas, Lawrence, KS, United States*

Scientific experimentation is the best approach currently available for examining nature and understanding facts of reality, including the behavior of organisms. However, a single experimental study is usually insufficient evidence to warrant high confidence in claims about the general facts of reality. Although findings from a single study can be interesting, original claims are considered validated when multiple, similar studies subsequently report similar findings (i.e., replication research). This means replication is a cornerstone of any scientific discipline where experimentation is used to understand a phenomenon of interest.

Replication functions as an instrument for verification of claims because original discoveries, though exciting, can be incorrect. Incorrect findings occur because scientific methods of investigation are imperfect, and scientists themselves may make errors or biased decisions. Also, extreme findings (especially an unprecedented result) often may reflect outliers that are the product of researcher error, bias, or limited understanding about the phenomenon under study. Outliers are likely to disappear or weaken after multiple, independent researchers, who are less likely to have an investment in or bias toward a particular outcome, conduct replication studies. The cycle of novel experimentation followed by multiple replications for verification characterizes the controlled albeit progressive nature of science and illustrates why science is successful for understanding, predicting, and improving our world.

Replication research also provides an opportunity to refine research methods to increase efficacy and accuracy of findings, including findings that may need correcting. If original findings are not subjected to rigorous scrutiny to verify and correct (via replication studies), then it is possible that erroneous claims will accumulate in a scientific corpus in ways that ultimately harm individuals and society (Ioannidis, 2005). The detection (and correction) of

Research Ethics in Behavior Analysis. https://doi.org/10.1016/B978-0-323-90969-3.00003-7

errors and inconsistencies in research is integral to maintaining ethical practice. Koocher and Keith-Spiegel (1998) outlined several ethical principles of psychological practice that have been valuable to applied behavior analysis researchers (e.g., Bailey & Burch, 2016). At least two of these principles, *benefitting others* and *do no harm*, relate to the importance of accurate research findings disseminated by researchers in scientific journals. For example, ABA professionals who rely on erroneous research findings to inform treatment decisions may intervene in ways unlikely to benefit clients, which can be considered an indirect form of harm. Interestingly, researchers in several scientific fields over past and recent decades appear to have published studies with novel findings that are not replicable (Earp & Trafimow, 2015).

In this chapter, we explain the replication crisis affecting most scientific fields and the circumstances that brought widespread attention to this concerning issue. We then provide perspectives about replication as it relates to single case experimental research (SCER) and behavior analysis. Attention also is allocated toward suggestions about how to make SCER more transparent in ways that facilitate replication research. Finally, we describe individual and institutional changes that can foster rigorous, honest, and transparent research practices, including replication research, to promote adherence to ethical principles that guide researchers (e.g., being just, being faithful, treating others with care and compassion, pursuing excellence, accepting accountability; Koocher & Keith-Spiegel, 1998).

The replication crisis

The replication crisis is a term used to refer to widespread concern about the accumulation of erroneous studies in scientific literature. Psychology researchers arguably have played a central role in the replication crisis (Wiggins & Chrisopherson, 2019), but other fields including medicine (Gehr et al., 2006; Ioannidis, 2005), economics (Duvendack et al., 2017), political science (Gerber et al., 2001), and education (Makel & Plucker, 2014) also appear to be affected. Although much attention to replication and the replication crisis is relatively recent, some researchers have long warned about limited replication in the psychology research literature. For example, Rosenthal (1979) described various barriers preventing publication of well-conducted replication studies that showed null results (i.e., publication bias). Such barriers included journal editors who favored studies with novel, positive, and sensational claims that bolstered citations, subscriptions, and researcher reputations. Editors simultaneously disfavored studies with results that showed small effects, no effects, or otherwise contradicted prior research. Publication bias meant many studies were ignored primarily because they showed a treatment was ineffective, a phenomenon was undetected, or a theory used to explain the observation was unsupported. Sensational but potentially inaccurate claims were therefore left uncorrected in scientific journals.

The significance of publication bias is difficult to underestimate. Failing to publish replication studies (particularly studies with null results) can have similar, harmful effects as failing to conduct replication studies at the outset. As previously explained, the accumulation of inaccurate research findings can cause harm when the literature leads professionals to use interventions that are unlikely to benefit their clients, and/or they may not have at their disposal the effective interventions necessary for positive client outcomes. Scientific researchers are ethically obligated to engage in scrupulous and honest research practices that increase the probability of trustworthy findings (Public Health Service Policies on Research Misconduct, 2005). However, publication bias may function as punishment for rigorous replication studies that do not reproduce previously positive effects, which can prevent clarifying for whom and under what conditions an intervention may (or may not) work. Publication bias also may motivate researchers to behave in ways more likely to generate sensational and positive (i.e., publishable) findings. Various contingencies of reinforcement associated with academic or scientific jobs may motivate researcher behavior toward biased outcomes and include enhanced reputation, more grant funding, tenure and promotion, invitations to speak, consulting opportunities, and others associated with the status conferred by frequent publication. In other words, publication bias and reinforcing contingencies can lead researchers to engage in questionable research practices (QRPs).

QRPs are researcher behaviors that influence study results toward a particular, desired outcome rather than an objective understanding of the actual state of affairs. Much of the discussion regarding QRPs has centered on group comparisons research and include manipulating data and statistical analyses to get significant results (e.g., p-hacking) as well as stopping or continuing data collection until favorable result are detected. QRPs in group research can also involve making specific "predictions" only after study results are known (i.e., hypothesizing after results are known [HARKing]; Kerr, 1998).

Wiggins and Chrisopherson (2019) explained how three events in 2011 brought publication bias and QRPs to the forefront for scientists across numerous fields. They first described a study by Bem (2011), who claimed to have found evidence of extrasensory perception (i.e., "pre-cognition") and published his findings in a prominent personality and social psychology journal. Researchers who attempted to publish replication studies exposing the flaws in Bem's study initially were unsuccessful because of the journal's policy to publish only original research and not replications (Aldhous, 2011). This obstruction of the self-correcting process of science resulted in vocal criticism toward the journal editors by members of the experimental psychology community (Wiggins & Chrisopherson, 2019).

Wiggins and Chrisopherson (2019) described a second event in 2011 that revealed rampant QRPs by prominent researchers. Leading social psychology researcher Diedrik Stapel was discovered to have blatantly fabricated data for several dozen, highly-cited studies in top psychology journals. As of March 2022, Stapel had 58 articles retracted from peer reviewed journals. Concerns about the scope of this problem led to the discovery of additional cases of questionable evidence in the scientific corpus (see https://retractionwatch.com for information and stories related to Stapel as well as other retractions of fraudulent research). These and other high-profile examples of researcher misconduct began to garner attention from psychology researchers and the broader scientific community, which prompted some scientists to begin examining more critically the published research in their respective fields (Wiggins & Chrisopherson, 2019). The replication crisis, as it was dubbed by researchers and popular media journalists alike, began gaining broader attention.

Wiggins and Chrisopherson (2019) finally credited an article by Simmons et al. (2011) for revealing how easily QRPs can be used to manipulate data and produce different (and desired) research findings. Simmons et al. showed that QRPs evident in group comparisons research could readily produce both statistically significant and statistically insignificant results from an identical dataset. Their compelling demonstrations revealed how different methods for analyzing the same data can produce very different findings that can be used to support or reject hypotheses. Collectively, the three events described by Wiggins and Christopherson stirred somewhat of an awakening among researchers in various scientific fields about the replication crisis as well as the potential and actual problems in their respective bodies of research (Wiggins & Chrisopherson, 2019).

Attention to the replication crisis perhaps reached a pinnacle of awareness with the publication of results from the Reproducibility Project (Open Science Collaboration, 2015). This group of researchers replicated 100 influential psychology studies that originally reported positive effects. The Open Science Collaboration found only 36% of original findings replicated, and when original results were reproduced, the effect sizes were only half as large as those obtained in original studies. The Reproducibility Project results garnered national media attention and the replication crisis became a mainstream topic of conversation.

The problems highlighted by publication bias, QRPs, and the replication crisis should make clear why replication is a central tenet of scientific research. Replication research is necessary to detect and advance accurate scientific knowledge and, when absent, the scientific corpus is vulnerable to accumulation of honest errors and deliberate misrepresentation. This is concerning for practical and empirical reasons. For example, professionals (e.g., behavior analysts, special educators, speech-language pathologists) may perceive a bogus intervention as potentially effective and, in turn, invest in the bogus intervention rather than something more likely to benefit the client. Similarly, behavior analysts may apply an intervention to decrease severe self-injurious behavior with no positive effect and negative (i.e., harmful) effects.

This example reflects how dignity is undermined (by way of perpetuating reliance on others for basic needs) and conflicts with prioritizing care and compassion of clients (Bailey & Burch, 2016). Also, a misleading corpus may direct researchers to pursue lines of inquiry that do not lead to valuable discoveries, thereby wasting intellectual and other resources that could otherwise be directed toward promising research. Such wastefulness of intellectual and material resources needed for knowledge generation stymies the pursuit of excellence in behavior analysis.

Maintaining an accurate scientific corpus is integral to ensuring beneficial outcomes for society, which constitute a central principle of ethical conduct (Koocher & Keith-Spiegel, 1998). Problems reflected by the replication crisis also underscore why researchers must make available various details about their studies, including details not traditionally published in journal articles (e.g., pre-study research plans, procedural manuals, raw data, code/syntax or databases used for data analyses, precise materials used). Such transparency undeniably fosters more reliable replication studies, facilitates the detection of honest errors, and (perhaps most importantly) may deter researchers from engaging in QRPs.

The issues that gave rise to the replication crisis may give the impression that QRPs and publication bias are limited to group comparisons research. Readers might therefore wrongly presume behavior analysis researchers, who largely use single-case experimental research (SCER) designs, need not be concerned about the integrity of their scientific behavior (Hantula, 2019). Experts have nevertheless highlighted how SCER is not immune to various QRPs (Laraway et al., 2019; Shadish et al., 2016). For example, Tincani and Travers, in press described several QRPs that are possible in SCER when selecting participants, defining variables, documenting procedural fidelity, and analyzing and reporting data (see Table 11.1). For example, Tincani and Travers suggested that variable selection or modification bias might affect single case researchers who change their dependent variable in specific ways after discovering that some responses are unlikely to improve following intervention (i.e., removing difficult responses in a task analysis). This could result in higher responsivity, which might wrongly convey to professionals a perceived value of the intervention for improving specific behavior.

There is some evidence that QRPs exist in SCER and may be motivated by similar incentives affecting group comparisons researchers. Shadish et al. (2016) surveyed 243 single-case researchers and found respondents were significantly less likely to submit or accept a manuscript for publication if experimental effects were small than if effects were large (i.e., publication bias). Publication bias in SCER was further evidenced by a study that found larger treatment effects in published SCER than unpublished (i.e., gray) studies of similar methodological quality (Sham & Smith, 2014). The limited findings and arguments suggest single-case researchers should attend closely to the rigor, integrity, and transparency of their research to foster replication

TABLE 11.1 Some questionable research practices (QRPs) in single-case experimental research.

QRP	Definition	Example
Participant selection bias	Occurs when researchers select participants based on foreknowledge or reasonable suspicion about exceptional (i.e., atypical) responding to the intervention.	Researchers discover a prospective participant has a history of conditional discrimination training and therefore include the participant in a study where such a history will likely amplify the perceived effects of the intervention. The researchers do not disclose this detail, which suggests individuals without the participant's history will respond similarly.
Variable selection or modification bias	Occurs when researchers select or modify independent and/or dependent variables in ways that enhance perceived effects of an intervention.	Researchers discover during the baseline condition that some steps in a task analysis (dependent variable) will be particularly difficult for one or more participants to master. Researchers therefore change the task analysis to omit those steps from the teaching procedures (independent variable) and do not measure those behaviors during the intervention condition.
Procedural fidelity documentation bias	Occurs when researchers add unnecessary and simple steps to a protocol in order to inflate perceived fidelity, or when difficult steps are omitted from a protocol to inflate perceived fidelity.	Researchers discover during the intervention condition that teachers who deliver the intervention have difficulty following portions of the procedure. The researchers decide to omit a few difficult steps (e.g., an error correction procedure) and add several easy and irrelevant steps to the protocol (e.g., smiling, looking toward the student). They then use video recordings to re-score the sessions for procedural fidelity.
Graphed data distortion	Occurs when researchers adjust the scale of x-axis or y-axis of a single-case research line graph in ways that amplify the perceived effects of an intervention.	Researchers conclude a study and notice their intervention had a consistent albeit small effect on percentage of tasks completed correctly. Researchers therefore adjust the maximum value on the y-axis from 100% to 60%, which enhances the perceived level change between baseline and intervention conditions. Researchers also extend the length of the x-axis to give an impression the data are more stable.
Statistical method and reporting bias	Occurs when researchers use various statistical methods to analyze study data and only report results for statistical analyses perceived to be advantageous.	Researchers calculate multiple effect size metrics for their single-case dataset and only report the metric that generated the largest statistic.
Selective reporting	Occurs when researchers exclude from their reports the results for participants or conditions that are perceived to be unfavorable (for publication or otherwise).	Researchers analyze results for five participants in a multiple-baseline across participants design. Results for the first four participants are positive and suggest a functional relation, but the fifth participant did not respond to the intervention. The researchers decide to exclude the fifth participant from their report.

Note. Adapted from Tincani, M., & Travers, J. C.. (in press). Questionable Research Practices in Single-Case Experimental Designs: Examples and Possible Solutions. In O'Donohue W., Masuda A., & Lilienfeld S. O. (Eds.), *Questionable research practices: Designing, conducting, and reporting sound research in clinical psychology.* Cham, Switzerland: Springer Publications.

and resist QRPs. Similarly, researchers who review their peer's research should consider whether bias or QRPs might have influenced study outcomes, and encourage researchers to be transparent about decisions that may have affected results (by examining them in their limitations section, for example). It also seems incumbent upon leading researchers, especially those training future researchers, to model ethical research behavior and create contingencies for reinforcing rigorous, transparent, and honest research activity.

SCER is, however, fundamentally different from group comparisons research in experimental logic and method. This means the conceptual foundations of replication are different for SCER designs than group designs. Also, scientific behaviors that enhance transparency and replicability (as well as potential ethical concerns resulting from increased transparency) can manifest differently in SCER.

Replication and single-case experimental research

Single-case experimental researchers who are committed to discovery and knowledge generation (i.e., pursuit of excellence) are obliged to support replication of their research. Specifically, researchers must describe their method with sufficient transparency and meticulous precision so that other researchers can (1) evaluate whether the study design was sufficient to allow for detection of a causal relation between independent and dependent variables and (2) conduct additional (i.e., replication) studies to establish the veracity of original claims. In behavior analysis research and practice, such circumstances lead to technological advances that stimulate new research and improved services. Researchers who support replication provide a clearer path for later discoveries that produce tangible benefit to individuals and society. Unlike group comparisons research, replication is a central feature of SCER.

Group comparisons research designs can involve a single assessment of a dependent (i.e., outcome) variable for each participant and experimental condition. For example, group researchers investigating a novel intervention might randomly assign participants to an intervention or treatment-as-usual condition (while ensuring both groups demonstrate equivalent baseline characteristics). Following the intervention, the researchers administer a standardized test to each participant and then statistically compare average test scores for each group to determine whether they are significantly different. This process must be repeated across multiple studies because group designs do not include opportunities to replicate treatment effects. Conversely, SCER design is characterized by repeated measurement of the dependent variable for each participant throughout the study (rather than at pre- and post-intervention only) as well as replication of experimental conditions. For example, a multiple-baseline design might involve (staggered) ongoing measurement of responding during replicated baseline and intervention condition across three different behaviors. The result is replicated demonstrations of intervention effects at different points in time that only occur following introduction of the intervention. This and similar replications are inherent in SCER designs and is necessary for demonstrating a functional relation between an independent and dependent variable.

Some single-case researchers may not report results for participants who show small or no responding to the independent variable (i.e., selective reporting; Shadish et al., 2016). Similarly, a single-case researcher might accidently enter the wrong information when transferring handwritten data to an electronic format or make a mistake when calculating percentage or rate. Although the impact of some of these errors may be negligible (e.g., reporting one incorrect but close-to-correct datum), other errors can have a significant influence on researcher claims (e.g., failing to report results for two of five participants). Furthermore, QRPs are not often evident to peer reviewers. For example, a reviewer usually has no way of detecting whether information for one or more participants has been omitted in a manuscript. This means the quality-control function of peer review is not sufficient to protect the scientific corpus from erroneous findings produced by QRPs. Instead, independent replication is the prevailing tool for ensuring the integrity of scientific knowledge.

Replication is also important for understanding, explaining, and improving the world outside of a tightly controlled experiment. A frequent goal of applied behavior analysis research is developing behavior change technologies that are relevant in more than one circumstance (Cooper et al., 2020). Generality (i.e., external validity) is the extent to which findings from a controlled experiment can be extended to different populations, settings, and conditions in the world at-large. A common misconception is that generality of research findings is primarily related to sample size (Walker & Carr, 2021). This misconception may lead to a claim that findings from SCER are inherently less generalizable than group comparison research findings (e.g., Purswell & Ray, 2014). However, sample size is neither the sole nor the most important factor for establishing the generality of findings.

Several variables other than sample size influence generality. These include, but are not limited to the heterogeneity of study participants, representativeness of participants to the population of interest, and methods for analyzing and reporting data (Branch & Pennypacker, 2013). Accordingly, some researchers have argued that replication within and across SCER studies may be a more reliable method establishing generality than studies with large sample sizes. That is, multiple SCER studies may better inform for whom and under what conditions an intervention appears effective than average effects for a large, representative sample (Branch & Pennypacker, 2013). The replication within and across SCER studies is especially relevant for professionals who must decide which intervention(s) to use for a client because average effects from a group comparison study may not generalize to the individuals they serve (Branch & Pennypacker, 2013). Replication in SCER is necessary for evaluating the extent to which claims hold true in different circumstances, including claims about the relationship between environment (e.g., interventions) and behavior. Understanding these relationships is important for ensuring that researchers (and professionals) do no harm, engage in behavior that benefits others, advance the pursuit of excellence, and are being truthful (Koocher & Keith-Spiegel, 1998).

Types of replication in single-case experimental research

Sidman (1960) distinguished between two different kinds of replication in SCER–direct and systematic replication. A *direct replication* is an experiment wherein researchers aim to verify findings from an original experiment (i.e., assess accuracy and reliability of findings). This means features of the original experiment are matched as closely as possible, though they might not always be identical (e.g., different but similar participants, different research team, different time; Walker & Carr, 2021). Direct replication is evident when single-case researchers repeat experimental conditions using a SCER design (e.g., repeating baseline and treatment conditions within a reversal design for one participant). Direct replication can also include repeating an SCER design with different but similar participants. For example, single-case researchers investigating an intervention to address challenging behavior might directly replicate a reversal design with three, similar participants with autism. Direct replication may discourage QRPs because later replication studies by independent researchers will reveal the original (biased) findings are untrue (see Makel et al., 2012) and therefore unlikely to benefit others.

Single-case researchers also conduct *systematic replications* to investigate whether and how effects differ or extend from original experimental findings (i.e., assess generality of findings; Sidman, 1960). Systematic replication involves deliberate variation of conditions from an original study along some non-trivial dimension (e.g., setting, materials, intervention agents, participants) to determine if similar effects are achieved. For example, research investigating a verbal behavior intervention might involve trained professionals who intervene in a tightly controlled clinical setting. This research could be systematically replicated by investigating the effects of the intervention when teachers deliver it at school or parents within the home, or within similar clinical settings but with participants who are different in seemingly important ways (e.g., disability severity). Systematic replication in applied behavior analysis ultimately helps to identify boundaries of effectiveness of behavior change technologies, thereby clarifying for whom and under what conditions an intervention appears effective. Accordingly, researchers should describe relevant details about differences between prior research in order to improve professional practice, clarify generality of effects, and support future replications. Replication studies should be conducted until effects of a behavior change method can be reasonably predicted for any given individual without further research (Walker & Carr, 2021).

Direct and systematic replications are critical for ensuring the veracity of findings in SCER and for individualizing treatment decisions, both of which are critical for ensuring researchers and professionals are truthful, do no harm, benefit others, and accord dignity. Evidence unfortunately suggests that systematic replication research in behavior analysis is decreasing (Locey, 2020), which should constitute cause for concern. Ethical principles like the pursuit of excellence and truth, as well as values associated with care and compassion, require behavior analytic researchers to provide clear and sufficiently detailed information to support direct and systematic replications. There are several ways to achieve this while increasing the transparency of SCER.

Increasing transparency of single-case experimental research

We reviewed in the sections above the justifications for replication research, how these are related to ethical principles, and the relevance of transparent research practices, QRPs, and establishing generality of interventions. Here we shift to describing how single-case researchers can demonstrate an ethical commitment to research transparency, which is the clear reporting and/or availability of relevant details about method, data, and data analysis, and other open science practices. Open science practices are those that enhance communication and transparency of researcher behavior (including decisions), as well as the perceived credibility of and access to scientific findings (van der Zee & Reich, 2018). Examples of open science practices include publicly posting or sharing data and research materials, study preregistration, and making research reports publicly available. Most open science practices have been proposed and adopted in response to QRPs, publication bias, and other factors related to group research methods. Despite this, open science practices can be used in SCER contexts (e.g., Cook et al., 2021). We believe that behavior analysis researchers are inclined to embrace some open practices that are already prominent features of SCER methods (e.g., data transparency via graphs), but they may perceive practical and ethical issues in adopting others.

The Center for Open Science (COS) is perhaps the most prominent organization for promoting open science practices. The premise of the COS is that replication research is fundamental to the scientific enterprise and transparency about researcher decisions across all phases of the research process is necessary (Samarrai, 2013). The COS promotes several practices that increase research transparency. These practices include (1) making available materials and data from research projects, (2) posting study purposes, hypotheses, and method prior to study execution, and (3) making readily accessible the findings from research, usually in the form of freely available manuscript versions of published reports or other written products. Each of these practices is described below (see Table 11.2 for a summary of relevant resources) along with specific ethical considerations for SCER.

TABLE 11.2 Open science resources.

	Resource	Website	Description
Comprehensive system	Open Science Framework	osf.io	Includes support for storing and sharing data, materials, analytic code, and conference presentations as well as study preregistration and preprint server integration, among other specialized features. Storage caps may limit video data storage and sharing.
Preregistration platforms	Registry of efficacy and effectiveness tudies	sreereg.icpsr. umich.edu/ sreereg/index	Includes support for a variety of quantitative and qualitative designs, including specific support for single-case experimental designs. Demo mode allows users to explore without creating an account. Integrated with What Works Clearinghouse (U.S. Department of Education).
	Open Science Framework	www.cos.io/ initiatives/prereg	Includes support for confirmatory and exploratory research. New user support (documents and videos) is available.
	As predicted	aspredicted.org	Includes support to preregister studies, but support for new users is limited. An open-answer format allows narrative descriptions of a study along seven standards and two supplemental details. A demo option allows users to explore the features.
Data repositories	Mendeley	data.mendeley. com	Provides data upload, management, archival storage, and access for data files. Account includes control over accessibility, including private, invited only, and public access settings. Datasets receive DOI numbers for citation, but all uploads must meet Mendeley policies. Can upload multimedia data.
	Databrary	nyu.databrary. org	Focuses exclusively on video and audio data upload, use, archival, and sharing sensitive data. Provides release forms, agreements, and resources for ethics board applications. Includes searchable volumes set for sharing purposes.

Continued

TABLE 11.2 Open science resources.—cont'd

	Resource	Website	Description
Data repositories *(Continued)*	Qualitative data repository	qdr.syr.edu	Archive for digital data and related documents associated with qualitative and multi-method research. Given some similarities in SCER and qualitative methods (e.g., video recording; observational data), this repository may be ideal for some single case researchers.
Preprint servers	PsyArXiv	psyarxiv.com	This preprint server is primarily used by psychology researchers and is hosted by Center for Open Science. Users may upload manuscripts and tag them with keywords and details to support searching and is indexed by Google Scholar. Users may upload supplemental materials with their manuscripts.
	EdArXiv	edarxiv.org	This preprint server was recently launched for education researchers and is hosted by Center for Open Science. Similar to other preprint servers based on the ArXiv format, this server is indexed by Google Scholar. EdArXiv allows researchers to post and search working papers, unpublished works, conference presentations and materials, and papers submitted to journals for peer review.
	OSF preprints	osf.io/preprints	Hosted by Center for Open Science, this preprint server had over 2.3million papers uploaded as of June 2021. Subjects vary considerably, but the social and behavioral sciences subject perhaps is most relevant to single case experimental researchers. All papers are indexed by Google Scholar.

Open data and open materials in single-case experimental research

Protection of human participants is a top priority of researchers and ethics review boards, and additional concern for that protection is warranted when participants are part of a vulnerable population (e.g., children with disabilities). This means researchers must carefully consider which and to what extent they will share data and materials (e.g., blank or completed data forms; all, partial, or no data). Importantly, open science is better considered in terms of degrees of transparency rather than an all-or-nothing approach, and research transparency is not more important than ensuring protections for research participants. Indeed, we are unable to conceive when an interest in supporting replication, transparency, and open science justifies any risk to participants that is not fully explicated in and evidenced by an informed consent. Researchers therefore may decide to share some but not all materials and/or data based on their ethical requirements and commitments to participants, with participant protection as the priority of concern.

Open data (i.e., making available all relevant data associated with a study) arguably represents the most fundamental practice associated with open science and research transparency (Cook et al., 2021). Whereas group comparisons researchers often deal with large data sets that are not included in published research reports, single-case researchers typically graph all data for each participant for visual analysis and to determine whether a functional relation is evident. This strength may give the impression that single-case researchers need not adopt new or additional practices regarding data transparency consistent with open science. For example, if future researchers are interested in the raw data from a study (e.g., for a meta-analysis or systematic review; Dowdy et al., 2021), then they can use software designed to obtain very precise estimates from line graphs that are included in SCER reports (e.g., Ungraph, WebPlotDigitizer, XYit; Moeyaert et al., 2016). However, uploading a database file with raw data to an open science platform or data repository (e.g., data.mendeley.com) will save future researchers considerable time while ensuring accurate data in future studies (like meta-analyses) and enhancing the perceived transparency of research. One potential additional benefit of data sharing is the assignment of a DOI number that can be cited by future researchers who use the uploaded data in their own research. This means researcher reputation may be enhanced by open science practices like data sharing when open data are cited by other researchers. If, however, data sharing may compromise participant confidentiality and undermine their dignity, or if harm may otherwise be caused by sharing data openly, researchers should abstain from posting their data on open science platforms. For a straightforward, stepwise guide to uploading data to the Open Science Framework at OSF, see Soderberg (2018).

Single-case researchers often use video recordings of study sessions to collect data. This approach means researchers have an opportunity to demonstrate the reliability of their original data by making available the videos from which their data were obtained. Furthermore, other researchers may find valuable data in the videos uploaded to an open science platform. Databrary is an online video data library and repository for behavioral scientists who need secure space to archive, access, and share their video data (see https://nyu. databrary.org/). However, most researchers take steps to ensure participant identity is anonymous and making videos available may compromise an informed consent that does not include permission/consent to show video. This means in many cases, a researcher cannot share video without violating research ethics, and that informed consent forms should include an option for participants to allow (or forbid) sharing video on open science platforms. The databrary website also provides excellent guidance about video data archiving and sharing, including template language to be used in applications for ethics board approval, language for obtaining participant permission to share video data, and sample videos of the data sharing release process (see https:// databrary.org/support/irb.html for ethics-related support for video data).

If informed consent forms explain that videos will be edited to preserve anonymity, and researchers take steps to ensure identity will not be revealed, then uploaded videos may be feasible. For example, researchers may use video editing software to blur faces, disguise voices, and omit names (or other important information) when spoken by individuals in the recording. Such editing may render the videos less valuable to other researchers (who must see the participant's face, for example, to measure engagement or self-stimulatory behavior). Also, anonymizing videos likely will require considerable time and resources that may not justify this degree of transparency, and errors that reveal identity or otherwise compromise informed consent agreements is still possible.

One potential alternative is to structure informed consent forms and research protocols such that participants can elect to have their identity revealed/shared in uploaded videos and other products and activities for dissemination. Researchers who upload videos for transparency purposes can make them accessible only to those whose permission has been granted. For example, Mendeley Data (data.mendeley.com) allows researchers to secure data and share only with specific individuals and with stipulations. However, researchers will need to take steps to make clear to participants the potential risks associated with identifiable information, and they must obtain informed consent that acknowledges potentially unanticipated effects associated with making videos available.

Single case researchers and methodologists have directed increased attention in recent years toward identification and development of statistical methods for analyzing and interpreting results from SCER studies. For example, considerable advances in metrics for quantifying the magnitude of intervention effects have been made in the past 10 years, but there is no consensus about which metrics should be used nor what formulas are most appropriate (Klingbeil et al., 2019). Visual analysis of graphed data as the primary method of data analysis in SCER (Cooper et al., 2020; Johnston et al., 2019; Ledford & Gast, 2018), researchers focused on statistical analyses of SCER data have found some interesting if not promising approaches that may enhance the perceived or actual rigor of SCER (Dowdy et al., 2021). Scientists who support open science and reproducibility should make available their raw data and statistical code or syntax for quantitative analysis and effect size calculations (Stodden, 2014). Such transparency promotes better understanding of the strengths and limitations of this emerging area of scientific investigation. For example, publishing reproducible code or syntax for statistical analyses may lead to discovery of errors as well as refinements when new methods and metrics are discovered.

Single-case researchers investigate the effects of environmental changes (e.g., an intervention) on participant responding. This means study authors usually have developed operationalized protocols that explain to intervention agents the stepwise procedures for applying the experimental intervention (e.g., procedural manuals). Important albeit sometimes overlooked details about a study can be more readily accessed and understood when study materials are made publicly available. For example, study materials are often used to clarify for intervention agents the intervention procedures and may ensure consistent absence and application of intervention procedures during the baseline and intervention conditions, respectively (i.e., control condition integrity and treatment integrity; Ledford & Gast, 2014). Such protocols have significant value to other researchers who may attempt to replicate original findings, but also to professionals who may use the intervention in applied practice.

Researchers may also integrate or develop for their studies various materials associated with an intervention protocol (e.g., visual supports, token economy board, commercial toys, games). They may use instruments developed for recording participant responses and procedures for assessing the reliability of those data. Also, researchers often generate materials to train others who will apply an intervention or collect data (e.g., PowerPoint presentations, training manuals, videos). Finally, researchers might have developed materials and procedures that explain how they recruited and selected participants for their study. Study materials may be developed in the form of checklists, narrative description of procedures (like those found in the method section of a study proposal or published research report), or multi-media guides that include photographs, video, text, and audio recordings. These materials may be perceived as superficial if not inconsequential, but seemingly minor details of a study can accumulate in significant ways and may influence study outcomes. It seems plausible that failed replications may be explained by the omission of − or differences between − study materials. Similarly, professionals who attempt to apply an intervention without the details revealed by examining study materials may find the intervention unsuccessful. Failed advances in knowledge about intervention effects and lost potential for benefit from a treatment are two among many negative effects that might be avoided when researchers adopt an open science approach to inquiry.

Relatedly, Cook et al. (2021) explained that single-case researchers should describe the criteria and/or process used for deciding when participants will advance from baseline to intervention conditions (or vice-versa; e.g., the ABAB design). This methodological detail may be part of a study protocol and should be included in published reports, but journal space limitations or reviewer oversight may mean publicly available protocols are the only place where this important detail is available. Single-case researchers who value replication and research transparency ought to ensure this important detail is represented in their own reports and/or materials. Doing so can facilitate discoveries that benefit others (e.g., clients, other researchers) and facilitate the pursuit of excellence by behavior analysts.

Single-case researchers should make available on an open science platform (e.g., OSF) the essential details about their study that otherwise would not be published in a research report. Inaccessibility of such details limits replication research and may hinder advances in professional practice. Conversely, posting such materials will support independent replication research in ways that enhances confidence in the original findings, facilitates systematic replication, and informs professionals whose clients may benefit from the intervention.

Although positive effects of open data and materials sharing are described alongside the specific practices above, there may be potential or actual ethical issues to consider before making this information available. First, raw data uploaded to a data repository or open science platform may include information about participants (e.g., names, settings) that can compromise anonymity (see Chapter 9 for strategies on ethical data handling and storage). Similarly, sharing recordings from which data were collected can compromise anonymity and violate informed consent. Data sheets, protocols, and other materials can sometimes include details that may, either independently or collectively, reveal the identity of participants along with sensitive information they did not consent to share. If edits are not made to remove identifiable information from datasets, then others who view the file may recognize or deduce participant identities.

Preregistration and registered reports in single-case research

Preregistration and registered reports may be confused as being synonymous because the terms sound similar. Preregistration refers to the publicly available record of a researcher's (or research team's) questions, hypotheses, and method of investigation for a prospective study (Nosek et al., 2018). There are several platforms that support preregistration of research. The OSF includes a dedicated online space for study preregistration (see https://osf.io/prereg/). The system provides a stepwise guide for different types of preregistrations and study designs (e.g., qualitative study, replication study), but not for SCER specifically. The Registry of Efficacy and Effectiveness Studies (REES) website offers a demo mode where curious individuals can preregister a hypothetical study and learn more about that process (see https://sreereg.icpsr. umich.edu/sreereg/demo/mode). The REES includes instructions for completing an eight-step process focused on study description, research questions, study design, and data analysis plan, among other details. Unlike OSF, REES provides specific support for preregistering SCER studies, and the entire registry is searchable by design type. At the time this chapter was written, there were 20 preregistered studies on the REES registry that reported using an SCER design (https://sreereg.icpsr.umich.edu/sreereg/search/search). For example, preregistration #6280.1v1 by Art Dowdy and Brittany Dumproff was logged on November 5, 2021 and can be accessed at the following link: https://sreereg.icpsr.umich.edu/sreereg/subEntry/6580/pdf?section=all&action =download.

Registered reports are only the introduction and method sections for a proposed study submitted to a journal for peer review that provide a rationale for the research and a detailed description of the method to be used. The main difference between preregistered studies and registered reports is that preregistration is merely a record of what one proposes to do–the study may never be conducted as described or, if conducted, may never be submitted to a journal. A registered report is a written proposal for a study that may be accepted by a journal before results are known. The registered report can be revised according to constructive feedback from peer reviewers before the study is executed, and it will receive a decision to publish (or reject) before the study is conducted (usually called "in principal acceptance" or "conditional acceptance"). This means registered reports that are accepted for publication will be published irrespective of results as long as the study is conducted as described and approved by the journal reviewers and editor(s). Although preregistration and registered reports both are a means of increasing research transparency, registered reports provide opportunities to identify methodological problems (i.e., increase rigor) before data are collected. Both preregistered studies and registered reports are a direct means of addressing publication bias, but only registered reports can prevent publication bias.

Registered reports remain relatively rare. We are not aware of any behavior analytic journals that explicitly state they accept registered reports for peer review. A related journal, *Journal of Educational Psychology*, does accept registered reports. The journal's website offers explicit guidance to researchers interested in submitting a registered report, including a flow chart and very detailed instructions for manuscript preparation and submission. The flagship journal in special education, *Exceptional Children,* accepts registered reports. These journal policies suggest others may begin accepting registered reports, but researchers, peer reviewers, and readers might facilitate journal submission policy changes by communicating to journal editors and publishers their value for registered reports. For a list of current journals that have explicit policies governing the publication of registered reports, see the curated list at the COS: https://www.cos.io/initiatives/registered-reports.

Increasing access to research reports

Traditionally, research has been published most often in peer reviewed journals. Journal subscriptions often are expensive, which means some scientists (e.g., those in countries where scientific infrastructure is limited) might not be able to access research relevant to their inquiry. Similarly, professionals who depend on research to guide their work (e.g., psychotherapists, behavior analysts, special educators) also may have limited access to relevant studies due to expensive association memberships or subscriptions. These and other concerns about limited access to peer reviewed and other scientific literature (e.g., books, book chapters) have resulted in two distinct approaches that circumvent the financial barriers to scientific literature–open access publication and pre-print servers.

Open access journals are journals that include articles that can be accessed by anyone with internet access (Fleming & Cook, 2021). These journals manage administrative and publication costs (which traditionally are covered by subscription revenue) through philanthropic support or article processing fees (paid by researchers). Some journals are entirely open access (i.e., every article published therein is publicly available), whereas other journals have adopted hybrid models that include some openly accessible articles and other articles behind paywalls. Although open access seems an effective way to increase access to research, the limited number of open access journals means many interested individuals will not find relevant information by searching openly accessible literature. Also, a large number of "open access" predatory journals (i.e., fake journals) have emerged in recent years that aim to exploit researchers who may pay article processing fees to publish their research (see https://predatoryjournals.com/journals/for an extensive list of known predatory journals). Some researchers may intentionally use predatory journals to publish poorly conducted or fraudulent research. Unsuspecting researchers may mistakenly presume the predatory journal is a legitimate outlet for their research, which can have negative implications for their careers (e.g., rejected tenure and promotion applications; negative reputation). Predatory journals have made it difficult to identify open access articles from reputable sources. We, therefore, suggest researchers rely on the Directory of Open Access Journals (doaj.org) to locate legitimate open access journals and articles.

Preprint servers have emerged in recent years as a way for researchers to continue publishing their research in journals that require subscriptions or fees while also providing access to the public at no cost. Preprints are the manuscript versions of journal articles and are often uploaded to a dedicated server when the researcher submits to a journal for peer review or when their manuscript has been accepted for publication (Fleming & Cook, 2021). Readers should note that a manuscript version of a completed registered report could be shared on a preprint server if consistent with the journal's policy. The PsyArXiv (pronounced "Psy Archive"; https://psyarxiv.com/) preprint server is primarily used by psychology researchers, and a recent server called EdArXiv ("Ed Archive"; https://edarxiv.org/) is dedicated to education researchers. Preprints also allow public access to rigorous research that may not be published due to null or negative results (i.e., publication bias). Also, preprints can offer public documentation of research method and results before and after peer review, which may help reveal when changes in method and results might be attributed to QRPs, reviewer recommendations, editor requests, etcetera. An additional benefit is that preprints can be assigned a DOI number to support tracking versions over time, facilitate citation (e.g., in grant applications), and establish a record of discovery/precedence and authorship.

Despite these and other benefits of preprints (Fleming & Cook, 2021), journals may have policies against submission or publication of manuscripts that have been posted on preprint servers, or they may not allow preprint versions to appear after the article version is published. This means single-case researchers who are interested in posting preprints of their research reports will need to closely examine journal and publisher policies before uploading their manuscripts. The Sherpa Romeo website can assist researchers in identifying policies (or lack thereof) regarding preprints by searching journal names or publishers (see https://v2.sherpa.ac.uk/romeo/). One ethical issue worth considering relates to the tension between timely dissemination of research afforded by preprint servers and the quality control associated with peer review. Some have proposed that preprints allow for rapid publication of information that can benefit society. For example, preprints for research related to the COVID-19 pandemic meant information was quickly available to public health officials, but the quality of information was unclear because the research was not yet subjected to peer review (Watson, 2022). Behavior analysis researchers should consider whether the claims associated with their findings (about a new intervention, for example) should first be subjected to peer review before uploading a copy to a preprint server to ensure rigorous review and important clarifications are incorporated into a final report. Also, researchers should consider whether a journal considers a pre-print a prior publication (and therefore may not be submitted for peer review) before uploading a copy to a preprint server to avoid violating journal submission requirements.

Generating and reinforcing a culture of openness

There is little doubt that students and professionals pursue behavior analysis research based on a genuine interest in contributing to scientific knowledge and a dedication to improving the lives of study participants. Prospective behavior analysis researchers are taught through coursework and supervised experience about the rigors of the scientific process, including but not limited to objective measurement, display, and interpretation of behavioral data as well as SCER design (Behavior Analyst Certification Board [BACB] 2017, 2021). Behavior analysts should, among other things, prioritize the welfare of clients, advocate for use of the most effective treatments, and abstain from engaging in practices that could lead to erroneous or deceptive results (BACB, 2014). Despite these and similar values (truth, honesty) in behavior analysis and science more generally, academic institutions often make hiring decisions, assign salaries, award promotions, and grant tenure based on a researcher's record of successful grant funding, quantity of publications, and the prestige of journals in which their research is published (Grimes et al., 2018; Nosek et al., 2012). Furthermore, refereed journals prioritize publication of novel or sensational findings over replications (Makel et al., 2012; Makel & Plucker, 2014; Martin & Clarke, 2017) and positive effects over null findings (Atkinson, 1982; Shadish et al., 2016).

Well-intentioned researchers who value scientific integrity may therefore find themselves in a position in which their reputation and livelihood (i.e., employment) are dependent upon publication of novel and positive findings. The values associated with a "publish or perish" culture in academia may be difficult for researchers to recognize and reconcile, particularly early career researchers who are expected to publish many articles to justify keeping their jobs and being promoted with tenure. Researchers may be inclined to make small decisions that accumulate toward positive effects, or they may value number of publications over the development of knowledge (i.e., separating data for one study into different publications can disjoint the literature and stunts progress). Early career researchers (and their more senior colleagues) who spend time getting familiar with issues associated with the replication crisis (e.g., motivating contingencies, publication bias, questionable research practices) may be better equipped to engage in rigorous research for knowledge generation in spite of the publish or perish culture of the academy.

Grimes et al. (2018) developed a formula to quantitatively estimate the impact on publication trustworthiness of various ethical issues encountered in a "publish or perish" culture. The formula included variables like researcher type (careless, diligent, unethical), funding availability, selective reporting rates, scholarly productivity, prevalence of research fraud, carelessness, replication and reproducibility rates, journal submission rates, and other related variables. The model suggested disproportionate rewards for publishing positive and sensational results that also decreased publication trustworthiness (i.e., proportion of replicable results) and increased the likelihood of false positives (i.e., reporting positive effects when they do not exist). Absence of publication bias unsurprisingly maximized trustworthiness of publications. Grimes et al.'s model also suggested QRPs are disproportionately reinforced in a "publish or perish" culture at the expense of honest and diligent research practices. High productivity (i.e., frequent publication) resulting from careless or fraudulent practices that go undetected can be reinforced by way of more research funding and better employment prospects than diligent research practices (Grimes et al., 2018). Interestingly, increasing detection and penalization (i.e., denial of future funding) of dubious publications did not markedly improve publication trustworthiness unless detection rates were very high (i.e., at least 75%), which is a finding that seems conceptually consistent with delay discounting (Madden & Johnson, 2010). Ethical and practical concerns (e.g., countercontrol; Skinner, 1953) may also arise from overly punitive systems that penalize honest mistakes to the same degree as egregious falsifications. For example, honest researchers who discover an error may be inclined to withhold details about the error for fear of penalties associated with research fraud. This chilling effect can inhibit scientific advances and technological innovation that, in behavior analysis, negatively affect clients who need effective interventions. Although Grimes et al. found that reinforcing diligent practices effectively improved publication trustworthiness, diligent practices did not wholly offset the deleterious influence of QRPs.

Grimes et al.'s (2018) findings demonstrate that current academic incentives can have damaging effects on the ethical behavior of researchers and the credibility of the scientific corpus. Fostering a culture of openness and diligence requires changes in practices across the scientific community (i.e., journals, academic institutions, researchers). Although researchers may adopt open science practices consistent with a grassroots approach, institutional and journal requirement changes also may contribute to a culture of openness and transparency.

One institutional effort for change was an initiative of the Transparency and Openness Promotion (TOP; Nosek et al., 2015) committee. The TOP committee developed eight standards designed to be adopted by refereed journals as policies for publication (see http://cos.io/top). These standards aim to promote open science practices and replication research. For example, the replication standard urges journals to explicitly encourage authors to submit replication studies and include registered reports as a submission option (Nosek et al., 2015). Such practices may decrease publication bias.

Each TOP standard includes three levels for adoption (Nosek et al., 2015). Level one offers some incentive for researchers to engage in the targeted practice and involves a negligible cost for journals. For example, level one for the data transparency standard requires authors to state in the manuscript whether data are readily available and, if so, where the data can be accessed. Data transparency level two explains that data is posted to a trusted repository and that any exceptions are described in the researcher's report at the time of submission. Level three data transparency means the data are posted to a trusted repository with exceptions identified at the time of submission, but that all analyses will be independently reproduced (i.e., by peer reviewers) prior to publication. Level three guideline for data transparency (and most other TOP Guidelines) will require additional resources (e.g., time, relevant software) because they involve peer verification prior to publication, but this investment may improve scientific rigor by detecting errors before publication (Nosek et al., 2015). Also, such activity may be ideal exercises for developing researcher skills, particularly doctoral students preparing for research careers.

The TOP committee also encourages journals to award badges for articles that meet open data, open materials, and/or preregistration standards (Nosek et al., 2015). These badges may offer further incentive for researchers to implement transparent practices. Finally, the TOP committee explained that journal editors may decide to gradually adopt standards (Nosek et al., 2015). For example, journals may begin by awarding badges for one or more levels one practices to establish new norms before instituting more rigorous (level two and three) practices. Gradual adoption is likely to make TOP standards more acceptable to researchers, journal reviewers, editors, and publishers than immediate adoption of all TOP Guidelines.

Preliminary evidence suggests the TOP standards can improve research transparency and replicability. Nosek et al. (2015) reported approximately 25% of articles accepted in *Psychological Science* were awarded at least one badge for open data, open materials, or preregistration in the first year the journal began this (low-cost) incentive. However, broad change is unlikely unless the TOP standards are adopted widely across journals, particularly by existing flagship and top-tier journals. This is because it is not in an author's best interest within the present "publish or perish" culture to publish in a small set of journals that promote open science or have adopted the TOP guidelines (Nosek et al., 2012). For example, *Journal of Applied Behavior Analysis* (*JABA*) is considered a flagship journal within behavior analysis. *JABA* explicitly encourages direct and systematic replication studies in the author submission guidelines, which would meet level one of the TOP replication standard (see https://onlinelibrary.wiley.com/page/journal/19383703/homepage/forauthors.html). However, no other TOP standards associated with promoting transparency and replicability (e.g., data and materials sharing, preregistration) or preventing publication bias (e.g., registered reports as a submission option) are evident in the journal's submission guidelines. It is unlikely that researcher publication practices in applied behavior analysis will substantially change if the publication practices of prestigious journals in behavior analysis do not substantially change.

An absence of incentives for open science practices in leading journals means individual researchers will need to independently adopt open science practices until journal editors recognize and adopt policies similar to the TOP standards. This also means researchers who serve as peer reviewers should begin to request, if not expect, open science practices to be reflected in the manuscripts they evaluate for journals. By setting an expectation for open science practices, even when journals do not have formal policies requiring them, reviewers may stimulate editors to begin considering and eventually adopt open science practices. Such changes in the culture may effectively discourage QRPs, enhance transparency (and, in turn, the perceived and actual credibility of SCER), and promote access to research by the public and broader scientific communities.

Conclusion

Science is the best but an imperfect approach to knowledge generation, and replication is a means of controlling for imperfected scientific methods. Unfortunately, the perceived value of replication appears to be diminished by reverence for novel and sensational findings. When these misplaced values occur in the context of publication bias, inaccurate research findings can accumulate. Replication research functions as a corrective mechanism for imperfect researchers, but a crisis of confidence in scientific findings can occur when replication is disfavored and important studies go unpublished (or are not conducted). This appears to have occurred in many scientific fields and has become known as the replication crisis.

Although the replication crisis is largely associated research that uses group comparisons designs, single case researchers have an ethical duty to engage in rigorous novel and replicative research to ensure the integrity of the SCER literature. Replication research decreases the likelihood that individuals who receive behavior interventions and supports benefit from treatment, and reduces the probability that professionals do harm to their clients. Professionals are better able to promote autonomy and preserve dignity of the people they serve when informed by sound, scientifically validated practices that have been repeatedly shown beneficial. Replication research is consistent with ethical principles associated with truth, justice (i.e., fairness), and the pursuit of excellence in human services. Finally, researchers are committed to knowledge generation and, when they err or exaggerate, accept correction and accountability from their fellow researchers.

This chapter overviewed some aspects of replication as it relates to SCER and offered recommendations to support replication research. We described how some SCER suspect QRPs may manifest in SCER, including participant selection bias, procedural fidelity bias, graphing manipulation and distortion, and selectively reporting results, among others. While replication research may help control for biased findings that stem from QRPs in SCER, open science practices also may increase transparency of research in ways the discourage QRPs while simultaneously enhancing replicability of original research. Researchers who commit to study preregistration, share their data, post research materials, and engage in other open science practices likely will advance knowledge progression, professional preparation, and the provision of effective services.

References

Aldhous, P. (May 5, 2011). *Journal rejects studies contradicting precognition.* New Scientist. https://www.newscientist.com/article/dn20447-journal-rejects-studies-contradicting-precognit ion/.

Atkinson, D. R. (1982). Statistical significance, reviewer evaluations, and the scientific process: Is there a (statistically) significant relationship? *Journal of Counseling Psychology, 29*(2), 189—194. https://doi.org/10.1037/0022-0167.29.2.189

Bailey, J., & Burch, M. (2016). *Ethics for behavior analysts.* Routledge.

Behavior Analyst Certification Board. (2014). *Professional and ethical compliance code for behavior analysts.* Author.

Behavior Analyst Certification Board. (2017). *BCBA task list* (5th ed.). Author.

Behavior Analyst Certification Board. (2021). *Board certified behavior analyst handbook.* Author.

Bem, D. J. (2011). Feeling the future: Experimental evidence for anomalous retroactive influences on cognition and affect. *Journal of Personality and Social Psychology, 100*(3), 407. https://doi.org/10.1037/a0021524

Branch, M. N., & Pennypacker, H. S. (2013). Generality and generalization of research findings. In G. J. Madden, W. V. Dube, T. D. Hackenberg, G. P. Hanley, & K. A. Lattal (Eds.), *APA handbook of behavior analysis, Vol. 1. Methods and principles* (pp. 151—175). American Psychological Association. https://doi.org/10.1037/13937-007

Cook, B. G., Johnson, A. H., Maggin, D. M., Therrien, W. J., Barton, E. E., Lloyd, J. W., Reichow, B., Talbott, E., & Travers, J. C. (2021). Open science and single-case design research. In *Remedial and special education.* Advance online publication. https://doi.org/10.1177/0741932521996452

Cooper, J. O., Heron, T. E., & Heward, W. L. (2020). *Applied behavior analysis* (3rd ed.). Pearson.

Dowdy, A., Peltier, C., Tincani, M., Schneider, W. J., Hantula, D., & Travers, J. C. (2021). Meta-analyses and effect sizes in applied behavior analysis: A review and discussion. *Journal of Applied Behavior Analysis, 54*, 1317—1340.

Duvendack, M., Palmer-Jones, R., & Reed, W. R. (2017). What is meant by" replication" and why does it encounter resistance in economics? *American Economic Review, 107*(5), 46—51. https://doi.org/10.1257/aer.p20171031

Earp, B. D., & Trafimow, D. (2015). Replication, falsification, and the crisis of confidence in social psychology. *Frontiers in Psychology, 6*(621), 1—11. https://doi.org/10.3389/fpsyg.2015.00621

Fleming, J. I., & Cook, B. G. (2021). Open access in special education: A review of publisher policies. In *Remedial and special education.* Advance online publication. https://doi.org/10.1177/0741932521996461

Gehr, B. T., Weiss, C., & Porzsolt, F. (2006). The fading of reported effectiveness. A meta-analysis of randomised controlled trials. *BMC Medical Research Methodology, 6*(1), 1—12. https://doi.org/10.1186/1471-2288-6-25

Gerber, A. S., Green, D. P., & Nickerson, D. (2001). Testing for publication bias in political science. *Political Analysis, 9*(4), 385—392.

Grimes, D. R., Bauch, C. T., & Ioannidis, J. P. (2018). Modelling science trustworthiness under publish or perish pressure. *Royal Society Open Science, 5*(1), 1—14. https://doi.org/10.1098/rsos.171511

Hantula, D. A. (2019). Editorial: Replication and reliability in behavior science and behavior analysis: A call for a conversation. *Perspectives on Behavior Science, 42*(1), 1—11. https://doi.org/10.1007/s40614-019-00194-2

Ioannidis, J. P. (2005). Why most published research findings are false. *PLoS Medicine, 2*(8), 696—701. https://doi.org/10.1371/journal.pmed.0020124

Johnston, J. M., Pennypacker, H. S., & Green, G. (2019). *Strategies and tactics of behavioral research and practice* (4th ed). Routledge.

Kerr, N. L. (1998). HARKing: Hypothesizing after the results are known. *Personality and Social Psychology Review, 2*(3), 196–217. https://doi.org/10.1207/s15327957pspr0203_4

Klingbeil, D. A., Van Norman, E. R., McLendon, K. E., Ross, S. G., & Begeny, J. C. (2019). Evaluating Tau-U with oral reading fluency data and the impact of measurement error. *Behavior Modification, 43*(3), 413–438. https://doi.org/10.1177/0145445518760174

Koocher, G., & Keith-Spiegel, P. (1998). *Ethics in psychobgy* (2nd ed.). New York: Oxford University Press.

Laraway, S., Snycerski, S., Pradhan, S., & Huitema, B. E. (2019). An overview of scientific reproducibility: Consideration of relevant issues for behavior science/analysis. *Perspectives on Behavior Science, 42*(12), 33–57. https://doi.org/10.1007/s40614-019-00193-3

Ledford, J. R., & Gast, D. L. (2014). Measuring procedural fidelity in behavioural research. *Neuropsychological Rehabilitation, 24*(3–4), 332–348. https://doi.org/10.1080/09602011.2013.861352

Ledford, J. R., & Gast, D. L. (Eds.). (2018). *Single case research methodology* (p. 377). New York, NY, Chicago: Routledge.

Locey, M. L. (2020). The evolution of behavior analysis: Toward a replication crisis? *Perspectives on Behavior Science, 43*(4), 655–675. https://doi.org/10.1007/s40614-020-00264-w

Madden, G. J., & Johnson, P. S. (2010). A delay-discounting primer. In G. J. Madden, & W. K. Bickel (Eds.), *Impulsivity: The behavioral and neurological science of discounting* (pp. 11–37). American Psychological Association. https://doi.org/10.1037/12069-001

Makel, M. C., & Plucker, J. A. (2014). Facts are more important than novelty: Replication in the education sciences. *Educational Researcher, 43*(6), 304–316. https://doi.org/10.3102/0013189X14545513

Makel, M. C., Plucker, J. A., & Hegarty, B. (2012). Replications in psychology research: How often do they really occur? *Perspectives on Psychological Science, 7*(6), 537–542. https://doi.org/10.1177/1745691612460688

Martin, G. N., & Clarke, R. M. (2017). Are psychology journals anti-replication? A snapshot of editorial practices. *Frontiers in Psychology, 8*(523), 1–6. https://doi.org/10.3389/fpsyg.2017.00523

Moeyaert, M., Maggin, D., & Verkuilen, J. (2016). Reliability, validity, and usability of data-extraction programs for single-case research designs. *Behavior Modification, 40*(6), 874–900. https://doi.org/10.1177/0145445516645763

Nosek, B. A., Alter, G., Banks, G. C., Borsboom, D., Bowman, S. D., Breckler, S. J., Buck, S., Chambers, C. D., Chin, G., Christensen, G., Contestabile, M., Dafoe, A., Eich, E., Freese, J., Glennerster, R., Goroff, D., Green, D. P., Hesse, B., Humphreys, M., … Yarkoni, T. (2015). Promoting an open research culture. *Science, 348*(6242), 1422–1425. https://doi.org/10.1126/science.aab2374

Nosek, B. A., Ebersole, C. R., DeHaven, A. C., & Mellor, D. T. (2018). The preregistration revolution. *Proceedings of the National Academy of Sciences, 115*(11), 2600–2606. https://doi.org/10.1073/pnas.1708274114

Nosek, B. A., Spies, J. R., & Motyl, M. (2012). Scientific utopia II: Restructuring incentives and practices to promote truth over publishability. *Perspectives on Psychological Science, 7*(6), 615–631. https://doi.org/10.1177/1745691612459058

Open Science Collaboration. (2015). Estimating the reproducibility of psychological science. *Science, 349*(6251), aac4716-1–aac4716-9. https://doi.org/10.1126/science.aac4716

Public health service policies research misconduct, 42 C.F.R. § Vol 93.103 (2005). https://www.ecfr.gov/current/title-42/chapter-I/subchapter-H/part-93.

Purswell, K. E., & Ray, D. C. (2014). Research with small samples: Considerations for single case and randomized small group experimental designs. *Counseling Outcome Research and Evaluation, 5*(2), 116−126. https://doi.org/10.1177/2150137814552474

Rosenthal, R. (1979). The file drawer problem and tolerance for null results. *Psychological Bulletin, 86*(3), 638−641. https://doi.org/10.1037/0033-2909.86.3.638

Samarrai, F. (March 4, 2013). *New center for open science designed to increase research transparency, provide free technologies for scientists.* UVAToday. https://news.virginia.edu/content/new-center-open-science-designed-increase-research-transparency-provide-free-technologies.

Shadish, W. R., Zelinsky, N. A., Vevea, J. L., & Kratochwill, T. R. (2016). A survey of publication practices of single-case design researchers when treatments have small or large effects. *Journal of Applied Behavior Analysis, 49*(3), 656−673. https://doi.org/10.1002/jaba.308

Sham, E., & Smith, T. (2014). Publication bias in studies of an applied behavior-analytic intervention: An initial analysis. *Journal of Applied Behavior Analysis, 47*(3), 663−678. https://doi.org/10.1002/jaba.146

Sidman, M. (1960). *Tactics of scientific research.* Basic Books.

Simmons, J. P., Nelson, L. D., & Simonsohn, U. (2011). False-positive psychology: Undisclosed flexibility in data collection and analysis allows presenting anything as significant. *Psychological Science, 22*(11), 1359−1366. https://doi.org/10.1177/0956797611417632

Skinner, B. F. (1953). *Science and human behavior.* Macmillan.

Soderberg, C. K. (2018). Using OSF to share data: A step-by-step guide. *Advances in Methods and Practices in Psychological Science, 1*(1), 115−120. https://doi.org/10.1177/2515245918757689

Stodden, V. (2014). The reproducible research movement in statistics. *Statistical Journal of the IAOS, 30*(2), 91−93.

Tincani, M., & Travers, J. C.. (in press). Questionable Research Practices in Single-Case Experimental Designs: Examples and Possible Solutions. In O'Donohue W., Masuda A., & Lilienfeld S. O. (Eds.), Questionable research practices: Designing, conducting, and reporting sound research in clinical psychology. Cham, Switzerland: Springer Publications.

van der Zee, T., & Reich, J. (2018). Open education science. *AERA Open, 4*(3), 1−15. https://doi.org/10.1177/2332858418787466

Walker, S. G., & Carr, J. E. (2021). *Generality of findings from single-case designs: It's not all about the "N."* Behavior Analysis in Practice. Advance online publication. https://doi.org/10.1007/s40617-020-00547-3

Watson, C. (2022). Rise of the preprint: How rapid data sharing during COVID-19 has changed science forever. *Nature Medicine, 28*(1), 2−5.

Wiggins, B. J., & Chrisopherson, C. D. (2019). The replication crisis in psychology: An overview for theoretical and philosophical psychology. *Journal of Theoretical and Philosophical Psychology, 39*(4), 202−217. https://doi.org/10.1037/teo0000137

Index